FIELD NOTES

FIELD NOTES

The Making of Middle East Studies
in the United States

Zachary Lockman

STANFORD UNIVERSITY PRESS
Stanford, California

Stanford University Press
Stanford, California

Printed in the United States of America on acid-free, archival-quality paper

Library of Congress Cataloging-in-Publication Data

Lockman, Zachary, author.

Field notes : the making of Middle East studies in the United States /
Zachary Lockman.

pages cm.

Includes bibliographical references and index.

ISBN 978-0-8047-9805-1 (cloth : alk. paper) — ISBN 978-0-8047-9906-5 (pbk. : alk. paper)

1. Middle East—Study and teaching—United States—History—20th century.
2. Area studies—United States—History—20th century. I. Title

DS61.9.U6L63 2016

956.0072—dc23   2015034990

Typeset at Stanford University Press in 10/14.5 Minion

ISBN 978-0-8047-9958-4 (Electronic)

Contents

Acknowledgments

THIS IS THE FIRST BOOK I have written based on archives in the United States, rather than in the Middle East and Europe. So I will begin by thanking the staff of the Rockefeller Archive Center, an impressively efficient and congenial institution, as well as the librarians and archivists who assisted me at the Library of Congress, Columbia, Princeton and New York University. The Middle East Studies Association allowed me to rampage through its files; for that, and for their hospitality, I thank Amy Newhall and Sara Palmer in particular. Irene Gendzier shared with me some of her personal papers as well as her memories, for which I am grateful.

The two people who reviewed my manuscript on behalf of Stanford University Press revealed themselves to me immediately after doing so, and I thank them profusely for their close reading and insightful comments. I've long thought of Robert Vitalis as my most fearsome reader and he lived up to that image in this case as well, no doubt fortified by the fact that he himself had recently completed a critical (and revisionist) history of an American academic field. This book is much better for his criticisms and suggestions. Edmund Burke III (better known as Terry) brought to bear on my manuscript both his deep scholarly understanding of how academic fields are constructed (and fought over), and his extensive experience with the study of the Middle East (and North Africa!) in the United States. I am very grateful to him as well.

A number of friends, colleagues and family members were kind enough to read and comment on part or all of the manuscript of this book. They include Joel Beinin, Benoit Challand, Melinda Fine, Irene Gendzier, Arang Keshavar-zian, Talya Lockman-Fine, Timothy Mitchell, Amy Newhall and Sara Pursley; my thanks to all of them for their willingness to read my work and for provid-ing their very helpful takes on it. It is entirely my responsibility if I foolishly failed to take their advice.

My thanks, too, to Kate Wahl, Nora Spiegel, John Feneron and their col-leagues at Stanford University Press for dealing with my manuscript so ex-peditiously and efficiently, and for their editorial skills which no doubt have improved it significantly.

I presented parts of what eventually became this book in my keynote ad-dress at the May 2013 Middle East History and Theory conference, organized by graduate students at the University of Chicago, and as the Wadie Jwaideh Memorial Lecture that I delivered at Indiana University in October 2013; my thanks to the organizers of MEHAT and to Professor Asma Afsaruddin, re-spectively, for hosting me so graciously. I also presented some of what has ended up in this book in talks at the University of California, Los Angeles and Berkeley, in April 2015; I am grateful to Emily Gottreich and Jim Gelvin, and the staffs of the two centers involved, for arranging my talks and treating me so well, and the attendees for listening so carefully and for asking me ques-tions that made me think, and think again.

I discussed the research project that culminated in this book at New York University's Hagop Kevorkian Center for Near Eastern Studies in February 2015, to kick off a new series titled "Research Off the Record." Anyone who was there can confirm that the account of my talk that promptly appeared on the Jihad Watch website (http://www.jihadwatch.org/2015/03/nyu-prof-admits-mesas-anti-israel-stance-rails-against-israel-lobby#comments) bore very little relation to reality, though it does nicely illustrate the kind of crazi-ness to which scholars in Middle East studies are routinely subjected.

A fellowship at New York University's Humanities Initiative (and the re-duced teaching load that came with it) enabled me to complete a first draft of this book, and it also provided both a stimulating intellectual environment very good company. I am grateful for all of these.

te this book to my mother, the last survivor of her generation in from whom I have learned so much and who has been both a an inspiration to my daughters.

Preface

I N THE SUMMER OF 1963 the School of Advanced International Studies (SAIS) moved into its newly completed building on Massachusetts Avenue in Washington DC. SAIS had been founded twenty years earlier, as the Second World War was raging. "Washington was coming alive with the prospects of new power," as a history of SAIS puts it, and a group of government officials, businessmen and academics decided that the capital needed a new institution to provide the kind of graduate training in world affairs that would serve the country's status as an emerging global superpower.[1] Seven years after its founding SAIS became part of the Johns Hopkins University. Now, thanks to funding from several of the country's richest foundations, including the Ford Foundation, the Carnegie Corporation of New York and the Rockefeller Foundation, it finally had a brand new home of its own, right in the heart of the nation's capital.

To celebrate both its twentieth anniversary and the dedication of its new building, SAIS invited a number of distinguished practitioners and scholars of international affairs to deliver lectures over the course of the 1963–1964 academic year. The highest-ranking government official to accept the school's invitation to participate in this lecture series was McGeorge Bundy (1919–1996), who held the post of Assistant to the President for National Security Affairs—more commonly referred to as the National Security Advisor. As a central figure in the executive branch's apparatus for formulating and coordinating military and foreign policy, Bundy was at the time a key architect of deepening U.S. military intervention in Vietnam.[2]

In his address at SAIS, titled "The Battlefields of Power and the Searchlights of the Academy," Bundy discussed the relationship between what he termed the "world of power" and the "world of learning." Hailing "the necessary and constantly expanding process of connection between the university and the government," Bundy cited as examples the role of science in public affairs and of economists in policymaking, and then went on to declare area studies a "third special area of powerful professional connection between the higher learning and government." He continued: "It is a curious fact of academic history that the first great center of area studies in the United States was not located in any university, but in Washington, during the Second World War, in the Office of Strategic Services. In very large measure the area study programs developed in American universities in the years after the war were manned, directed, or stimulated by graduates of the OSS—a remarkable institution, half cops-and-robbers and half faculty meeting."[3]

Bundy was not wrong to highlight the importance of the OSS, the country's first civilian intelligence agency, in helping to spawn area studies as a distinctive component of the postwar academic scene in the United States. Established by President Franklin D. Roosevelt in 1942, the OSS recruited heavily among scholars with expertise on parts of the world in which the United States was, or would soon be, deeply engaged. But as this study shows, area studies had important prewar roots as well, and other visions, institutional sites and factors contributed to its emergence and development. And while there is certainly some basis in fact for Bundy's assertion in this same speech that "it is still true today, and I hope it will always be, that there is a high measure of interpenetration between universities with area programs and the information-gathering agencies of the government of the United States," I argue in this book that it is nonetheless simplistic to depict area studies in the United States as in essence a product or servant of the national security state built during the Cold War.[4]

At SAIS Bundy went on to call for "a much wider and stronger connection niversities and governments than we yet have. . . . What there is of yet, and what I come to praise, is the kind of academic work eeds from the same center of concern as that of the man who is mitted to an active part in government. That center of concern is the taking and use of power itself."[5] Bundy's appeal to scholars to more fully engage with, and more effectively serve, state power may well have resonated positively for many when he issued it. But within a few years his own career in government service would come to an ignominious end, undermined by the increasingly obvious failure of the American war in Vietnam that he had helped initiate and direct. At the same time, growing numbers of academics, in area studies and elsewhere, were coming to recognize the potential costs and consequences—moral, political and intellectual—of the kind of state service to which Bundy had exhorted them. This development would contribute significantly to the transformations that area studies fields underwent from the late 1960s onward, even as Bundy himself, as president of the Ford Foundation from 1966 to 1979, exercised the power that position gave him in ways that helped to shape these fields, along with many other dimensions of American life.

Bundy's reference to university-based area studies as a key domain in which the "world of learning" intersected with the "world of power" manifests its presence by the 1960s as a well-established and apparently durable feature of the landscape of the American research university and of American academic life. As this study shows, the early visionaries and funders of area studies promoted it as an intellectually innovative and naturally interdisciplinary new mode of producing and disseminating knowledge. Alongside the disciplines, each of which was (at least nominally) organized around some body (or competing bodies) of theory specifying that discipline's distinctive object of inquiry (and thus its boundaries), along with a set of methods enabling investigation of that object, each of the area studies fields would in principle focus on a distinct geographic region and draw on multiple disciplines to produce a new kind of knowledge that would advance the world of scholarship but also be of benefit to government and to the American people. That vision was never fully realized; nonetheless, over time, as the various area studies fields developed, they became increasingly bound up with new kinds of scholarly institutions and networks, and were firmly established within the university setting and on the national academic scene.

In this book I explore key dimensions of how that came to pass, especially for Middle East studies in the United States.[6] In so doing I take a very different approach, and draw on entirely different sources, than I did in my earlier book *Contending Visions of the Middle East: The History and Politics of*

Orientalism. In that study I offered a broad survey of Western engagement with, and popular and scholarly representations of, the Middle East, Islam and Muslims. A good part of that book addressed the linkages between the power which since the Second World War the United States has exercised in the Middle East and the Muslim world, on the one hand, and on the other the knowledge produced about those regions in this country. It was in that context that I discussed the emergence and evolution of Middle East studies in the United States from the end of the Second World War to the near present, with the aim of delineating what I termed that field's "politics of knowledge," along with the transformations which it underwent over that period. While that overview included some discussion of the origins of area studies in general, its main concern was the intellectual trajectory of U.S. Middle East studies, especially its engagements with Orientalism and modernization theory in the 1950s and 1960s, and the critiques of these two paradigms that made themselves increasingly felt within the field from the 1970s onward. Moreover, the account of the history of Middle East studies that I offered there was based largely on secondary sources and on analyses of specific texts which I argued could be taken as emblematic of certain features of, and trends in, scholarly writing on the Middle East and the Muslim world at particular points in time.

I continue to stand by the big picture that I drew in *Contending Visions*, though I have never claimed that it is the last word on the subject. Indeed, after its publication I became increasingly aware of how little we actually knew about many dimensions of the history of this field or the contexts that gave birth to it and helped shaped it. That realization impelled me to head for the archives and ultimately to write this book, which is quite different in purpose, focus and scope than *Contending Visions*. Drawing mainly on material found in the archives of foundations, academic organizations and universities, this book seeks to reconstruct the origins and development of area studies, initially envisioned as a distinct way of achieving and imparting knowledge about the world and eventually embodied in a new set of institutions and practices within American higher education. Within that broader context, this study focuses on the history of Middle East studies, including the elaboration of what I term the field's infrastructure: the establishment of new academic institutions, including centers, departments and/or programs focused on a specific geographic or cultural space; the provision of funding for new modes of research and training; the development of language-train-ing methods, materials and programs as well as of library and bibliographic resources; and the launching of new academic organizations and networks, scholarly journals, and models of graduate education and undergraduate pedagogy. To put it somewhat differently: this book narrates the construc-tion and trajectory of Middle East studies as an academic field while seeking to situate that history in relation to the rise of area studies as a whole, to some of the transformations that American higher education underwent after the Second World War, and to developments in American society and politics, including of course the rise of the American national security state.

Much, perhaps most, of the scholarly work on area studies in the United States has foregrounded that last dimension, on the premise (implicit or ex-plicit) that area studies was basically a byproduct of the Cold War, launched primarily to produce knowledge and trained personnel of use to the gov-ernment. There is thus a sizable literature that explores the ways in which, during that era, American scholars (especially political scientists) involved with one or another area studies field and sometimes funded directly or in-directly by government contracts and/or by the big foundations strove to elucidate issues of concern to policymakers and intelligence agencies, and thereby to produce "policy-relevant" knowledge.[7] The questions on which this literature focuses are clearly important, and there have recently been several valuable studies of the linkages between American power in the Middle East and American expertise on that region.[8] However, in my view this framing needs to be supplemented, and enriched and complicated, by serious attention to what actually went into imagining and building the new kind of academic field that area studies (and, for my purposes, Middle East studies in particular) purported to be, and how they evolved over time. The Cold War context (and, more broadly and perhaps more usefully, visions and exigencies of the United States as a global power in the age of decolo-nization) played their parts, to be sure, but as this study shows so did devel-opments in philanthropy, higher education, the humanities and the social sciences in the United States before, during and after the Second World War, as well as factors specific to each regional field. So I do not in this book as-sume that what area studies produced can be understood as only, or even mainly, a Cold War form of knowledge. A range of factors contributed to the conceptualization, launching and specific historical trajectories of the various regionally focused academic fields which were also, each of them in its own way, internally complex and diverse, shaped by distinctive legacies and cultures, and experiencing significant change over time. The Cold War context and these fields' linkages with the national security state therefore do not tell us all we need to know in order to make sense of the history of any one of them.[9]

In the course of exploring how U.S. Middle East studies took shape as a distinct academic field, I do not devote a great deal of time to discussing the intellectual content of the books, articles and conference papers that individual scholars produced, or the theoretical paradigms and methodological presuppositions, explicit or implicit, that informed their work, or how scholarly expertise on the Middle East related to policymaking. I made this choice for several reasons. For one, I have already discussed dimensions of the field's intellectual history at some length in *Contending Visions*, which might profitably be read alongside this study, and see no reason to repeat myself. It also does not seem to me that scholars in this field actually had much of an impact on policymaking. But perhaps most simply, my priorities in this book lie elsewhere: I seek here to elucidate the broader visions, rationales and decision-making processes which underpinned the development of area studies as a mode of understanding the world and of pursuing research, graduate training and undergraduate education, while delving most deeply into the agendas, contention, anxieties, mechanics and logistics that informed field-building in U.S. Middle East studies.

To reconstruct and narrate this complex story, I focus largely on institutions and networks of various kinds, and the people involved with them. Emily Hauptmann has noted that "when externally funded research becomes crucial to universities and individual academics, asking whether and how the entities that supply it influence academic disciplines become important questions. To answer them . . . one must identify the channels through which external funds flow into and then reconfigure the terrain of academic disciplines."[10] This understanding has encouraged scholars to investigate the perspectives, motivations and decision-making processes of the institutions, networks and individuals whose patronage, initiatives and leadership helped shape key developments in twentieth-century American intellectual and academic life—not just in the social sciences but in the humanities as well, and not just during the Cold War but before and after it too. In keeping with this approach, this study begins by discussing the growing engagement after the First World War of the Carnegie Corporation of New York and the Rockefeller Foundation with the social sciences and the humanities at America's universities, and proceeds to explore the efforts of the foundation-funded American Council of Learned Societies (ACLS), from the late 1920s to the outbreak of the Second World War, to induce scholars and disciplines in the humanities to pay greater attention to what was thought of as the non-Western world and to develop more effective methods of language training. I argue that these initiatives fostered new networks and institutions that can be seen as forerunners of (and sometimes models for) the area studies fields that would emerge after the war.

This book goes on to explore how, during the Second World War, an emerging vision of a new kind of regionally focused knowledge about the wider world crystallized at a range of sites, including the Office of Strategic Services but also other government, academic and university-based entities and programs. Key foundation and academic leaders (many of the latter associated with the Social Science Research Council, SSRC) embraced that vision early on, and soon after the war ended Carnegie and Rockefeller, joined in the early 1950s by the even wealthier Ford Foundation, allocated a great deal of money to translate it into reality. In fact, these three foundations play key roles in this story: long before the federal government began supporting area studies, it was behind-the-scenes decision-making at the foundations, and of course the large-scale funding they provided, which from the mid-1940s onward enabled the establishment at universities across the country of new area studies centers, departments and programs, as well as the launching of other vehicles through which to sustain and advance the new regionally focused academic fields, including Middle East studies.

Among those vehicles were the committees set up for each regional field to oversee and promote its intellectual and infrastructural development. Since my focus here is on Middle East studies, I devote a great deal of attention in this book to the work of the various committees appointed (with foundation funding and oversight) from the late 1930s onward by the ACLS, by the SSRC, or jointly by both, to build this field, institutionally but also intellectually. In particular, I reconstruct in some detail the history of the Committee on the Near and Middle East established in 1951 by the SSRC and from 1959 sponsored jointly with the ACLS. Long before the founding of the Middle

East Studies Association in 1966, it was this committee which was deemed responsible for providing intellectual leadership for Middle East studies in the United States, for coordinating among the field's centers and programs, and for developing its infrastructure. Even after MESA was established, this committee continued to regard the formulation and implementation of a coherent research program that would propel the field forward as one of its main missions. My research shows that this committee's conception and execution of its field-building mission was deeply ambiguous and that, despite notable achievements in the later 1950s and the 1960s in putting in place key components of the field's infrastructure, it never quite accomplished other elements of its mission as originally envisioned.

This book narrates a good part of the history of Middle East studies in the United States through the lens of this committee's history. Some readers may feel that I have paid inordinate (and excessively detailed) attention to its doings and exaggerated its significance. But I believe that a close look at what this committee tried to do, how it tried to do it, and what its shifting roster of members (most of them leading scholars in the field) thought they were doing and why, can contribute to a deeper and fuller understanding of how this field was built; it enables us to see how the sausage was actually made, so to speak. I must hope that my fellow scholars who know how academic life works, who may, for example, have had to sit through seemingly endless hours of committee meetings, often deadly tedious but sometimes surprisingly productive, will understand my choice and why it may offer a potentially interesting and valuable perspective. This is often where important academic decisions get made, or not made, with real consequences.

But there is another reason why I devote so much effort to reconstructing what this committee in its various incarnations was up to, one which highlights a key theme of this study. From 1991 to 1995, relatively early in my own academic career, I served on this same SSRC-ACLS Joint Committee on the Near and Middle East toward what turned out to be the very end of its lifespan, though of course we did not know that at the time. We did a good job, I think, of awarding research fellowships to smart graduate students, which in its own way helped advance the field, and we had many excellent meals in interesting places. But I also have vivid memories of witnessing, from my perch at the bottom of the committee's social hierarchy, the angst that beset the senior scholars who led the committee as they sought to fulfill their mandate to frame and implement a research agenda that could move U.S. Middle East studies forward.

Decades later, in the course of my archival research for this book, I was surprised to find that this same committee, charged with overseeing the intellectual (and, for a period, institutional) development of Middle East studies, had been plagued by this same anxiety virtually from its inception in 1951. Over the decades that followed many of the committee's members, generally senior figures in the field, perceived Middle East studies as intellectually isolated and backward, and often despaired about its prospects. They were convinced that while the social science disciplines (and perhaps some of the other regional fields as well) were making great intellectual advances, they in Middle East studies were failing to fulfill their mission of formulating and implementing a productive research agenda for their field rooted in some coherent intellectual paradigm. In reality, of course, much of what was going on in disciplines like political science in the 1950s and 1960s turned out to be a dead end, and many in those disciplines (and other area studies fields) had their doubts and anxieties as well. Nonetheless, the sense among leaders in Middle East studies that they were failing to delineate a paradigm that could generate cutting-edge research, and thereby enable them to emulate their colleagues' apparent triumphs, generated widespread feelings of anxiety, self-doubt and intellectual inferiority that would be a salient feature of Middle East studies into the 1980s, even as the field became increasingly developed, institutionalized, stable and (in terms of scholarly output) productive. Investigating this committee's complex trajectory offers a way to elucidate this phenomenon and thus to help understand the vagaries and travails of building this field.

In the course of reconstructing how Middle East studies as an academic field was actually built, I pay considerable attention to the efforts made to endow it with greater organizational coherence as it began in the early 1960s to approach what might be termed critical mass, in terms of numbers of centers, programs, faculty and students as well as of scholarly publication. One manifestation of those efforts was the now largely forgotten American Association for Middle East Studies, which for some years played a significant role in the field and whose rise and fall I reconstruct here. Another was of course the Middle East Studies Association (MESA), founded in 1966 after many twists and turns, which quickly became (and remains) the leading academic organization in the field. The circumstances that led up to MESA's formation and the association's early history, which witnessed not a little contention and conflict, are extensively discussed here, as they too are part of the field-building story.

The historical narrative that I offer in this book, which begins in the 1920s, comes to its end in the mid-1980s. This is not because the field has no history worth relating after that time. Rather, well before the end of the Cold War and the fraught discussions that ensued about the rationale for the continued existence of area studies, Middle East studies (among other area studies fields) had already been undergoing significant transformations that would leave it very different than it had been in its first three or so decades. I chose to end this book on the cusp of these changes, because to adequately unravel their origins and trace their impact would require a study of a very different kind.

Over the succeeding decades a great deal of empirically rich and theoretically sophisticated scholarship has been produced in this field, much of it in active dialogue with work done in other fields and disciplines. Indeed, as I have suggested elsewhere, while Middle East studies as a field and many of its practitioners have over the last several decades been subjected to vituperation, threats and assaults by outside individuals and organizations with political agendas, in strictly intellectual terms the scholarly work done within it has generally been of very high quality, and has been increasingly recognized (and engaged with) as such by scholars in other fields.[11] Along the way, however—and this is a central argument of this book—the vision that Middle East studies (and presumably other area studies fields as well) should or could have some unique or distinctive intellectual paradigm had to be abandoned. Instead, there has been at least de facto recognition that what gives this field its coherence is, simply, the fact that those engaged in it, while doing a great many different things in intellectual terms, all relate to part or all of more or less the same geographic space and are involved with a common set of institutions and networks.

In the course of my narrative of field-building in U.S. Middle East studies I occasionally zoom in for a closer look at university-based Middle East studies programs, particularly Princeton which before the Second World War was something of a pioneer in the study of the region in the period since the rise of Islam and which in 1947 launched what was portrayed as the first interdisciplinary Middle East studies program in the United States. However, this study operates largely at the U.S. national scale, with developments in Canada largely ignored, as is the Middle East Institute, which played an important (if largely nonacademic) role in the field early on and merits a serious study of its own. I certainly realize that much of the crucial field-building in U.S. Middle East studies was accomplished not by the big foundations, or by the academic organizations through which they worked, or by the Middle East Studies Association. Rather, it happened at colleges and universities across the country, where in each case a small number of highly motivated and energetic scholars and teachers struggled to get languages and survey courses taught, battled departments to allocate faculty lines, trained and mentored students, labored mightily to convince colleagues and administrators to support the creation of Middle East departments, centers and programs, secured Title VI and other funding for them, and so on. Some of the work needed to recover the local histories of how institutions and practices associated with area studies were actually implanted at specific universities, which would complement the perspective offered here, can be done in foundation and Department of Education archives, but much of it will require research in university archives and in collections of personal papers, along with oral interviews. That work has barely begun, suggesting that we still have a lot to learn about the history of this field and about the contexts that shaped it. I should also acknowledge that while I do at times discuss developments in other area studies fields, some of which have significant parallels with Middle East studies, there is simply no way I can delve into them in any depth.

The scholarly literature on the history of postwar Middle East studies in the United States as an academic field is surprisingly sparse. In addition to work cited earlier, there is R. Bayly Winder's 1987 article surveying "Four Decades of Middle Eastern Study" and, in a class by itself, Timothy Mitchell's 2004 essay on the trajectory of Middle East studies (and area studies more broadly) in the United States and their relationship with the social science disciplines.[12] As I discuss in the Epilogue, while Mitchell's essay is insightful and thought-provoking my research does not support the genealogy of the field that he outlines, which suggests that postwar Middle East studies in the United States was centrally shaped by Arnold Toynbee's vision of world history, transmitted through H. A. R. Gibb. I also benefited from two collections of interviews with leading scholars in Middle East studies, many of them no longer alive: Thomas Naff's *Paths to the Middle East: Ten Scholars Look Back* (1993) and Nancy Elizabeth Gallagher's *Approaches to the History of the Middle East: Interviews with Leading Middle East Historians* (1994).

There has been some important work on the histories, politics and cultures of other area studies fields in the United States, as well as on area studies as a whole. David C. Engerman's *Know Your Enemy: The Rise and Fall of America's Soviet Experts* (2009) offers a remarkable study of one regionally focused field, though my purposes and approach in this book are rather different from his; I am also doubtful that, at least for the period covered in this book, the kind of investigation Engerman has accomplished for Soviet studies could be done for Middle East studies. I cite other work in these genres along the way or in the Bibliography, and I discuss some of the issues they raise (including the depiction of area studies as essentially a product of the Cold War) in the Epilogue. I also draw on the valuable scholarly work that has been done on the critical role played by the leading foundations in many dimensions of American higher education as well as in shaping the contours of social science research in the United States during the twentieth century, though for the most part that work does not delve into Middle East studies or even area studies as such. I have benefited as well from the rich and growing literature on the new conceptions and forms of knowledge generated during the Second World War and the Cold War. For example, Nils Gilman's *Mandarins of the Future: Modernization Theory in Cold War America* (2003) offers a powerful overview of the rise and fall of modernization theory in postwar American social science, while Irene L. Gendzier's *Managing Political Change: Social Scientists and the Third World* (1985) remains a landmark.

Then there is Robert A. McCaughey's 1984 study *International Studies and Academic Enterprise: A Chapter in the Enclosure of American Learning*, which traces the process by which (as McCaughey sees it) primary responsibility for the pursuit of international studies—which he defines as "serious inquiry by Americans into those parts of the world Americans have traditionally regarded as having histories, cultures, and social arrangements distinctly different from their own"—was "enclosed," that is, was transferred from the American intellectual community writ large to the narrower world of academia.[13] There is much of value in this book and McCaughey's thesis is provocative, but his definition of international studies is so broad as to be of limited use for my purposes. He is, in fact, not particularly interested in area studies as such and so does not seek to reconstruct or assess the specific trajectory of this field, as opposed to the many other things that he includes under the rubric of international studies.[14]

I am well aware that there are aspects of the history of area studies and Middle East studies into which this study does not delve; all I can say is that one can do only so much in a single book. There is certainly plenty of room (and need) for more research on the questions I explore here (and others that I don't), and more broadly on how knowledge about the "non-West" has been produced and disseminated in the American academic world over the past century or so.[15] I focus in this book on what I see as key dimensions of how one (relatively small) region of the American academic world took shape. Some of what I relate here fits with the story that I and others have told about the trajectory of area studies in general and of Middle East studies in particular, but it also includes a great deal that I for one had not known about or expected. Like every process of academic field-building, indeed like all human endeavors, the field of Middle East studies as we know it today turns out to be the product of all sorts of contingencies, of politics of many kinds, of visions and projects that had consequences their initiators did not intend or anticipate, of interventions by people and institutions with divergent hopes and motives, of conflict and contention, and of much else besides. I must hope that the way this study reconstructs and relates this complex history does it at least partial justice.

FIELD NOTES

1 "We Shall Have to Understand It"

... at the minute the Arabic world is not drawn to our alarmed attention as is the Far East, but everything indicates that within the next couple of decades we shall have to understand it. We should not wait until the need is too obvious, for by that time it will be too late to do anything.

—Mortimer Graves, 1936 or 1937

T HE SECOND WORLD WAR has been described as the metaphorical "midwife" or "mother" of area studies, the historical conjuncture which brought it into being as a distinct mode of organizing the production and dissemination of scholarly knowledge.[1] There is clearly some truth in this depiction, but postwar area studies in the United States also had significant prewar antecedents that provided important visions of, models for and experience with regionally focused academic research, training, networks, programs and institutions which would later contribute to the formation of area studies. Moreover, as with area studies in the decades that followed the war, these initiatives were supported, indeed made possible, by funding from several of the country's richest foundations, often working through a new kind of academic organization that connected them with the objects of their beneficence.

The Rise of the Great Foundations

The enormous, indeed unprecedented, accumulations of wealth which led to the creation of the Carnegie and Rockefeller "families" of philanthropic institutions were the product of the rapid industrialization which the United

States experienced after the Civil War, accompanied by the rise of powerful corporations which came to dominate entire sectors of the American economy as virtual monopolies and generated vast wealth for those who controlled them. Around the turn of the century Andrew Carnegie (1835–1919), who had built a business empire that at its height encompassed much of the country's steel industry, began establishing a number of philanthropies with distinct missions. For our purposes the most important of these was the Carnegie Corporation of New York, founded in 1910 with an endowment of $135 million (the equivalent of over $3 billion in 2015) as the main vehicle through which Andrew Carnegie's vast fortune would be disbursed for philanthropic purposes. John D. Rockefeller Sr. (1839–1937), who had built the Standard Oil empire and at the beginning of the twentieth century was reckoned the richest person on earth, followed Carnegie's example by donating large sums to educational institutions and to medical research. He went on to establish the Rockefeller Foundation, formally chartered in 1913 "to promote the well-being of mankind throughout the world," with an endowment totaling $100 million. As of 1934 the Carnegie Corporation had an endowment of $157 million (equivalent to about $2.8 billion in 2015) and was distributing about $4.7 million ($83 million) in income each year. The Rockefeller Foundation, close behind with an endowment of $154 million ($2.7 billion), was distributing almost $12 million ($213 million) in income annually.[2]

Carnegie and Rockefeller no doubt regarded themselves as altruists. But much of the American public saw them as "malefactors of great wealth," as President Theodore Roosevelt put it in 1907, and their new philanthropic enterprises were established in part to ameliorate their founders' negative public image as well as to avoid the looming threat that their vast fortunes, widely perceived as ill-gotten, might be subjected to heavy taxation. More broadly, this wave of philanthropy can be seen as part of an effort to mitigate the deleterious consequences of the economic and social transformations that the United States was experiencing in the late nineteenth and early twentieth centuries, and to combat the rising tide of resistance to the enormous economic and political power now concentrated in the hands of the owners and managers of the giant corporations and banks. As Edward H. Berman has put it, those who created and led these foundations hoped to achieve

> the stabilization of the rapidly evolving corporate and political order and its legitimation and acceptance by the majority of the American population; the

institutionalization of certain reforms, which would serve to preclude the call for more radical structural change; and the creation through educational institutions of a worldwide network of elites whose approach to governance and change would be efficient, professional, moderate, incremental, and nonthreatening to the class interests of those who, like Messrs. Carnegie, Ford, and Rockefeller, had established the foundations.[3]

They thus shared substantial common ground with the Progressive movement of the period, which sought to address widespread social distress and discontent through moderate social and political reform led by an enlightened elite, to be achieved by the deployment of scientific (including social-scientific) and technical expertise to address social problems and by the provision of enhanced educational opportunities.

During and after the First World War, key leaders at the great foundations, and at the organizations and institutions they funded (and had often created), also embraced an increasingly internationalist perspective.[4] They were particularly concerned about the leading role which they believed the United States, as a rising global power, could and should—indeed, must—play on the world stage, and so they sought to instill in Americans a greater awareness of what they regarded as the country's global responsibilities.[5] Hence the creation, with Rockefeller and/or Carnegie funding, of such entities as the Foreign Policy Association (1921), the Council on Foreign Relations (1921), the Institute of Pacific Relations (1925), which would play a key role in promoting the study of modern and contemporary Asia, and the Yale Institute of International Studies (1935).[6]

The Foundations and American Academic Life

The elaboration of this new network of foundation-funded organizations and institutions focused on international affairs and foreign policy was accompanied in the interwar period by efforts to enhance teaching and research about other parts of the world at America's colleges and universities. In this endeavor a key role was played by the American Council of Learned Societies (ACLS), founded in 1919 to represent American academic organizations in the humanities in the Union Académique Internationale. The ACLS brought together representatives of the American Historical Association, the American Oriental Society, the Modern Language Association, the American

Economic Association, the American Political Science Association, the American Antiquarian Society, the American Academy of Arts and Science, and the American Sociological Society (which in 1959 renamed itself the American Sociological Association, thereby escaping an unfortunate acronym), among others. Many of these professional associations were the product of the reorganization along disciplinary lines of teaching, research and professional life in American higher education in the late nineteenth and early twentieth centuries, a process which also yielded distinct disciplinary departments at colleges and universities.[7]

The founders and early leaders of the ACLS shared the intellectual and political vision of the Progressive movement: as such they were part of what Alfred De calls "an emerging network of modernizing and forward-looking academics that connected humanists to the goal of improving society through rational knowledge and democratic action."[8] Beyond serving the ACLS' constituent learned societies, they hoped not merely to promote but also to reshape the humanities in the United States, by supporting the upgrading of professional standards and the adoption of scientific research methods. While it was still getting itself up and running, the ACLS was joined on the American academic scene by another organization with which it would often collaborate but was sometimes in competition. This was the Social Science Research Council, established in 1924 to do for the social sciences more or less what the ACLS hoped to do for the humanities: protect and extend the interests of the social science disciplines and promote social science research, especially on contemporary social problems—again, very much in keeping with the Progressive vision of developing and deploying scientific expertise to address social problems. The SSRC brought together a set of academic organizations that included the American Anthropological Association, the American Historical Association, the American Political Science Association, the American Psychological Association, the American Statistical Association, the American Economic Association and the American Sociological Society; some of its members belonged to the ACLS as well.

It was only in 1926 that the ACLS secured a reliable source of support, from the General Education Board, established in 1902 as one of several philanthropies created by John D. Rockefeller Sr. and his family and associates.[9] The ACLS would thereafter receive the great bulk of its funding, for its programs as well as for its operating expenses, from Rockefeller philanthropies;

indeed, for much of its life it was widely regarded as more or less an arm of the Rockefeller Foundation. From its inception through the 1930s the SSRC also received most of its funding from Rockefeller philanthropies, especially the Laura Spelman Rockefeller Memorial (founded in 1919) which, before it was merged into the Rockefeller Foundation in 1929, disbursed tens of millions of dollars for social science research, mainly on education, public health and welfare, race relations and child study in the United States but on a smaller scale on international affairs as well.[10] Both the ACLS and the SSRC thus served as intermediary organizations linking the foundation world with scholars, universities and academic institutions and organizations, and as conduits for foundation funding.

The Rockefeller philanthropies made substantial grants to individual scholars, academic institutions and programs in the humanities through the 1920s: for example, they gave $780,000 to the University of Chicago's new Oriental Institute to train archaeologists, and $500,000 to Harvard University's Fogg Museum to train curators and art historians.[11] The ACLS, especially its leading figure in this period, the historian-archivist Waldo T. Leland (1879–1966) who served as the organization's executive secretary and then director until his retirement in 1946, hoped to make the allocation of grants funded by Rockefeller (and on a smaller scale by the Carnegie Corporation as well) less haphazard and more strategic, and also to encourage the humanities disciplines to produce more—and more practically useful—knowledge of the non-Western world.[12] In this mission Leland was joined by a younger colleague, Mortimer Graves (1893–1987), who would succeed Leland as the ACLS' preeminent figure and dominate the organization until the late 1950s. As De puts it, Graves "criticized the traditional focus of the humanities on the preservation and transmission of western culture. In the 1930s, he complained that humanities scholars too often isolated themselves from current events, despite the education and training that uniquely equipped them to analyze broad international changes." Scholars in the humanities should, Graves believed, "educate the public and create a class of knowledgeable policy elites capable of navigating complicated international waters, especially those of East Asia."[13] To achieve this Graves advocated, among other things, the reform of the undergraduate curriculum so that it much more effectively exposed students to the histories and cultures of the non-Western world.

The ACLS and the Humanities in the Long 1930s

This international orientation helped the ACLS carve out for itself a distinctive role in American academia. In 1928, as the Rockefeller Foundation was beginning to fund projects in China, the ACLS began to convene meetings on Chinese studies in the United States which attracted some of the leading figures in the field and out of which emerged an ACLS-sponsored standing committee on Chinese studies along with ambitious proposals to promote and develop this field.[14] Progress was halting, but over time there were signs of change in Asian studies, including the establishment of a new Program in Oriental Civilizations at the University of Michigan in the late 1920s. This field's development, and later that of other fields, gained new impetus after 1932, when David H. Stevens (1884–1980), previously involved in other Rockefeller-related projects, became director of the foundation's Humanities Division and increased support for culture and the arts but also for research and training in the humanities focused on specific regions of the non-Western world.

Foundation funding enabled the ACLS to provide postdoctoral research fellowships (if on a modest scale) for what was at the time usually referred to as Far Eastern studies. Working with the separate committees for Chinese and Japanese studies that it appointed and supported, and with the Carnegie Corporation providing funding for fellowships, beginning in 1932 the ACLS also helped organize a series of summer institutes that brought together scholars and students for intensive training on East Asia, generally including accelerated language training and courses on the history and culture of the region. The summer institute (or summer seminar) quickly became a model that was emulated in other regional fields and served as an important instrument of field-building; it also provided a context within which to develop new and more effective methods of language training, such the use of native speakers as drill instructors.[15] The ACLS also supported the development of bibliographical resources, including (with grants in 1933 from the Rockefeller Foundation) the creation of a center for Far Eastern studies at the Library of Congress to enable students in the field to receive advanced training and make better use of that institution's rich collections.[16] Plans were also made for the Library to catalogue Chinese and Japanese books in American collections.

The ACLS Committees on Far Eastern Studies, encompassing separate committees for Chinese and Japanese studies, began publishing a newsletter in 1937 and later a journal, *Far Eastern Quarterly*, and sponsored conferences that brought together scholars in the field.[17] As Robert A. McCaughey notes, during the Depression years the committees also "acted as an academic placement bureau, anticipating openings wherever they might occur and trying to keep unemployed PhDs in the field through stopgap fellowship support."[18] Though growth was slow, over time the field expanded and courses in East Asian languages gradually became more common; for example, in the fall of 1936 Robert K. Reischauer, a young political scientist then teaching in Princeton's School of Public and International Affairs, began offering courses in Japanese through the university's Department of Oriental Languages and Literatures.[19]

Along roughly similar lines, Latin American studies also slowly began to coalesce as a distinct and increasingly institutionalized field in the 1930s, owing in large measure to foundation support. As Helen Delpar shows, the Rockefeller Foundation had long funded research on Latin America, a region of special interest to the Rockefeller family which had large oil investments there. It now began to encourage Latin American studies in a more sustained way, and as early as 1932 the ACLS formed an advisory committee to help develop the field. The committee initially focused on literature, but a group of social scientists soon began to collaborate with it and in 1935 the Social Science Research Council funded a small conference of Latin America scholars. The conference participants decided to continue to work together and to pursue annual publication of a select and critical bibliography of scholarly research on Latin America, encompassing a broad range of disciplines. The *Handbook of Latin American Studies* began to appear in 1936, with modest support from a Carnegie philanthropy (channeled through the ACLS) and, a few years later, with much more substantial support from Rockefeller; it continues to be published today, though its format has changed considerably over time. In 1939 the ACLS sponsored the creation of a formal Committee on Latin American Studies, which the following year received a three-year grant of $52,000 (the equivalent of almost $900,000 in 2015) from the Rockefeller Foundation. As with Far Eastern studies, Rockefeller in this period also funded summer institutes on Latin America sponsored by the committee, as well as projects by several American university libraries to acquire Latin American materials and the work of the Hispanic Foundation of the Library of Congress and its Archive of Hispanic Culture.[20]

Studying the Near East

By the early 1930s Leland and Graves had begun to take an interest in other regionally defined fields as well, forming committees to promote Indic and Iranian studies (successor to a similar committee established by the American Oriental Society in 1926) and Mediterranean antiquities.[21] They also began to attend to the Near East, though in this regard we must distinguish between the scholarly study of the Near East in the ancient and "classical" (i.e., Greek and Roman) periods, on the one hand, and on the other the period from the rise of Islam onward. The former was actually relatively well developed in the United States. The American Oriental Society had been founded in 1842 to foster the study of the "Bible lands," but over time its geographic scope expanded to include much broader swathes of the ancient Near East (including both Egypt and Mesopotamia), and India and China as well. Its journal was a key venue for the publication of scholarship in these fields, which was overwhelmingly philological in character. The journal *Hebraica,* established in 1884, was renamed the *American Journal of Semitic Languages and Literatures* in 1895 to reflect its expanding scope and provided another important outlet for scholarly work on Semitics and the ancient Near East.[22]

The scholars and departments of Bible studies, Semitics and related fields based at colleges and universities around the country were joined soon after the First World War by a new institution, the Oriental Institute of the University of Chicago, founded in 1919 with lavish funding from the Rockefeller philanthropies and directed by James Henry Breasted (1865–1935), the preeminent American Egyptologist of his day. The Oriental Institute quickly became an academic powerhouse and provided what many saw as a new model of multidisciplinary or even interdisciplinary academic enterprise.[23] McCaughey notes that

> Breasted envisioned the institute as a means by which American Oriental studies would be transformed from what they had been, a primarily linguistic endeavor identified almost exclusively with ancient civilizations, into a historical discipline "in which art, archaeology, political science, language, literature, and sociology, in short all of the categories of civilization shall be represented and correlated." To the extent that Breasted succeeded in this effort, the Oriental Institute anticipated the "area center" approach that became fashionable among proponents of international studies after World War Two.[24]

Breasted's institutional vision was bound up with his insistence on treating the ancient Near East, including both Egypt and the civilizations of the "Fertile Crescent" (a term he originated in 1914) as not only a distinct historical-civilizational unit but also as central to the story of the origins of Western civilization. As he saw it, Egypt and Mesopotamia had passed their rich heritage—the heritage of the "Great White Race," the "fundamental carrier of civilization"—on to the Greeks who in turn bequeathed it to the Romans; in the process the foundations of Western civilization were laid.[25] The idea that this region possessed a high degree of historical continuity stretching back to ancient times, and therefore that Near Eastern studies as a scholarly field should properly encompass both ancient times and all later periods, would persist in scholarly circles for decades to come.

By contrast with the relatively developed state of ancient and classical Near Eastern studies, and unlike the situation in Europe, until well into the twentieth century Arabic and Islamic studies had only a tenuous existence as an academic field in the United States. There were certainly American scholars who studied or taught Arabic (along with Syriac and Aramaic) as an adjunct to Hebrew and Biblical studies, but there were very few who pursued serious research on Arabic literature, on Islamic thought and culture or on the histories of the Near Eastern lands in the period after the rise of Islam. Change came slowly, sometimes in the service of other agendas. For example, in 1892 Duncan Black Macdonald (1863–1943), trained in Oriental studies at Glasgow and Berlin, arrived at Hartford Theological Seminary to teach Semitic literature. Macdonald would later declare that "I had come to Hartford determined to have a school of Arabic, although I was warned that there was no opening for Arabic in America. I found the way through Missions." Or as he put it on another occasion, he discovered "that you could smuggle Muslim studies into a theological school under the guise of training missionaries."[26] In fact, Macdonald seems to have shared Hartford's commitment to Protestant mission, but he was at the same time determined to promote the study of Arabic and of Islam, and neither he nor his colleagues and successors at Hartford saw any contradiction between their religious commitment and serious scholarly work.

The same was true of the founders of the country's first journal focusing on the modern and contemporary Muslim world. *The Moslem World*, launched in 1911 as a quarterly in the wake of the Edinburgh World Missionary Conference held the previous year, bore a subtitle which made clear the strong Protestant missionary impulse that informed it: *A Quarterly Review of Current Events, Literature, and Thought among Mohammedans, and the Progress of Christian Missions in Moslem Lands.* As the editorial opening the very first issue put it, in the same "know your enemy" vein that decades later would underpin Soviet studies in the United States: "If the Churches of Christendom are to reach the Moslem world with the Gospel, they must know of it and know it."[27] Its strong missionary slant notwithstanding, *The Moslem World* was for decades the only journal in the United States which followed and regularly reported on religious, political and social developments in contemporary Muslim communities worldwide. As time went on it published informative and relatively neutral articles on Islam by some of the leading scholars of the day, including the eminent Orientalist David Samuel Margoliouth (1858–1940), Laudian Professor of Arabic at Oxford from 1889 to 1937 and the immediate predecessor in that position of H. A. R. Gibb.[28]

Despite developments at Hartford and a few other institutions of higher education, Arabic and Islamic studies, and the teaching of the relevant languages—much less the teaching of Arabic, Persian or Turkish as modern living languages by means of up-to-date methods—remained grossly underdeveloped into the interwar years. While the American Oriental Society provided an academic home for scholars in these fields, most of them philologists, their numbers were small and the organization was dominated by those primarily interested in ancient times. The same was true both of the AOS' own journal and of the *American Journal of Semitic Languages and Literatures*, though they did publish some articles on Islamic topics. At the same time, college-level courses on Islamic thought and history were very rare. Decades later, J. C. Hurewitz would assert that "as far as can be ascertained, there was a lone two-semester survey course on the history of the Middle East in Islamic times, offered in alternate years at the University of Illinois at the graduate/undergraduate levels by Albert H. Lybyer, starting in 1928 or even earlier." Lybyer is best known today for his 1913 book *The Government of the Ottoman Empire in the Time of Suleiman the Magnificent*, which informed Gibb and Bowen's analysis of the Ottoman state in their influential study published in the 1950s, *Islamic Society and the West*.[29] He does in fact seem to have begun to offer a two-course sequence—"The Mohammedan World: The Saracen Empire and the Crusades" followed by "The Mohammedan World: The Ottoman Empire and the Question of the Near East"—in 1928–1929.[30] Whether Lybyer was actually the first to offer this kind of survey, or in the 1920s the only one to do, is uncertain; but it is clear that undergraduate courses on the Middle East in the period after the emergence of Islam were at best extremely rare. More broadly, before the 1930s an academic field focusing specifically on the Near East after the rise of Islam can hardly be said to have been in existence.

The ACLS and Arab-Islamic Studies

Yet in the 1930s there were signs of change in this arena as well, with Philip K. Hitti (1886–1978) of Princeton University playing the leading role. Born in Lebanon, Hitti had graduated from what was then still called the Syrian Protestant College (it would be renamed the American University of Beirut in 1920) and went on to receive his doctorate from Columbia in 1915, after which he began teaching at AUB. Princeton had acquired a rich collection of Arabic manuscripts and wanted someone who could catalogue and edit them, and use them for research and teaching, and so in 1926 it recruited Hitti for a new position as assistant professor of Semitic philology, funded by the William and Annie S. Paton Foundation.[31] A year after Hitti's arrival at Princeton, the university established a Department of Oriental Languages and Literatures for its Orientalists, most of them philologists specializing in Semitic or Indo-European languages; its first chair was Harold H. Bender, who bore the title of Professor of Indo-Germanic Philology. In this new framework, while working on his *magnum opus, A History of the Arabs,* first published in 1937, Hitti gradually began to move beyond Semitic philology by promoting the teaching of Arabic as a living language along with the study of Arab and Islamic history and culture, and by working with colleagues to convince the university to expand its offerings in this field.

In March 1933 Hitti and several of his Princeton colleagues, constituted as an interdepartmental Committee on Near Eastern Studies under the chairmanship of the university's head librarian, issued a report urging the university to devote greater attention to the history, literature and art of the Islamic world. Studies in this field were, the report asserted, "becoming of constantly increasing importance on account of their intrinsic value as a discipline, their place in the history of thought and culture, and the decisive part which the newly established nations are destined to play in world affairs," while Princeton was deemed "peculiarly fitted" to take the initiative owing to its rich faculty, library and manuscript resources. The report noted that over the past two years some twenty-five graduate and undergraduate students had enrolled in Arabic classes.

In his segment of the report Hitti highlighted the importance of Arabic for philologists and scholars of medieval Europe but also the practical utility of Arabic and Islamic studies. Arabic, Hitti declared, was "the living language of some fifty million people, and the religious language of about two hundred and fifty millions. . . . Next to Christianity, Islam is the most vital and aggressive religion today; its adherents are thrusting themselves more and more into the foreground of world affairs. There is today hardly a country in Eastern Europe, Asia and Africa that does not have its Moslem problem. About half a million Moslems, the Moros, live in the Philippines under the rule of the United States. Another half a million Arabic-speaking immigrants have found a new home in our land." The committee recommended that the university allocate as much as $457,000 (over $8 million in 2015) over a period of three to five years in order to acquire books, periodicals, manuscripts, photographs and maps to fill gaps in Princeton's collections; fund several research fellowships or lectureships "in the general field of Near-Eastern studies" that would strengthen course offerings; establish an annual lecture series; and secure an endowment for a professorship of Arabic language and literature. The report also expressed the hope that, along with Arabic, Turkish and Persian would eventually be taught at Princeton on a regular basis.[32]

We have no record of any response by the university, and it would be years before the report's recommendations were even partially fulfilled. Nonetheless, this initiative signaled to ACLS leaders that Princeton was by far the most likely site for the more systematic development of this field, over and above the kind of grants that the ACLS (and the foundations for which it was a funding conduit) had been handing out to individual scholars and organizations for specific projects.[33] Mortimer Graves and his boss Waldo Leland hoped to go beyond this kind of piecemeal support and do for the study of the Islamic and modern Near East what they had already begun to do for other fields.

In this context Philip Hitti stood out as the most promising prospect in his field, and by the spring of 1934 Graves was expressing directly to Hitti his desire to "advance the study of the modern Near East in this country." Graves asked Hitti to let him know about promising younger scholars the ACLS might support and encouraged him to consider organizing at Princeton a summer seminar on the Near East, on the model of the ACLS-funded Far Eastern studies seminar planned for the coming summer at the University of California, Berkeley.[34] By late 1934 or early 1935 Hitti had agreed to organize a seminar in Arabic and Islamic studies in the summer of 1935, with the goal of enhancing the ability of mature scholars in other fields to incorporate these topics into their courses. For its part, the ACLS ("with considerable difficulty," Graves noted) raised $2000 to match Princeton University's contribution to covering the costs of the seminar.[35]

The seminar took place over a period of six weeks in June and July of 1935, with thirty-three participants from nineteen educational institutions; $40 was charged for tuition and $20 a week for room and board. The one required course was a survey by Philip Hitti of Islamic culture and Arabic literature up to the Ottoman conquest. The electives offered were elementary and advanced Arabic, a survey of Islamic art taught by Mehmet Aga-Oglu (1896–1949) of the University of Michigan, elementary Ottoman Turkish and a survey of Ottoman history; the latter two courses were taught by Walter L. Wright Jr. (1900–1949), then assistant professor of history at Princeton. Senior scholars from other universities gave special lectures for seminar participants.[36] Graves later acknowledged that of the participants "only a very few continued to devote themselves to becoming Arabists or scholars of Arabic civilizations." However, he continued, others "went back to their posts in universities and colleges teaching medieval history, fine-arts, Romance languages, etc. but better equipped to present the Arabic phases of their own fields, to show the Arabic contributions, and to awaken an interest in the pursuit of Arabic studies for their own sake." He therefore deemed the seminar "a modest step forward in the direction of rounding out university and college curricula to a point where they are adequate to the job before them."[37]

In a series of memoranda produced soon thereafter Graves located the development of Near Eastern studies in the context of his vision of the ACLS' broader mission:

> As the repository of organized American thought in the field of the Humanities the Council is responsible not only for the best possible development of those studies within themselves, but for their interpretation to and their integration in

society. So long as the Humanities are defined merely as the studies of the Greek and Latin classics and the philological and linguistic disciplines ancillary to or derivative from them, they may be developed internally to the furthest degree, yet their interpretation and integration cannot proceed much further than is the case at present. Further, as the Humanities taken in this sense prove less and less to be essential as an implement of understanding the world, we can expect them to become less and less maintained and cultivated by a society interested primarily only in activities useful to it. A number of us, consequently, have come to believe, first, that the Humanities must be defined as the study of all human life at the intellectual level, that is at the level of activity which differentiates humanity from the rest of Nature, and second, that the Humanities so defined are certainly equally important with the sciences as an implement in understanding the world.[38]

Hence the imperative that the ACLS promote and develop Arabic-Islamic studies as it had Far Eastern studies. It was true, Graves admitted in another memorandum, that "at the minute the Arabic world is not drawn to our alarmed attention as is the Far East, but everything indicates that within the next couple of decades we shall have to understand it. We should not wait until the need is too obvious, for by that time it will be too late to do anything."[39]

Though the ACLS was unable to raise the funds to support summer seminars in Arabic and Islamic studies in 1936 or 1937, it was able to provide fellowships to participants in two more seminars held at Princeton, in 1938 and 1939. These offered a wider range of courses and lectures by faculty from several universities as well as instruction in Persian, along with Arabic and Turkish.[40] The success of the seminars had consequences for Near Eastern studies at Princeton as well: with funding from the Rockefeller Foundation, a newly hired instructor began in the fall of 1939 to offer graduate students and qualified seniors instruction in Persian and Turkish on a regular basis, along with lectures on Islamic archaeology.[41] Teaching these two languages as well as Arabic, and teaching them as living languages, made Princeton unique among American universities before the Second World War.[42]

Encouraged by what he saw as signs of life in Arabic and Islamic studies, Mortimer Graves engineered the dissolution of the ACLS committees on Mediterranean Antiquities and on Byzantine Studies in January 1937 and replaced them with a new provisional Committee on Mediterranean and Near Eastern Studies, to which were recruited some of the country's leading scholars of Egyptology, Assyriology and Biblical archaeology.[43] This committee was charged with surveying the fields of Mediterranean and Near Eastern studies and making recommendations for their further development. It convened just once, in October 1937, concluded that there was a need for greater attention to medieval and modern Near Eastern studies, and to Turkish as well as Persian, and recommended that a Committee on Studies in Islamic Culture be established; it then disbanded.[44]

Another indication that things in this field were at long last moving, albeit slowly, was the luncheon organized at the American Oriental Society's April 1938 annual meeting in Philadelphia by members interested in Islamic studies—apparently the first time they had done such a thing. Participants, including Hitti (who in 1936 had been appointed the William and Annie S. Paton Professor of Semitic Literature), Lybyer and the Islamicist Edwin E. Calverley (1882–1971), since 1930 a professor at Hartford Seminary (where he had been trained by Duncan Black Macdonald) and newly appointed co-editor of *The Moslem World*, discussed ways of promoting Arabic and Islamic studies in the United States, "both as subject of instruction in colleges and universities and as subject of research and scientific publications," and constituted themselves a committee within the AOS.[45]

In the course of 1938, building on these developments and on the recommendations of its provisional Committee on Mediterranean and Near Eastern Studies, the ACLS launched two new committees, a Committee on Near Eastern Studies for the ancient and classical periods and a Committee on Arabic and Islamic Studies (CAIS) for the period since the rise of Islam. The latter was charged with giving special attention to Turkish and Persian language and culture, deemed to be even less developed in the American scholarly world than Arabic. To chair the CAIS, the ACLS recruited Gardiner Howland Shaw (1893–1965), scion of a prominent Boston family who had joined the Foreign Service in 1917 and for stretches in the 1920s and 1930s held various positions at the U.S. embassy in Turkey, then located in Istanbul rather than in Ankara; he lived in Turkey for some twelve years altogether and was regarded as one of the country's foremost experts on the contemporary Near East.[46] In addition to Shaw, the other members of the newly established CAIS were Philip Hitti; Edwin E. Calverley; the Qur'an scholar Arthur Jeffery (1892–1959) of Columbia University; and the Harvard Semiticist and Arabist William Thomson (1886–1972), soon to be appointed the first James

Richard Jewett Professor of Arabic.

At their first meeting in May 1939 the committee members agreed that their mission to foster Arabic and Islamic studies in the United States should entail "the development of American trained personnel, a survey of facilities and materials, particularly manuscript, in America, and the creation of a center of interest in these studies at the Library of Congress."[47] This last priority was a reference to the efforts made by the ACLS in 1939–1940 to convince that institution to devote more attention and resources to the Near East, as it had earlier begun to do for the Far East. A leading role in this campaign was played by Myron Bement Smith (1897–1970), who had amassed a collection of tens of thousands of photographs, architectural drawings, maps and other items relating to various aspects of Islamic (especially Iranian) art and architecture. Smith, who had come to call his materials the "Islamic Archives," served as a consultant to the Library of Congress and hoped to house his collection there as the nucleus of the new Center for Islamic Studies the ACLS proposed establishing at the Library.[48] In October 1941 Librarian of Congress Archibald MacLeish agreed in principle to something much more modest: the establishment of a new section within what was then called its Division of Orientalia that would cover "the Near East, the Middle East and South-east Asia." By then, of course, the country was already preparing for war, and so MacLeish noted not only the cultural contribution this section could make but also "the services it could render to defense organizations." But he insisted that the ACLS would have to come up with the funds to pay the salaries of the personnel who would run the new section.[49] A Near East division would be established at the Library of Congress in 1945, but the Islamic Archives, with Smith's collection at its core but also including materials acquired from or donated by other collectors and scholars, eventually ended up at what is today the Smithsonian Institution's National Anthropological Archives.[50]

The CAIS seems to have been involved at least peripherally in this project, and by 1941 Myron Smith was listed as the committee's secretary. But the committee exhibited few signs of life in the years that followed, and it seems to have convened only once during the war. In 1941 it was reported to have "joined with the Committee on Near Eastern Studies in supervising the compilation of an index to the Near Eastern and Islamic material in the *Journal of the American Oriental Society*," and somewhat later some of its members apparently helped edit a chrestomathy compiled by Nabih Amin Faris (1906–1968), who for a time worked under Hitti at Princeton and edited, translated and published a number of Arabic manuscripts from its rich collection. The chrestomathy was published in facsimile as *Mukhtatat min al-Adab al-'Arabi* around 1946.[51] It seems that, with the approach and then arrival of the war, the CAIS' members, along with the ACLS, became increasingly preoccupied with other concerns and projects, and so this committee—unlike that for Latin American studies, for example, which mobilized itself for the war effort—simply languished, existing only as a set of names on paper.

Between the late 1920s and the Second World War, the ACLS thus channeled substantial foundation funding into, and devoted a great deal of energy to fostering, projects that had the effect of enhancing the development of academic fields focused on particular geographic regions. Though the scale of funding was modest compared to what would come later, it was not insubstantial: it is estimated that the Rockefeller Foundation's grants between 1934 and 1942 to support non-Western language training, scholarship and related projects totaled somewhat under $1 million—the equivalent of roughly $15 million in 2015.[52] These investments had a significant impact, and fields that could be thought of as Far Eastern and Latin American studies—and in a much more rudimentary way perhaps even Near Eastern studies—began to grow in size, and to develop a certain coherence and institutional density, well before the war. They did not necessarily define themselves or function as they would come to do after the war, but they were characterized by a growing number of students and of trained scholars, by increasingly ramified scholarly networks with experience in collaborative endeavors, including conferences, publications and new kinds of intensive language-training programs, and by heightened attention to the modern period and contemporary issues. All this indicates that at least some elements of the intellectual and institutional infrastructure of what would become area studies, and models of what this new mode of knowledge production and dissemination might look like, were taking shape well before Pearl Harbor.

Meanwhile, if the notion of organizing the production and dissemination of scholarly knowledge along regional lines predated the war, so did another key feature of postwar area studies as initially envisioned: what we today refer to as interdisciplinarity. As Ellen Condliffe Lagemann has shown in her study of the Carnegie Corporation, key foundation and academic leaders came in the 1920s to regard the transcendence of disciplinary boundaries as an important goal and began funding efforts to achieve it. She cites the example of Yale's Institute for Human Relations, founded with Rockefeller Foundation support in 1929 in order to "foster collaboration among scholars from all divisions of the Yale faculty" but also to "make the study of human behavior in its individual and group relations one of the major objectives of the University's investigative and educational programs," thereby prefiguring the behavioralism that would be so powerful in postwar U.S. social science. The desire to promote interdisciplinarity also contributed to the establishment of the University of Chicago's Oriental Institute, Yale's Institute of International Studies and other academic entities in the interwar period.[53] Wartime developments would seem to further validate this vision of interdisciplinarity, and the belief that knowledge production organized along regional lines could provide the vehicle by means of which interdisciplinary training and research could at long last take root in, and reshape, American scholarly life would be a powerful argument in favor of what would in the 1940s become known as area studies. In short, as David C. Engerman usefully reminds us, "many of the key elements that shaped American social science in the Cold War years flowed directly from concerns that long predated the Soviet threat," and some of these would later help buttress (and shape) postwar area studies.[54]

One last point needs to be made here, a point that applies as much to the post-Second World War era as to the prewar years. In the 1930s ACLS officials were in close and regular contact with the foundation leaders who funded their organization and its projects, and they were acutely aware of and responsive to the foundations' perspectives and priorities. The same was from the start also true of the SSRC, which like the ACLS depended almost entirely on foundation funding. The relationship between these academic organizations and the big foundations was not entirely one-sided: ACLS and SSRC officials, in close touch with developments in the academic world, frequently sought to "sell" foundation officials on projects and initiatives that they argued would address problems or lacunae in various disciplines and fields. But these proposals generally had to fit within what one or another of the foundations considered to be its sphere of interest, and in the final analysis it was the foundation officials who held the purse strings, and thus the power to influence the character and direction of academic disciplines and fields.

Underpinning and facilitating this close working relationship was the fact that both sets of men—and they were virtually all men—for the most part belonged to the same social world. They tended to come from well-to-do families of white Protestant stock, were mostly educated at Ivy League institutions (and sometimes before that at the same exclusive private schools), and broadly speaking shared a common outlook on the world and on their mission in it, an outlook that might be characterized as Progressive (in the sense discussed earlier in this chapter), internationalist and informed by a sort of elite-technocratic (and very American) sense of *noblesse oblige*. Their common origins, values and vision of the world would enable ACLS and SSRC officials to maintain a highly efficient working relationship, and collaborate more or less seamlessly, with Carnegie and Rockefeller staff, and later with Ford Foundation officials, as together they conceived and laid the foundations of area studies during and after the Second World War.

2 "The Regional Knowledge Now Required"

The immediate need for social scientists who know the different regions of the world stands second only to the demand for military and naval officers familiar with the actual and potential combat zones.
—*World Regions in the Social Sciences,* 1943

A S WITH MANY modern wars, the Second World War not only dramatically accelerated the pace of changes already under way but also spawned powerful new visions which quickly took on institutional form. So it was that wartime exigencies brought into being a new set of sites, projects, practices and networks through which the contours of area studies were delineated, ultimately yielding both an apparently coherent and efficacious vision of how useful knowledge about the world might be produced and disseminated, and an assemblage of new academic programs, institutions and funding flows.

The Early War Period

As the Roosevelt administration began mobilizing the country for war in 1940–1941, the ACLS and other academic entities increasingly oriented their activities accordingly. Two months before Pearl Harbor, Archibald MacLeish was already justifying the expansion of the Middle Eastern and Southeast Asian sections of the Library of Congress in terms of national defense. Around the same time Mortimer Graves of the ACLS circulated a proposal to create a School of Modern Oriental Languages and Civilizations in Washington; his models were France's state-supported École nationale des langues orientales vivantes, whose origins went back to 1795, and Britain's School of Oriental and African Studies, founded in 1916.[1] But this proposal failed to gain traction, and as academic and foundation leaders began to think about how the nation's need for knowledge about the rest of the world might best be met, they focused on America's universities and their faculties, not on new institutions to be created or funded by the federal government.

Once the United States actually entered the war in December 1941, the ACLS and its sister organization the SSRC immediately sought ways of making themselves useful to the war effort. On January 15, 1942, ACLS director Waldo G. Leland wrote a letter to Walter A. Jessup, president of the Carnegie Corporation of New York. Citing what he called "my still very vivid recollections of 1917," Leland told Jessup that the current situation with respect to the "mobilization of the intellectual resources of the nation" was much better than had been the case the last time the U.S. went to war, "because the four councils have really achieved a high degree of intellectual activities and have made possible a very effective sort of cooperation." The "four councils" to which Leland referred were his own ACLS, the SSRC, the National Research Council (NRC), established in 1916 to help mobilize the country's scientific and technological resources for war, and the American Council on Education (ACE), representing institutions of higher education. But as Leland saw it, a "problem of demand and supply" had arisen that was making it difficult for government agencies to get the scholarly knowledge they urgently needed, even as scholars across the country were asking what they could do to serve the war effort.

What was required, Leland told Jessup, was "a central agency located in Washington which would be charged with maintaining close contacts between the councils and the Government, interpreting to the councils the needs of the Government that they might be able to meet, and also interpreting to the Government the ways in which the councils can be useful to it." Funding for this new agency would presumably come from a Carnegie philanthropy.[2] But Leland seems to have been playing catch-up: Jessup had in fact already been discussing the question of how scholars could most effectively aid the war effort with Robert Crane, executive director of the SSRC. Neither Jessup nor Crane seem to have thought that a "central agency" of the kind Leland was proposing was a good idea and the proposal never went any further, but in the months and years that followed large numbers of scholars and students would be recruited for the war effort by other means, with the collaboration of both the ACLS and the SSRC.[3]

The entry of the United States into the war provided further impetus for the institutionalization and development of regionally focused academic networks, perhaps especially in Latin American studies. In March 1942 the ACLS Committee on Latin American Studies was merged into a new Joint Committee on Latin American Studies (JCLAS); the committee was referred to as "joint" because it was co-sponsored by the ACLS, the SSRC and the NRC. It was chaired by the noted University of Chicago anthropologist Robert Redfield, who had been a member of the now-dissolved ACLS committee, and like its predecessor enjoyed substantial Rockefeller funding.[4] The new committee threw itself into the war effort, among other things by enabling four social scientists to pursue war-related research in Latin America. Of these four, three—the geographer Carl Sauer (1889–1975) of the University of California, Berkeley; Earl J. Hamilton (1899–1989), a scholar of Spanish and Latin American economic history at Duke University; and especially Robert B. Hall (1896–1975), a geographer and Japan specialist at the University of Michigan—would go on to play leading roles in launching area studies in the United States. Hall's wartime research project focused on Asian settlements in the Western hemisphere, a topic of security interest to the government and military. During the war the JCLAS worked closely with the federal government's Office of the Coordinator of Inter-American Affairs, headed by Nelson A. Rockefeller (grandson of John D. Rockefeller Sr., and a future governor of New York and vice president), which sought to counter German and Italian influence, and pro-Axis sentiment, in the Western hemisphere through a propaganda campaign but which also supported projects to foster intellectual and academic cooperation.

"Foreign Area and Language" Programs on the Wartime Campus

In the months after Pearl Harbor the ACLS played a central role in launching a program which would contribute significantly to the crystallization of the area studies vision. ACLS secretary Mortimer Graves had long campaigned for, and channeled foundation funding into, improved language teaching in the United States, especially of Asian and Middle Eastern languages. Even before the United States entered the war, the Rockefeller Foundation began making large grants to the ACLS "to develop personnel and resources in modern Oriental languages."[5] In the months after Pearl Harbor, with additional Rockefeller funding, the ACLS built on the language-teaching methods pioneered during the 1930s (especially in the summer seminars and institutes it had sponsored) and on Mortimer Graves' extensive network of contacts to develop a new Intensive Language Program (ILP). This was an innovative vehicle through which to quickly teach a broad array of languages (including Arabic, Persian and Turkish) to military and civilian personnel on college and university campuses, and to further develop the new kinds of teaching methods and materials needed for such intensive courses. Within six months ILP-sponsored programs had trained some 700 students in twenty-six different languages.[6]

Graves did not regard the ILP as an end in itself: he was already thinking about its implications for the postwar period. In a 1942 memorandum—one of a great many he churned out over the years—he proposed that, with foundation and perhaps government funding, the ILP be expanded beyond language training in order to meet what he saw as the country's great need for people equipped to oversee postwar rehabilitation and reconstruction around the globe, drawing on the idle or underutilized humanities resources of American colleges and universities. "An educational program of this character consequently would," he argued,

> 1) train the persons who are to implement reconstruction; 2) utilize our humanistic facilities in an operation closely connected with the War effort; 3) preserve humanistic scholars (and incidentally the universities and colleges) through the emergency in activities not too far removed from their major interests; 4) give a foretaste of the kind of experiment in education necessary for the second half of the twentieth century; 5) possibly develop a few persons who would make scholarship in these underworked fields their life's work.[7]

Much sooner than he could have imagined, Graves' vision would be at least partially realized by means of a massive new government program. As David C. Engerman notes, the ILP was "quickly dwarfed by the arrival of the military services, which incorporated the intensive approach as the keystone of their work."[8] In December 1942 the Army Specialized Training Program (ASTP) was established; the same period also witnessed the creation of a similar (but much smaller) Navy program as well as of the Civil Affairs Training Program

(CATP), designed to prepare personnel for military government service in oc-
cupied territories. Under their auspices, with large-scale funding from the federal government and support from the ACLS and the ACE, some 227 colleges
and universities across the country offered intensive, accelerated training to
tens of thousands of military and civilian personnel in a range of fields, including engineering, medicine, dentistry and veterinary science. But the ASTP
and the CATP also established "foreign area and language" programs at fifty-
five of those institutions, with a peak enrollment of 13,185 as of December 1943,
to train military personnel in the languages, cultures, politics and histories of
parts of the world which U.S. military forces were likely to fight in, occupy and
administer. This component of the ASTP absorbed the ILP, adopting and applying the language training methods which the ACLS had helped pioneer in
the 1930s and had then refined further in its short-lived ILP.[9]

Not everyone felt that the ASTP, which at its peak had an enrollment of
150,000, made a significant contribution to the war effort; for example, Major General Harry L. Twaddle, Assistant Chief of Staff to General George C.
Marshall and from 1942 commander of a division in General Patton's Third
Army, later wrote that "The underlying reason for institution of the ASTP
program was to prevent some colleges and universities from going into bank-
ruptcy [because so many of their current and potential students had been
drafted]. From a strictly mobilization viewpoint, the value of the program
was nil."[10] Twaddle's assessment is probably too cynical: the ASTP and its
companion programs did produce substantial numbers of trained personnel
in a range of fields while also pioneering on a large scale what many at the
time perceived as a significant pedagogical innovation.

Some six months after the ASTP was established, the indefatigable Graves
began pushing for a study of how its foreign area and language training component was working out; he was already contemplating the implications of
the ASTP for postwar higher education in the United States. A survey was
soon commissioned and two anthropologists were hired to visit university
campuses and assess their programs. One of them—the anthropologist William Nelson Fenton (1908–2005), later a leading scholar of Iroquois history
and culture—would draw on the survey's findings to produce a series of appraisals of ASTP programs at the universities that he and his co-investigator
had visited, released in the spring and summer of 1945 under the rubric of
"Reports on Area Studies in American Universities." These reports, compiled

into a comprehensive study published in 1947, contributed to a growing sense that area studies, and the division of the world into distinct world regions on which it was based, had the potential to become a durable and valuable dimension of the American academic scene.[11]

A number of university-based scholars also began to argue early on that the ASTP courses offered, as two sociologists put it in a 1944 assessment of their experience with the program at Vanderbilt University, "a stimulating experimental situation in general social science education inasmuch [sic] as they provided an unprecedented experience in integration." They concluded that

> integrative, that is to say regional, courses in the social sciences should accompany and follow rather than, at best, precede specialization. We agree with Professor Whitney Griswold, organizer and director of the Foreign Area studies at Yale University, that considerations such as these "may well cast the shadow before the coming event of a change in our university curricula." . . . We think that in the wake of the educational movement which we have sketched as gathering momentum from the experience gained in the ASTP, a sustained effort should be made to supplement our habitual [thematic] courses in pure sociology with additional courses in applied sociology, almost all of which could best be delivered on a regional basis.[12]

The ASTP and related programs thus gave colleges and universities extensive experience with curricula and programs focused on regions of the world hitherto largely ignored, and with intensive instruction in languages that had previously not been taught, or taught only at a small number of elite universities, supported by a massive infusion of federal funds. As a consequence, some in academia began to embrace the notion that regionally focused training could and should be a valuable component of postwar higher education; among them were university leaders who would prove reluctant to give these programs up altogether—or to lose the external funding that had made them possible. As Neil Smith puts it, the ASTP "probably changed the country's campuses more profoundly than it changed the country's army."[13]

Disciplines into Areas: The Ethnogeographic Board

The ACLS, in collaboration with the SSRC and the NRC, was also centrally involved in creating another new entity that explicitly defined its mission as the production of interdisciplinary and regionally focused knowledge to serve the country's wartime needs. This was the Ethnogeographic Board, established within the Smithsonian Institution with SSRC, NRC and ACLS sponsorship and funding from the Rockefeller and Carnegie foundations. The board's mission was outlined at its first meeting in August 1942: "Government agencies, in seeking information upon man's existing and potential activities in various regions, tend to think mainly in terms of areas, whereas the sources of such information in the scholarly world are classified in terms of disciplines. Therefore representatives of the scholarly world have created the Ethnogeographic Board to serve as a more efficient means of translating the scholarly resources of the several disciplines into the geographical categories used by the governmental agencies."[14] A Rockefeller Foundation internal document approving additional funding for the board explained that it had "been set up primarily to function during the emergency as a clearing house of specific regional information and personnel data between the sponsoring institutions, their numerous affiliated scientific and educational organizations and civil, military and war agencies within the government."[15]

To serve the war effort the board compiled a "World File of Area and Language Specialists" with some five thousand names, which helped government agencies more efficiently identify and recruit people with expertise on different parts of the world and their languages. The ACLS and the SSRC participated in the compilation of this roster, and they also helped government agencies recruit personnel through personal connections and informal networks. The Ethnogeographic Board also produced reports, and organized conferences, on strategic issues and regions for government agencies. For example, in September 1942, at the request of the Office of Strategic Services, scholars who had "special knowledge through personal experience and study of the Indians of Bolivia" were convened at Yale University to discuss "factors in Indian culture which bear on the problems of: 1. Utilizing these Indians as industrial labor in the Bolivian mines. 2. Inducing the Indians to increase the agricultural output of Bolivia."[16] This conference typifies the new ways in which scholarly knowledge of specific locales and regions now began to be mobilized to serve the war effort. These and other studies and projects of the Ethnogeographic Board bolstered the notion that regionally focused expertise was important and useful to the nation and should be developed further, thereby contributing to the emerging vision of area studies as a valuable component of postwar higher education.

The OSS and Area Studies

In addition to prewar models, the experience garnered by colleges and universities across the country with the ILP, the ASTP and the CSTP, and the interdisciplinary frame of the Ethnogeographic Board's work, the notion of organizing research along lines that focused on geographic regions and crossed disciplinary lines also reflected the practice of a key wartime government agency in which a great many scholars were deeply involved. During the war both the War Department and the State Department generally divided the world into a set of regions and "theaters of operations," and they demanded actionable knowledge that corresponded to this framing. A good deal of that knowledge would be produced by the Office of Strategic Services (OSS), the country's first civilian foreign intelligence service (and forerunner of the Central Intelligence Agency). In July 1941 President Roosevelt appointed General William J. Donovan (1883–1959) as Coordinator of Information, charged with laying the groundwork for a new civilian intelligence capacity. A year later Roosevelt issued an executive order creating the OSS, giving Donovan the institutional and legal framework he needed to build a full-scale foreign intelligence service.[17]

The new agency created branches to gather secret intelligence and run clandestine agents and operations; the latter included support for resistance movements operating in areas under German or Japanese occupation. But it also quickly built up a large and effective Research and Analysis branch (referred to here as R&A), headed by Professor William L. Langer of Harvard. He and his senior colleagues in R&A, drawn largely from elite universities, recruited large numbers of other scholars from colleges and universities across the country, including many former and current graduate students, who possessed expertise on parts of the world in which American military forces were, or soon would be, operating, and about which U.S. military and civilian policymakers desperately needed accurate information and reliable prognoses. Both the SSRC and the ACLS helped the OSS identify scholars with particular expertise who could be recruited to R&A, and the OSS also contracted out research projects to faculty and institutes at a number of universities.[18] It was actually R&A that McGeorge Bundy had in mind when, two decades later, he called the OSS the "first great center of area studies in the United States."[19]

The Research and Analysis branch was initially organized along what were referred to as "functional" (i.e., quasi-disciplinary) lines, with separate "Economic, Geographical and Psychological (Political)" divisions. However, in what Barry M. Katz's study of R&A characterizes as a "traumatic" reorganization early in 1943—traumatic because it "violated the received wisdom [among scholars] that the world is organized in the manner of a university catalogue"—the "functionalists" were "forced into a framework dictated by the patently interdisciplinary realities of the European and Asian theaters. . . . The basic work of research and analysis was henceforth carried out by the staffs of four regional divisions, each of which had functional subdivisions assigned to particular technical matters." The four regional divisions covered "Europe-Africa" (with Africa referring mainly to French-ruled North Africa, which the Allies invaded toward the end of 1942 as the prelude to a planned invasion of southern Europe), the Far East, the Soviet Union and Latin America; other regional divisions were added later. Katz concludes: "By forcing a degree of cross-disciplinary collaboration . . . the reform of January 1943 harnessed the latent epistemological ferment and enabled [R&A staff] to transcend the bounds of traditional scholarship and to bring to bear all types of knowledge on problems of a particular region, with dazzling results."[20]

The strategic importance of the Middle East and North Africa soon led to the establishment of a separate Near East section of R&A, which scoured the country for people with expertise on the region. Edwin M. Wright (1897–1987), who was born to missionary parents in Iran and spent many years working in education there, decades later told an interviewer how his knowledge of Iran and of Persian led to his recruitment for intelligence work. His account also nicely illustrates the great value to the war effort of information gleaned by specialists from publicly available sources—what is today called "open source" intelligence.

> When the war came on, the OSS put out a general request to find people who knew the Middle East. As I recall, there were only six people in America at that time (of American parentage) who could read or write Persian. I was one of them. Practically all of us got dragged into the Government. We had no political background in the Middle East and practically no interest in politics there. There was [a great dearth] of what you might call specialists or experts in the Middle East. There were a few from archaeology, a few missionaries' children, and a few from business. Many of us were dragged into the research branch of

the OSS, to prepare materials for the U.S. Government in case the United States became involved in that area.

Eventually, Mr. [Winston] Churchill called up President [Franklin] Roosevelt and said that they did not have the facilities to handle supplies for Russia across Iran. Immediately the OSS asked me to prepare a study on the railways and transportation systems of Iran. I wrote a very complete one because I found in the Library of Congress all the sources, in Persian, of the railway maps and whatnot that had been sent in earlier. I was able therefore to prepare a full study on the Iranian railway system. This got into the Department of Defense [*sic*] and Mr. Roosevelt said, "Well, we'll take over the Iranian railways and operate it under the Persian taskforce."

They found my name on this study and immediately offered me a captaincy in [U.S. Army] Intelligence. They assigned me to go to the Middle East and work in the intelligence side of the operations (E-2).[21]

The Near East section of R&A had its ups and downs. Robin Winks reports that it "suffered from too many changes of hands, as the Near East rose and fell and then rose again in priorities and as its members sought to get into the field. In time the section consisted of older prewar specialists who, having the complex language abilities necessary to the area, were viewed as a bit snobbish about their earlier academic achievements, which outranked the fresh-faced postgraduate scholars of the other sections."[22] Ephraim Avigdor Speiser (1902–1965), who would serve as head of the Near East section of R&A in 1943–1945, was one of those "older prewar specialists." Born in what was then Habsburg-ruled Galicia, he came to the United States in 1920, earned his doctorate at Dropsie College for Hebrew and Cognate Learning in Philadelphia, and joined the faculty of the University of Pennsylvania as a professor of Semitics.[23] His expertise was in the ancient civilizations of Mesopotamia and he had participated in archaeological expeditions in Iraq since the 1920s. Shortly after the war, in a survey of U.S. Near Eastern studies prepared at the request of the American Council of Learned Societies, Speiser would write about the wartime experience of older scholars like himself:

> . . . the work which they were called upon to do had only a remote relation to the work for which they had been trained. The great majority of Near Eastern specialists [recruited for government service, including the OSS] had started out as students of the ancient Orient, whereas the need was now for many more workers on the modern phase than were available or could be trained on short

notice. Calls came from various government departments and agencies: the State Department, the War Department (G-2, Signal Corps), Naval Intelligence, the Office of Strategic Services, the Office of War Information, and the like. It was not at all unusual for an Egyptologist to serve as an analyst on Arab affairs or for a cuneiformist to investigate the manifold problems of Afghanistan. Nevertheless, much constructive research was accomplished, which should—once the results are released—add appreciably to our knowledge and understanding of the whole region.[24]

Many of the scholars who worked for the OSS during the war would go on to play leading roles in the development of Middle East studies after the war. For example, Jacob C. Hurewitz (1914–2008) served under Speiser in Washington as an OSS research analyst on Palestine. The anthropologist Carleton S. Coon (1904–1981), who had in 1931 published an ethnography of tribal groups in Morocco's Rif region and was on leave from Harvard, was sent to North Africa to help prepare for the November 1942 Allied invasion and then served elsewhere in North Africa and in Europe. Richard N. Frye (1920–2014), then a doctoral student at Harvard, was sent by the OSS to Afghanistan but also served elsewhere during the war.[25] Middle East studies was by no means unique in this respect: a great many of the scholars who played central roles in laying the intellectual and institutional foundations of the new postwar area studies fields had together experienced a stint doing team-based, policy-relevant, interdisciplinary research and analysis in the OSS.

Indeed, it was to a significant extent within the OSS Research and Analysis branch that some of the new regional fields were in practice established, with consequences that persisted for decades. For example, William Langer brought the Russian historian Geroid T. Robinson of Columbia University to Washington to head the Soviet division of R&A. At that division's height it employed some sixty scholars, many of whom (including Robinson himself) would go on to play leading roles in the network of Russian studies centers founded soon after the war and would dominate the field, intellectually and institutionally, for a generation.[26] So although we must be careful not to ignore prewar antecedents of what would come to be termed area studies, as well as other wartime and postwar factors, the role of the OSS Research and Analysis branch as a proving ground and model for this enterprise should not be underestimated. The OSS was abruptly disbanded by President Truman in September 1945, just weeks after the surrender of Japan and the end of the Second World War, but it would leave a powerful imprint on American academia for decades to come.

World Regions

Through its articulation, adoption and deployment by a range of government and academic entities during the war, the notion of organizing research and training around specific geographic regions quickly gained widespread acceptance and significant momentum, in ways that sometimes built on but rapidly went far beyond prewar antecedents. The SSRC's annual report for 1941–1942 already noted "the probability that academic work will in the future be organized in some part on a regional basis," rather than along conventional disciplinary lines, and its officers soon became increasingly convinced that the wartime programs, created hurriedly to meet urgent wartime needs, would have long-term intellectual and institutional consequences for American academia. At a January 1943 meeting of the SSRC's Committee on Problems and Policy (hereafter P&P), responsible for overseeing the Council's operations and programs, a member asserted "the certainty of far-reaching effects on future university programs as a result of whatever government action is taken, and the probability of a continuing need for training [i.e., after the war] which will enable personnel to work in terms of the [foreign] environments concerned."[27] Around the same time, Carnegie Corporation officials visiting William Langer of the OSS told him that they "were impressed by the R. and A. approach to the analysis of complicated situations and, in the course of lengthy discussions, raised the question of whether some similar system might not be introduced in our universities."[28] Officers of the Rockefeller Foundation were thinking along the same lines; as David C. Engerman has put it, "Even as its program officers scurried to contribute to the war effort, the foundation focused on long-term goals, not on wartime emergencies. It wanted to promote area studies not as a means for knowing enemies, friends, or subjects, but as a means of spurring more cosmopolitan general education, promoting interdisciplinary research, and reducing the 'provincialism' of the social sciences."[29]

The officers of the Carnegie and Rockefeller foundations were, by and large, liberal internationalists in the Wilsonian vein. They felt that President Wilson's failure in 1919–1920 to convince the Senate to ratify the Treaty of Versailles and join the League of Nations, and more broadly to have the United States irrevocably establish itself as a world (rather than a largely hemispheric) power, had been a historic setback, a lost opportunity that they were determined to avoid repeating. After Pearl Harbor it was clear to them that, when the current war ended, the United States would without question be a global superpower, and they were determined that the country not again shirk what they regarded as its proper role in shaping and running a postwar world order that would serve American interests. Many of them were also critical of European colonialism and expected that, after the war, the colonial empires would either be dismantled or, at a minimum, opened up to American trade and investment, which strengthened their conviction that Americans had to become much better informed about the non-Western world in particular.[30] They therefore continued to fund organizations like the Council on Foreign Relations and the Institute of Pacific Relations, but they also became increasingly convinced that the wartime programs for training Americans in foreign languages, histories and cultures, and for producing regionally focused knowledge, which the government would abruptly terminate once the fighting stopped (and sometimes even earlier), needed to be made an integral and permanent component of the mission of institutions of higher education in the United States. They thus encouraged both the ACLS and the SSRC to explore ways of achieving this goal, which would obviously require substantial foundation funding.

In January 1943, just over a year after the United States entered the war, the SSRC took the step of creating a new Committee on World Regions (CWR), appointed "to scrutinize the implications for social sciences of the government's training programs for service in foreign regions" and to begin formulating a long-term approach to the development of what was by now widely referred to as "regional," "area" or "areal" studies. The committee was chaired by Guy Stanton Ford (1873–1962), a professor of history at the University of Minnesota, long-time dean of its graduate school and the university's president from 1938 to 1941. At the time of his appointment as chair of the CWR he was serving as executive director of the American Historical Association and editor of its journal *The American Historical Review*. The CWR's other members were E. Pendleton Herring (1904–2004), who was then still a political scientist on the Harvard faculty but would assume the leadership of the SSRC after the war; Carl Sauer, who was associated with the prewar ACLS

Committee on Latin American Studies and its successor the JCLAS; Thorsten Sellin (1896–1994), a sociologist at the University of Pennsylvania and a pioneer in the field of criminology; Waldo Leland of the ACLS; Frederick P. Keppel (1875–1943), who had served as president of the Carnegie Corporation from 1922 to 1941, during which period it had given away some $86 million—the equivalent of well over one billion 2015 dollars; and the ethnographer William Duncan Strong (1899–1962), director of the Ethnogeographic Board. By linking a set of key people, institutions and networks, the CWR constituted a critical site at which the emerging vision of area studies began to take shape.

At its first meeting, on February 10, 1943, the CWR discussed a memorandum on approaches to the development of regional studies submitted by Mortimer Graves, secretary of the ACLS, and developed an outline of the report on the content and contours of this newly envisioned field whose formulation was its main task. In light of that discussion the Duke historian Earl J. Hamilton, who had recently received Rockefeller research funding through the JCLAS and was now serving as the CWR's staffer, began drafting the committee's report. Hamilton's initial draft was discussed by the committee at meetings in February and April 1943 and subsequently revised; its final version was released in June 1943 as *World Regions in the Social Sciences* and circulated to universities, foundations, government departments and the military, including civilian and military intelligence agencies.[31] Clearly informed by the experience of Hamilton and CWR members with Latin American studies, and by early impressions and assessments of regionally focused work at other academic entities and in government agencies, this report seems to have been the very first attempt at providing an explanation of what area studies might be, and a coherent intellectual rationale for it, that would appeal to the SSRC's constituencies, including the foundations and social scientists.

World Regions in the Social Sciences began by explaining why knowledge of world regions was now critical:

> The present war has focused attention as never before upon the entire world. Interest in foreign regions has been intensified and sharp attention drawn to areas over which we have felt little or no concern.
>
> The immediate need for social scientists who know the different regions of the world stands second only to the demand for military and naval officers fa-

miliar with the actual and potential combat zones. Since few overseas areas have hitherto attracted research, we lack the regional knowledge now required; and traditional curricula and methods of instruction have left inert such information as we possess. . . . The consequent scarcity of professional and scientific personnel combining linguistic and regional knowledge with technical proficiency seriously hampers every war agency.

But developing region-based knowledge was not to be understood as merely a wartime exigency. *World Regions in the Social Sciences* asserted that whatever happened after the war ended, "the United States will enjoy unexampled opportunities and face heavy responsibilities" requiring "thousands of Americans who combine thorough professional or technical training with knowledge of the languages, economics, politics, history, geography, peoples, customs, and religions of foreign countries. . . . America will not be able to assume her economic, political, and cultural responsibilities as a member of the United Nations after the war without enlarged spatial concepts and a more comprehensive knowledge of the world." Hence "failure to consider permanent needs in the formulation of plans for the emergency will distort and diminish the service rendered future generations by our institutions of higher learning."

The report noted that while university instruction and research in the humanities had for some time been organized largely in terms of specific nations or regions, the social sciences (except for history) had witnessed much less regional concentration: "The regional approach in both research and instruction has been virtually neglected in favor of the disciplinary and functional approach." The Pan-American Union (predecessor to the Organization of American States) that beginning in 1889 sought to foster stronger ties among the republics of the Western hemisphere had for a time had some impact on American universities, and during the First World War Latin American studies had briefly surged. But, the report went on, "institutes for areal [*sic*] research have never taken root on American soil," few social scientists "can be regarded as experts in any particular area of the world, and only a negligible fraction of the outstanding research has attacked regional problems." In contrast, some of the European powers had established institutions that fostered a regional approach, for example the University of London's School of Oriental and African Studies and its School of Slavonic and East European Studies. In France and Germany too, and to a lesser extent in Italy, research institutes focusing on particular regions had operated effectively in the interwar period.

In its final form the report did not propose that the United States emulate this European model by establishing centralized, state-supported, policy-oriented research institutes on regions outside the United States; instead, "the first step should be the establishment of university centers for research and graduate instruction" which would "extend our knowledge of the major areas of the world; supply government and business with experts; and provide materials and teachers for lower levels of instruction." This network of centers should be built up gradually, with the Far East and Latin America as two areas of most immediate concern. In the longer term, greater knowledge of world regions would be imparted to undergraduates and to elementary and secondary students as well. Fostering regional knowledge and a better understanding of the wider world might thereby help avert a repetition of what one CWR member characterized as America's "disappointing" experience in the aftermath of the last war; as another committee member put it, "we want people educated into antiprovincialism."[32]

In addition to serving the needs of a country currently at war and destined to be a global power when the war ended, *World Regions in the Social Sciences* argued that the reorientation of knowledge production and dissemination along regional lines would also benefit the social sciences, by producing findings with a stronger claim to universality and by fostering something like what would later come to be called interdisciplinarity:

> The primary task of the social scientist is to master and contribute to his discipline. . . . But the laws and generalizations of the social sciences are relevant to time, place and culture; and much can be gained by the concreteness derived from the regional approach. Some of the most fruitful results have been obtained through the comparative method, and more precise regional data will greatly extend and improve its use. Regional study offers the same advantages as the case method and reduces the temptation toward vague generalities—one of the besetting sins of the social scientist. Concentration on regions may conceivably open the road to one of the major and most distant goals of many outstanding social scientists: a weakening of the rigid compartments that separate the disciplines.

As Donald Young of the SSRC staff put it at a meeting in 1944, "we have long been aware that the social disciplines have been provincial in their failure to

check their experiences against those of cultures not under Western civilization. This kind of checking is very much needed. . . ." Young also noted "the
possibility that a regional focus may be one way of integrating the social sciences, effectively encouraging the interdisciplinary work so long discussed."[33]

However, implementing this new intellectual agenda would require a great
deal of investment, among other things in the development and diffusion of
new teaching methods and materials (especially for language training), the
establishment or expansion of libraries and collections, and the provision
to students and scholars of opportunities to travel abroad for research and
training. All this would entail considerable expense, as would the creation of
the many additional teaching and research positions that would be necessary
to staff the envisioned new regional studies centers. The report offered the
hope that, "owing to the magnitude of the financial burden and to the obvious benefits to the whole nation it is not unreasonable to anticipate that the
federal government may continue to subsidize regional instruction when the
emergency is over." This new mode of organizing the production and dissemination of knowledge carried risks, the report acknowledged, including the
danger that regional studies might become "the resort of mediocrity." Nonetheless, World Regions in the Social Sciences expressed confidence that such
knowledge "will prove essential to peace, security, and international order in
the postwar era" while also enabling the social sciences to "gain in precision
through intensive study of concrete areas; and scientific progress should result from an extension of regional comparison" and from "weaken[ing] the
rigid barriers that separate the social sciences." And so, the report concluded,
"we must plan carefully and proceed cautiously."

Once World Regions in the Social Sciences was completed and circulated,
the CWR was deemed to have done its job and disbanded. But SSRC leaders
continued to consider how their organization could play a leading role in the
development of regional studies; after all, it had long experience with mecha-
nisms for awarding fellowships and grants for social science research which
could be scaled up to handle expanded programs during and after the war.
Some fifty universities had already established regionally oriented training
programs for the army and navy, with powerful effects on those institutions;
however, as one Council member put it, these programs had been organized
in a haphazard manner and the SSRC could provide a useful service by monitoring their development and effectiveness, with an eye to the postwar era.[34]

But the SSRC (like other academic and scholarly organizations) was also still grappling with the question of what this new field should be in intellectual terms, how it might relate to the social science disciplines, and what institutional form it should assume. For example, in September 1943 anthropologist Robert Redfield told the Council (on which he represented the American Anthropological Association) of his "fear that the role of anthropology in developing regional studies might be larger than the anthropologists ought to fill," because of anthropologists' more extensive knowledge of specific regions. He may have felt the need to raise this concern because of a recent claim advanced by fellow anthropologists that they could make a distinctive contribution to the war effort first and foremost because they were, as one report put it, "the only social scientists who systematically study all aspects of a given culture—language, technology, social organization, use of environment, etc. . . ."[35] Redfield nonetheless suggested that "the study of regions should be organized around the notion of culture rather than around current regional problems, such as the making of tariff agreements," both because such an approach would be intellectually sound and because "a cultural focus in regional studies is more compatible with the organization of teaching and research than are the present government plans."[36]

Contending Visions of Area Studies

Despite a growing consensus among foundation and academic leaders about the need to incorporate regional studies into postwar American higher education, there was considerable disagreement about the form, content and priorities of the emerging new field or approach. The SSRC's evolving vision of area studies as properly constructed around social science research on the modern and contemporary world, coupled with graduate-level training, was vigorously opposed by Mortimer Graves of the ACLS, who had long espoused a different conception of what needed to be done. In a letter to John Marshall of the Rockefeller Foundation, Graves characterized Hamilton's 1943 report as "almost fantastically futile" because it "never got around to the problems of area studies. It recited the well-known fact that the social sciences have not concerned themselves particularly with large sections of the world and then demonstrated that there were certain difficulties in changing this state of affairs. It had nothing constructive to offer, though it contained considerable information which displayed the assiduity of its compiler."[37] Graves believed that priority should be given to making foreign area and language studies an integral component of undergraduate education, and he had for some time been persistently urging the Rockefeller Foundation to support the extension of undergraduate language and area training on the ASTP model to American colleges and universities.[38] Strong backing from Rockefeller would also help Graves overcome what he regarded as the conservatism of the ACLS executive committee: as a Rockefeller Foundation officer put it, Graves feared that area studies would "appear so revolutionary to his people that compromises will be necessary."[39]

A development early in 1944 led Graves to seek to advance his agenda with even greater urgency. In February the War Department suddenly announced that some 105,000 of the 140,000 Army personnel then enrolled in the Army Specialized Training Program at colleges and universities across the country would be transferred to combat units in order to ameliorate manpower shortages in the run-up to the invasion of France. This aroused fears, particularly at the ACLS which had been deeply engaged with the ASTP but also at the Rockefeller Foundation which had for years funded most of the ACLS's area studies-related endeavors, that the scholars and institutional resources mobilized to serve this program (and the smaller CATP) would be dispersed and the momentum created for intensive language and area studies would be lost. As a Rockefeller Foundation staff member put it, "As of some early date, all the able people in the AST program will be at loose ends. I suppose that this must really be a 'blue Monday' for them. We know that they are really able people and the very ones who ought to have a leading part in an adaptation of this phase of war-time training which would make it a permanent element in peace-time education. . . . It seems to me that a prompt move on our part now might open up a whole chain of developments such as we should be very glad to see."[40]

Ten days after the War Department's announcement, ACLS and Rockefeller Foundation staffers met to discuss ways of preserving the momentum these programs had generated in the face of the army's retrenchment, among other things by compiling a list of key "area men" at various universities who should be "held together as much as possible," with the Rockefeller Foundation assisting "these men in developing a means of carrying over the advantages gained in this war-time teaching into post-war education." Philip K.

Hitti of Princeton was among those on the list; he was described by Graves as someone who "has really been talking in area terms for a decade. That is one reason why he has not been accepted by the philologians [*sic*] in the philological discipline of Arabic studies." Near Eastern and Turkish studies were cited as particularly vulnerable to dispersal.[41]

To follow up on this meeting the ACLS, with funding from the Rockefeller Foundation, convened a somewhat larger two-day conference in Philadelphia in mid-March 1944 to consider the place of area studies in American higher education—apparently the very first conference devoted specifically to area studies. Participants included officers of the ACLS, the Rockefeller Foundation, the Ethnogeographic Board and the SSRC, along with representatives from several universities, among them Philip Hitti. The tone of the conference's deliberations was set by its key organizer, Mortimer Graves of the ACLS, whose assertion that "people are pretty well decided that something called area studies is going to be part of the postwar educational experience" reflected what was already the prevailing view at Rockefeller and beyond.[42] Graves continued to believe that area studies should focus first and foremost on undergraduate education, and so he proposed that, in order to make area and languages studies an integral part of the undergraduate curriculum, colleges require students to devote the equivalent of a full year to intensive language studies and to courses on a specific world region.[43]

SSRC officers were unhappy about both Graves' conception of the purpose of area studies and the outcome of the conference he had organized. In their own memo to the Rockefeller Foundation—a key potential funder of any initiative in this arena—staffers Donald Young and Paul Webbink argued that "curricula constructed around a core of linguistic study which perforce shuts out thorough education in other disciplines will fail as completely as did the pre-war curricula."[44] In his report to P&P on the conference, Donald Young asserted that it had focused "primarily on undergraduate work and there were no concrete results, but the questions revealed the nature of the humanists' interests in the regional approach. They regard it as a substitute for the classical studies in the attainment of the liberal arts education, and also as providing vocational training to meet postwar demands; and they are of course greatly concerned with the role of language study." Unfortunately, Young went on, research had been ignored and "the program envisaged by the humanists pays little heed to the interests or possible contributions of social science." There was thus a danger that the outcome would be "a superficial areal approach" that would disregard "the interests of social science." To counter this there was discussion of the SSRC establishing its own committee on area research, possibly with Robert Redfield as chair, but nothing came of this during 1944.[45]

The SSRC's negative reaction to Graves' conception of area studies as constructed largely around language training and the humanities was echoed by Joseph Willits (1889–1979), since 1939 director of the Rockefeller Foundation's Social Sciences Division. In a July 1944 memo to his colleague David H. Stevens, who as head of the foundation's Humanities Division had recently proposed that it adopt a "National Plan of Work" focused on language training, Willits set forth some of the pitfalls that he believed area studies (and the foundation) should try to avoid, including efforts by one discipline to "capture" area studies at the expense of others. Unfortunately, Willits argued, "Mortimer Graves' statement circulated in advance of the Philadelphia conference seemed to contemplate such a capture by the language departments although he may not have been aware of the implications. Such a procedure seems calculated to develop the worst rather than the best possibilities of the situation."

To drive his point home, and to warn against the exploitation of area studies by university departments in their competition with one another, Willits quoted from a memorandum which Robert Redfield had produced for the March 1944 area studies conference:

> Universities are, among other things, places where professors and departments compete with one another for students, courses, influence and a larger share of the budget. Any new program of instruction or research, or any realignment of old programs, offers new opportunities to increase power and new dangers of losing power. It would be unfortunate if the development of area programs for civilian purposes should become merely the efforts of Professors of Bessarabian to bring it about that the area chosen for emphasis in their institution be Bessarabian rather than Cambodgia because Bessarabia is what they happen to be professors of, with the Professors of Cambodgian taking an opposing position for corresponding reasons.

Like Redfield, Willits went on to strongly endorse area studies as a very promising new direction for American academia, as long as high standards were maintained in both teaching and research, the humanities and social sciences were well and truly integrated, area teaching was built on research, and universities agreed to what he called a "rigid division of labor," with each focusing on the region or two for which it had superior resources rather than trying to cover everything, which would lead only to superficiality. On this basis Willits favored Rockefeller Foundation support for the new field; and in fact, by 1944 Rockefeller was already stepping up grants to universities for area studies programs and would within two years begin funding the establishment of new area studies centers on an unprecedented scale.[46]

Defining Area Studies

SSRC leaders were of course well aware of growing foundation interest in fostering area studies. They had worked very closely with Rockefeller and Carnegie foundation officials since the SSRC's founding in the mid-1920s, and the two foundations had provided the great bulk of the funding that supported the organization's research and fellowship programs and its operating expenses; the Rockefeller Foundation alone gave the SSRC $6.6 million between 1924 and 1947.[47] But while the SSRC and the foundations were in virtually constant conversation, about area studies and much else, pressure to get area studies off the ground in some coherent fashion also came from the universities. As Robert B. Hall, already a central figure in the nascent area studies field, noted in the fall of 1945, "interested groups" at universities which had hosted area and foreign language programs for military personnel during the war were "attempting to perpetuate similar programs of research and study," creating demand for new programs and institutions (and the outside funding with which to support them). In fact, Hall claimed, "nearly every college in the country is trying to join the movement, regardless of the adequacy of their resources for supporting such programs."[48] That same year the American Council on Education commissioned a study of the wartime language and area studies programs for military personnel and their implications for higher education in the postwar United States. The study concluded that the wartime programs "went far to establish . . . the fruitfulness of concentration on the study of an area" and the gains to be "achieved by the intensive study of area and language in a combined program."[49] At the same time, the armed forces and civilian agencies were beginning or continuing to organize research on a regional basis, including intelligence research at the State Department and the army's program for training military attachés.[50]

All this led the SSRC to more actively consider establishing a new committee through which it could play a leading role in shaping this emerging field and ensure that the interests of the social sciences were fully represented. Clearly, things could not be left to the ACLS, whose vision of area studies the SSRC regarded as deeply flawed. There was, however, ongoing discussion, as Paul Webbink of the SSRC's Washington office staff put it, about "whether a Council committee should establish close relationships with the State Department on research matters; and whether a committee should be concerned primarily with advancing research to increase knowledge of foreign areas or to develop American strategic intelligence. What would be the implications of stressing the latter in terms of objective research and access to data, and avoidance of subordination to government interests and policies of the moment?" However, Robert Hall "advised against any official connection, in order to protect the position of the American scholar working abroad. The independent scholar can work anywhere. An official connection is a great handicap, shutting one off from many sources and threatening the freedom of research and of the individual."[51]

Late in 1945 the Ethnogeographic Board, in the process of being dissolved, circulated a proposal to establish a committee on ethnogeographic research that would carry on its work, to be run jointly by the SSRC, the ACLS and the NRC. In December 1945 the Conference Board representing the three councils revised the Ethnogeographic Board's proposal, which in its original form was deemed too narrow, and formally endorsed the creation of a new Joint Exploratory Committee on World Area Research (JECWAR), to be chaired by Robert Hall.[52] Hall, who has already surfaced at several points in this narrative, had served in U.S. Army intelligence during the First World War and then pursued his undergraduate and graduate education at the University of Michigan, where he became professor of geography and helped initiate and lead his university's Program in Oriental Civilizations, an important prototype for postwar area studies programs. He also directed Michigan's Institute for Far Eastern Studies, which with ACLS support organized summer sessions in 1937, 1938 and 1939 offering intensive language training in Chinese and Japanese as well as a range of courses on East Asia past and present.[53] Before the Second World War Hall conducted research in Haiti and Japan, and in the early war years he had received Rockefeller funding (via the JCLAS) to study Asian settlements in the Americas. After the United States entered the war he joined the OSS, directing its Pacific Coast office and then running its Research and Analysis operation for China and India.[54] Given Hall's training, intellectual orientation, and experience both in intelligence-oriented research and in an academic program that could now be seen as a model for the emerging field of area studies, he was a natural choice to lead the new committee—and to play a central role in the SSRC's efforts to launch and shape area studies.

The new committee's other members were Mortimer Graves of the ACLS, who had been promoting his own vision of regionally focused studies for a decade and a half; the Yale anthropologist and authority on Andean archaeology Wendell Bennett (1905–1953), who during the war was executive secretary of the JCLAS (another key model for organizing area studies) and also a member of the Ethnogeographic Board, and who in 1945 joined the board of directors of the SSRC;[55] and Maurice Halperin (1906–1995) of the State Department. In light of P&P's recent discussion about relations with the State Department and whether or not area studies should seek to "develop American strategic intelligence," the decision to include a State Department official as a member of the ECWAR is interesting. It was, presumably, Halperin's expertise on Latin America and his experience with regionally focused work while serving in the Research and Analysis branch of the OSS during the war that led to his appointment to the JECWAR. But he would serve on the committee for only a few months during 1946 and does not seem to have played any significant role in its deliberations; no other serving government official would be appointed to this committee or its immediate successor.[56]

The agenda set for the JECWAR's first meeting, in February 1946, proposed that its role should be to "produce a practical program for the development of Area Studies by the three Councils or any of them" while defining area studies as "the focusing of all the disciplinary competences . . . upon a cultural area for the purpose of obtaining a total picture of that culture." It asserted that "the world's civilizations can be grouped into thirty or forty significant Areas," with the Far East, "the Slavs," the Near East and "the Indic World" as the top priority for research, and Western Europe, Latin America, the United States and Canada as the lowest priority.[57] When the new committee actually convened for the first time, however, there was deep disagreement over how to proceed. A minority of its members (Mortimer Graves and his allies) argued that the time for "drastic action was long overdue," presumably along the lines Graves had laid out at the March 1944 conference in Philadelphia, while the majority (those affiliated with the SSRC and the NRC) felt that "large scale action was not advisable until the facts were more fully ascertained and the problems were more clearly delineated." Summing up the committee's second meeting in April 1946, Graves declared in frustration that internal divisions had prevented it from formulating a program, and so "any of the Councils which can formulate a program of its own had better proceed with it."[58]

The only significant action taken by the paralyzed joint committee was to commission a survey of what could now be categorized as existing or planned area studies research and training programs at American colleges and universities, to be conducted by Robert Hall. There was precedent for this: for example, one of the first priorities of the JCLAS after it was constituted in 1942 was to commission a survey of university-based training, research and library resources on Latin America, in large part to serve the war effort.[59] Even before Hall's study was completed, however, the SSRC decided that it needed to take action on its own, by replacing the ineffective joint exploratory committee with a standing committee exclusively under its own purview. The new SSRC Committee on World Area Research (CWAR), which would in subsequent years play a central role in getting area studies off the ground, initially consisted of Robert Hall (appointed as chair) along with Latin America specialist Wendell C. Bennett; the Harvard historian of France Donald C. McKay, like Hall a veteran of the OSS Research and Analysis branch; and Geroid T. Robinson (1915–1965), the Columbia historian of late tsarist Russia who had led R&A's Soviet division and would shortly become director of the very first major new area studies center established after the war. All four of the new committee's members thus had extensive wartime experience of producing regionally focused knowledge to serve military and policy ends, and the CWAR can be seen as a key link between the kind of work done by the OSS Research and Analysis branch and the postwar field of area studies as it first took shape.[60] They and other academic leaders connected to the SSRC also benefited from that organization's close working relationship with foundation officials, a relationship lubricated by social interaction as well. For example, in the late 1940s and into the 1950s, many of the conversations between

SSRC and foundation officials during which key programmatic and funding decisions about area studies were made took place over lunch at the Century Club on West 43rd Street in Manhattan, just off Fifth Avenue—a private club where the power elite convened out of public view and from which women were barred from membership until 1989.

The CWAR's main task in its first year of operation (1946–1947) was to review and finalize Hall's report on the survey he had conducted, published in May 1947 as *Area Studies: With Special Reference to their Implications for Research in the Social Sciences.*[61] Between April and September 1946 Hall visited twenty-four universities across the country in order to gather information about their existing or planned area studies programs, graduate and undergraduate. Overall, he identified fifty-two undergraduate programs, thirty-seven graduate programs and "25 group projects for research in a particular area." (7) Of these 114 programs, which included programs in American studies and American civilization, seventy-six were actually in operation or about to commence, while the others were still in the planning stage. Hall's decision to count American studies programs, the first of which emerged at U.S. universities in the mid-1930s, is worth noting.[62] It may have been prompted by a desire to offer a recognizable model for area studies, and perhaps to inflate the number of programs that could be included in his count. But it also points toward a feasible conception of area studies in which social scientists would investigate American society, politics and culture in the same way they approached foreign societies, and vice versa. This was, however, a road not taken, and thereafter few would insist on counting, or treating, American studies as part of the area studies field, which came to focus exclusively on societies and peoples outside the United States and Canada.

But Hall's study was in any case less a survey than a meditation on the intellectual character, current role and future prospects of area studies in American higher education. More broadly, it can be seen as a statement of the SSRC's perspective on the content and direction of area studies, a sort of founding charter for the field. As such it gave clear priority to the social sciences and to research, and was thus very different in tone and content from the ACLS' vision of area studies, which continued to emphasize the undergraduate curriculum, language instruction and the humanities. Hall began by adopting a broad definition of area studies and by taking pains to provide it with a long and distinguished intellectual pedigree in American academia. Insisting that "World War II was not the mother of area studies," as was widely assumed, Hall declared that "much of the basic concept of area study is to be found in the very beginnings of American higher education and scholarly research. The classical programs [i.e., Greek and Latin studies] were area studies. . . . The original aim was to give as complete an understanding of the Greek and Roman worlds as was possible." (12) Of course, Hall acknowledged, we do not yet know as much about other regions of the world as we do about ancient Greece and Rome, but that only points up the need to learn more about them.

To support his depiction of classics as a form of area studies Hall drew on Redfield's 1944 paper on area studies, which had included a quote from John Stuart Mill defending the study of Greek and Latin literature as a way of "frequently using the differently colored glasses of other people" in order to get beyond one's preconceived notions and ingrained cultural assumptions. Such an approach, which Hall suggested was at the heart of area studies, could also be a source of power for the United States in the postwar world: "It is no exaggeration," Hall asserted, "to hold that 'those differently colored glasses' went a long way in destroying British provincialism in the days of her 'one world' when British ships, British opportunities, and British responsibilities were finding the most important corners of the 'seven seas.' Is there not a similarity in our position today? Do we need 'those differently colored glasses' to live wisely in our new 'one world'?" (14) For generations, Hall claimed, scholars had grasped, implicitly or explicitly, "the need for a total knowledge of areas (national, cultural, and other)," (15) but all previous attempts to achieve such knowledge had failed; however, the present generation of scholars was now equipped to succeed, because of the great intellectual, institutional and financial resources at its disposal, the progress of the social sciences toward maturity and the greater accessibility of all parts of the world owing to improved transportation.

Hall noted that a number of area studies programs had been established before the war, including his own Program in Oriental Civilizations at Michigan. The war had of course greatly accelerated interest in area studies and many people had been "converted" to the area approach, though the hastily established wartime programs should not, he felt, be seen as proper models for the field in the postwar era. The time had now come, Hall declared, to put area studies on a solid footing for the long term: "Our old methods of education and direction of research proved unequal either to maintaining the peace or most effectively winning the wars. . . . There is a demand for both an interdisciplinary and intercultural approach to many of the problems which we have so far failed to answer. Area study is at least one approach to the partial solution of these problems. For the present it would seem to be the most direct approach and as promising as any other." (21)

Hall went on to review the arguments for and against area studies. The arguments in favor were similar to those advanced by Hamilton in 1943. "We have studied men isolated in the milieu of the North Atlantic," Hall asserted, "thinking that we have been studying man. . . . We need the data of other areas to check our assumptions." (23–24) An area focus would also enable scholars to overcome the disciplinary compartmentalization of knowledge. Critics of the area studies approach were doubtful that it had any "hard core," but Hall insisted that area training and research did not require abandoning disciplinary competence; instead, it meant supplementing disciplinary competence with a new competence, area knowledge. Moreover, Hall was confident that the problem of securing positions for people trained as area specialists in a system of higher education organized along disciplinary lines could be solved. As for the specific objectives and methods of area studies training, Hall argued that (as was currently the case at most of the area studies program he had surveyed) such training should normally be restricted to the master's degree stage, with doctoral programs based within a specific discipline. As for research, the social sciences must form the core of this field, with "responsibility for the essential unity of area studies." (50)

Over time, Hall concluded, it was necessary for "the national good" to foster a "national program for area studies," consisting crucially of programs for graduate training and research based at the country's major universities. Priorities would have to be set, with regions deemed more strategically important receiving attention earlier on; but "once the more important areas are taken care of, or at the same time where opportunity is favorable, we should move rapidly toward filling out the map." (83) Each important area should have several centers devoted to its study, geographically dispersed across the country, while less significant areas might do with a single center, at least for the time being. At present, Hall found, the United States was best equipped with programs focusing on Latin America, with the Far East coming in second and Russia third.[63] By contrast, "the Near East is completely neglected and there are few scholars in the country who know anything about the area except in the field of languages," though he added that Princeton "has both plans and resources on this area." (84)

Well before the Second World War ended, then, and well before anyone was anticipating the onset of what came to be known as the Cold War, a vision of university-based area studies as a potentially productive mode of producing and imparting knowledge—knowledge that could transcend divisions among the disciplines and would be useful to scholars and students as well as to policymakers and the general public—had crystallized at key institutional sites, from the Carnegie and Rockefeller foundations to the SSRC and the ACLS to major research universities to government agencies, and beyond. To those who embraced this vision, the experience of the OSS, the Ethnogeographic Board, the ASTP and other wartime entities and programs seemed to prove its potential efficacy and utility. As they saw it, the key tasks now were to elaborate a theoretical paradigm for area studies, flesh out what it should actually look like as an academic field, and translate the resources which the foundations were ready to make available into new centers, departments, programs and curricula—and new faculty and students—at American universities.

3 Launching a New Field

We must develop aggressive long-term research programs covering each of
the various areas of the world; and we must expand and improve the quality
of our present pitifully small corps of experts on these various areas.
—John W. Gardner, 1948

I N HIS 1947 CHARTER for area studies, Robert Hall did not explicitly
discuss who might fund the many new university-based centers and
programs he saw as necessary. But even as he conducted his site visits and
drafted his report, both the Rockefeller Foundation and the Carnegie Corporation of New York were already beginning to pour very serious money into
the new field, turning area studies from a wartime vision into a postwar reality. So Hall's formulation of both an intellectual and a geopolitical rationale
for area studies, and efforts to delineate the content and contours of this new
academic field, barely kept pace with its actual materialization in the form of
institutions, personnel, curricula and research projects.

Area Studies and the Cold War

The process of elaborating an institutional and funding infrastructure for
area studies was already under way when the war ended, but soon thereafter a
new and largely unanticipated geopolitical context took shape which significantly affected, and dramatically accelerated, the field's development. Widespread American goodwill toward the Soviet Union as the most important
ally of the United States in defeating Germany, at horrific cost for the soldiers

and peoples of the Soviet Union, and hopes for a peaceful postwar global world order, quickly faded as tensions flared between the two newly emergent superpowers, initially over the fate of Soviet-occupied Central and Eastern Europe. After barely a year of peace, the two countries increasingly came to be seen as engaged in what would soon come to be termed a "Cold War." By 1947 the idea that the United States and the "Free World" it led were threatened by aggressive Soviet expansionism (of which the international communist movement was deemed a key instrument) had taken firm hold among American policymaking and media elites, resulting in a massive mobilization and reorganization of resources to confront the perceived threat and the unleashing of an increasingly virulent anticommunist campaign at home.[1]

In February 1947 President Truman, determined to crush a communist-led insurgency in Greece, announced the foreign policy doctrine that bears his name, an apparently open-ended commitment by the United States to oppose what was framed as Soviet expansionism, or the threat thereof, anywhere in the world. In March, largely to deflect Republican claims that government agencies had been infiltrated by communists, Truman issued Executive Order 9835, which empowered the FBI to investigate all government employees and established "loyalty boards" which could dismiss those deemed to be communists or associated with organizations the Attorney General designated as subversive. In June the European Recovery Program (better known as the Marshall Plan), through which the United States would spend billions of dollars to help the economies of western Europe recover from the war, was announced. July 1947 witnessed the signing into law of the National Security Act, which created the Central Intelligence Agency and the National Security Council and reorganized the military forces of the United States.[2]

During the war, academic and foundation officials had embraced the idea that area studies could offer a more effective way to produce and impart scholarly knowledge about long-neglected parts of the world and to educate the American public about them. Now, in the new postwar context, there also developed a growing sense that with a global conflict getting under way between the United States and the Soviet Union, and their respective allies, clients and proxies, the country urgently demanded of its scholars and the academic institutions that housed them better and more useable knowledge about the world—particularly the non-Western world—than was currently available. As had been the case during the Second World War, regionally focused and interdisciplinary research—now recast as area studies—seemed to many the best way to secure that knowledge and to train new cadres to produce more of it.

This also led to closer contact and coordination between government officials and the academic world. As Sigmund Diamond has demonstrated most fully, in the late 1940s and into the 1950s many foundation officials and university leaders were in close and regular contact with the CIA and other U.S. intelligence agencies. They expected, or at least hoped, that the new area studies centers they were funding or hosting would cooperate effectively with those agencies, and more broadly would serve the needs of the state during a protracted period of global crisis and conflict, whether by producing policy-relevant research or by training personnel for government service.[3] It was to this linkage that McGeorge Bundy would allude in his speech at SAIS a decade and a half later when he asserted that "there is a high measure of interpenetration between universities with area programs and the information-gathering agencies of the government."[4]

Not everyone explicitly acknowledged or addressed the connection between the place of the United States in the postwar (and Cold War) world and the importance of area studies. One who did was Pendleton Herring, about to become a central figure in both the social sciences and area studies in the United States: in 1948 he assumed the presidency of the SSRC, where he would remain in charge for two decades and, as Nils Gilman puts it, "positioned himself as kingmaker for postwar social science, a sort of one-man pressure group for promoting his ideas about how social science should be conducted."[5] Matthew Farish quotes Herring as writing in 1947 that a better understanding of the Soviet Union and other world regions was essential for "a cool and calculated execution of the Truman Doctrine or its equivalent." Moreover, given unrest and turmoil around the world, the United States and the Soviet Union were now clearly rivals for global influence: "The struggle, in other words, is rather a competition to win adherents friendly to the United States and more disposed to accept our values than to follow the course of Russian leadership. . . . To the extent that we are able to exert our influence upon these areas and win their adherence through our understanding of their problems and, in turn, through their understanding of our objectives, we shall be able to win out in our competition with the Soviets."[6] For Herring, whose career straddled the worlds of government, the foundations, the universities and academic organizations like the SSRC, but also for many others engaged in launching area studies in the United States, the intellectual value of this enterprise was thus intertwined with its potential importance to a country now striving for global hegemony and mobilizing to face a new era of geopolitical crisis and confrontation. John Willits of the Rockefeller Foundation put it a bit more benignly in the spring of 1948: "The objectives [of area studies] would seem to be derived from the fact that this country has been propelled into a position where we have power all over the world and the question is whether we will exert it with intellectual responsibility, without which there is no basis for moral responsibility. It took Great Britain 500 years to develop knowledge of world areas and we are in danger of continuing to be incredibly naive."[7]

It was large-scale funding from the Rockefeller and Carnegie foundations which actually got area studies off the ground in 1946–1947, and the programmatic initiatives that led to these systematic investments were obviously not uninfluenced by rising global tensions in those and subsequent years. However, in exploring how this new academic field took on institutional form, we must be careful not to treat it as exclusively a product of the Cold War, even as we try to understand how the Cold War helped shape it. It can plausibly be argued that at least some of the new area studies centers and programs discussed in this chapter would have been established even without the coming of the Cold War, because Cold War concerns were never the only rationale for area studies advanced by the field's founders and funders. So, for example, Robert Hall told his SSRC colleagues in April 1948, a moment of acute Cold War crisis in Europe, that social scientists had been too preoccupied with "disciplinary interests" rather than specific problems, such that the "potential usefulness of area research will lie in its ability to stimulate cross-fertilization of disciplines." At that same meeting John Willits, after asserting that the United States needed a fuller understanding of the world if it was to exercise its newfound global power effectively, went on to cite a more expansive rationale for area studies. He pointed to "the tendency for the social sciences except for geography and anthropology to be preoccupied with Western society and the North American continent. Of course we should know more about them but in the face of recent developments other disciplines should turn their attention to problems of interest to them as they appear in the various countries of the world, particularly in the 'backward' countries, because they have something to learn as well as to give."[8] The process of launching area studies as a new academic field in the postwar United States was thus certainly inflected by contemporary geopolitical concerns, in ways that need to be elucidated, but it cannot be reduced to them.

The "Golden Age" of American Higher Education

The emergence of area studies also needs to be situated within yet another context that fostered and shaped it: the dramatic transformations that American higher education underwent in the decades following the Second World War. For one, the postwar period witnessed a huge increase in the number of students enrolled in colleges and universities, in absolute terms and as a proportion of the relevant age group. In 1919–1920, almost 600,000 people were enrolled in institutions of higher education in the United States, less than 5 percent of the cohort of eighteen- to twenty-four-year-olds; by 1939–1940 that total had more than doubled and now constituted about 9 percent of the age cohort.[9] By the end of the 1940s that number would double again, reaching some 15 percent of the cohort.

A major factor in this rapid postwar expansion was massive government funding in the form of the "GI bills," under which the federal government paid college tuition for veterans of the Second World War and later the Korean War. By 1947–1948 the Veterans' Administration was paying the tuition of almost half the male college students in the United States, and by 1962 the federal government had disbursed some $5 billion in tuition payments for veterans—roughly $40–50 billion in current dollars.[10] This program enabled much broader segments of American society to pursue higher education than ever before and opened the way for the dramatic acceleration of growth in enrollment that followed.[11] The number of students in college tripled between 1960 and 1980, encompassing an ever larger proportion of eighteen- to twenty-four-year-olds; by 1990 enrollments were ten times what they had been in 1940, far outstripping overall population growth. This growth in numbers was accompanied, and facilitated, by a massive increase in government funding for higher education, which rose from $2.2 billion in 1950 to $23.4 billion in 1970 and $31 billion in 1991. In particular, as discussed in Chapter 6, the National Defense Education Act of 1958 opened the floodgates for a tidal wave of government funding in the years that followed by providing a national security rationale for federal support of higher education.

The impact of these changes on the country's universities was particularly dramatic. As Thomas Bender notes, "by 1970 or so, research and [graduate] training was no longer dominated by a select few institutions—Chicago and the Ivies. Distinction was as likely to be found in major public institutions (Berkeley, Ann Arbor, Madison) as private ones. . . . All areas of the country became home to major research institutions, and the number of institutions with stature as major research and graduate training campuses increased from about twenty to more than 125 in the half century." It is no wonder that Bender called the five decades following the end of the Second World War the "golden age" of the American university.[12]

But what universities did, and how they did it, also changed enormously in the decades after the Second World War, in significant measure as a result of what Clark Kerr, president of the University of California, would characterize in 1963 as their "common-law marriage" with the federal government. Seeking to capture this transformation as a whole, Kerr declared that the prewar research university, generally modeled on German universities of the late nineteenth century, had since the war been replaced by what he called the "multiversity," "a whole series of communities and activities held together by a common name, a common governing board, and related purposes." He cited the example of what his own institution had become:

> The University of California last year had operating expenditures from all sources of nearly half a billion dollars, with almost another 100 million for construction; a total employment of over 40,000 people, more than IBM and in a far greater variety of endeavors; operations in over a hundred locations, counting campuses, experiment stations, agricultural and urban extension centers, and projects abroad involving more than fifty countries; nearly 10,000 courses in its catalogues; some form of contact with nearly every industry, nearly every level of government, nearly every person in its region.[13]

Kerr's vision of the corporatized multiversity smoothly and efficiently serving the needs of government and industry would be criticized from both the right and the left. For example, in 1971 the conservative sociologist Robert A. Nisbet (1913–1996) denounced what he saw as the deleterious effects of the "immense amount of money" that in the 1940s began to flow into American universities, which for the most part took the form of "direct grants from government and foundation to individual members of university faculties, or to small company-like groups of faculty members, for the purposes of creating institutes, centers, bureaus, and other essentially capitalistic enterprises within the academic community" to further "the express purpose of research," first in the natural sciences, then in the social sciences and finally in the humanities.[14] In the 1960s the emerging New Left also formulated a powerful critique of the postwar American university; in fact, it was students at Kerr's own University of California who led the way in rejecting the model of higher education he had celebrated and what they saw as its complicity with corporate and state power. As Mario Savio, a leader of the Free Speech Movement at Berkeley, put it on the steps of Sproul Hall in December 1964:

> . . . If this is a firm, and if the Board of Regents are the board of directors, and if President Kerr in fact is the manager, then I'll tell you something. The faculty are a bunch of employees, and we're the raw material! But we're a bunch of raw materials that don't mean to be—have any process upon us. Don't mean to be made into any product! Don't mean—don't mean to end up being bought by some clients of the University, be they the government, be they industry, be they organized labor, be they anyone! We're human beings![15]

Students and scholars on the left would go on to argue that the Cold War had brought about the emergence of a "military-industrial-academic complex," with American universities increasingly transformed into instruments of the national security state and handmaidens of the giant corporations which dominated the economy, while themselves becoming ever more corporatized in their mode of governance and educational priorities.[16]

One significant feature of the postwar transformation of American universities was thus the emergence of new modes of, and new institutional vehicles for, research and training, often launched and sustained by large-scale funding from the big foundations, the government and other external sources. The rise of area studies as a framework for graduate training, scholarly research, undergraduate education and language instruction at universities across the country was a relatively small but nonetheless significant manifestation of this broader phenomenon. In this same period, area studies also gradually coalesced on the national scale as a set of distinct regionally focused academic fields with their own professional associations, journals, funding streams and cultures, often in uneasy co-existence with the humanities and social science disciplines which had themselves largely taken shape in the late nineteenth and early twentieth centuries and were also undergoing profound changes in the postwar period.

The Foundations Take Action

The Rockefeller Foundation had supported the ACLS' efforts to promote and develop regionally focused research and training since the late 1920s, and even as the Second World War was still raging it began making substantial grants for programs built around this approach in a range of fields, for example $75,000 each to Stanford, the University of California and the University of Washington for Far Eastern studies, plus $35,000 to Pomona College.[17] Soon after the war ended the foundation decided to appropriate even larger sums to support the establishment of new university-based centers for research and graduate training on regions deemed critical to the country's future. A December 1946 memorandum by Charles B. Fahs (1908–1980), who was then assistant director of the Rockefeller Foundation's Humanities Division and as its director from 1950 would oversee the foundation's area studies program into the early 1960s, elucidates its broader conception of the purposes and character of area studies in this period:

> Intellectual and practical experience of the last few years makes clearer than ever before what sort of men are needed to deal with present national and international problems. First, of course, men with a sound training in the analytical techniques of one or more of the humanistic and social science disciplines. Second, men who have learned to apply these techniques to the concrete human problems in specific situations in space and time. To do so they must have both a factual knowledge that is both deep and broad of the society under consideration and be alive to the need for interrelated application of all pertinent disciplines. This is area study and is [sic] applicable most easily to the area we know best—the one in which we live. Third, however, men are needed who have learned the perspective which comes only from study of an area other than one's own.

Fahs, who during the war had worked in the Far Eastern division of the OSS R&A branch, proposed that the Rockefeller Foundation support "the establishment of local and foreign regional or area studies as an integrated part of the general education of students in the social sciences and humanities and the related development of strong centers of graduate research."[18]

Toward this end, Rockefeller envisioned foundation support for one or two strong university-based centers in each regional field; but, Fahs concluded, "when the minimum has been established on a sound basis R. F. should withdraw. It is our job to help someone start the band wagon. We have no responsibility to help the late comers to climb on."[19]

Among the regions Russia (by which was meant the Soviet Union) was probably the Rockefeller Foundation's top priority in the immediate postwar period, followed closely by East Asia. In its annual report for 1945 the foundation devoted a special section to "Relations with Russia." "Two vast continental systems have emerged from the war—Russia and the United States—facing each other across the Pacific," the report declared. "Our relations with Russia are too immediately important, too freighted with all sorts of possibilities, to be left to the mercy of uninformed emotion, whether ecstatic or denunciatory. What is required is a determination to be accurately informed, to see things as they are."[20] In fact, a proposal for a new Russian Institute at Columbia University, drawn up by Geroid T. Robinson while he was still in charge of the OSS Research and Analysis branch's Soviet division, had been submitted to the Rockefeller Foundation before the end of 1944, and the institute was established with large-scale Rockefeller funding two years later, with Robinson appointed its first director.[21] That same year the Rockefeller Foundation also provided substantial funding to Yale to support Far Eastern and Russian studies, and to the University of Washington for a new Far Eastern Institute. These programs and institutions would serve as important models for other new area studies centers and programs soon to be established.

Until 1947 the Carnegie Corporation of New York moved more cautiously than Rockefeller had toward a firm decision to support area studies as part of a ramped-up program of activity in the field of international affairs. At an October 1945 meeting of Carnegie's board of trustees, the foundation's president had outlined a proposal to direct "a substantial portion of our income toward stimulating adult thinking in respect to foreign relations," perhaps as much as one million dollars a year, and there were consultations with SSRC leaders about a new Carnegie-funded program to provide fellowships to train area specialists at American universities.[22] There then ensued months of discussion among the foundation's officers and staff about the character of its new international program, to include continuing funding for such long-time recipients of Carnegie beneficence as the Council on Foreign Relations, the Foreign Policy Association and the Institute of Pacific Relations but also support for new initiatives in area studies.[23] Finally, in January 1947, Carnegie Corporation officers secured their board's approval to appropriate $1.1 million for a new program in area studies, to be disbursed in grants of up to five years with the aim of "enriching and invigorating college and university contributions to international understanding, because from this source come the teachers, the influential citizens and the practitioners. The officers believe that the first step should be a few pilot programs in selected universities, particularly at the graduate level, and also an experimental program at the undergraduate level," with a focus on universities that already had significant resources in a particular field. This program constituted the largest component of Carnegie's total grants for 1946–1947 in the field of international affairs, which came to $1,828,700—almost three times as much as in the preceding years and equivalent to about $20 million in 2015. All told, between the beginning of 1947 and the end of 1949 the foundation authorized spending almost two million dollars for the establishment or support of area studies centers at universities across the country, plus an additional $1.1 million for "programs or projects which are closely related to the study of foreign areas."[24]

In this critical period it was John W. Gardner (1912–2002) who at Carnegie played the leading role in launching its new initiative in area studies. Gardner had received his PhD in psychology from the University of California in 1938 and then taught at Mount Holyoke College; during the war he served as a captain in the Marine Corps and worked for the OSS, and then joined the Carnegie Corporation staff early in 1946. By 1955 he had risen to become president of the Carnegie Corporation; ten years later President Lyndon B. Johnson appointed him Secretary of Health, Education and Welfare, in which capacity he helped launch Medicare and other "Great Society" programs. Gardner resigned from the Johnson administration in 1968 because of his opposition to the war in Vietnam and later chaired the Urban Coalition; in 1970 he founded Common Cause, which he would lead for seven years. Gardner vigorously embraced Carnegie's commitment to university-based area studies early on: he had met with William L. Langer in 1943 or 1944 to express the foundation's admiration for the analytical approach developed by the OSS R&A branch and explore how it might be applied in a university setting. He soon came to see the development of area studies as an urgent priority for the United States, as he explained in an article published in *The Yale Review* in March 1948:

> We must develop aggressive long-term research programs covering each of the various areas of the world; and we must expand and improve the quality of our present pitifully small corps of experts on these various areas. In seeking to solve this problem, it is primarily to the universities that we must turn. The government is able to carry on a limited amount of research; private research agencies can handle a small portion of the job; but the task is enormous, and the only institutions prepared to do the job with the continuity and on the scale it demands are the graduate schools of the universities.[25]

Once Carnegie's board had approved the new initiative in area studies, its officers worked hard to determine how to allocate the funds. In March 1947 the board was informed that a Corporation representative—almost certainly John Gardner—had "visited every institution in the United States which is carrying on important work in foreign area study and has talked personally with most of the leading experts on each of the foreign areas concerned. Extended discussions have also been held with Department of State officials, who are developing a concern as to the problems of training expert personnel."[26] Gardner played a central role in deciding which universities should receive Carnegie funding for which area studies programs, and along the way he and other Carnegie officers were in regular conversation with government officials about how to meet their needs for accurate and timely information and analysis. By May 1947 Carnegie had made grants totaling $445,000 (equivalent to some $4.75 million in 2015) for area studies programs: to the University of Michigan for a new Center for Japanese Studies, headed by Robert Hall, who also chaired the SSRC's Committee on World Area Research (CWAR); to the University of Minnesota for Scandinavian studies; to Columbia for fellowships in Russian studies; and to Yale for Southeast Asian studies. An additional $415,000 had been committed but not yet disbursed.

Unsurprisingly, the Carnegie Corporation followed the lead of the Rockefeller Foundation by choosing Russian studies for one of its largest early initiatives in area studies. In 1947, in close consultation with government agencies, Carnegie worked hard to convince Harvard to agree to create a new Russian Research Center whose goal it would be "to attempt to develop a thorough understanding of Russian behavior through a systematic study of the available historical and current data," and to support the new center Carnegie provided a very large multiyear grant.[27] At this center, as at Columbia's, veterans of the Soviet division of the OSS R&A branch played a central role, and a significant percentage of the research done there in the late 1940s and 1950s was contracted and funded by the military or intelligence agencies.[28]

By September 1947 all but $208,500 of the $1.1 million appropriated by the Carnegie Corporation the previous January had been allocated.[29] In addition to granting substantial funds to individual universities for new or existing area studies programs, Carnegie now also moved ahead with the new national fellowship program in area studies that it had long been contemplating. Here too John Gardner seems to have played the key role, within the Carnegie Corporation and in discussions with the SSRC.[30] In February 1947 the SSRC's Problems and Policy Committee responded positively to an "informal inquiry from the Carnegie Corporation of New York concerning the Council's willingness to accept funds for fellowships for area study," to be administered by the CWAR.[31] Gardner participated in the subsequent meeting of this committee at which it began to formulate the outlines of the proposed fellowship program, and when committee members proposed a national conference on area studies that would bring together the key figures in the new field, Gardner quickly provided $5000 with which to fund it and offered his advice about whom to invite in each regional field.[32] The collaboration between Carnegie and the SSRC was such that only two weeks elapsed between the SSRC's formal submission of its request for $130,000 (equivalent to almost $1.4 million today) to fund its new area studies fellowship program, which would include predoctoral and postdoctoral research fellowships as well as travel grants for scholars, and Carnegie's confirmation that it had approved the request.[33]

November 1947: Taking Stock at Columbia

The national conference on world areas and area studies—the first of its kind—that Carnegie had agreed to fund some months earlier met for three days at Columbia University in November 1947. On the day on which it convened, the Carnegie Corporation formally notified the SSRC that it would in fact fund a new national area studies fellowship program under its auspices. This development not only substantially brightened the emerging field's prospects, it also put the SSRC rather than the ACLS in its vanguard. Over the next seven years this program would disburse some $700,000 in fellowship funding to 214 scholars and students—the equivalent of $6–7 million in 2015.

The conference brought together more than a hundred people, mainly from universities but also government officials, foundation staffers and representatives of scholarly organizations. For many participants it must have felt like a reunion of OSS veterans. Many of the key players in the nascent area studies field were present, from Latin American, Soviet, Southeast Asian, Indian, Near Eastern, European and Far Eastern studies, to take stock of what had been achieved thus far and discuss where to go from here. It was evident that area studies had developed very quickly in the two years since the end of the war. As CWAR chair Robert Hall—by now the central academic leader in the field—noted in his preface to the published account of the conference, compiled by anthropologist Charles Wagley (1913–1991), then serving on the SSRC staff, 1946–1947 had witnessed the establishment of area centers "which together approximate complete world coverage of all the major regions" except for Africa and parts of Europe, and additional centers were under development. Government agencies were expressing interest in university area research and training, new scholarly bodies and regionally focused academic organizations had come into existence, and universities were continuing to expand their offerings in area training. Area studies, it would seem, was at long last up and running.[34]

Conference participants were by no means unaware of the connection between what they were meeting to discuss and the current fraught state of the world. In his preface to Wagley's synopsis of the conference, Hall noted—with humorous intent, one must hope—that "it is perhaps fortunate for the continued development of area studies, if for nothing else, that our world has remained even after the war in a state of critical uncertainty." (iii) But Wagley felt the need to insist, rather defensively, that "international understanding—not military intelligence—is the goal" of area studies (8), and he went on to quote E. A. Speiser, former head of the Near East division of R&A, as having declared that there was no conflict "between academic and national needs, between scholarship and government objectives, scientific progress and basic intelligence. . . . Where scholarship and research are involved, the academic and national needs are one and the same thing. Sound research is valuable to the nation, whereas the national need cannot be served by inadequate scholarship. Only the soundest sort of area research can be in the genuine national interest and thereby also a factor of international well-being." (8–9)

Speiser had that same year published *The United States and the Near East*, which offered readers a survey of the history of the region from ancient times onward, outlined its current problems and assessed U.S. interests there. He argued that the country urgently required more trained personnel who could provide the expertise needed to develop an effective and realistic American policy for the Middle East.[35]

The conference opened with an address by Pendleton Herring on "The Objectives of Area Study" in which he reiterated an argument that advocates of area studies had been making since 1943: any provincialism within the social science disciplines "will quickly be revealed when the expert applies his formulations to alien cultures." (7) Talcott Parsons (1902–1979), widely regarded as the country's preeminent sociologist, was among those invited to respond to Herring's opening remarks. He was a vocal advocate of cross-disciplinary social science research; indeed, he had been instrumental in the creation of Harvard's new Department of Social Relations, established a year earlier not merely to foster interaction across the disciplines but ultimately to unify them through the development of a common "basic social science."[36] In his remarks at the Columbia conference Parsons suggested that area studies offered specialists in different disciplines a way to collaborate productively, though he saw the uneven development of various social science disciplines as a challenge still to be overcome on the way toward achieving what Wagley paraphrased as "an integrated treatment of the total social system of an area." (6)

The conference's regional panels highlighted the great differences among the various area studies fields. For example, many of the Latin Americanists had worked together for years, in the framework of the joint ACLS-SSRC-NRC Committee on Latin American Studies and elsewhere, and they were well-organized and already quite engaged with interdisciplinary approaches.[37] In Soviet studies business was of course booming, with the very well-endowed centers at Columbia and Harvard in operation and lots of interest (and contracts) from government agencies. In contrast, Near Eastern studies had yet to attain much coherence or momentum as a field and at that point could boast of only a single avowedly interdisciplinary graduate program, at Princeton.

In Search of a Model: From Puerto Rico to Peru and Mexico

The published report on the Carnegie-funded November 1947 area studies conference insisted that it had "clarified many general and specific problems of area instruction and research" and secured "a good deal of agreement
among the participants, even though they represented diverse disciplines
and a variety of kinds of area specialization, as to the main outlines of what
constitutes area study and area research." (48) But the conclusions that the
report's compiler cited were in fact rather general and vague, and though the
SSRC would publicly declare the conference a success, in private there was
less enthusiasm. Some years later Hall would acknowledge to the SSRC that
the conference had been "plagued by dead-end discussion," especially about
the definition of "area" and the place of language study in area studies, and he
continued to express concern about what he saw as the nascent field's lack of
theoretical and methodological clarity and rigor.[38]

In his preface to Wagley's conference report, Hall chose to emphasize the
immaturity of area studies as a field and how much remained to be done:

> In this period of initial development, of necessity, much has had to be taken on
> faith. General objectives, to be sure, have been clearly stated but these must now
> be refined, adapted, and demonstrated. A great deal remains to be done in the
> designing of desirable research projects, in the perfection and testing of area re-
> search techniques and procedures, and in the intellectual appraisal of scholarly
> area efforts to date. The next logical step would seem to be the planning and
> execution of a pilot study of some selected foreign area. Only in this way can
> existing theory be tested and amplified. (iv)

In the wake of the conference Hall and some of his colleagues strove to put
area studies on a firm foundation by clarifying the vexed question of what
this new academic field could and should be. They believed that it needed
to be equipped with what they held the traditional disciplines to possess: a
theory or paradigm that specified its proper object, and a methodology by
means of which that object could be studied, framed within the scientistic
understanding of social-scientific knowledge production that was gaining
ground in this period.[39] At the time, key figures at Rockefeller and Carnegie
were struggling with similar issues as they sought to develop a coherent rationale for their funding decisions in the social sciences. As Mark Solovey
has shown, they were uncertain about "what exactly scientific work in the

social field meant" and about "whether and how social scientists might pursue wisdom, vision, and ethical inquiry."[40] Many of their anxieties and confusions, never to be definitively resolved, overlapped with, and informed, those of the founders and leaders of area studies in the late 1940s and beyond.

As he told his SSRC colleagues in 1948, Hall wanted first of all to secure a comprehensive "intellectual appraisal of the whole theory of area studies and their accomplishments."[41] Happily for him, Julian Steward, chair of Columbia University's Anthropology Department and a participant in the November 1947 conference, had been giving some apparently related questions considerable thought, and his perspective was deemed particularly valuable because of the research project he was involved in at the time, which CWAR members thought might provide an appropriate model for the kind of "demonstration project in area research" that Hall had called for in his preface to Wagley's report on the Columbia conference.

Steward (1902–1972) is best remembered among anthropologists for his formulation of "cultural ecology," an approach which focused on the interactions between a community's culturally available technology and its environment.[42] In the late 1920s and 1930s Steward's research focused on the indigenous peoples of the western United States and Canada, and it was this work which gave birth to his concept of cultural ecology. But in 1947, a year after becoming chair of Columbia University's Anthropology Department, he had assumed leadership of what was formally called the Puerto Rico Social Anthropology Project, an in-depth study of the island's population (especially its rural majority), with fieldwork carried out mainly by several of Steward's graduate students, among them Sidney Mintz and Eric R. Wolf. As a note accompanying the guide to the archival records of the project puts it, "In contrast to previous anthropological studies that investigated communities as isolated units, the Puerto Rico Project not only assessed the impact of industrialization among rural communities, it produced an analysis of the relationship between those communities and the Island through oral history, labor studies, and comparative surveys of sociocultural patterns." The Puerto Rico Project coincided with the launching of Operation Bootstrap, a program through which the federal and local governments sought to diversify the island's economy, traditionally dominated by sugar cultivation and processing, and alleviate rural unemployment by attracting American corporate investment in manufacturing through tax incentives and easier access to the island's abundant supply of cheap labor.[43]

Field research for Steward's Puerto Rico project began early in 1948, just as Hall and his colleagues were pushing to clarify the character and future direction of social science research in area studies. For them, the kinds of theoretical and methodological problems with which Steward was grappling in Puerto Rico seemed the very problems which area studies writ large had to face; hence their hope that Steward's work in Puerto Rico might blaze a trail for this new field in formation. There is, however, considerable irony in the CWAR's embrace of the Puerto Rico project as a model: as Steward's biographer Virginia Kerns points out, he "had never engaged in the type of field research that his students [in Puerto Rico] would undertake" and "had no firsthand experience with field methods such as participant observation."

> He had collected census material, but his method [in his previous research] depended on plumbing the memories of one or two elderly informants and had no relevance for his students. . . . In Puerto Rico, Steward thus found himself in the peculiar position of advising a community study project without ever having taken direct part in one himself. . . . Moreover, he still knew rather little about Puerto Rico. . . . And he did not speak Spanish or read it with great ease, which limited his access to published material and his contact with any Puerto Ricans who did not speak English.[44]

Nor, as Kerns also notes, did Steward evince much interest in "the issues of class power and U.S. control of Puerto Rico that quickly seized the attention of the students."[45]

Nonetheless, in the first half of 1948 the CWAR, anxious to develop a model for area studies research, proposed undertaking "a fairly intensive study of the problems involved in interdisciplinary area research" in Puerto Rico as well, whether through a project of its own or by adding specialists to Steward's project already under way.[46] But Steward's Puerto Rico project was only one of several models for the kind of collaborative research that Hall and his CWAR colleagues hoped could secure area studies' social-scientific legitimacy and clarify the methods proper to it. Both Steward and CWAR member Wendell Bennett were in this same period also deeply involved with the Viru Valley project, a multidisciplinary team effort launched in 1946 in the coastal plain of northern Peru to investigate settlement patterns and their environmental contexts. Participants in the November 1947 area studies conference at

Columbia had in fact heard a report on the Viru Valley project, described as "studying the development of the culture of one north Peruvian valley from its earliest archaeological horizons to the contemporary society." Conference participants were also told about the Tarascan project, launched in 1940 and run collaboratively by Mexico's Department of Indian Affairs, its National Polytechnic Institute and the University of California, Los Angeles; its goal was to learn "as much as possible about the Tarascan-speaking Indians who inhabit an area west of the Valley of Mexico through an analysis of their contemporary culture and its relationship to the environment, and through an archaeological and historical study of Tarascan culture." Both these projects, intended to produce something like the "total knowledge" of a region that early advocates of area studies upheld as the new field's ideal, were presented to the conference as possible models for area studies research.[47]

Important as these projects were, it is also worth keeping in mind that many of the key figures in area studies early on had spent a good part of the war working together in the OSS Research and Analysis branch or at other sites that similarly fostered new modes of collaboration across disciplinary boundaries. More broadly, as Joel Issac notes,

> . . . World War II produced a culture of scientific research in which a premium was placed on getting one's hands dirty and mucking in with specialists from other fields. . . . The human sciences were inexorably drawn into this research culture. Even as seemingly tradition-bound an activity as the training of "overseas" (i.e. colonial) administrators in academic military programs encouraged thoughts of cross-disciplinary synthesis. . . . Team-based, problem-focused, applied research was helping to bring down divisions between disciplines, thereby creating a new institutional landscape for the human sciences.[48]

Their wartime experience thus inclined them to believe that such focused, intensive and cross-disciplinary methods could yield in-depth, interdisciplinary knowledge of a well-defined area or topic and thereby demonstrate the utility of area studies both for postwar social science and for policymakers.[49] At the same time, team projects of this kind would be a feature of much postwar government (and government-funded) as well as corporate research, in the sciences and beyond. A similar vision informed Harvard's new Department of Social Relations, committed to overcoming disciplinary divisions and producing a unified social science.[50]

In this context, it is not surprising that, in the late 1940s and early 1950s,

Hall and his CWAR colleagues expected (or at least hoped) that such projects, and the approaches and methods associated with them, could serve as models for area studies research—even though one could in fact argue that neither the Puerto Rico project nor the Viru Valley project nor the Tarascan project actually constituted interdisciplinary research. All were essentially conceived and executed by anthropologists (though of course that rubric could and did encompass people doing a variety of substantively different things).[51] They also focused on much smaller geographic areas than was typical of other social science disciplines, for example political science which when it came to non-Western societies tended to operate on the scale of the nation-state, at a minimum. Their relevance as models for interdisciplinary area research as Hall and his colleagues conceived it was thus questionable.

A Theory of Area Studies?

Julian Steward would share his own understanding of the theory and practice of area studies in several formats between 1948 and 1950. In 1948 he drew up a memorandum on "Area Program Planning," of which he seemed to have much first-hand knowledge from his research projects in the American West and in Puerto Rico, and in March 1949 he published an article, "An Anthropologist's Concept of Area Studies," in the inaugural issue of the SSRC's *Area News Letter*, which he edited. The former was framed very generally, while the latter was clearly informed by Steward's experience with the Puerto Rico project and much more concretely addressed how he thought anthropologists should go about integrating the study of what he termed "Phenomena of local or horizontal sociocultural segments" and "Formal, area-wide institutions."[52] In 1948 the SSRC also commissioned Steward to produce a much more extensive assessment of the concepts and methods of area studies; after revision in light of comments by CWAR members and others, it was finally published in 1950 as Council Bulletin 63, under the title *Area Research: Theory and Practice.*[53]

In his preface to *Area Research*, Steward explained that while "the practical demand that area research supply information to guide our foreign relations is perhaps as great now as it was during the war . . . the sense of urgency has diminished sufficiently to enable scholars once again to give thought to the theoretical and methodological implications of their research." The time had thus come to try to "put area research on a solid scientific basis." (xii–xiii) But he immediately acknowledged that "the theory of area research poses some difficult problems," and overall *Area Research* is characterized by a cautious and tentative tone; it certainly made no claim to being authoritative, or even applicable to disciplines beyond anthropology. Indeed, Steward stated at the outset that his thoughts about area studies "are primarily those of a cultural anthropologist who has some firsthand experience in area programs"; scholars from other disciplines would have to modify the concepts and methods he was presenting, or propose alternatives (xiv). He also readily acknowledged that the term "area" could have very different uses and meanings: it might refer to a "world area" (like South Asia), a "culture area" (like Latin America or the Maya Indians), a nation, a colony or dependency (like Puerto Rico) or a region (like the Southeastern United States). As a result, "the units selected for area study programs are determined by a number of considerations which may have little to do with scientific theory: the institution's facilities, availability of funds, and others." (8–9)

Nonetheless, Steward asserted, there was "general agreement on the following four objectives of area research: 1) To provide knowledge of practical value about important world areas; 2) To give students and scholars an awareness of cultural relativity; 3) To provide understanding of social and cultural wholes as they exist in areas; 4) To further the development of a universal social science." (2–3) Elaborating on the third objective, Steward explained that the culture of each area "is necessarily recognized as an entity which differs from our own culture in its entirety as well as in many of its particulars. . . . As knowledge of a foreign area increases, it not only becomes evident that the culture differs from our own in particulars but that these have a consistency or interrelationship that suggests the need for some larger frame of reference for understanding them." (4–5) Hence the need for an interdisciplinary approach, though in what would seem to be an allusion to the grandiose vision of Parsons and his Harvard colleagues Steward deemed the development of a universal social science "at present little more than a hope." (5)

In what followed Steward surveyed what he cautiously characterized as "Some Practices of Area Research," including community, regional and national studies, mostly the work of either anthropologists or sociologists. A subsequent chapter, just as cautiously titled "Some Concepts and Methods of Area Research," presented aspects of his own understanding of anthropological theory, in a manner seemingly intended to be accessible to non-anthropologists; this was followed by a chapter discussing the conceptual framework that informed the Puerto Rico Social Anthropology Project, though Steward acknowledged that "the methodological conclusions to be drawn from the Puerto Rico project do not of course apply to all areas." (127) Steward concluded by offering the hope that while such "world-wide trends" as the decline of subsistence farming and growing political centralization had "distinctive local characteristics . . . by proper cross-cultural comparison it should be possible to formulate recurrent regularities in developmental processes and functional relationships," yielding problems or hypotheses for further research. Here as throughout the essay, he struck a tentative and subdued tone about the prospects of area research. (155–156)

By the time *Area Research* was finally published in 1950—some two years after it had been commissioned—it no longer seemed of much relevance or interest to most of those engaged in area studies across the country. For one, the outbreak of the Korean War earlier that year had dramatically changed the atmosphere in Washington as well as the context within which area studies operated, which may have made Steward's essay seem irrelevant to current concerns and priorities in the field. But more broadly, Hall's vision of developing a rigorous and coherent theory and methodology of area studies social science research and of demonstrating their effectiveness through a model research project had not been widely embraced by the area studies community. In fact, he faced a great deal of skepticism from the start: as early as July 1948 the SSRC's new president, Pendleton Herring, had agreed with John Gardner that the CWAR, "though well fitted to deal with problems involved area teaching programs, was not ideally equipped to explore the problems of area research." Gardner was unenthusiastic about funding the kind of demonstration project Hall was hoping for and eventually even the CWAR stopped discussing it, leaving Hall to move ahead on his own through the area studies center over which he presided.[54] Meanwhile, efforts by the SSRC to arouse interest in theorizing area studies among practitioners also failed to elicit much of a response. In the March 1949 inaugural issue of the *Area News Letter* published by the SSRC to enable those engaged in area studies to exchange ideas, Julian Steward had admitted that, even as programs and centers were being established, "the precise meaning and purpose of an area study have, however, not yet been clarified." He invited researchers in this new field to discuss how their projects might address broader issues; how they would go about defining what an area was; how disciplinary boundaries might be transcended; and which of their field methods might be of use to others. The SSRC urged area studies researchers to respond to Steward's queries, but few if any did so, and the first issue of its *Area News Letter* also seems to have been the last.[55]

In this changed atmosphere, when Steward's *Area Research* finally appeared the SSRC seemed anxious to distance itself from the study it had commissioned. In his foreword to Steward's study SSRC staffer Paul Webbink wrote:

> The appraisal is frankly that of one man, and has been approached, as the author himself states, principally from the point of view of an anthropologist. It is clear that at many points geographers, historians, political scientists, or persons trained in other disciplines would have proceeded with different assumptions and somewhat different objectives. Some area specialists within and outside the Council's Committee [i.e., the CWAR] question whether any generalized and theoretical definition of area research can span the range of situations from, for example, Puerto Rico to the Soviet Union, which fall within the scope of area research. Nevertheless, many of those who disagree with the author at specific points will agree that he has performed a major service in attempting for the first time to block out a generalized approach in a field notable for the variety and discreteness of the research thus far undertaken. The bulletin [i.e., Steward's study] should not only challenge further intensive self-analysis on the part of proponents of other approaches, but may also serve to stimulate individuals competent in other disciplines to attempt their own formulation of the goals which area research should seek to achieve and the techniques it should use. (viii–ix)

A few months later, in a report to the SSRC Council, Robert Hall referred to *Area Research* simply as "an able statement by an anthropologist" and remarked that "it is a question whether the committee [i.e., the CWAR] should encourage comparable expressions from other disciplines of their views of area research and what they can contribute to it."[56] In fact, the CWAR never solicited any similar contributions, nor did it ever really grapple with the question Steward had raised of how to define the term "area," which would seem to be important for a field calling itself area studies. By this point many of those who had come to see themselves as engaged in area studies, including even members of the CWAR, seem to have lost interest in elaborating a coherent and comprehensive theory to define and guide this new field, accompanied by a toolkit of rigorous methods, or at least they no longer deemed it an urgent priority. Instead, they pursued research on the basis of a much looser, vaguer, more common-sense notion of area studies then taking shape, which in practice often meant that area studies was whatever they happened to be doing.

This does not mean the search for a theory and a method appropriate to area studies was altogether abandoned. For example, Robert Hall would eventually launch and oversee a demonstration project of the kind he had long envisioned, under the auspices of his own Center for Japanese Studies at the University of Michigan. In 1950, after arduous efforts, the center opened a field research station in Okayama, Japan, at which graduate students (all reserve officers in the Army or Navy) could assist faculty with their research while pursuing their own master's degrees. The three young scholars stationed in Okayama when the facility opened included an anthropologist, a geographer and a political scientist. While each pursued his or her individual project, their research was regarded as part of a larger long-term project focused on three nearby villages, with the aim of producing "an approximation of a total knowledge of these representative communities." The field station closed in 1955, apparently because funding ran out.[57] Whatever scholarly benefits the field station may have yielded for those directly involved with it, it did not produce the kind of theoretical and methodological breakthrough for area studies that Hall had once hoped for, nor did it have any significant impact on the wider field. However, Hall's failure in the late 1940s and early 1950s to achieve a paradigm for area studies, to develop a generalizable model and method that practitioners in the field could put to work, did not bring this quest to an end; nor did the vexed question of the relationship between area studies and the disciplines go away. Grappling with these issues would henceforth be the responsibility of the committees established by the SSRC for each regional field and charged with formulating and implementing a coherent research agenda that would shape and advance it, presumably rooted in some productive and presumably interdisciplinary paradigm. With respect to Middle East studies, at least, this was a mission which the SSRC (later joint SSRC-ACLS) committee for this field would for decades struggle mightily to fulfill.

4   Princeton, the ACLS and
Postwar Near Eastern Studies

At this moment in American history it is not necessary to justify, if indeed it ever was, some immediate and drastic improvement in the study of the Near East.

—Mortimer Graves, 1947

A S THE ROCKEFELLER FOUNDATION and the Carnegie Corporation began to invest in area studies in 1946–1947, they deemed Middle East studies—almost universally referred to at the time as Near Eastern studies—a much lower priority than Russian or Far Eastern studies, and so the field benefited from much less foundation largesse. Such foundation support as this field received early on went at first exclusively to Princeton University, and an examination of the establishment there of what was characterized as the country's first "integrated" area studies program for the Middle East can elucidate important aspects of how this field took shape in the early postwar period. But the development of Middle East studies was also affected in the later 1940s and early 1950s by contention between the American Council of Learned Societies and the Social Science Research Council over its character, direction and leadership, a rivalry whose outcome would shape its course for decades to come.

"For the First Time in America":
Near Eastern Studies at Princeton

As it had been with Russian studies, the Rockefeller Foundation was first into the breach with Near Eastern studies. In December 1946 Charles Fahs of Rockefeller's Humanities Division lamented in an internal memorandum that neither Princeton nor Chicago, both of which he considered possible sites for centers for Arabic studies, "has modern interest or has decided on field of specialization."[1] But in its annual report for 1946 the foundation framed the situation at Princeton more positively: with Philip K. Hitti clearly in mind, it declared that "since the establishment 20 years ago of its Department of Oriental Languages and Literatures, with a group of scholars whose mother tongue was Arabic and whose training in Near Eastern and American universities fitted them to understand both East and West, Princeton has departed from the traditional practice of American universities and has treated Arabic as a living rather than a dead language." The report also recalled the summer seminars that Hitti and his colleagues had organized in 1935, 1938 and 1939, with Rockefeller funding channeled through the ACLS, "in which, for the first time in the history of American education, the three major Islamic languages—Arabic, Turkish and Persian—were made the core of a regional program which embraced religion, culture, history and art."[2]

By 1939 Princeton was offering instruction in Persian and Turkish as well as in Arabic on a regular basis, and during the war it had organized intensive programs in Arabic and Turkish for army personnel as part of the ASTP while also building up its collection of books, periodicals and maps on the contemporary Middle East. In 1944 Philip Hitti became chair of Princeton's Department of Oriental Languages and Literatures, whose tenured faculty at that point consisted of himself and the semi-retired Sanskritist Ernest Bender. Soon after the war Hitti was finally able to secure several new hires that significantly bolstered the university's faculty strength in Near Eastern studies. In 1946 Walter L. Wright, Jr. was appointed as professor of Turkish language and history, a year later T. Cuyler Young (1900–1976) joined the department to teach Persian language and history, and around the same time Farhat J. Ziadeh (born 1917) was hired to teach Arabic.[3] Princeton also had longstanding links with the American University of Beirut and the wider Arab world, through Philip Hitti but also through the Dodge family, members of which had served as president of AUB.[4] Unsurprisingly, then, it seemed to foundation officials that Princeton was the only institution of higher education in the country that had the human and material resources necessary to offer something approaching comprehensive, interdisciplinary training on the modern and contemporary Middle East.

This led the Rockefeller Foundation to announce in 1946 that it was giving Princeton a grant of $42,500 over a five-year period (the equivalent of almost half a million 2015 dollars) to support the establishment of a new Program in Near Eastern Studies. As the foundation put it in its annual report for that year:

> The Department of Oriental Languages and Literatures has ... assumed primary responsibility for the study of the Near Eastern area, in much the same way that the Department of Classics has responsibility for the study of all phases of the ancient world of Greece and Rome. ... The eventual aim is to develop a program of study comparable to that offered by the School of Oriental Studies and African Languages [sic] of the University of London and the École National des Langues Orientales Vivantes in Paris. Under this broader program the Department will offer undergraduates an opportunity to elect Near Eastern studies as an upper-class field of concentration, requiring the study of at least one Near Eastern language and courses in the culture, religion, history and political institutions of the area; and a two-year graduate course designed as training for government, business or educational service in the Near East, requiring mastery of at least one Near Eastern language.[5]

The new program, the first of its kind in the country, began operating in the fall of 1947 under the direction of Philip Hitti.

The Carnegie Corporation also soon appeared on the scene offering money. According to R. Bayly Winder, Hitti (who was Winder's father-in-law) would in later years tell the story of a visit from a Carnegie officer—most likely John Gardner as he toured universities in 1947 in order to meet with potential grantees. "As the gentleman got up to leave, he said that if there were anything he or Carnegie could do, to please get in touch. Hitti said it took about five minutes for the significance of this remark to sink in, but also that he had an appointment with the president of the university within the hour and a large grant some months later."[6] In soliciting that grant Princeton's president Harold W. Dodds told Carnegie's president Devereux C. Josephs that the university's new Program in Near Eastern Studies, would, "for the first time in America, provide the college undergraduate with an opportunity to choose the Near East as a field of concentration . . . and enable the graduate student to study for an M.A. degree in this area, for the purpose of utilizing his training as business man, teacher, missionary or governmental official."[7] Not long thereafter Princeton received exactly what it had requested: a Carnegie grant of $61,500 over five years to support the new Program in Near Eastern Studies—the equivalent of more than $650,000 in 2015.

Though substantial, this Carnegie grant was by far the smallest amount allocated or committed by the foundation to a new area studies program during 1947, and Carnegie Corporation officers had their doubts about Princeton. In soliciting a grant for Near Eastern studies from Carnegie, Princeton's president Harold W. Dodds had called the proposed new program "a logical development of the Summer Seminar in Arabic and Islamic Studies, which was at different times held at Princeton, of the Army Specialized Training Program in Arabic and Turkish, which was maintained in 1943–44, and of existing joint programs with the Department of History and the School of Public and International Affairs," and he highlighted the university's rich faculty and library resources in the field.[8] Though Carnegie quickly approved Princeton's request for funds, the foundation's president expressed his concerns in a personal letter to Dodds:

> In making this grant, Gardner and I are anxious to reaffirm something that we have said before in discussing the Near Eastern Studies with your very able associates. We have been disturbed by the fact that, although distinguished work has been done in this country on the ancient Near East, attention to the modern Near East has been entirely inadequate. We have been concerned, too, with the fact that the social sciences have been almost entirely inactive with respect to this area. We shall be happy if the present grant should prove useful to you in your efforts to broaden the Studies and make them even more relevant to present international problems.[9]

Dodds immediately sought to allay Josephs' concern "regarding the modern Near East in the light of the traditional emphasis [at Princeton] on the ancient Near East. . . ."

> There were those who told us that our Department of Oriental Languages and Literatures, and Professor Hitti in particular, were so oriented to classical times that they would not be able to adjust even to the war program in this area which

Princeton undertook. The events fully disposed of those fears. I doubt if any area program in the country during the war was more "relevant" than the show Hitti ran here. His recent extended trip through the Near East and the influence and respect he commands with the governments of this area are, I think, indicative of the fact that he cannot retire in an ivory tower even if he wanted to do so.

Dodds went on to assure Josephs that "since it is impossible to separate politics from religion and heritage in this area," Princeton's new program would certainly plan to offer training in the social sciences.[10]

All told, in its first five years Princeton's Near Eastern studies program received a total of almost $210,000 (over $2 million in 2015) in outside support. In addition to grants from Rockefeller and Carnegie, funds were provided by the William T. Grant Foundation and the Cleveland T. Dodge Foundation as well as by Aramco, other oil companies and the engineering and construction firm Bechtel.[11] Princeton Near Eastern studies' standing at the big foundations, and its ability to attract generous grants and donations, were probably bolstered by visits to the university by royalty from the region. Saudi princes (and future kings) Faysal bin 'Abd al-'Aziz (then his country's foreign minister as well as viceroy of Mecca) and Khalid bin 'Abd al-'Aziz visited together in 1943, Crown Prince Sa'ud bin 'Abd al-'Aziz visited in 1947, and to top it all off His Imperial Majesty Mohammed Reza Shah Pahlavi of Iran paid a visit in 1949.[12] Another innovation that raised the public profile of Near Eastern studies at Princeton and probably helped convince foundation officials and corporate donors that Hitti and his colleagues would indeed attend to the contemporary Near East was the annual conferences that they now began to organize. The first such conference, a three-day event on "Near Eastern Culture," was held in March 1947, one of many events organized to mark Princeton's bicentennial. Philip Hitti declared that in addition to American, Canadian and British scholars, the conference would feature "the most distinguished and largest group of Oriental scholars ever to confer on United States soil." And indeed, in addition to faculty from Princeton and other North American universities, participants included Constantine Zurayq (1909–2000), at the time a member of the Syrian delegation at the United Nations; Charles Malik (1906–1987), then Lebanon's ambassador to the United States and the United Nations; and the noted editor and publisher Emile Zaydan.[13]

In 1949 Ottomanist and Turkicist Lewis V. Thomas joined the faculty of Princeton's Department of Oriental Languages and Literatures; the following year R. Bayly Winder (1920–1988) did the same, immediately after completing his doctorate there. Winder's best-known scholarly work is *Saudi Arabia in the Nineteenth Century*, published in 1965, but in 1957 he and Farhat Ziadeh also published a textbook of modern Arabic that for a time was widely used, successor to a primer developed earlier by Ziadeh. Meanwhile, Dodds' 1947 commitment to bolster the contemporary social science dimension of Near Eastern studies at Princeton would only be realized some years later, thanks largely to a 1951 Rockefeller Foundation grant of $100,000 over five years to support the hiring and professional development of two young social scientists. According to William Marvel of the Carnegie Corporation staff, Hitti had long resisted this development, but "other interested faculty seem to have done such a good selling job on this point that now Hitti has embraced it warmly and discusses it as though it had been his idea all along."[14]

The two social scientists hired in 1952, both very recent PhDs, were Morroe Berger and Dankwart A. Rustow, appointed as assistant professors in the Sociology and Politics departments, respectively. Berger (1917–1981) served in the U.S. Army during the Second World War, and it was in that context that he was introduced to the study of the Middle East: he was later described as "one of the few outstanding students" in the Army Specialized Training Program at Princeton and subsequently served with military intelligence in Egypt, Iran and India. After the war he pursued graduate study at Columbia, receiving his PhD in 1950, after which he briefly taught at NYU before joining the Princeton faculty.[15] Rustow (1924–1996) was the son of a refugee from the Nazis who in the early 1930s had secured a teaching position at the University of Istanbul; he received his doctorate from Yale in 1951. Princeton's Rockefeller grant made it possible for Berger and Rustow to teach part-time in their first year and have their second year free of teaching for study and travel in the Middle East; only in the third year of their appointments would they assume full-time teaching responsibilities in their respective disciplinary departments.[16]

The hiring of Berger and Rustow was intended to remedy what a visiting Carnegie staffer described in 1951 as the "decidedly linguistic" bias of Princeton's Near Eastern studies enterprise. That same year the Program in Near Eastern Studies was removed from the exclusive control of the Department of Oriental Languages and Literatures and designated a separate program to be overseen by representatives of several departments.[17] Thus encouraged, Carnegie renewed its grant to Princeton for Near Eastern Studies the following year. The Rockefeller Foundation also saw Princeton as worthy of continuing support: in 1954, reflecting a new policy of helping a small number of area studies programs achieve long-term financial stability, it provided a grant of $500,000 (almost $4.5 million in 2015) to the university to support Near Eastern studies, with the proviso that for the first ten years the university could spend only the income from this fund. "It is believed," the foundation's annual report explained, "that the existence of this assured income will be of assistance to the university in stabilizing its present offering in Near Eastern studies, and in its effort to secure the larger support which is needed for its longterm maintenance."[18] Two years later the Ford Foundation, a relatively recent arrival on the American philanthropic scene, gave Near Eastern studies at Princeton $275,000 over five years (about $2.4 million in 2015), making it the third university (after Michigan and Columbia) whose Near Eastern program Ford was supporting.[19]

Near Eastern studies at Princeton thus enjoyed lavish and sustained foundation support between the mid-1940s and the mid-1950s, with its Program in Near Eastern Studies staking a claim to be the very first program of its kind in the country. This helped the university build on its long history and rich resources as a center for the study of the region and the wider Muslim world. From the start, however, foundation officials were not quite sure that Princeton Near Eastern studies could (or really wished to) transcend its philological heritage and sustain a properly interdisciplinary area studies program of the kind they envisioned. These doubts would persist through repeated changes in the personnel and leadership of Princeton's Near Eastern studies enterprise, and some of its rivals would vie for foundation support in part by denigrating its model of graduate training as old-fashioned and inadequate to the demands of the times. Nonetheless, foundation funding for Near Eastern studies kept flowing into Princeton's coffers, supplementing the university's own substantial support and making it for decades one of the best-resourced programs in the country.

"A Critical Area": The ACLS and Postwar Near Eastern Studies

Even as Princeton University was launching its new area studies program, the ACLS was devoting renewed attention to ways of promoting Near Eastern studies more broadly. Yet at a time when area studies was gathering momentum and the SSRC was staking its claim to guiding the field's trajectory, the vehicles that the ACLS had created in the prewar period to advance Near Eastern studies were languishing. In the late 1930s the ACLS had established a Committee on Near Eastern Studies (CNES) for the ancient and classical periods, and a Committee on Arabic and Islamic Studies (CAIS) for the period since the rise of Islam. During the war the former had maintained some level of activity, but the latter (whose membership remained unchanged from 1939 to 1946) was almost completely inactive and remained so even after the war ended. Egyptologist John A. Wilson (1899–1976), who had recently stepped down after many years as director of the University of Chicago's Oriental Institute, was added to the CAIS late in 1946 or early in 1947, but this does not seem to have ameliorated its paralysis. Neither did the appointment of Edwin E. Calverley of the Hartford Seminary as the committee's new chair, replacing G. Howland Shaw who after resigning from the State Department had turned his attention to philanthropic work.

This was an unacceptable state of affairs for Mortimer Graves, still ACLS secretary. Anxious to ratchet up area studies as he understood it, it was clear to him, and more importantly to the Rockefeller Foundation officials with whom he worked closely and who were beginning to pour money into area studies, that neither the CAIS nor the CNES was adequate to the task of achieving (as Graves put it in a memorandum) "some immediate and dramatic improvement in the study of the Near East." Graves therefore began formulating a plan to replace both the CAIS and the CNES with a reconstituted, and hopefully more vigorous, committee that would cover both the ancient and the modern Near East, and everything in between. This organizational form was rooted in a widely held belief, going back at least to James Henry Breasted, in the continuity and essential unity of the region's history over the millennia from ancient times down to the present; but it stood in increasingly sharp contrast to the SSRC's prioritization of the modern and contemporary periods and of social science research.[20]

The last event in which the moribund CAIS, or at least some of its members, was involved brought together leading figures in the field from Britain and the United States. In the fall of 1946 Graves informed Rockefeller Foundation officers that Hamilton Alexander Rosskeen Gibb (1895–1971), who since 1937 had been the Laudian professor of Arabic at Oxford, wished to come to the United States the following spring and hold a conference on translation from, and the teaching of, what were termed "Oriental languages."[21] In the months that followed this idea morphed into a proposal for a conference of British and American scholars of Near Eastern studies (broadly defined), similar to the March 1944 ACLS/Rockefeller conference on area studies and a more recent Rockefeller-funded conference on Slavic studies in New York. But these plans did not work out, and in the end the Rockefeller Foundation hosted a small meeting at its New York offices in March 1947, billed rather grandiosely as a "Conference on Near Eastern Studies" and attended by Gibb, the anthropologist Carlton Coon of Harvard, Philip Hitti of Princeton, John Wilson of the Oriental Institute, Millar Burrows of the American Schools of Oriental Research, and several Rockefeller and ACLS officers.[22] Mortimer Graves, who kept a close eye on what the SSRC was up to, very much wanted to get things moving in this particular area studies field, in which he and the ACLS had long been involved, and hoped that this meeting would contribute to that end.

The conference participants discussed a range of issues concerning Near Eastern studies in the United States, with Hitti in particular lamenting what he saw as the persistent gross inadequacy of available resources for teaching:

> We need encyclopedias, we need dictionaries. We haven't got a decent Arabic dictionary. . . . If a man comes to you and says, 'This word is Arabic and Turkish and Persian; what is the etymology of it? Did it come from Arabic to Turkish and Persian?' Where would you tell him to look it up? There is no place, no place. You can't refer him to anything. If you want to dig it up yourself, it may take you half an hour to find one word. We have no tools, we have no instruments, we have no implements. We have absolutely nothing. . . . I spend hours teaching my students how to look up a word in the Arabic dictionary. The Arabic dictionary is arranged, as you know, in a very funny way. It takes a long time. If we could only get a primer in Arabic to teach our students the elementary material! What do you use, or don't you begin with the elementary stuff, as we do? What do you use as an elementary book, introducing the student to the simple Arabic? Have you anything, Professor Gibb?

Gibb did not respond directly to Hitti's plaint, which reflected the ACLS' understanding of the field's main deficits and priorities. Gibb did, however, express his conviction (which he would reiterate over the years) that "the only methodologically correct approach to the study of the modern Near East is to begin with the study of the classical Near East."

Make sure your student of research in this field has a pretty firm grasp of his classical background, then bring in the modern Near East, and let him work out for himself what, in fact, is continuous and what is new; the element of continuity, the element of difference between the old civilization and the civilization of the present day, whether it be on literature or whether it be in political life or whether it be in community structure.

Neither Gibb's perspective nor the ACLS' broader conception of area studies was shared by the SSRC and its friends at Carnegie. Whereas Gibb believed that it was the Orientalists who must oversee interdisciplinary regionally focused research, because they alone understood the essence of Islamic civilization and thus how all the pieces fit together, Robert Hall of the CWAR was at this same moment arguing that it was the social scientists who bore "responsibility for the essential unity of area studies."[23] In the same vein, John Gardner of the Carnegie Corporation, just now beginning to pour funds into area studies, offered a vision of area studies that was very different from that of the ACLS. In a 1948 article he hailed what he saw as the field's "new emphasis on the social sciences" and on "the problems which face us today." "Preoccupation with the past and refusal to consider present realities had done much to stultify earlier work by scholars dealing with foreign areas. . . . We must study the past and study it well, but we cannot afford to get lost in the past." Moreover, Gardner added, "We now realize that if we are to arrive at any genuine appreciation of another society, we must study its economic structure, its industrial potential, natural resources, social organization, political myths, class structure, and so on."[24] Hall, Gardner and their allies were thus critical, if not disdainful, of the ACLS' conception of area studies, with its disinterest in, or even rejection of, research and graduate training and its prioritization of undergraduate education and language instruction. The vision of area studies they propagated would eventually prevail, at least in institutional terms, largely because it seemed much more likely to yield useful (including policy-relevant) knowledge about the contemporary world and was thus what the foundations wanted and were willing to support, even though actually realizing the SSRC's early hopes of developing a productive research agenda for area studies would prove elusive.

At his March 1947 meeting with scholars and foundation officials in the ACLS-Rockefeller orbit, Gibb also reported on the work of the Interdepartmental Commission of Enquiry on Oriental, Slavonic, East European and African Studies in Britain, generally referred to as the Scarbrough commission after its chair. This body had been appointed by the British government to investigate how that country's teaching and research resources on various regions might be sustained and developed; the commission's report, issued that same year, recommended additional funding for universities to strengthen their capacities in this area.[25] The Americans may have taken heart from the British government's willingness to invest in area studies and hoped that their own government would eventually do the same. But more immediately, the meeting seems to have contributed to the determination of the ACLS and the Rockefeller Foundation to at long last get things moving in Near Eastern studies. As the Rockefeller Foundation's annual report for 1947 acknowledged, "during recent years Near Eastern studies in the United States have lagged behind studies of China, Japan and the Soviet Union. The decline in relative emphasis on the ancient Near East has not been offset by adequate attention to what goes on in the minds of Near Easterners today."[26]

The final meeting of the CAIS took place in March 1947, with Gibb attending. Soon thereafter the ACLS disbanded both it and the CNES, and constituted a new Committee on Near Eastern Studies (CNES) composed of a dozen members—unusually large for an ACLS committee. Years later Bayly Winder would remark facetiously that the new committee consisted of "17 people representing seven universities, two seminaries, the Library of Congress, and the Department of State."[27] Moreover, despite Rockefeller's expressed interest in "what goes on in the minds of Near Easterners today," the new committee included both scholars of the ancient Near East as well as Arabists and Islamicists. Not everyone was happy about this, and in the months that followed tensions between "ancientists" and "modernists" would hamper the committee's work. Some of the members of the new CNES were holdovers from the disbanded CAIS or CNES, among them Edwin E. Calverley (designated chair), Philip Hitti, John Wilson, E. A. Speiser and the Biblical archaeologist William F. Albright (1891–1971). But there were also some new faces, including Walter L. Wright, Jr., who had recently returned to Princeton to teach Ottoman and Turkish history and language; the historian of Islamic art Richard Ettinghausen (1906–1979), then working at the Freer Gallery; and Halford L. Hoskins (1891–1967), first dean of Tufts University's Fletcher School of Law and Diplomacy, a member of the board of governors of the new Middle East Institute in Washington and at the time director of the recently established and still independent School of Advanced International Studies, which had begun to offer a range of courses on the modern and contemporary Middle East as well as Arabic.[28] In the spring of 1948 Edwin M. Wright, mentioned earlier as a recruit to wartime intelligence work and at the time a Middle East specialist at the State Department, would join the committee as well.[29]

The Rockefeller Foundation, chief patron of the ACLS, welcomed the formation of the new committee, declaring that it "proposes to explore the contributions which studies of the Near East might make to our civilization, to survey and evaluate the research facilities and personnel already available, and to formulate programs to fill the more important gaps between opportunity and performance thereby revealed." More importantly, Rockefeller awarded the new committee a grant of $12,000 over three years to support its planning and development work.[30] The following year, noting that the Near East was "a critical area" whose "political importance has been emphasized by recent events," the foundation gave the ACLS an additional $75,000 to expand its translation program to include Near Eastern languages, with special emphasis on modern materials.[31]

A Program for the Field

The new ACLS Committee on Near Eastern Studies committee convened for the first time in October 1947. The following month several of its members participated in the three-day national conference on world areas and area studies at Columbia discussed in Chapter 3. In that setting it was clear that Near Eastern studies was lagging behind several of the other area studies fields: it had yet to attain much coherence or momentum as a field and could boast of only a single avowedly interdisciplinary graduate program, at Princeton. A few months earlier John Gardner of Carnegie had noted that for the Near East, "Princeton (Hitti, Wright), Pennsylvania (Speiser) and Chicago (John Wilson) are the only institutions which seem to be at all hopeful. Neither Speiser nor Wilson have programs of the sort that interest us but that isn't their fault, and both are potentially very useful men for Near East area studies. I think in any case it would be helpful for these men to sit down together."[32]

The November 1947 conference's Near East panel offered them an opportunity to do so but did not yield the kind of results Gardner had hoped for. It included four people associated with Princeton's Department of Oriental Languages and Literatures, which had just launched its Program in Near Eastern Studies: department chair Philip Hitti along with Walter L. Wright, T. Cuyler Young and Lewis V. Thomas. Four of the panelists (Hitti, Wright, E. A. Speiser and Halford L. Hoskins) were members of the new CNES as well. Also on the panel were the Harvard anthropologist Carleton Coon (who until 1951 secretly served as a consultant for the CIA); Frank S. Hopkins, assistant director of the Department of State's Foreign Service Institute; John A. Morrison, a Soviet and Eastern European expert at the National War College; and Mortimer Graves of the ACLS. It is perhaps worth noting that of the panel members Coon, Morrison, Speiser, Thomas, Wright and Young had all served in the OSS during the war.

Given that so many of the panel members were associated with the CNES, it is not surprising that the panel's report to the conference manifested the vision of the Near East as a coherent and historically continuous civilization that had underpinned that committee's formation and composition. The report insisted on the need to respect the "essential unity of Near Eastern history," meaning the continuities that allegedly characterized the region's history from the most ancient times down to the present. It also asserted that the field faced special problems because of the very long time-span of its history and the "number and complexity of its peripheral areas," by which was apparently meant everything beyond what was characterized as the region's "Arabic-Turkish-Persian core." The panel went on to lament the continuing lack or inadequacy of basic teaching materials and resources for Near Eastern studies, another longstanding ACLS concern.[33] Given this perspective, the Near East panel was something of an outlier at the conference: in keeping with the general tone in area studies and with the priorities of Carnegie and the SSRC, the other regional panels tended to give greater emphasis to social science research and contemporary concerns.

In the wake of this conference the CNES met with some regularity, but its deliberations were rather meandering and desultory, and it achieved little progress with regard to its mission of surveying the field and developing a coherent program for it. As a result, by the middle of 1948 it appeared that the new committee was replicating its predecessors' torpor.[34] Richard N. Frye, who after his wartime OSS service had returned to Harvard to complete his doctorate and in 1948 was appointed the committee's executive secretary, would decades later characterize it as composed of

> old professors who wanted no changes in their time honored methods. For ex-
> ample, Arabic was taught by all of them from an English translation of a nine-
> teenth century German grammar of Albert Socin, following a Latin model.
> Warning the members of the committee that it would be abolished if some ac-
> tion to adapt to the times were not taken, I for one could observe the coming
> changes in academia and realized that adaption was in order. John Marshall of
> the Rockefeller Foundation spelled out what changes the foundation would sup-
> port.[35]

The committee was also clearly too large and unwieldy, and divisions between its members who specialized in the ancient Near East and those specializing in later periods led to paralysis. In an internal memorandum Graves
blamed the ACLS executive committee and board of directors for appointing
such a large committee while he was traveling abroad. "Now," he went on, "it
is quite possible to have a large committee if some political purpose will be
served thereby, but one or two people will do all the work and have all the
ideas. It has been a great struggle to keep my hands off this committee but
the thesis was it could go it alone,—I almost said 'my hands off the throat of.'
... The Ancient Near Easterners should be on the Committee for whatever
help they can give in developing the Modern field, and I am sorry that it is
turning out to be less than I had hoped."[36] Political differences also played
their part: in his February 22, 1949 letter of resignation from the CNES, E. A.
Speiser (who had repeatedly complained that the Islamicists and modernists on it outnumbered the "ancientists") declared that "With the best will
in the world, a rabid pro-Zionist or an equally fervent pro-Arab cannot act
as dispassionately as is necessary for the best interest of the Committee and
its work." He seems to have been referring to his fellow committee members
Zellig Harris and Edwin Wright, respectively.[37]

Anxious to get things moving, and concerned that the terms of the committee's Rockefeller grant required that two-thirds of it be spent by the middle of 1949, frustrated ACLS officials moved to replace Calverley with someone who might provide more effective and energetic leadership. They turned
to the Princeton Turkicist Walter L. Wright, because of his relatively mod-
ernist orientation but probably also because as a former college president
he presumably had substantial experience with making things happen in the

academic world. Wright was, however, reluctant to accept appointment as chair. He told members of the SSRC's Committee on World Area Research in November 1948 that the purpose of merging the two old ACLS committees had been to "bridge the traditional gap between these two fields of interest within the same area," and he believed that "it is exceptionally important to break down any division between the 'ancient' and the 'modern' in this area where the historical continuum is so long and so well documented."[38] But in a letter to ACLS Executive Director Cornelius Krusé he acknowledged that he was very concerned about what he politely termed "the divergence in interests of the Committee's members."

> Some of those who cultivate the more ancient fields of scholarship seem to be very resentful of the fusion of their originally separate committee with the committee concerned with modern and medieval studies. At each of our meetings discussion of this real or imagined grievance has taken up much time and has involved questions regarding the choice of members which seemed to imply that some of us had no legitimate business being there. Since I am branded even more openly than Professor Calverley as a "modernist," I must expect a certain lack of cooperation from the "ancients." Further, my output of published scholarly work has not been sufficient to provide the prestige which might enable a chairman to speak with real persuasiveness.[39]

Krusé assured Wright that he was just the person needed to get things moving and produce the kind of results the times demanded: "My slogan during the past year has been that we no longer simply want to cultivate orchids, but we wish now, through the humanities, to bake bread for the humanities."[40] After several months of hesitation Wright finally accepted appointment as chair and began working closely with Richard Frye to draft the program for the future development of Near Eastern studies whose formulation Wright saw as the committee's top priority.

Drafting the medieval (Islamic) and modern sections of the report proceeded apace, but Wright found it difficult to get the "ancientists" to produce their section. Given the very slow pace of the CNES' work, there were also fears that its claim to leadership of U.S. Near Eastern studies might be undermined by more vigorous competitors. For example, Myron Bement Smith, who was associated with the CNES, submitted to it a lengthy, detailed and confidential report on a two-day "Conference on Modern Middle East Studies" held at Dropsie College in Philadelphia in April 1949. Smith found much

to praise in the conference proceedings and warned that Dropsie's new Institute for Israel and the Middle East "is a challenge to Princeton, the School
of Advanced International Studies (Middle East Institute) and to any other
institution which plans to enter the field of Near East Area Studies." The
CNES thus stood "in grave danger of losing its leadership by default to the
co-ordinating and planning group which is projected as the outcome of the
Philadelphia meeting. Should the ACLS Committee fail to produce positive
and adequate results in the immediate future and give adequate promise of
being able to continue resolute and spirited leadership in its field, the Council must seek other means for meeting our country's needs in planning for
Near Eastern Studies."[41]

Wright's leadership of the committee was cut short by his sudden death
in May 1949. But by then drafting of the document on which he had been
working was well advanced, and it was discussed by the CNES in June, redrafted with input from Mortimer Graves and released by the ACLS later
in 1949 as a thirty-eight-page pamphlet titled *A Program for Near Eastern
Studies in the United States*.[42] This document clearly manifested the vision of
Near Eastern history that had informed the reconstitution of the CNES some
twenty months earlier, a vision that posited civilizational continuity across
vast stretches of time and space. "The past of the Near East is largely our
own past," the program declared, "most obviously through the Bible, which
reflects Near Eastern life and thought on every page." (5–6) But it had a presentist cast as well:

> The position of the Near East just on the hither side of a civilization which is
> competing with our own for world leadership, its location astride some of the
> world's most important transportation routes in peace and war, and its posses-
> sion of fabulous wealth in oil ensure that Americans will have to make many de-
> cisions affecting the peoples of that area. Without widely diffused knowledge of
> the Near East, public understanding of the issues involved is impossible. With-
> out competent experts in universities, in the professions, and in government,
> there will be no way to enlighten the public. Therefore, ways and means must be
> found to fill the need for men and women with scholarly knowledge and under-
> standing of the Near East, past and present. (6–7)

The program went on to lament the country's "pitifully inadequate" resources with regard to the Near East and endorsed the creation of university-
based centers for research and training on the Near East. But its more urgent

focus was on the improvement of language training, among other things through the development of new textbooks and curricular materials. It also called for injecting the Near East into existing disciplinary departments; a field training program in the Middle East which would also conduct research (for example, a five-year community study in Damascus); a translation program, for which the ACLS had already received Rockefeller funding; and fellowships for intensive language study and other purposes. However, the program explicitly refused to address questions of research: "The Committee believes that for the moment a focus on research is impossible, this because the basic requirement of flourishing research—a *cadre* of trained personnel—does not yet exist. . . . Only when we have more in trained personnel and more of the modern implements can we begin to put research on the modern Near East in its proper place in higher education."[43] (32)

The End of the Road

The CNES would later assert that the program it had so painstakingly formulated "had met with considerable public enthusiasm and not a little critical comment. . . ."[44] In fact, its formulation of the field's priorities and how to achieve them met with dismay over at the SSRC, which believed research on the contemporary Middle East should be a top priority from the outset and regarded the ACLS' focus on language training and undergraduate education as old-fashioned and unlikely to produce useful results. Moreover, the ACLS soon came to play an increasingly limited role in the nascent field of Middle East studies, further reducing the long-term impact of the program for the field whose formulation it had overseen.

One manifestation of this was the termination of the CNES in its original format and membership. It was obvious that, though the committee had managed to crank out a program for the field, it was not suited to implement its own recommendations for action; as Myron Bement Smith put it to the executive director of the ACLS, ". . . I trust the Board has no illusion as to the fitness of this Committee to administer anything."[45] For a time Mortimer Graves hoped that the Middle East Institute might be convinced of the importance of the ACLS program for the field and take on its implementation, but when that did not pan out he and his colleagues decided to reorganize the CNES with a much smaller membership.[46] In July 1950 the ACLS discharged the members of the CNES and appointed a wholly new membership. T. Cuyler Young, who had begun teaching Persian history and literature at Princeton in 1947, was designated to chair the reconstituted committee. He had studied theology as an undergraduate at Princeton and then spent eight years (1927–1935) in Rasht, Iran, as a Presbyterian missionary. That experience led him to decide he did not wish to be a missionary and he returned to the U.S. to pursue graduate studies at the Oriental Institute, after which he taught Hebrew and ancient Near Eastern history at the University of Toronto from 1938 to 1947. But in that period he twice took periods of leave from his academic post. In 1942–1944 he was a research analyst in, and then deputy chief of, the Near East section of the OSS Research and Analysis branch, and in 1944–1946 he served as public affairs officer at the U.S. Embassy in Tehran, after which he accepted a position at Princeton. Given his long experience in the region, his linguistic abilities, his record of government service and his Princeton position, complemented by his relative youth (he was forty years old at the time), it is not hard to see why ACLS officials thought he was the right man for the job.[47]

Also appointed to the committee was Wilfred Cantwell Smith (1916–2000), who had received his doctorate from Young's department at Princeton in 1948 and went on to teach comparative religion at McGill University. Smith was clearly perceived as a rising young star, one of the few Islamicists in North America whose research focused on contemporary trends and movements in Islam. The Rockefeller Foundation had given him a research grant in 1949, and in 1951 it would provide an additional $214,800 (almost $2 million in 2015) to establish an Institute of Islamic Studies at McGill under Smith's direction. Rockefeller also allocated funding for travel grants that would enable Western scholars, Smith among them, to "revisit Islam and thus to study at first hand the thought and movement that characterize Islam today." Smith's Institute of Islamic Studies would, as noted earlier, benefit from another very generous round of Rockefeller funding a few years later, in the form of a large capital grant.[48]

As Young would acknowledge, under his leadership the CNES mainly sought to follow up on some of its predecessor's projects. The committee administered an ACLS program providing small grants to participants (mainly graduate students) in one of the summer programs with Middle East-related content offered in 1950 by Harvard, the University of Michigan, New York

University and the University of Kansas City (known today as the University of Missouri-Kansas City). It also oversaw the compilation of an annotated bibliography of books in Western European languages relevant to Near Eastern studies, edited by Richard Ettinghausen and published by the Middle East Institute in 1952 (discussed in Chapter 5), as well as the preparation of *A Guide to Iranian Area Study* by L. P. Elwell-Sutton. Finally, it launched the Rockefeller-funded Near Eastern Translation Program, established to translate into English significant modern works in Arabic, Persian and Turkish; publication was made possible by Aramco's commitment to buy enough copies to cover costs. The first translation from Arabic actually published through the program was Sayyid Qutb's *al-ʿAdala al-Ijtimaʿiyya fi'l-Islam* (*Social Justice in Islam*), which appeared in 1953.[49]

In February 1951 the committee's chair T. Cuyler Young took another break from academia in order to assume a temporary appointment as political attaché in Tehran, where he worked with U.S. Ambassador Henry F. Grady on "special aspects of U.S.-Iranian relations." This was an oblique reference to the deepening crisis over control of the British-owned Anglo-Iranian Oil Company that in March 1951 would lead to the company's nationalization, the U.S.-British campaign to reverse that measure and, when that failed, their secret collusion to overthrow Iran's government.[50] With Young abroad for an extended period, Wilfred Cantwell Smith presumably busy with his new institute at McGill, and J. Kingsley Birge dying in August 1952, the CNES had more or less run its course. In June 1953 the ACLS board of directors terminated it, along with its Committee on Far Eastern Studies and the Joint Committee on Southern Asia. A new Committee on Review of Oriental Studies, chaired by T. Cuyler Young, was appointed to take a fresh look at all three of these regional fields, but it apparently never produced a report or recommendations.[51]

Thus by 1953, if not earlier, the ACLS' long effort to guide the development of Near Eastern studies in the United States had reached a dead end; by that time, as I discuss in Chapter 5, the SSRC had already launched its own Committee on the Near and Middle East and established its claim to leadership of this field. The ACLS' vision of the field's priorities and future, embodied in its 1949 *Program for Near Eastern Studies in the United States* and in the various incarnations of its committee for Near Eastern studies, had failed to provide a basis for effective action to develop the field in the postwar period. Its emphasis on undergraduate education, its inability to overcome the field's traditional focus on ancient times and on philology, its inattention to what we today call interdisciplinarity and its refusal to prioritize research (especially social science research) on the modern and contemporary periods rendered it increasingly out of touch with what the foundations wanted to see (and were ready to fund) in area studies. The ACLS' efforts, in Near Eastern studies at least, thus came to seem a relic of what was now widely perceived as an old-fashioned and increasingly irrelevant conception of the humanities.

The ACLS was also increasingly hampered by a lack of resources with which to sustain—much less promote—its vision. While the Rockefeller Foundation remained very interested in developing Islamic and Near Eastern studies, it increasingly preferred to do so through direct grants to universities which had academic entrepreneurs ready to use them effectively, rather than through yet another hapless and ineffective ACLS committee. Moreover, Rockefeller, which had for decades been the ACLS' main patron and funder, had made it clear soon after the war ended that it wanted to reduce funding for the organization, which as a result struggled in the early 1950s to find adequate sources of support for its operations and programs. Rockefeller, and the Carnegie Corporation and Ford Foundation as well, had become increasingly convinced that the ACLS needed thorough renovation if it was to fulfill its mission of advancing the humanities. As the foundations came to see it, that would require, among other things, the departure of Mortimer Graves, who had for years been the dominant figure in the organization but was now widely seen as intellectually old-fashioned and out of touch; even worse, he had managed to alienate top foundation officials. Graves was finally forced out in 1957, whereupon Ford and Carnegie quickly provided generous new funding to support the new leadership and new direction of the ACLS.[52]

As it became increasingly clear in the later 1940s that the ACLS was ill-equipped to provide the requisite leadership, for area studies in general and Near Eastern studies in particular, foundation officials embraced alternative visions and vehicles. Already in 1947 Carnegie had chosen the SSRC to administer its new area studies fellowship program, and in the years that followed the SSRC, backed first by the Carnegie Corporation and then by the Ford Foundation, would take the lead in seeking to advance underdeveloped fields like Near Eastern studies along lines very different than those that the ACLS had pursued.

5 A Committee for the Near and Middle East

... it is still true that most distinguished Near Eastern experts are totally uninterested in the social sciences and almost totally uninterested in anything
that has happened since the tenth century, A.D.
—John W. Gardner, 1951

SURVEYING WHAT HAD BEEN accomplished in building area
studies as of the fall of 1948, thanks largely to large-scale infu-
sions of Carnegie and Rockefeller funding, Charles Fahs of the Rockefeller
Foundation concluded that "Far Eastern, Russian, and Latin American studies at the graduate level have been widely enough established to produce
about as many scholars as are likely to be able to find employment until
an effective place for area studies in undergraduate education is found. We
may even soon have overproduction." But several other area studies fields,
including the Near East, were in his view "still weak or one-sided"; centers
for African, Canadian and Australasian studies were altogether lacking; and
some critical languages (like those of Soviet Central Asia) remained largely
or entirely untaught. Moreover, Fahs asserted, "No university or college has
yet adopted foreign area studies as a coherent part of undergraduate general
education. Area studies is still thought of as a luxury variety of specialized
training which only an institution with its snout firmly in the foundation
trough can afford." Fahs believed that additional grants from Rockefeller,
together with funding from Carnegie and the U.S. government, could help
remedy these shortcomings.[1]

Though no government funding was forthcoming, over the next several years foundation support made possible the launching of additional univer-sity-based area studies centers and the strengthening of existing programs. The field also gained impetus, coherence and status from the implementation of the Carnegie Corporation's national area studies research fellowship and travel grant program, announced in the fall of 1947. The work of selecting the research fellows and the recipients of travel grants was assigned not to the CWAR but to a separate SSRC Committee on Area Research Fellowships, which in May 1948 made its first set of awards: twenty-six fellowships and sixteen travel grants totaling some $47,000—equivalent to some $464,000 in 2015. The first awardees included graduate students and scholars from a wide range of disciplines, but only four among them focused on the Near East.[2] The Carnegie Corporation deemed the program's first year a success and in October 1948 authorized funding for a second round of fellowships and grants at the same level; the following year Carnegie approved two additional years of funding, on the understanding that a plan would then be worked out for the gradual termination of Carnegie support a year later.[3]

Leaders in area studies continued to hope that government funding could be secured for the new academic field. For example, in November 1948 CWAR's chair Robert Hall went to Washington "to study the possibil-ity of university cooperation with the U.S. Government in area studies," indicating the committee's continuing interest in developing ways of mak-ing area studies knowledge available to, and useful for, government agen-cies—but also in securing government funding for the nascent field. Noth-ing came of this initiative, but when the Cold War suddenly turned hot less than two years later the issue was immediately back on the committee's agenda. In the interim the CWAR began planning a second national confer-ence on area studies, which was eventually postponed until the spring of 1950, by which time most of the recently established area studies programs and centers would have had at least two full years of operation to report on. Following a March 1949 meeting of representatives of universities with area studies programs, sponsored by the Carnegie Foundation for the Ad-vancement of Teaching, the CWAR also began to plan a new survey of area studies programs and resources for training and research, in order to get a sense of how the field had developed since Hall's survey in 1946 and of the problems it currently faced.[4] Meanwhile, the SSRC took steps in this period to elaborate a national institutional infrastructure for area studies: it established two new committees responsible for advancing specific regional fields. In 1948, as part of the very rapid expansion of Russian and Soviet studies in the United States that had been made possible by Rockefeller and Carnegie funding and accelerated by Cold War concerns, the SSRC and the ACLS established a Joint Committee on Slavic and East European Studies; the following year they also launched a Joint Committee on Southern Asia, which, however, lasted only until 1953.[5]

But Cold War priorities could also have deleterious effects on area studies fields. As Helen Delpar has discussed, the wartime flourishing of Latin American studies was not sustained in the later 1940s. The Carnegie Corporation made grants toward the end of the decade to a number of universities for new centers for Latin American studies, but these were generally smaller than those made in the regional fields deemed to have the highest priority; and data from a 1951 survey suggest that while both Russian and Far Eastern studies had surged since the mid-1940s in terms of the number of university programs and of graduate students, Latin American studies had stagnated.[6] Moreover, in 1947 the ACLS, SSRC and NRC decided to disband their Joint Committee on Latin American Studies, apparently for lack of sufficient funding. Delpar argues that this decision, and the relative stagnation or decline in the flow of funding to the field, can be attributed at least in part to political factors: "During the decade after the end of World War II, Latin America, except for the case of Guatemala, seemed remote from the main areas of cold war contention and therefore peripheral to the concerns of policy makers, social scientists, and other scholars who had no prior interest in the region."[7] The Joint Committee on Latin American Studies would only be revived in 1959, when the Cuban revolution suddenly made Latin America seem not a side-show in the Cold War but a critical region that merited much more scholarly attention in the United States.

"The definition of 'area' did not come up at all!"

Nonetheless, by 1950 the area studies field as a whole was clearly much more institutionally developed than it had been just a few years earlier, progress that the second national area studies conference, held in March 1950 at Columbia and like its November 1947 predecessor funded by a Carnegie grant, was intended to showcase.[8] Richard H. Heindel, the SSRC staffer who

produced the official account of the conference (published only in mimeograph), reported that there were ninety-seven participants, including nineteen government officials; fifty of those attending had also participated in the
first area studies conference.[9] Overall, Heindel asserted, "the theory, practice,
and contributions of foreign area teaching and research are evolving satisfac-
torily but slowly," though "the extension and rationalization of professional
and academic organization will be required to advance and consolidate the
academic tradition in the making." (2) Language training remained a serious
problem: as one conference participant was reported to have declared, "We
are about to face a language competence crisis, especially in such languages
as Chinese, Russian, and Arabic. . . . We are using up our language war babies,
and we need some new incentive, less terrible than war, to encourage our
youngsters to put in the extra time and energy for acquiring such languages."
(28)

Reporting that the conference had witnessed a "frank stocktaking of
the theory, techniques, objectives, and resources of area research," Heindel
added that "it would be misleading not to report that there is considerable
uneasiness about the use of words like 'integration,' 'interdisciplinary,' 'cooperation,' 'disciplines,' 'departments,' 'synthesis,' 'generalist,' and 'specialist.'"
(33) The participants were clear, however, "that successful interdisciplinary
research calls for a well-defined research problem as a focus for any coop-
erative and integrated study to be carried out by a team of specialists." Such
problems, Heindel asserted, had thus far been selected "with a high regard
for both scientific and public interest. Area research is not operating in an
ivory tower." For example, he went on, "many area specialists consider Point
4 as their greatest peacetime challenge and opportunity for demonstrating the value of area training and research." (34) This was a reference to
the Point Four program, announced by the Truman administration in 1949,
which offered economic aid and technical assistance to underdeveloped
(and often newly independent) countries in order to demonstrate that the
U.S.-led camp in the Cold War could improve the living standards of the
poor masses deemed vulnerable to communist propaganda, recruitment
and mobilization.

Conference participants also heard presentations on "examples of area
research practices," including the Okayama field station run by Robert Hall's
Center for Japanese Studies at Michigan. But the Okayama model was ex-

ceptional: the other examples of area research presented at the conference generally involved much more loosely defined research programs implemented by individual researchers. For example, research at the Far Eastern and Russian Institute at the University of Washington reportedly focused on "the social whole of Chinese society in transformation in the 19th and 20th centuries," and Heindel's account asserted that research projects at the Harvard and Columbia Russian centers were generally pursued by individual scholars under such broad rubrics as "the general problem of the capabilities and intentions of the Soviet Union" (44–51)—though in fact intelligence and other government agencies played a key role in setting and funding these centers' research agendas. More broadly, despite Heindel's claims of progress in developing a theory and methodology for area studies, it was not at all clear that any progress had been achieved or was likely to be achieved in the foreseeable future. In any case, many in the field had already set different priorities for themselves, whether by focusing their research on more narrowly defined questions, sometimes policy-related but more often not, without devoting too much thought to interdisciplinarity or related issues, or by attending to the practical tasks of teaching and field-building, whether locally or nationally.[10]

The March 1950 conference featured several plenary sessions. Karl Wittfogel delivered the main address over dinner, titled "The Relationship of Area Studies to World Affairs," displaying what John Gardner called "great erudition" and making "a great impression upon his listeners" who included "the top specialists in the country on Russia, China, India, the Near East, and Eastern Europe." For much of the conference, however, participants divided along regional lines, with separate "round tables" for Russia, the Far East, South Asia, the Near East and Africa, Latin America and Europe. Reporting on their round table, the Near East specialists at the conference lamented that "not a single academic institution in America has embraced [for the Near East] the area program as a whole." This would seem to be an implicit acknowledgment of the persistent shortcomings of Princeton's Program in Near Eastern Studies, now in its third year of operation. Heindel went on:

> If the field [of Near Eastern studies] is top-heavy with humanistic studies it should be added that the humanities are weak, excepting those of ancient content. . . . Because of the lack of university centers adequate training can be provided at the graduate level only in Biblical studies, ancient Mesopotamian

studies, Egyptology, and medieval Islamics. Without the foreign scholars in this country, the shortage would be worse. There are gaps on areas such as the Caucasus, Central Asia, the Afghanistan-Pakistan area, North Africa (exclusive of Egypt), and Ethiopia; and in languages such as Berber, Kurdish, Persian dialects, Pashto, Urdu, Turkish dialects, Caucasian languages, Ethiopic, and Arabic dialects. (7)

The Near East round table discussed and endorsed the program for the development of Near Eastern studies in the United States formulated the previous year by the ACLS Committee on Near Eastern Studies. However, SSRC and Carnegie officials remained convinced that, like its ACLS predecessors, the CNES and its program were not only excessively oriented toward the premodern period but also unproductive. Given that program's prioritization of language training, a traditional ACLS focus, and its continuing strong interest in the ancient Near East, they were not optimistic about its potential for advancing the field, particularly social science research on the contemporary Near East. As a leading figure in the SSRC's own Middle East work during the 1950s recalled decades later, the SSRC rejected the ACLS committee's program "because it looked backward rather than forward in recommending practical steps for coping with the unprecedented challenge of the Cold War."[11] Soon after the May 1950 area studies conference John Gardner of Carnegie told CWAR member George E. Taylor, a historian of modern China, that "although the field of Area Studies has progressed enormously since the last conference, this general progress only serves to high light [sic] the striking lack of progress in African and Near Eastern studies."[12]

Notwithstanding the persistent backwardness of certain fields, CWAR chair Robert Hall saw the 1950 conference as a step forward: he reported to the SSRC Council that unlike the 1947 conference, which had been "plagued by dead-end discussion," such empty talk had been "held to a minimum in the second. The definition of 'area' did not come up at all!"[13] Hall seems to have been pleased by the lack of attention to conceptualizing this term, though one might regard it as tacit acknowledgment that even he was losing interest in coming up with a paradigm for area studies, one element of which would presumably be a theoretically coherent and methodologically productive definition of what was meant by area. For his part, John Gardner observed that "the field of area studies has shaken down a great deal since the meeting two years ago."

A good many of the "fundamental issues" which were hotly debated in the first conference (e.g., the place of language in area study) are gone and forgotten, partly because people just got tired of talking about them, and partly because they discovered that these issues somehow got themselves settled in practical working situations. The level of competence of the participants was very high— probably higher than at the first conference—and this is unquestionably due to a sifting process which has gone on during the past two years.[14]

The Korean War: Threat and Opportunity

The March 1950 area studies conference made no formal recommenda- tions for future action, but there was clearly widespread support among the participants for the creation of more regional committees, by the SSRC alone or if feasible jointly with the ACLS.[15] However, in June 1950, before action could be taken, the Korean War broke out and dramatically changed the at- mosphere in which area studies had been developing. As the Carnegie Cor- poration's staff reported to the board of trustees before its November 1950 meeting, "the mood of Washington is the mood of December 1941."[16]

Philip Hitti at Princeton was quick to offer the services of his department and program to the government, much along the lines of the ASTP dur- ing the last war.[17] More usefully, the SSRC helped establish an interagency Committee on Area and Language Specialists to survey available area studies personnel and facilities, and present a report to the Office of Defense Mo- bilization; in this respect its role during the Korean War was something of a replay of its role during the Second World War.[18] To many movers and shak- ers in the young and still fragile field of area studies, it seemed that the war posed dangers as well as opportunities. Carnegie Corporation officials were particularly concerned about the potential impact on colleges and universi- ties of large-scale conscription and of recruitment of faculty for government service. Robert Hall shared this concern: he told the SSRC Council in Sep- tember 1950 that as a result of the war "the need for knowing more about world areas is again of vital importance in government agencies," but he was worried about the war's potential impact on the still underdeveloped human and institutional infrastructure of area studies, especially as key personnel in area centers were already being "raided" by the government and the military. "A few more years would have made an enormous difference in the supply of trained personnel," Hall told his colleagues. "It is a question of playing our part in maintaining the national welfare, and at the same time of preserving training facilities at critical points so that qualified personnel will continue to flow into these fields. Protection of the process by which the skills needed over the next 25–50 years are created is of crucial importance."[19]

But the Korean War seemed to open up new possibilities as well. Hall's CWAR colleague Wendell Bennett saw in the crisis a not-to-be-missed opportunity to finally secure government funding for area studies, and in the fall of 1950 he began developing a proposal that over the following months evolved into what the SSRC came to call "A Project for Training Area Specialists," or "the Project" for short. This was a plan to have the federal government provide a thousand three-year graduate fellowships to train social scientists as area specialists, at a cost of $15.5 million—the equivalent of ten times that amount in 2015 dollars. When the plan was discussed with government officials, however, it became clear that, even assuming funding could be secured, they were much less interested in supporting university-based graduate training in area studies than in quickly acquiring employees with some modicum of area knowledge. Moreover, as Pendleton Herring explained to Charles Dollard, since 1948 president of the Carnegie Corporation, "apparently, everybody gives lip service to the idea but no one person or agency wants to carry the ball aggressively. PH facetiously suggested that the whole negotiation might make an interesting item in the program of the [SSRC] Committee on Public Administration Cases."[20] Various alternatives were discussed: for example, in April 1951 it was proposed that the State and Defense departments simply establish their own area studies fellowship programs, to be administered by the SSRC, but this too went nowhere.[21] By the second half of 1951 the momentum of "the Project" had dissipated and this effort to exploit the crisis atmosphere induced by the Korean War in order to secure federal government support for area studies came to an end.

It was in this atmosphere of wartime emergency that, in the spring of 1951, Wendell Bennett conducted the new survey of area studies that the SSRC had been planning since 1949; it was published by the SSRC in June 1951 as *Area Studies in American Universities*. As Osamah Khalil shows, Bennett's survey was conducted amidst ongoing discussions involving government and SSRC officials about how academic area studies might best serve the government's need for trained personnel. But the survey, and articles in the press on its findings, were also intended to support Bennett's campaign to secure large-scale government funding for area studies.[22] In his introduction Bennett declared that such a survey was particularly important at the present time because, "aside from the traditional [scholarly] function of research training, the universities may be called upon to meet the increasing government needs for area personnel and special area training. . . . Can the universities provide the needed expert personnel and practical area training without serious curtailment of all-important research activities?" This was a question that Bennett, Hall and their CWAR colleagues had been worrying about since the outbreak of the Korean War the previous summer. But Bennett's survey provided no clear answer: it was essentially a compilation of data briefly describing every university-based "integrated area program" in the United States, along with planned programs and related offerings, as well as international affairs programs at Columbia and Harvard. Bennett did not bother to elaborate a rationale for area studies, nor did he include American studies in his count of area studies programs, as Hall had in 1947: it had by now become increasingly clear that area studies was fundamentally about the study of foreign regions.[23]

From the data Bennett presented, it was evident that area studies had expanded dramatically since Hall's survey five years earlier, even without counting American studies programs. Bennett found a total of twenty-nine functioning integrated area programs, varying significantly in structure, requirements and relationship to the disciplines, up from the thirteen Hall had identified. Of these, eight focused on the Far East, six on Latin America, five on Russia and four on Europe; only one or two programs existed for each of the other areas. Of the 375 faculty engaged in area programs, the largest single disciplinary affiliation was literature (presumably including language instructors), at ninety-seven, followed by history, political science, anthropology and economics; by contrast, sociologists and specialists in international relations seemed to be in short supply. According to Bennett's survey 669 graduate students were studying in the integrated area programs, with Russia and the Far East accounting for some two-thirds of the total. The number of non-Western languages being taught through the advanced level, and the number of universities at which such training was offered, had also increased greatly. Despite the growth of area studies in recent years, however, Bennett argued that, "Ultimately, the federal government must furnish financial support for the type of training that its activities demand. Proposals for establishing government area fellowships, modeled on those for studies of atomic energy, are now being considered." (41)

"Good Committee Men" for the "Near and Middle East"

In the early 1950s Near Eastern studies remained among the less developed of the area fields, though it was perhaps not quite as deficient in terms of programs and faculty as African, South Asian and Southeast Asian studies. Bennett reported just two integrated Near East area programs, at Princeton and the University of Michigan, with eighteen faculty and twenty-seven graduate students between them. Princeton offered a master's degree in Near Eastern Studies and taught Arabic, Persian and Turkish through the advanced level, while Michigan offered master's and doctoral degrees through disciplinary departments and taught only beginning Arabic. Bennett also noted Near East-related programs and offerings at the University of Chicago, Columbia, Dropsie College, SAIS and the University of Pennsylvania. Overall, Bennett counted a total of twenty-four students of Arabic, seventeen of Turkish and four of Persian at the institutions he surveyed; the difference between these low numbers and the hundreds he found studying Chinese or Russian is striking.

The annotated bibliography whose compilation the ACLS Committee on Near Eastern Studies had sponsored provides another way of gauging the state of this field as of its completion in the summer of 1951. This bibliography of books and periodicals in Western-languages (mainly English, French and German) on the Middle East was edited by Richard Ettinghausen and published by the Middle East Institute in 1952.[24] Though its subtitle promised "Special Emphasis on Medieval and Modern Times," about one-third of its pages were devoted to books and articles on the ancient Near East, including Egypt, the Fertile Crescent, Iran and Bible studies, while "Islamic Civilization to the Early 1800s" accounted for another third or so. The sections on the modern Near East indicate how thin the scholarly literature on this period still was at this time. For example, the bibliography lists a total of fifteen books on the modern history of Egypt (three of them by British colonial officials), and just four on the modern history of Syria and Lebanon. While it includes a substantial number of publications in anthropology and ethnology, most of these (for the predominantly Arab lands, at least) are by British or French researchers; nor do the works listed under the rubric of political science bear much resemblance to the kind of work American political scientists would produce on the Middle East in subsequent decades. At the time, very few such specialists existed: Dankwart Rustow would later estimate that in 1950 there were no more than half a dozen members of the American Political Science Association with a working knowledge of Arabic, Persian or Turkish.[25]

To address these perceived deficiencies and advance the field in keeping with its vision of area studies, the SSRC began in the fall of 1950 to explore the establishment of its own committee on Near Eastern studies. The joint committees on Slavic and South Asian studies established in 1948–1949 were reported to be doing well, and Near Eastern studies seemed to be next in line. There was some discussion early on of forming a committee for the Middle East jointly with the ACLS, but SSRC leaders and the scholars associated with them rejected the ACLS approach to area studies and regarded its still extant but barely functioning Committee on Near Eastern Studies as a failure, so they soon abandoned that idea and decided to go it alone.

The CWAR's consideration of this question at its October 1950 meeting took place in the context of a broader discussion of what the minutes refer to as "the present and future contributions and prospects for area training and research as related to immediate and long-term problems of national interest," despite the lamentable absence of "a clearer picture of governmental requirements and thinking."[26] The war in Korea and more broadly the Cold War, as well as the SSRC's effort to secure government funding for area studies, were thus very much on the minds of CWAR members and SSRC leaders as they contemplated the future prospects of Middle East studies. But the CWAR was also moved to action by a memorandum it had recently received from a self-appointed "working committee" of eight men, affiliated with universities or the Department of State, which had been formed at a meeting held at the Middle East Institute in March 1950 and referred to itself as the Middle East Social Science Committee. The group's chair and leading light was William Wendell Cleland, who began teaching at the American University in Cairo in 1920 and is probably best known for his 1936 book *The Population Problem in Egypt*, based on his Columbia doctoral dissertation and often described as the first comprehensive treatment of the subject.[27] CWAR members met with Cleland and urged SSRC president Pendleton Herring to move ahead with forming a committee for what they termed "the Near and Middle East."[28]

This was the first time that in SSRC circles the region was denoted in this way: previously it had always been called simply the Near East, and the academic field that focused on it Near Eastern studies. It is striking that no explanation would ever be offered as to why the SSRC decided to give its new committee the name it did, nor would any precise definition of the geographic space for which it was responsible be forthcoming. It is possible that "Near and Middle East" was chosen because it more or less reflected the State Department's usage: since 1944 the department had had a Division of Near Eastern Affairs covering Greece, Turkey, Iraq, Palestine, Transjordan, Syria, Lebanon, Egypt and the Arabian peninsula, and a Division of Middle Eastern Affairs covering Afghanistan, Burma, Ceylon, India and Iran.[29] SSRC officials were in close and regular contact with government officials, at the State Department and elsewhere, and at this moment of crisis, with the United States and its allies fighting a land war in Asia and the SSRC particularly concerned with how area studies might serve the needs of national security, they may have decided to adopt a version of the government's nomenclature—notwithstanding the fact that some of these countries were not to be under the proposed committee's purview, while the lands of North Africa west of Egypt, not obviously encompassed by the rubric "Near and Middle East," presumably would be.

This terminology may also have been adopted in order to indicate that the new SSRC committee would cover the whole stretch of territory between Europe (including the Soviet Union) and Africa to the north and west, and South Asia and East Asia to the east—that is, an expansively (if vaguely) defined chunk of the globe that filled the gap between regions that were under the purview of other SSRC committees, or soon might be. Finally, one may speculate that this name was chosen to differentiate the SSRC's initiative in this field from that of the ACLS, which never used anything but "Near East," and perhaps also to signal the SSRC's strong interest in this region in the modern and contemporary periods, because "Middle East" had a somewhat more up-to-date ring to it, whereas "Near East" could by now sound a bit old-fashioned. In any case, despite the committee's official designation, for many years to come "Near East" would continue to be the term most commonly used in internal committee discussions and documents to refer to the region whose study it was charged with advancing.

In the late fall of 1950, after consulting with John Gardner at Carnegie and securing his assent, Pendleton Herring discreetly began to solicit suggestions for members of the projected new committee.[30] Among others Herring asked Bryce Wood, who as head of the SSRC's Washington DC office was familiar with the scene there, to formulate a list of some twenty-five or so suitable social scientists, with background information on each, from which eight or ten people might be selected as "good committee men." Herring told Wood that most of the committee's members should be based in universities rather than the government and that "the major focus of the committee should be on the Arab world and Moslem countries, and apparently it is wise to keep in mind the conflict of opinion over Israel."[31]

By early December 1950 Wood had submitted a tentative list, which favored people with experience and connections in Washington.[32] His top candidates for chair of the new committee were Raymond F. Mikesell (1913–2006), an economist who had obtained his PhD in 1939 and worked in the Treasury Department's Division of Monetary Research from 1942 to 1947, and Benjamin U. Ratchford (1902–1977), a professor of economics at Duke University who worked at the World Bank. Among those under consideration for committee membership were Peter Franck of Wendell Cleland's group; Richard Frye, now teaching at Harvard and former executive secretary of the ACLS Committee on Near Eastern Studies; J. C. Hurewitz, who after his wartime OSS service worked for the United Nations, had just completed his doctorate at Columbia and was teaching at both Columbia and Dropsie College in Philadelphia; Afif I. Tannous, head of the Near East section of the Department of Agriculture's Office of Foreign Agricultural Relations; and Majid Khadduri, a former Iraqi diplomat with a PhD in international relations from Columbia who joined the faculty of the School of Advanced International Studies in 1949 and founded its Middle East program the following year.[33] On the SSRC's list of potential nominees the names were categorized by discipline, occupation and institutional affiliation, but also by their known or presumed position on the question of Palestine, clearly a significant consideration for the SSRC. Among the top choices, Hurewitz's views were characterized as "moderate Zionist," Afif Tannous' stance as "moderate Arab"; among the alternates Raphael Patai was described as a "moderate Zionist" and Majid

Khadduri as a "moderate Arab." All the others were described as "presumably neutral but have worked in or with Arab states or Turkey."

In a candid January 1951 memo to Carnegie president Charles Dollard, John Gardner explained the problems Herring faced in constituting a new Near East committee. It is clear that he had the negative experience of the (by now largely inactive) ACLS committee very much in mind.

> As you know, most of the prominent and well-established experts in the field of Near Eastern studies are *humanists*. You know, too, that most of them have thrown their weight heavily and consistently against any increased attention to the problems of the modern Near East. The Oriental Institute at the University of Chicago represents the finest collection of Near Eastern scholars in the country, but they staunchly refuse to concern themselves with any phase of the modern Near East.
>
> The ACLS has received a good deal of foundation money for Near Eastern studies, but the same crowd has controlled the spending of it (up until the last year or so). The situation has changed considerably, of course, in the past few years, but it is still true that most distinguished Near Eastern experts are totally uninterested in the social sciences and almost totally uninterested in anything that has happened since the tenth century, A.D.
>
> For this and other reasons, Pen Herring has for several months been attempting to bring together a group of social scientists interested in the modern Near East. In spite of the fact that the ACLS already has a committee on Near Eastern studies, he has not followed early precedent of attempting to set up as joint ACLS-SSRC committee. After a very extensive search, in which I helped wherever possible, he has managed to uncover a rather promising group of men, and is calling them together for a meeting.

If that meeting succeeded, Gardner told Dollard, Herring planned to established an SSRC committee for Near Eastern studies and "would like to see such a committee financed on the same basis as the committee on Southern Asia studies which we helped to set up a year and a half ago." But, Gardner cautioned, "we should make it clear that we do not intend to support such a committee beyond the terms of the original grant; that we are not generally in the business of supporting area committees; and that we do not conceive it as the main task of the committee to dream up proposals to be submitted to Carnegie Corporation." Dollard tentatively approved a grant of up to $10,000 for the new committee.[34]

Soon thereafter Herring convened a meeting, formally dubbed a "Conference on Near Eastern Studies," that would give him the opportunity to observe and vet potential committee members in person. The participants urged the SSRC to establish a committee on Near Eastern studies expeditiously; among other factors, there were rumors that with war raging in Korea the federal government was about to launch a drive to recruit specialists in this and other area studies fields, and thus a danger that "the satisfaction of governmental needs might be made at the sacrifice of the capacity of [academic] institutions to train future specialists." They also expressed their strong preference that the SSRC launch its own separate committee, which might collaborate with the ACLS Near East committee but not function jointly; they thus shared the SSRC's conviction that the ACLS' CNES had not only failed to accomplish very much but was on the wrong track altogether. Attendees also lamented the great gaps in social science research on the region, and to fill these gaps they offered examples of possible future research questions: "What is the relation between agricultural production, and the growth and age distribution of population?"; "what forms of modification of land tenure are feasible and desirable?"; "what is the precise character of the tribal and family patterns in various countries, and how do they affect political and economic life?"; and "is the Point Four program likely to promote stability or instability in the Near East?"[35] The presentist thrust of the research questions and the significant involvement in the conference of government and World Bank officials offers insight into its organizers' conception of the role and direction of social science research on the Middle East at a historical moment in which the Cold War had turned hot and the country was at war in Asia.

Forming the CNME

Herring and his colleagues now felt ready to decide whom to invite to join the SSRC's new Committee on the Near and Middle East (CNME). George Cameron (1905–1979) of the Department of Near Eastern Studies at the University of Michigan was asked to serve as committee chair and quickly accepted, though because he would be out of the country until the fall of 1951 Robert Hall would temporarily take his place. Cameron might seem an unlikely choice to lead this committee whose primary mission it was to plan and oversee social science research and training on the modern and contemporary Middle East: he was a scholar of ancient Iran, especially Elam, whose work focused on epigraphy and philology. In 1936 he had become assistant editor of what had since 1895 been called the *American Journal of Semitic Languages and Literatures*; after he became principal editor in 1941 he renamed it the *Journal of Near Eastern Studies*, but its content continued to focus almost exclusively on the ancient period. The biographical sketch that opens the volume offered by his colleagues to honor him when he retired is titled "Portrait of an Orientalist."[36]

In addition to his qualities as an individual, what seems to have made Cameron attractive to the SSRC in 1951, despite his premodern and humanistic scholarly interests, was the character of the Near Eastern studies program he was building at the University of Michigan, which would soon attract substantial foundation funding. In 1948 Cameron had left the Oriental Institute of the University of Chicago, where he had done his graduate training and then taught for fifteen years, and accepted a position in the University of Michigan's Department of Near Eastern Studies, newly formed out of components of what had been called the Department of Oriental Languages and Literatures. Cameron was at first the new department's sole member and soon became its chair, in which capacity he moved quickly to build a strong faculty (George Hourani, George Makdisi, Andrew Ehrenkreutz and Oleg Grabar were among those he would eventually bring to Michigan), strengthen ties with other departments and develop a multifaceted Near Eastern studies program.[37] Cameron's program embraced a model of graduate education that required students to meet all the requirements of their disciplinary department, with their training in Near Eastern studies regarded as supplementary. This model differed from Princeton's, where graduate students generally did most or all of their training in the Department of Oriental Languages and Literatures rather than in a disciplinary department; and Michigan also seemed to have a strong focus on the modern and contemporary Middle East. As Richard Frye would later put it, Cameron "had seen the writing on the wall, and led the way."[38]

Cameron clearly seemed to be doing things right: in 1952, a year after he became the first chair of the CNME, Cameron secured a $100,000 multiyear grant (equivalent to almost $900,000 in 2015) for his program at Michigan from the Ford Foundation, a newcomer to the philanthropic scene. This was in fact the very first grant that Ford made in support of a Middle East area studies program, though over the course of the 1950s it would become the field's biggest funder by far. Cameron used his Ford funding, along with Carnegie and university support, to hire new faculty, launch a program of summer session courses on the Middle East, including language training, and develop his program in other ways.[39] In this light it is understandable that Cameron was perceived by the SSRC, and by the foundation officials with whom that organization's leaders were in constant contact, as someone who, his own scholarly interests notwithstanding, had displayed effective academic entrepreneurial skills. Two years after Cameron's arrival at Michigan, Wendell Bennett's survey would cite it as one of two universities in the country that had an "integrated area program" for the Near East (the other was of course Princeton), and it would later be asserted that by 1952 Michigan "already had greater coverage of the Near East as an 'area program' than any other university."[40] It probably also helped that CWAR chair Robert Hall was Cameron's colleague at Michigan and that both had launched new area studies programs, with a great deal of foundation funding, at roughly the same time.

But there seems to have been another factor which played a part in Cameron's appointment as chair of the new SSRC committee. He already had substantial experience conducting research in the Middle East, even if it was on the ancient period; but in the period leading up to his selection as chair of the CNME he conceived and implemented what seemed to SSRC and foundation officials to be just the kind of interdisciplinary field research project that they (and perhaps especially CWAR chair Robert Hall) had long been hoping for. In the fall of 1950 Cameron asked his university to help fund a "field project" that from February to August 1951 would take him and a team of scholars to "the rugged vastnesses of northern Iraq and the adjacent portions of Iran." Cameron's own scholarly interests were clearly involved, since in his pitch to the university he highlighted the presence in this region (which he described as geographically "uncharted") of "two steles with bilingual inscriptions uncopied since their preliminary examination in 1898; these inscriptions are known to be the key or 'Rosetta Stone' by which we can decipher another of the hitherto unknown languages of the past." But Cameron also advanced a broader and more present-oriented argument for the critical importance of this expedition:

Historically, the area was the center of early Medes and Persians, and toward it, four years ago, Soviet armies moved in a great show of force. Since it is here that the civilizations of the Turks, Arabs, and Persians are impinging on each other, with the Caucasus just on the horizon, the area presents a superb case study for the modern sociologist, political scientist, and anthropologist. . . . Thus, through the teamwork of members of its staff, it is now within the power of the University to make a contribution to science which will not only bring it considerable fame but also advance our knowledge and improve the relations of our own government vis-à-vis the inhabitants and governments of the peoples of the Near East.[41]

Cameron secured $10,000 from his university and $6000 from Carnegie to fund his expedition, and assembled a team consisting of his Michigan colleagues Douglas Crary (geography), William D. Schorger (anthropology) and N. Marbury Efimenco (political science), along with Ralph Solecki of the Smithsonian Institution (prehistoric archaeology), a zoologist named Andersen and two Michigan graduate students, Ernest N. McCarus (linguistics) and Carter Zeleznik (history). As Ernest McCarus would later recount, the expedition spent the spring and summer of 1951 in Iraq, in Baghdad or camped out at Rowanduz in the north, "with a three-week motor trip to Iran."[42]

Cameron apparently got to copy his inscriptions, McCarus was able to complete his dissertation research on Kurdish grammar, and the other expedition members also presumably benefited from their time in Iraq. But to characterize the project as "an extraordinary experiment in interdisciplinary cooperation in a common endeavor," as a Carnegie staffer did in a breathlessly enthusiastic report a few months after Cameron's return to Michigan, is clearly exaggerated. As far as one can tell, there was nothing really interdisciplinary about the expedition: each participant pursued his own separate research project, though in more or less the same geographic area at the same time, with little apparent intellectual interaction, much less cross-fertilization. Nonetheless, SSRC and foundation officials perceived Cameron's expedition as a successful model for regionally focused interdisciplinary field research, just the kind of thing Robert Hall hoped would be the hallmark of area studies. Moreover, Cameron had demonstrated that he was capable of planning and carrying out a complex field-research project in the Middle East, which further elevated his standing at the SSRC and beyond. The Carnegie staffer just mentioned described Cameron to his foundation colleagues as "eminently qualified to conduct field work of this kind in the Near East—the best qualified, in fact, that CPH [the author of the report] has seen," and "unsurpassed" as a potential leader in the field.[43] With this kind of encomium, and given that at the time the United States had very few senior social scientists specializing in the Middle East, someone with Cameron's energy, experience and interest in the modern and contemporary periods looked very attractive. He was thus deemed an excellent choice to lead the new committee and get research on the Middle East moving.

The other initial appointees to the CNME were anthropologist Carleton Coon, now at the University of Pennsylvania, whose popular book *Caravan: The Story of the Middle East* would be published later that year and who was still one of the few American anthropologists with research experience in the Middle East or North Africa;[44] Douglas Crary (1901–2005) of Michigan's Geography Department; Peter G. Franck of Wendell Cleland's group, working on his doctorate in economics at Berkeley; Richard Frye of Harvard; J. C. Hurewitz of Columbia: E. A. Speiser of the University of Pennsylvania; and Afif Tannous of the Department of Agriculture, with Herring and Wood serving as *ex officio* members. In its initial composition, the CNME was thus (like the Near East panel at the 1947 area studies conference) something of an OSS reunion: Coon, Frye, Hurewitz and Speiser had all served in the agency during the war.

Given the SSRC's strong interest in fostering social science research on the contemporary Middle East and its longstanding unhappiness with the ACLS' approach, it may seem surprising that it nonetheless chose to appoint a Committee on the Near and Middle East three of whose eight members—Cameron, Frye and Speiser—were not social scientists but humanists whose work focused on the ancient or premodern Middle East. Middle East studies was of course not unique in this regard; for example, as Nicholas Dirks puts it with reference to another area studies field,

> serious academic study in the U.S. of the contemporary political, social, and economic predicament of the new postcolonial nations of South Asia was initially mediated by forms of knowledge focusing either on ancient India or its most remote hinterlands. It is hard to imagine a group of Hellenic scholars being called together with fieldworkers experienced for the most part only in the village life of peasant societies to found, say, a modern European studies program.[45]

But it is also worth keeping in mind that Speiser had served as chief of the R&A Near East section for much of the war, which had given him extensive experience of supervising policy-relevant research; Frye was a young and energetic scholar who had demonstrated his mettle with the OSS in Afghanistan and beyond; and Cameron seemed to have amply demonstrated his leadership potential. So despite their humanistic and premodern scholarly interests, SSRC and foundation officials could plausibly regard them as well-equipped to help formulate and implement the kind of research program they expected from the committee.

The absence on the committee of anyone from Princeton is also noteworthy, given that the country's first purportedly interdisciplinary Middle East studies program had been launched there in 1947, the university possessed much greater human and library resources on the Middle East in the period since the rise of Islam than any other institution, and Princeton men (notably Walter L. Wright and T. Cuyler Young) had played leading roles in various initiatives to build Near Eastern studies. However, those initiatives were associated with the ACLS, and Young was at the time still serving as chair of the parallel ACLS committee, so he was in any case not available for service on the SSRC's committee. In addition, it would seem that, despite their initial optimism about Princeton's program, by this point neither SSRC leaders nor Carnegie officers were all that impressed by what it had actually accomplished. In April 1948, after a conversation with Hitti, John Gardner reported that "Near Eastern Studies at Princeton appears to be developing in a very healthy fashion," including initiating a training program for military personnel. But three years later Gardner told his boss Charles Dollard that "the Near Eastern program which we are supporting at Princeton is anything but bold and imaginative, and the present pattern of Near Eastern studies in this country is pitifully inadequate."[46] In 1952 Carnegie would renew its grant to Princeton for another five years, but its skeptical appraisal of Near Eastern studies there may have made George Cameron's newer operation at Michigan, already attracting substantial foundation funding, look vigorous and promising by contrast.

Immediately after launching the new SSRC Committee on the Near and Middle East, Pendleton Herring formally asked the Carnegie Corporation for a grant of $10,000 to support its work. Carnegie quickly approved the grant, though Gardner told Herring that "I hope you will make it clear to

Dr. Cameron and his colleagues that this is a one-shot grant to get the Committee well launched and that we do not look forward to continued support of the Committee."[47] Carnegie's reluctance to provide open-ended funding did not concern this committee alone: both Rockefeller and Carnegie often warned that their large-scale support for area studies in general would not continue indefinitely. They had been prepared to spend a great deal of money in the late 1940s and early 1950s to get programs and centers up and running, but they repeatedly declared that they would ultimately have to be sustained by the universities which housed them or by other sources. This prognosis soon proved unrealistic, however, and foundation funding for area studies would keep flowing to universities for many years to come.

The Ford Foundation, the Cold War and Area Studies

From the mid-1940s into the early 1950s the Carnegie Corporation of New York and the Rockefeller Foundation between them provided the great bulk of the external funding that enabled universities to establish area studies centers and programs. By its own reckoning, the Rockefeller Foundation spent some $8 million on area studies between 1946 and 1954 (the equivalent of $70–100 million in 2015), though this figure would seem to include programs abroad—for example, American studies in Germany, Great Britain and Japan—as well as funding to U.S. universities for area programs and centers.[48] For its part, in addition to the large-scale funding it channeled to many of the new university-based area studies centers and programs, Carnegie approved annual grants of $130,000 for the SSRC's area studies fellowship program in 1950–1951 and 1951–1952, in light of "the international situation"—i.e., the Korean War and heightened Cold War tensions—so that "the flow of highly trained area studies specialists not be in any way impeded." But the second year's funding was made subject to a review of the situation in early 1952 and the discretion of the foundation's president. Carnegie officers had concerns about the direction of the new area studies programs: now that they had been established, the foundation's board of trustees was told in 1951, they "are beginning to show the need of some focus for their approach to a country. For an area study program to have no other goal than all-inclusive study of the area is an essentially aimless and intellectually sterile procedure. It seems certain that each area program will have to adopt certain central lines of inquiry which will give continuing focus to its work."[49]

Even as the SSRC tried during the first year of the Korean War to secure large-scale government support for area studies, it also looked elsewhere for additional sources of funding. Happily for it and for area studies, a new and extremely well-endowed funder with a strong interest in international affairs appeared on the American philanthropic scene in the early 1950s. This was the Ford Foundation, which soon became by far the largest funder of area studies and international studies at American universities. Henry Ford (1863–1947), founder of the Ford Motor Company, had established the foundation with a modest endowment in 1936. After he died the foundation assumed control of 90 percent of the company's non-voting stock, which suddenly made it the richest philanthropic foundation in the world. It took several years for the foundation's leadership to determine its funding priorities; though these did not explicitly specify support for area studies, the foundation's commitment to "the establishment of peace" was deemed to include enhancing the ability of nongovernmental institutions (presumably mainly universities and independent institutes) to provide objective, policy-relevant information and analysis to the government so that it could formulate and implement an effective foreign policy.[50] The Ford Foundation's lavish support for area studies over the decade and a half from the early 1950s to the late 1960s played a critical role in establishing the new regional fields on a secure basis. In addition to providing support for the development of the infrastructure of many area studies fields, directly and through the SSRC, Ford's channeling of massive funds to universities for area and international studies in the late 1950s and early 1960s in many instances provided the resources which enabled institutions of higher education to significantly expand such programs and make them an integral and durable part of university life.

Ford's motivations for this kind of expenditure were much more closely and directly tied to the needs of the national security state that the Cold War had brought into being than had been the case with Carnegie and Rockefeller, both of which had long experience of engaging with the humanities and social sciences in ways that were not intended or designed to serve state power. Robert A. McCaughey points out that the Ford Foundation's president in the early 1950s, Paul G. Hoffman, had served as the chief administrator of the Marshall Plan and "had always insisted that the Marshall Plan was not an exercise in disinterested philanthropy but an imaginative weapon in the Cold War the United States was waging with the Soviet Union." Thus Hoffman "envisioned the Ford Foundation doing for the rest of the world what the Marshall Plan had done for Europe: to provide it with the technical and administrative wherewithal to acquire a level of economic well-being that would allow the development of democratic institutions, thereby effectively eliminating both the threat and the appeal of communism."[51] Moreover, in developing and implementing Ford's new international and area studies initiatives, foundation staff kept in close contact with government officials and agencies as well as with the SSRC and the academics connected with its regional committees, and they encouraged the latter to attend to the needs of the former. In the 1950s and well into the 1960s Ford maintained particularly close links with the CIA, which among other things used it to covertly channel funds to various anti-communist organizations and periodicals and to support research of interest to U.S. intelligence.[52] It was also the case that, in addition to having a lot more money to give away than Carnegie or Rockefeller, tax and other considerations impelled Ford to disburse funds quickly and on an unprecedented scale. Its involvement with area studies in general, and Middle East studies in particular, therefore made a crucial difference for the trajectories of these fields.

In the spring of 1951, with its efforts to secure government funding for area studies making little headway, SSRC president Pendleton Herring approached the Ford Foundation about "the possibility of stop-gap support which will hold the area centers together [during the wartime crisis] and get the plan in to operation [sic] for later government sponsorship." Herring was thinking big: he planned to ask Ford for $4 million to expand existing area studies centers and training programs, preparing the way for eventual government funding to meet national needs.[53] Ford was not at this point ready to make a commitment of this kind, but it would soon enter the field of international and area studies on its own in a big way, thereby enabling (or inducing) Carnegie and Rockefeller to withdraw from certain programs and spheres of interest and to devote their resources to other areas. In 1953, for example, the Carnegie Corporation announced that it would stop allocating funds for the area studies research fellowship and travel grant program, administered by the SSRC, that it had established in 1947. As noted earlier, over the seven years of the Carnegie-funded program's existence it had made awards totaling $700,000 to some 214 individuals—the equivalent of nine or ten times that amount in 2015 dollars. Of these awards, only fourteen went to scholars studying the Middle East, compared to thirty-seven for Eastern Europe and the USSR, thirty-one for Latin America and the Caribbean, twenty-nine for Japan and the Philippines, twenty-eight for Western Europe and twenty-two for China (including Mongolia). In fact, the Middle East had received the fewest awards of any region, fewer even than Africa, Southeast Asia or South Asia; in this sense its relative standing had actually declined since the late 1940s.[54] Carnegie had repeatedly said that it would not fund this fellowship program indefinitely, so the termination of this program could not have come as a complete surprise to the SSRC—though it was certainly perceived as a serious loss.[55]

The end of Carnegie's direct funding for area studies fellowships was somewhat mitigated by the fact that it continued to provide support to specific area studies centers and programs, though by the mid-1950s it was telling grantees that it planned to gradually withdraw entirely from area studies, as well as by the continuation of the SSRC's own longstanding social science research and training fellowship program.[56] But much more important was the fact that in 1952 the Ford Foundation, accumulating wealth faster than its trustees could spend it, had announced the creation of its own Foreign Study and Research Fellowship Program, initially targeted at Asia and the "Near and Middle East" but later expanded to encompass other regions, to be administered by an external Board on Overseas Training and Research (BOTR). In effect, Ford replaced, redefined and greatly expanded Carnegie's program for the funding of overseas study and research. The scale of Ford's new program was from the outset significantly larger than Carnegie's: whereas the latter had given the SSRC $130,000 a year for area studies, BOTR in 1953 alone awarded eighty-three grants totaling $473,850, twenty-seven of which were for projects relating to the Middle East. On the other hand, whereas Carnegie had specifically sought to bolster university-based area studies training and research, Ford's new program did not specifically target universities, academic area studies training and research, or the social sciences. According to Ford, its goal was "to help meet the urgent need for more American men and women who are trained in business, education, agriculture, labor relations, communications, and the professions, and who have an understanding of cultures and problems of Asia and the Near and Middle East."[57] Ford fellowships—from 1953 administered by its in-house International Training and

Research (ITR) division, which replaced BOTR—were therefore available to a broad range of applicants, including students who had just completed their undergraduate education, people with experience in business, government and a range of other fields, and people who had done or were doing graduate work in a variety of specified areas.

But Ford's dramatic entry into the international and area studies fields soon went well beyond its new program of fellowships for individual scholars. In 1952 it appropriated a million dollars to support specific projects "on a wide range of economic, social, and political problems relating to Asia, including the Near East."[58] Under that rubric it began to emulate the example of the Carnegie and Rockefeller foundations by making substantial grants directly to area studies programs, beginning with $100,000 for Near Eastern studies at the University of Michigan in 1952 and $150,000 for Near Eastern studies at Columbia the following year.[59] Given Ford's largesse, along with that of Carnegie and Rockefeller, and toward the end of the decade the beginning of federal funding for area studies, Robert A. McCaughey aptly calls the decade and a half stretching from the early 1950s to the late 1960s "bonanza years" for area and international studies in the United States.[60]

In deciding to fund the Near Eastern studies programs at Michigan and Columbia, Ford accepted the rationale advanced by Schuyler Wallace, director of Columbia's School of International Affairs, which grew out of the wartime Naval School for Military Government and Administration the university had hosted. In a clear allusion to Princeton, Wallace explained to Ford's Director of Research Cleon Swayzee why he thought the foundation should make grants to both Columbia and Michigan:

> First, and perhaps foremost, it seems to me that no one or two institutions should be permitted to dominate a field of such great importance. The danger of the development of what I might call a party-line or ideological monopoly is most clearly apparent in the Russian field. It is, it seems to me, no less serious in connection with the study of the Near and Middle East. And just as those of us, who established the Russian Institute at Columbia University, thought the danger of such ideological monopoly so great—even though we were administering the Russian Institute—that we campaigned for the establishment of the Russian Institute at Harvard University and contributed I think no little to its establishment; so I would argue now that the Ford Foundation should support not one but several institutions in the Near and Middle East field.

A second reason why I believe that there should be more than one Center of Near and Middle East studies is the simple fact that there are several ways of approaching the same problem. And that diversity of approach can best be secured through independent administrative units. Indeed, the existence of a number of independent administrative units in the same field is almost a sure guarantee that a diversity of procedures and methodology will develop.

Moreover, Wallace told Swayzee, while he would not compare what Columbia was doing with what was going on at any other university, "certain differences will quickly become apparent." Columbia's program "is and will continue to be under the leadership of the social sciences. . . . We shall not be interested in belle letters, in archaeology or in antiquities for antiquities sake. We shall be interested exclusively in an investigation of those factors and forces which have some relevance to the modern world which must be taken under consideration in the development of contemporary public policy." Again, the implicit denigration of Princeton was obvious; and also unlike Princeton, at Columbia (as at Michigan) graduate students would be trained primarily in one of the disciplinary departments.[61] The Ford Foundation's support for the Near Eastern studies programs at Columbia and the University of Michigan in 1952–1953 can thus be seen as an effort to create alternatives to Princeton's approach to graduate training in Near Eastern studies, though Ford would a few years later itself begin funding Near Eastern studies at Princeton as well. It would seem that, despite their misgivings, the foundations could simply not resist giving Princeton money.

The CNME in Action

The newly formed SSRC Committee on the Near and Middle East, which despite initial funding from Carnegie was almost from the outset strongly oriented toward the Ford Foundation as its prime potential patron, held its first meeting in February 1951. Two distinct perspectives on how the committee should define its mission immediately emerged. Those committee members who shared Robert Hall's vision of area studies as properly constructed around well-defined social science research projects argued that its primary goal should be to contribute "to a more complete understanding by the Government, people and scholarship of the United States about the area of the Near East, through the development of the resources of the social sciences as applied to the study of that area." Rather than trying to "include all aspects of Near Eastern history, linguistics or geography . . . the committee should try to state what is distinctive about, and necessary to, a research approach by social scientists . . . and fix upon one or two projects which could be completed within a relatively short time." However, other committee members, with former OSS R&A Near East section chief E. A. Speiser probably among them, argued that (as the minutes put it)

> the goal of the committee would be to develop an over-all program which would be something like that attained by the OSS during World War II, in which a group of able and informed people from the fields of sociology, psychology, law, history, etc., who were possessed of expert knowledge about individual countries of the Near East, could pool their judgments in such a way as to represent and reflect the region as a whole. It was suggested that while the committee might avoid an all-inclusive program, it should know what that program was if it were to carry on an effective activity. Further, the opinion was expressed that work in the fields of social science could not be separated from other fields of scholarship.

Where the SSRC leadership stood seems clear: as J. C. Hurewitz would recall much later, "From the first meeting, Pendleton Herring, the SSRC president, and Bryce Wood and Joseph Casagrande, the committee's successive staff associates, pressed us to think about research projects that would contribute to the solid anchorage of each social science discipline to the region." The minutes from February 1951 sum up this discussion by asserting that "these two points of view were not considered to be mutually exclusive, and it was agreed that progress might be made along both lines simultaneously." But the fault lines and confusions revealed by this very first discussion of the CNME's mission would not be easy to overcome, and they would for years to come hamper its work—and its ability to secure research funding from the Ford Foundation.

This lack of clarity was manifested in the very broad and ill-defined suggestions for research projects made by committee members, solicited to help define a "constitution" for the CNME's work. These included "Land tenure," "Causes of social instability in the Near East," "Results of the impact of western civilization on the cultures of the Near East" and "Forces and factors of tension in the Near East." The committee eventually settled on this last topic as its priority, because it was deemed "as being related to policy concerns of the United States Government, as being sufficiently inclusive to permit participation by all those interested in the field, and as permitting the study of both the intrusive and internal sources of tension and unrest"; the hope was that it could be developed into a well-focused research project that might secure foundation funding. Meanwhile, the CNME discussed conducting yet another survey of the Near Eastern studies field in the United States and reviewed the programs under way at the home universities of committee members. In the course of that discussion someone suggested holding "a discussion of the theory of area studies in general"—just the kind of question to which Robert Hall had devoted so much time and effort—but this was put off to a later date and never actually happened.[62]

In the months that followed the CNME struggled to formulate a coherent research program that might secure funding from Ford or one of the other big foundations. The Cold War concerns that informed its deliberations and underpinned its hopes for foundation funding were made explicit in a June 1951 statement of the committee's broader mission:

> American interests in the Near East before World War II were primarily cultural; the United States enjoyed a large measure of good will throughout the area because it had not become involved in political or economic disputes within the region. Since 1945 the maintenance of the security and stability of the Near East has become clearly associated with the national interest because of the threat of communist pressure on Iran and Turkey, the danger of the loss of the petroleum production of the region, and the desire of the United States to stimulate a democratic orientation on the part of the local peoples and governments.
>
> The growth of political concern about the Near East has created a demand, within and without the government, for information about the area and comprehension of its problems, and for personnel competent to perform research and serve as technicians in the field. The type of information now at a premium is the basic data of the social sciences; the training of personnel is a cooperative opportunity for social scientists, linguists and classical scholars.[63]

But turning these broad concerns into a concrete research agenda proved a difficult task. A draft outline of a research program was formulated by April–May 1951, under the broad rubric of "Dynamic Forces in the Middle East"; it listed a series of tentative projects all but one of which were to be directed by scholars who were not members of the CNME and nearly all of which had clear relevance to government policy concerns. They ranged from a project to be directed by Majid Khadduri on "Political Forces Operating in the Arab League" to Firuz Kazemzadeh on "Political Implications of Soviet-Near Eastern Relations" to Raymond Mikesell on "Economic, Political and Cultural Impact of Petroleum Development upon the Middle East."[64] But none of the committee's proposals aroused much interest at the Ford Foundation, now emerging as an increasingly important funder of area studies, or elsewhere, and after an initial flurry of activity the pace of the committee's activity slowed down considerably.

The committee did not convene again until January 1952, after a hiatus of nine months, and during its second year of existence its main focus continued to be drafting a proposal for the development of research in Near Eastern studies which could be presented to foundation officials for funding.[65] Along the way the committee also proposed the establishment of a permanent field station, possibly at the American University of Beirut, as a base for ongoing social science research and training in the region, similar to Robert Hall's field research station at Okayama. A Ford Foundation staffer reported that the proposal

> apparently grows out of the experience of Mr. Cameron's recent studies there [i.e., his 1951 expedition to Iraq]. It seems that the major problem in conduct of research is one of administration. For example, it is necessary to disguise social science research behind ostensible archeological digging. . . .
>
> As I understand it, the basic proposal is that arrangements be made for teams of social scientists to go each year over a period of years under the experienced guidance of a person such as Cameron. . . . In terms of substance, the social scientists would be concerned primarily with the dynamics of change. They would report back each year [on] current situations and changes, for example with respect to rising nationalism.[66]

This sounds more like political monitoring, if not intelligence gathering, than it does social science research; in any case, neither Carnegie nor Ford was interested in funding a field station and the idea was soon dropped. So the CNME finally agreed to focus its energies on what seemed to be a more achievable project: a conference at which research on what were deemed to be key social categories and institutions in the region would be presented and discussed, under the broad rubric of "Dynamic Forces in the Middle East." As the committee's annual report for 1951–1952 explained, "the present time is a critical one in the Near East. Processes of change are gradually causing the people of the area to relinquish old values for new. Analysis of these processes may indicate the directions that the new forces are taking."[67] Despite some initial reluctance Carnegie ultimately agreed to fund the proposed conference.[68]

Social Dynamics at the Princeton Inn

Retitled "The Near East—Social Dynamics and the Cultural Setting," the conference took place on October 24–25, 1952, at the Princeton Inn, which now houses a residential college for Princeton undergraduates but at the time was a hotel with suitable meeting space. In his opening remarks to the fifty or so attendees, George Cameron declared that in the Middle East

> this is a time of crisis; that it is necessary to understand what changes are taking place in the Middle East and what the direction of these changes is likely to be. He indicated that it was essential for the conference to consider the people as members of groups, as representatives of institutions and as personalities; to understand the group's structures, ideas and motivations; to take the neuter out of individuals, changing them into "he" or "you"; and to ask the questions "why," "how," and "who."[69]

In keeping with plans developed over the previous year or so, each paper presented at the conference sought to delineate the key characteristics of a specific (albeit broadly and loosely defined) social category: the intellectual, the clergyman, the nomad, the villager, the bazaar merchant, the political leader (this paper was actually a study of Ataturk's career), the army officer, minorities, the entrepreneur class, the worker, economic planners, the Israeli farmer, the "Palestine Arab refugee" and the immigrant in Israel.[70]

The event was the CNME's intellectual debut, intended to showcase the progress and promise of social science research on the Middle East. However, recalling the conference decades later, committee member J. C. Hurewitz aptly asserted that the papers "revealed that social science research on the region was still swaddled," by which he meant that it was still in its infancy. To judge from both the summaries of the papers in the conference record and the versions eventually published, they were all highly descriptive, generalizing, and devoid of both analytical rigor and a clear theoretical or methodological perspective. The one exception, Hurewitz apparently could not resist adding, was a paper titled "Cultural Factors in Social Dynamics in the Near East" by fellow CNME member E. A. Speiser, which Hurewitz later characterized, tongue firmly in cheek, as "an original analysis in the author's usual multimillenial perspective."[71]

Speiser did indeed incline to the long view: in his 1947 article on Near Eastern studies in the United States he had declared that "in this region of immemorial and persistent cultural traditions it is impossible to splinter off the modern phase from its antecedent periods without serious loss to our knowledge of any given stage, especially the current one. Near Eastern studies are indivisible in a very real sense."[72] In his 1952 conference paper Speiser advanced a concept of his own recent invention, the "ethneme," defined as "the minimum effective political organism in its socio-cultural setting" that denoted "the irreducible minimum of productive features without which one contemporary socio-political organism might not be readily distinguished from the next in the long perspective." This new analytical tool would, Speiser insisted, "enable the social scientist to go beyond the present group manifestations, e.g. the nation, to cut through the strata of the past, and to trace the social and cultural genes still operative." Speiser argued that there were a minimum of three distinct Arab ethnemes—Egypt, Saudi Arabia and the Fertile Crescent—each of which was essentially a unit unto itself. It would appear that the conference participants were deeply unimpressed by Speiser's theoretical innovation, and it is hard to avoid concluding that Columbia political scientist Schuyler C. Wallace was being facetious when, in his summing up of the conference proceedings, he expressed "his satisfaction that for the third time in his life he had been present at the birth of a new professional term: the ETHNEME."[73]

William Marvel, on the staff of the Carnegie Corporation which had funded the event, told his colleagues that "CC got its money's worth out of this conference." It was, he reported, "one of the more successful efforts in the field of scholarly conferences" and "indicative of the strides that have been made in Near Eastern studies over the last ten years." Nonetheless, he went on, "by and large, both the papers and the discussions were more descriptive or in some cases analytical of the present institutional structure of the Middle East than they were informative as to perceptible trends of development," and he also noted "a lack of effort to place the analysis of conditions in that area in a context of United States interests or United States foreign policy."[74] In fact, doubts about the conference papers' scholarly value would delay their publication in an edited volume and demoralize the committee.

Research Topics

In its first incarnation (1951–1955), the CNME was in fact active for only about a year and a half: after its October 1952 conference at Princeton the committee largely ran out of steam. It does not seem to have convened even once during 1953, and the projects for which it sought foundation funding continued to fall far short of the coherent research program that both the SSRC and the Ford Foundation expected it to formulate and implement. For example, in March 1953 the SSRC submitted a proposal on behalf of the CNME to Ford's Board of Overseas Training and Research requesting $500,000 over a five-year period to support research on the Middle East. But the sample research projects CNME proposed were much like those it had presented the previous year: they addressed a disparate set of questions and did not add up to anything like a coherent research program. E. A. Speiser wanted funding for a team project on "law and religion"; Raymond Mikesell wanted to study "petroleum development"; J. C. Hurewitz proposed research on "the foreign policies of the United States and Great Britain"; Morroe Berger, the young sociologist hired by Princeton the previous year, put forward a project on the Egyptian civil service; and so on. Ford clearly did not see these proposals as the kind of thing it was interested in and took no action on the proposal; as CNME chair George Cameron correctly surmised in a September 1953 message to his colleagues, this was probably because Ford "could not see what the cumulative effect of such work would be or what (if any) efforts had been made to integrate the various undertakings—in general, where it was all leading to."[75] An internal Ford staff memo attributed the CNME's paralysis to "1) the shortage of qualified research personnel; and 2) the limited and fixed interests of many of those who were qualified to do top level research."[76]

Cleon O. Swayzee, the Ford Foundation's Director of Research, actually met with CNME members in 1953 to urge them to develop a coherent, integrated research agenda. But in any case they could not have been unaware of what Ford (and the U.S. government) wanted to know more about because the SSRC, as always in tune with the foundations' desires and priorities, made sure they were aware. For example, it circulated to them a list of "Suggested Topics for Social Science Research" dated December 1953 and drawn up jointly by the State Department's External Research Staff (established in 1947

as the department's interface with the academic world) and its Psychological Intelligence and Research Staff. Topics on this particular list, which the
State Department (and the CIA) wanted scholars to investigate, included the
"evolution of the Army's role in Egyptian politics" and many other aspects
of contemporary Egyptian politics and foreign policy, especially the internal
workings of the military regime which had come to power the previous year
and which the United States was trying to cultivate.[77]

Swayzee's efforts to shape the CNME's research program do not seem to
have been very effective, owing in part to what was by that point the committee's profound inertia but perhaps also to the disinclination of many academics to have their research agenda dictated to them by someone else. But
Swayzee could also be much more direct. For example, as he acknowledged to
colleagues at the SSRC in October 1953, he had recently approached Princeton's T. Cuyler Young, who had spent a year or so at the U.S. Embassy in
Tehran in 1951–1952, and asked him to study "subversion in Iran," apparently
at the suggestion of Paul F. Langer who was in this period helping Ford identify scholars whose research would be of interest to the government. This
exchange took place less than two months after the CIA had orchestrated
a military coup d'état in Iran which overthrew the parliamentary government of Prime Minister Mohammad Mossadegh and installed Shah Mohammad Reza Pahlavi as absolute ruler, so in this context "subversion" apparently
meant resistance to the Shah's autocracy. Young reported Swayzee's request to
his university's administration and was told that he should not take on such
"directed" research but should instead pursue his own projects. As I discuss
later, Young had in any case been rather sympathetic to Mossadegh's National
Front government.[78]

Another incident involving Iran at the highest levels of the Ford Foundation further illustrates the linkage between its funding priorities and the
foreign policy of the United States government. On September 16, 1953, about
a month after the coup in Iran, Ford's board of trustees approved the following proposal: "In view of the recent political change in Iran, resulting in
the emergence of a government favorable to the West, the officers suggest
that the Board consider authorizing its Executive Committee to appropriate
up to $500,000 if investigation indicates a significant possibility to assist in
strengthening the new government in making progress toward democratic
objectives."

Ford's alacrity in approving funding for work in Iran so soon after a U.S.-orchestrated coup had installed the Shah as the country's autocrat and destroyed any hope of "progress toward democratic objectives" speaks for itself.

But there was a potential glitch. Kenneth R. Iverson (1909–1980), the Ford Foundation's chief representative in the Near East, had been in Tehran during the coup (one wonders why) and sent foundation officials an exciting blow-by-blow account which they wished to share with the board of trustees. However, before that could happen, John Howard, director of Ford's Division of Overseas Activities, felt compelled to ask Iverson to revise "two sentences of it, at the bottom of page two, about the [communist] Tudeh party which, if taken out of context, could cause a certain amount of questioning." Howard told Iversen:

> We understand you to mean that, given the present state of political organization and consciousness in Iran, the Kremlin-controlled Tudeh party, because of its systematic and disciplined enrollment, is the only party sufficiently well organized to fight and win an election if it were held now under the conditions which obtain in the western democracies. However, you were told that Iranian elections are controlled, that they are not by secret ballot, and that therefore a Tudeh victory was unlikely. Another way of saying this, I suppose, is that Iran is not yet ready—just as guerrilla-ridden Greece immediately after the war was not ready—for a democratic election.
>
> Would you care to suggest an alternative wording of this portion of your report so that we can distribute the report more widely without the danger that this portion, if quoted out of context, might be misinterpreted.
>
> Since we are talking to the Trustees about Iran, there is some urgency in the matter, and I would be grateful if you would reply as soon as possible.

Iverson, now back in Beirut, apparently complied and provided Howard with a revised version of his account that did not seem to suggest that the Tudeh might have done well in free elections and was thus deemed safe for the trustees to read.

Soon thereafter, Iverson returned to Iran where, "after discussions with many government officials, including the Prime Minister, General Zahedi, as well as private citizens, both local nationals and foreigners, he concluded that there is a genuine desire on the part of the new government to be responsive to the needs of the people." In light of his report the Ford Foundation's president told his executive committee that "the investigation has shown that there are significant opportunities to assist the new government in its efforts to achieve democratic objectives" and recommended that the foundation begin spending the $500,000 already approved by the board. Over the next twelve years Ford would devote substantial sums to rural development in Iran, before concluding that its programs there had failed and withdrawing from the country.[79]

There were some within academia who objected early on to the close association between university-based area studies, on the one hand, and the U.S. government and American business interests on the other. One of these was anthropologist Jerome Rauch, who in 1955 published an article in the *Journal of Negro Education* in which he argued that "this over-riding association of foreign area research with United States corporate and government objectives must arouse considerable concern not only on political grounds pertaining to the policies with which this research is identified and supports—and on the success or failure of which the correctness of the research itself may be judged, but also on substantive, scientific questions relating to the very integrity, independence and validity of area social science." Rauch was particularly distressed that the "heightened interest in African studies is sharply attuned to political developments in Africa. . . . Raw materials and investment opportunities, strategic and military import, the status quo and/or colonialism—and not only European, are the themes underlying African research." Rauch went on to quote sociologist Werner J. Cahnman, a Jewish refugee from Nazi Germany: "The first and foremost danger is that area studies are being viewed as the chambermaid of politics. Area studies may be only a covering term for a more effective mapping of the world for the purpose of imperialistic penetration and ultimately for war. The growth of area studies may mean that science is bent to motives that are extra-scientific and even anti-scientific in character. This would be German Geopolitics with a vengeance."[80] Rauch would pay a price for his outspoken criticism: David Price reports that he came to be deemed unemployable in academia and was compelled to pursue a career elsewhere.[81] Voices like his were in any case few and far between in American academia in the 1950s, and it would not be until the mid-1960s, under the impact of the U.S. war in Vietnam and of revelations about the government's misdeeds, indeed criminality, that significant numbers of faculty and students in area studies would begin to publicly question their fields' links with the national security state.

"Have we as a group shot our bolt?"

Unable to formulate, much less implement, an effective (and fundable) research agenda, the CNME now also lost some of its original members. Douglas Crary and Richard Frye resigned from the committee in 1953 and E. A. Speiser the following year; Afif Tannous also dropped out at some point. Lewis V. Thomas of Princeton and Majid Khadduri of SAIS were appointed in their place, but this did not perceptibly reinvigorate the committee. In a September 1953 memorandum to his colleagues Cameron expressed his despair about its inactivity and ineffectiveness:

> Have we anymore [*sic*] reason for existence? Have we as a group shot our bolt, contributed all we can to the development of Near Eastern research in America, and are content and remain content to carry on through our own individual work, teaching, and contacts? If so, let's disband, or have Pen Herring disband us. If not, where do we go now? Frankly, I have a guilt complex. I am unhappy with what little we have accomplished (we have had no summation or evaluation of ourselves so far) and I blame much of it not on you but on myself. The Chairman should provide at least some direction and you have had precious little. You would think even now that he could make some concrete proposals for your consideration, but "where are we?" is in his own mind, too.
> . . . Do you have nothing to say on [Ford's inaction on CNME's funding proposal] or on other things, such as the need for social science research tools? If so, is what you have to say worth being heard by the full committee perhaps around the middle of November, if not before? Does what the Ford Foundation do or fail to do carry so much weight with us that if we don't get what we want from them, we are done, finished, kaput? Please let me know.[82]

This was among the earliest in a long line of laments by CNME leaders and members about what they perceived as the committee's shortcomings and failures, which almost exclusively concerned its efforts to formulate and implement an effective research agenda for the field whose intellectual leadership it claimed. SSRC leaders were equally unhappy with the CNME's torpor. In a November 1953 meeting with William Marvel of Carnegie, Pendleton Herring and Bryce Wood expressed their "acute feelings of dissatisfaction with the role of the SSRC Committee on the Near and Middle East" and "a real inclination to dissolve it in the near future," possibly in order to replace it with one or more "working groups" focused on specific research projects.[83] But the SSRC failed to take prompt action and the CNME continued to languish. In October 1954, after another failed attempt to formulate a research agenda for the committee, its chair George Cameron reiterated to Bryce Wood his conviction that "either our Committee should be disbanded, some new blood brought in, or we have a job to do by ourselves. . . . Is it not about time that we, ourselves, began to make sense?" But the "lines of research" that he went on to suggest were essentially those proposed repeatedly over the previous two years.[84]

Cameron's despair, and the low standing of the CNME in the eyes of the SSRC, were no doubt exacerbated by the fate of the manuscript assembled from the papers presented at the one and only conference the committee had sponsored. The task of editing the volume ended up in the hands of Sydney N. Fisher (1906–1987), who taught Middle Eastern history at Ohio State University, and it was eventually submitted for review to Princeton University Press under the title "Social Forces in the Middle East," only to be rejected in October 1954. The anonymous readers' reports were scathing about several of the chapters and unenthusiastic about the volume as a whole. One reader described most of the chapters as "a program for, rather than the result of, sound scholarship," though he or she went on to explain that this "is not a criticism so much of the MS as of the state of scholarship in the field as a whole." "The real revision of this ms. would," the report added, "require absolutely every contributor (except Speiser and Hurewitz) to start all over again and ask himself what the purpose of the conference was and the volume is, and to follow it. What they have done is to pass out a few speculations directly bearing on the general problem raised by the stated goal of the book, but only after much attention has been given to the traditional treatment that was obviously to be avoided." Specific chapters also came in for tough criticism; for example, the reader's report asserted that in the chapter on "the bazaar merchant" "all the author does is to describe the Beirut shopping district, which is interesting but hardly constitutes an analysis of the bazaar merchant and certainly doesn't stand as a contribution to the study of social change, cultural diffusion, or the economic history of the Middle East—all of which the author apparently wants the reader to believe." The volume was eventually published, apparently without much (if any) revision, by Cornell University Press in 1955 as *Social Forces in the Middle East*.[85] This first published scholarly product of the committee's work would remain its only publication for many years to come.

Writing to Pendleton Herring soon after the manuscript was rejected by Princeton University Press, Cameron again voiced his regret that he and his CNME colleagues were such "laggards." The committee could do its job of directing research "only if it does not continue to serve as a clearing house and propagandizing board for such research as any one individual may *like* to undertake." He was in any case doubtful that the current committee could successfully plan research, "for it lacks a geographer, a psychologist, a sociologist, an anthropologist, and is overweighted with historians." To remedy the problem and get the committee moving he proposed holding a mini-conference with more social scientists participating, though he acknowledged that this might be a "screwy idea."[86] Though in the summer of 1955 the SSRC submitted to Carnegie an upbeat account of the CNME's activities and achievements over the previous four and a half years, in private discussions it was readily acknowledged that the committee in its current composition was hopelessly moribund and needed to be reconstituted if there was to be any chance of getting Middle East studies moving.[87] Before taking action, however, Pendleton Herring consulted with John Howard, director of the Ford Foundation's International Training and Research division, and secured assurances that Ford—well on its way to becoming the leading foundation funding area studies—would provide financial support for a revitalized committee.[88] With these assurances in hand the SSRC finally took action in the middle of 1955, effectively disbanding the committee and revamping its membership.

Over the previous four and a half years the committee had failed to formulate a coherent intellectual agenda for the field whose leadership it claimed, it had proven unable to secure additional foundation funding, the one conference it had organized had yielded a published volume of little scholarly value, it had accomplished almost nothing in terms of developing the nascent field's infrastructure, and its chair and members were demoralized and inactive. Personalities may have had something to do with these failures, but so did the fact that in the early 1950s Middle East studies was still a small and underdeveloped field, with very few university-based scholars available who possessed the skills and vision to carry out the field-building tasks that the SSRC expected of the committee or who could conceive, plan and implement effective research projects on the modern and contemporary Middle East. It was only in the second half of the 1950s that a massive influx of foundation (and later federal) funding began to create a more viable material basis for this field. This funding fueled its dramatic expansion in the late 1950s and early 1960s, and enabled a new set of CNME members to achieve a significant measure of success in developing the field's infrastructure and providing research funding to promising candidates. Success at the other key task expected of the committee—guiding the field's intellectual agenda and fostering cutting-edge research—would be another matter altogether.

6 Field-Building in Boom Times

> I accepted because of my increasing conviction that in this pioneering field
> with very limited resources, a substantial effort at cooperation is necessary,
> and after some observation and experience over the years I think the con-
> text that the Council affords is now the most promising one in which to
> contribute to the development of this field. . . .
> —T. Cuyler Young, 1956

F ROM THE MID-1950S through the mid-1960s, owing in large
measure to a huge influx of foundation and then government
funding, Middle East studies in the United States underwent a qualitative
transition, in terms of the number of centers, departments, programs, faculty
and students in the field but also in terms of its infrastructure and resource
base as well as its institutional density and coherence. As a result it may be
said to have approached critical mass by the early 1960s, such that it was now
for the first time possible to seriously contemplate the formation of a national professional association for the field. The SSRC's Committee on the
Near and Middle East, reconstituted in 1955 and for the first time backed by
significant Ford Foundation funding, played a key role in building this field
during this critical decade.

Reconstituting the CNME

To chair the CNME in its new incarnation and to try to at long last get
things moving in this seemingly backward field, the SSRC recruited Prince-

ton's T. Cuyler Young, and then appointed its other members in consultation with him.[1] As we have seen, Young had taught Persian language and literature at Princeton since 1947 and had chaired the ACLS Committee on Near Eastern Studies in 1950–1953, the last phase of its existence. He was thus very much a known quantity to SSRC officials, who clearly had confidence in his leadership abilities—though as he himself would admit, the lack of a suitable senior social scientist specializing in the Middle East also played a role in his selection. That Young had substantial experience in the Middle East as well as in the U.S. foreign policy world, including a lengthy prewar sojourn in Iran as a missionary, wartime service in the OSS and two periods of service at the U.S. Embassy in Tehran (in 1944–1946 and 1951–1952) clearly weighed heavily in his favor.

Young's second stint at the U.S. embassy in Iran is particularly noteworthy: he accepted the post of political attaché under Ambassador Henry F. Grady just before Iran nationalized the British-owned Anglo-Iranian Oil Company, leading to a crisis in relations with both the United Kingdom and the United States.[2] Grady was unhappy with Washington's subsequent drift toward fully embracing Britain's campaign to force Iran to reverse the nationalization, which put him on bad terms with Secretary of State Dean Acheson. Grady announced his retirement from the Foreign Service in July 1951 and was replaced as ambassador by the more pro-British Loy Henderson, who helped orchestrate the August 1953 CIA-led coup that overthrew the government of Prime Minister Mohammad Mossadegh, installed the young Shah as absolute ruler and crushed the nationalist-democratic and communist movements, opening the way for a resolution of the oil crisis on a basis satisfactory to the United States and Britain.[3] By then Young was long gone, having returned to Princeton in January 1952. An article he published not long after his return suggests that he was sympathetic to the Mossadegh government, then still in power; he certainly made clear his belief that Mossadegh had the support of the majority of the Iranian people.[4] Kermit Roosevelt, who coordinated the CIA's operation to overthrow Mossadegh, made several references in his 1979 book *Countercoup* to one Roger Black, described as a former OSS operative and Yale professor then teaching history in Tehran—"a crusty, quixotic, opinionated professor who spoke fluent Farsi" and "knew far more of Iran and of the people than any of us actually in the Agency did—or probably ever would."[5] Many believe that Roger Black, whom Roosevelt denigrated as a strong supporter of Dr. Mossadegh and (like Mossadegh) as "vain, opinionated, domineering," was in fact Roosevelt's pseudonym for T. Cuyler Young. Young, who had deep roots in Iranian society and friends among the leaders of Mossadegh's National Front, may in fact have unwittingly played some minor role in Roosevelt's machinations, which he is said to have deeply resented.[6]

In later years Young would continue to voice criticism of the Shah's regime and urge U.S. policymakers to press for reform in Iran. For example, in a 1962 article in *Foreign Affairs* Young asserted that "the overwhelming majority of the politically concerned and aware among the people are back of the National Front" and noted that "recent governments have had to maintain stability and themselves in power by force" and rigged elections. Young went on to acknowledge the distrust, if not dislike, that many Iranians felt toward the United States and to decry the "widening gulf" between the Shah's regime and the Iranian people. "The present pattern cannot persist without explosion or significant change," he concluded.[7] In this same period Young, along with other Iran experts, urged the Kennedy administration to use aid as leverage to pressure the Shah to form a more broadly based government, since economic reform was unlikely to succeed without political reform.[8]

However, Young's misgivings about the 1953 coup and his doubts about the Shah's regime did not prevent him from putting his expertise at the service of the CIA. For many years Young was a member of an informal group of senior scholars known as the "Princeton Consultants," though some were in fact based at other universities or institutions, convened to provide the CIA with an outside perspective on its intelligence assessments. The group seems to have been established in 1950 and held regular secret meetings with Allen Dulles, Princeton alumnus and CIA director from 1953 to 1961, with Sherman Kent, chair of the CIA's Board of National Estimates, and later with other CIA officials. While Dulles was director these meetings usually took place when he came to Princeton for the quarterly meetings of the university's board of trustees, but they continued for a decade after Dulles was compelled to resign in the wake of the 1961 Bay of Pigs invasion fiasco. No information is available about Young's specific contributions as a member of this group, and we do not know what if anything Young's academic colleagues knew about his CIA connection. Nonetheless, his maintenance of that connection while playing a leading role in U.S. Middle East studies during the later 1950s and early 1960s offers food for thought.[9]

In 1954, two years after his return to Princeton, Young succeeded Philip Hitti as chair of his university's Department of Oriental Languages and Literatures and as director of its Program in Near Eastern Studies. (The department's name would be changed to Oriental Studies in 1956, when it acquired its first tenure-line East Asianist).[10] In the spring of 1956, a few months after his appointment as chair of the CNME, Young would explain to the SSRC Council why he had agreed to accept this task:

> Last summer I was persuaded reluctantly to accept the chairmanship of your committee, when it appeared that no sufficiently mature social scientist could be found for the assignment. I should explain that I am an Orientalist and something of a historian, so perhaps have one leg to stand on. I accepted because of my increasing conviction that in this pioneering field with very limited resources, a substantial effort at cooperation is necessary, and after some observation and experience over the years I think the context that the Council affords is now the most promising one in which to contribute to the development of this field. . . .[11]

The most senior as well as the most prominent of the CNME's newly appointed members was H. A. R. Gibb, by that time widely regarded as the doyen of Anglo-American Orientalism. Gibb had recently left Oxford and moved to Harvard, where he was appointed the James Richard Jewett Professor of Arabic and University Professor.[12] When Gibb arrived at Harvard in 1955, William L. Langer, of OSS and CIA fame, was serving as director of the university's new Center for Middle Eastern Studies. That entity, the university's second area studies center (the first had been the Russian Research Center), had been established in 1954, after consultation with the State Department, the CIA, U.S. Army Intelligence, Standard Oil of New Jersey (later Exxon) and of New York (later Mobil) and Aramco.[13] In his autobiography Langer highlighted the oil companies' special interest in the new center, which they hoped would provide them with trained personnel.[14] It is also likely that, as with Columbia and the University of Michigan a few years earlier, it was hoped that Harvard would do what Princeton seemed incapable of doing: producing knowledge about the modern and contemporary Middle East that would be useful to policymakers. Thus Harvard's broader rationale for the new center's establishment was largely framed in instrumental terms: "Our international commitment to counter the Soviet threat in the Middle East, the fundamental importance of Middle-eastern [*sic*] oil to our economy, and the continuing crisis in the area make it imperative that American universities turn their attention to this vitally important but hitherto relatively neglected region." The center's mission would be "to train selected men for service in private industry and government and at the same time to encourage scholarly basic research on the modern Middle East in the fields of economics, political science, anthropology, history, and social relations including social psychology."[15]

Gibb succeeded Langer as center director in 1957. His scholarly eminence and the close ties he soon forged with foundation officials brought lavish funding to Harvard's center. In 1956 the Rockefeller Foundation awarded Gibb $205,000 (about $1.8 million in 2015) over a six-year period for a project he would supervise on "the evolution of Middle Eastern societies from the beginning of the nineteenth century to the present, and on the social and economic problems of these societies in terms of their evolution."[16] Gibb had recently argued that "there exists hardly a single work of genuine historical research into any aspect of the inner historical development of the Middle East in the nineteenth century," and he had also lamented that if "in England and Europe there are at most only some three or four orientalist scholars who are professional historians . . . in the United States it would be hard to find as many." So the task, as Gibb saw it, was to produce historians with "orientalist qualifications," something that this grant, and others soon to arrive, would presumably help him achieve at Harvard.[17] In 1957 the Ford Foundation gave the Center for Middle Eastern Studies that Gibb now directed a $300,000 five-year grant; two years later Rockefeller gave Harvard a grant of half a million dollars for the center, and in 1960, as part of a massive surge in foundation funding for area and international studies, Ford provided additional grants amounting to almost one million dollars (the equivalent of some $7–8 million in 2015) to help fund two new chairs in the Middle East field and to support the center's activities. No other Middle East center enjoyed foundation beneficence on so lavish a scale.[18]

In October 1955 Gibb accepted Pendleton Herring's invitation to join the CNME, "provided that you will allow me to be guided by later experience as to how far I can be of material service to the ends at which the Council aims."[19] Gibb would in fact soon be pleading that while the CNME was a priority for him, his advancing age, his research, and his teaching and other duties at Harvard required some "conservation of energies" on his part. This, from Gibb's perspective, justified his effort in February 1957 to send anthropologist Derwood Lockard, then executive secretary of Harvard's Center for Middle Eastern Studies, to a committee meeting in his place. Young remonstrated that committee membership was personal rather than institutional.[20]

Also appointed to the reconstituted committee was Wilfred Cantwell Smith of McGill University's Institute of Islamic Studies, which had just received a large capital grant from the Rockefeller Foundation. Smith, who had until two years earlier served under Young's chairmanship on the last incarnation of the ACLS Committee for Near Eastern Studies, expressed some reluctance to accept Herring's invitation: "My first impulse, on receiving your invitation to join the SSRC committee on the Near and Middle East, was to feel flattered but to decline on the grounds of incompetence—since I am not (and, frankly, do not want to be) a social scientist in any of the accepted disciplined senses."[21] Indeed, in an address earlier that same year to the American Oriental Society (AOS), Smith had vigorously defended the humanities and what he termed "oriental studies" as traditionally conceived. He told the AOS that the emergence of area studies centers on North American campuses aroused his concern because they had "arisen not primarily out of the inner impetus toward disinterested knowledge, but in response to a stringent practical demand—the need for 'experts,' for men who can deal with concrete and specific problems that have arisen because of intercultural activity, particularly at the governmental level." The rapid expansion of oriental studies, Smith went on, had been a "source of money, of students, of whole new programs." But, he warned, "it would be equally idle to deny that it is full of danger, both to our studies and to the world. There is the danger of 'being used'; of subordinating knowledge to policy, rather than vice versa. There is the subtler danger of acquiring seeming knowledge that is, in fact, false. For it happens to be a law of this universe in which we live that you cannot understand persons if you treat them as objects. You misinterpret a culture if you approach it in order to manipulate it."[22] Nonetheless, Smith declared himself willing to put his concerns aside for the time being and join the CNME. As he put it to Herring:

> On second thoughts [sic], however, I have decided to accept; partly in view of the proposed membership—your chairman's name wins me over completely— and partly on the grounds that the responsibility is, I suppose, basically yours. If the kinds of approach and concern to which I am wedded prove in the end

inacceptable [*sic*] to the Social Science authorities, I shall be ready without hard feeling to accept any suggestion of resignation.

If, on the other hand, your initiative means that you and the Council feel that this kind of work should comprehend both social sciences and humanities, in co-operation rather than in any subordination of either to the other, then I am enthusiastically with you. When I was secretary of the ACLS committee, I urged co-operation with yours, and hoped for some kind of joint programme. I strongly feel that this kind of planning and co-ordinating of studies needs doing, and am happy to be given an opportunity to participate with your group in this activity.[23]

The Michigan anthropologist William D. Schorger (1921–2003) was also appointed to the reconstituted committee in the fall of 1955; he had accompanied George Cameron on his 1951 expedition to northern Iraq, though he spent most of the time ill with hepatitis at the American University of Beirut hospital. So was Harvey P. Hall, who had been editor of the *Middle East Journal*, organ of the Middle East Institute in Washington, since it began to appear in 1947; however, he would leave the committee after just a year to join the staff of the Ford Foundation. J. C. Hurewitz of Columbia and Majid Khadduri of SAIS, both political scientists, were the only members of the old committee invited to join its new incarnation. In June 1956 committee chair Young, "feeling in some need of reinforcement on the social science side," also recruited the young political scientist and Turkey specialist Dankwart Rustow to the reconstituted CNME as its non-voting secretary, because there could not be two voting members from the same university.[24] As discussed in Chapter 4, Rustow had (along with Morroe Berger) joined Princeton's faculty in 1952; he remained on the committee through the end of the 1957–1958 academic year and left Princeton for Columbia in 1959.[25]

As J. C. Hurewitz would frame the change decades later, "the face and pace of the committee changed emphatically. Gone were the archaeologists [i.e., Cameron and Speiser]. To fill their slots came humanists (one from Canada) with modern scholarly concerns and dedicated commitment to language teaching and religion."[26] The committee as initially reconstituted in 1955 in fact consisted of three humanists (Gibb, Smith and Young) and three social scientists (Hurewitz, Khadduri and Schorger), plus Harvey Hall who does not seem to have played any active role before stepping down. The SSRC's decision to appoint a committee about half of whose members were from the humanities may have reflected its recognition that, in the absence of a parallel ACLS committee focusing on the humanities side of things, the reconstituted SSRC committee would have to give considerable attention to field-building concerns normally the province of the ACLS, including language training and the development of library resources. Given this reality, as early as January 1956 Pendleton Herring raised the question of whether the SSRC should invite the ACLS to become a joint sponsor of the committee and was authorized by his organization's Committee on Problems and Policy (P&P) to pursue this course. But the members of the CNME felt that the time was not ripe for co-sponsorship, and the matter was put aside for several years.[27]

Meanwhile, the reconstituted committee was assured of a substantially higher level of foundation support than its predecessor had enjoyed. In December 1955 Pendleton Herring wrote Young to report that he had had "a very satisfactory talk yesterday afternoon with John Howard [director of Ford's International Training and Research division] and Swayzee [the foundation's director of research]. They had read the minutes of our committee meeting with thoughtful attention and expressed a warm interest in the problems that we had selected for further exploration. They assured me of their readiness to support the committee over a period of years."[28] Funding was soon forthcoming: in May 1956 Ford approved a $50,000 grant (the equivalent of almost $440,000 in 2015) to support the committee's work. For the first time it had significant funds at its disposal which it could use to try to play a much more active role in developing Middle East studies than had its predecessor.[29]

Missions, Possible and Impossible

From the time of its reconstitution in 1955 and into the 1980s, the SSRC's committee for this regional field, and then its successor jointly sponsored with the ACLS, focused on three distinct missions. First, before the establishment of a national professional association for scholars, teachers and students in the field, the CNME took on critical field-building tasks that no single Middle East studies department, center or program could have undertaken on its own. It thus played a key role in developing what I have termed the infrastructure of Middle East studies in the United States. Second, it secured funds which enabled it to award a number of postdoctoral research fellowships (and later dissertation research fellowships) each year, which cumulatively had an important intellectual impact on the field over the long term. Finally, it sought to formulate and implement a research agenda that would advance the field intellectually and produce the kind of knowledge about the region that the founders and funders of area studies had anticipated. The committee was, I argue, much more successful at the first two of these missions than it was at the third.

Over the years the CNME devoted considerable time, energy and attention to enhancing the resources and training available to those involved in Middle East studies in North America. In the first place this meant the development of effective programs for the teaching of Middle Eastern languages, as well as the materials and methods they required. This had long been recognized as a major problem in the field, and to help address it the committee played an important role in securing a Ford Foundation grant of $176,500 (about $1.5 million in 2015) which in 1957 made it possible for a consortium of five universities (Columbia, Harvard, Johns Hopkins, Princeton and Michigan) to launch an annual intensive summer language training program in Arabic, Persian and Turkish, and which also supported the development of new materials and teaching methods for these languages. T. Cuyler Young chaired the interuniversity committee which oversaw the program from its inception until his retirement in 1969. Ford would renew and increase its grant for the program in 1962, and other universities joined the consortium (which also secured federal funding) in the course of the 1960s.[30]

In addition, the CNME helped fund such small-scale but important projects as Milton Cowan's translation into English of Hans Wehr's modern Arabic dictionary (originally published in German in 1952) and George Makdisi's translation of Régis Blachère's *Eléments de l'Arabe Classique*. It also hired a bibliographer to consult on developing Middle East-related bibliographical resources and encouraged the Association of Research Libraries to appoint a Committee on the Near and Middle East. As the Library of Congress and university libraries began to build their Middle East collections using funds made available through the PL 480 program, discussed later in this chapter, the committee took on the vexed issue of Arabic transliteration in 1957. As Dankwart Rustow would later recount:

> I had found, to my surprise, that the Library of Congress was keeping boxes and boxes with thousands of Arabic books in its storage vaults uncatalogued because scholars had not agreed on any standard system of transliteration for

Arabic. Here I thought the committee could make a major contribution by set-
tling this issue. In our preliminary discussion, one committee member, Wilfred
Cantwell Smith of McGill University, remarked that, of course, he "would never
yield on a matter of principle, such as transliteration." So I quietly saw to it that
this particular "man of principle" would not be part of the transliteration subcommittee. The most knowledgeable subcommittee member turned out to be
Sir Hamilton A. R. Gibb, who had recently moved from Oxford to Harvard; and
while I did not concur in all of *his* principles, I gladly yielded in the end, since it
was obviously more important to resolve the issue of transliteration than to get
hung up on its details.[31]

The subcommittee's proposed revisions to the Arabic transliteration guidelines developed by the Library of Congress finally helped resolve the problem.[32]

The flurry of activity in which the reconstituted committee engaged during its first two years helped it secure a three-year commitment from the
Ford Foundation in 1957 to provide $50,000 a year (about $423,000 in 2015)
to be disbursed as grants to scholars conducting postdoctoral research on
the modern Middle East—the first time the committee had funds of its own
to award for scholarly research and thereby help shape the field.[33] In the late
1950s and early 1960s the committee awarded nine or ten grants a year; though
not numerous, the cumulative impact of these grants on this still quite small
field was nonetheless significant.[34] Over the first three years of this program
(1957–1958 to 1959–1960) the CNME awarded a total of twenty-seven grants
(out of eighty applications) averaging $5144 each—an amount equivalent in
terms of buying power to over $40,000 in 2015, and even more munificent
when spent in the Middle East, where living costs were generally very low at
the time. Eleven of the twenty-seven recipients were in political science and
six in history, with the remainder divided among anthropology (three), economics (two), psychology (two), sociology (one) and "other" (one).[35]

The committee's focus on language training, bibliography, translation
and similar issues aroused some concern within the SSRC. At a January 1957
meeting of P&P it was noted that

> There is an impression that the committee is more concerned with fields of the
> humanities than with social science. . . . disappointment was expressed that the
> committee's present program does not include plans for systematic analyses in
> social science terms of sociological and economic aspects of the Near and Mid-

dle East. Members of P&P considered these so important that they should over-weigh the tendency of historians to define the committee's concerns mainly in terms of the humanities. Too great emphasis could not be placed on the need for opening up economic and sociological research on the Near and Middle East.

Pendleton Herring responded to these concerns by noting the difficulty of finding an economist or sociologist to recruit to the committee and by ex-plaining that he had hesitated to "discourage the committee's concern with general research tools since its strength lay in that area."[36] But the fact re-mained that while CNME achieved substantial success in its efforts to de-velop instructional and bibliographic resources and to support the work of individual scholars, it was consistently less successful when it came to its mis-sion of setting an intellectual agenda for the field by promoting social science research on the Middle East.

P&P's concerns may have been at least somewhat allayed by the confer-ence that the CNME organized in May–June 1957 on "Fields of Research in Middle East Cultures: Anthropology, Politics, History," held at Dobbs Ferry, New York, and intended to help elucidate needs and directions for Middle East research. The paper presenters included William Schorger on Middle East anthropological research, Richard P. Mitchell on the Muslim Brothers, and Leonard Binder on Islamic political thought in Pakistan.[37] But the star attraction was no doubt H. A. R. Gibb, whose paper "The Study of Islamic History in North America" reiterated how underdeveloped he thought this field remained. Gibb asserted that "original research in classical Islamic his-tory is all but non-existent in North America" and went on to declare that "the plain fact is that Islamic history, as taught in all but a handful of univer-sities (and this applies as much to England and Europe as to North America), hardly deserves the name of a real academic discipline; indeed, as Cl. Cahen has forcibly reminded us in an incisive paper in *Studia Islamica*, it has still largely to be written. . . . There is not in any North American university to-day one qualified Islamic historian." Gibb insisted that proper Islamic histo-rians would need to be trained in history departments, by historians: "The Grunebaums, the Gibbs, and others do their best, no doubt. . . . But until a thoroughly qualified Islamic historian is to be found in North America, the future historian must complete his technical education by working for a time under the direction of one or other of the Islamic historians in European institutions."[38] In fact, few members of the coming cohorts of Islamic historians in North America would be trained as Gibb proposed. More broadly, though the CNME discussed organizing additional conferences focusing on anthropology and political science, it failed to follow up and its efforts to stimulate and guide research on the region yielded meager results.

The "Bonanza Years"

The CNME's ability to begin playing a much more active role in building Middle East studies in the second half of the 1950s was obviously bolstered by the fact that, thanks to the Ford Foundation, it finally had substantial financial resources at its disposal to support its own activities and to help fund research by others. But this new reality, and its heightened level of activity, must be seen in the context of a much broader development: the dramatic surge in the growth of area studies as a whole that began in the later 1950s, thanks to a large-scale influx of funding from foundations and somewhat later from the federal government. This period witnessed the unprecedented expansion of Middle East studies as well as of other area studies fields, with some older centers and programs acquiring significant new resources that allowed them to expand, and new Middle East centers and programs popping up at universities which had not previously had them.

The Rockefeller and Ford foundations had made substantial grants to a number of area studies centers in the mid-1950s, including Princeton's Program in Near Eastern Studies, Harvard's Center for Middle Eastern Studies and McGill's Institute of Islamic Studies, along with Columbia and the University of Michigan. Later in that decade and into the early 1960s, these foundations (especially Ford) began to pour money into international and area studies on an unprecedented scale. Meanwhile, Ford's foreign study fellowship program, initially intended to promote "careers in international affairs" in a wide range of professions and fields, increasingly served those pursuing academic careers, a tendency that accelerated after 1962 when Ford transferred administration of what was now known as its Foreign Area Fellowship Program (FAFP) to a joint ACLS-SSRC committee.[39] Between its inception in 1952 and 1964, this program awarded 1,214 individuals (mainly advanced graduate students and younger scholars) a total of $10 million in fellowships—the equivalent of roughly eight times that amount in 2015 dollars.[40] More broadly, from the later 1950s onward Ford's International Training and

Research program would increasingly focus on supporting the study of, and training in, international relations and foreign areas at American institutions of higher education.

In the late 1940s and early 1950s the Rockefeller Foundation and the Carnegie Corporation had repeatedly declared that while they were prepared to invest large sums of money to get area studies off the ground, in the long run these programs would have to be supported by the universities at which they were based. But by the mid-1950s there was growing recognition that this vision was unrealistic. In a 1954 assessment of the Rockefeller Foundation's long-range policy for area studies, Charles B. Fahs, director of its Humanities Division, took pride that Rockefeller had been "the first Foundation to enter the area studies field in significant degree," blazing a trail along which Carnegie and Ford had followed. But, Fahs went on, though area studies

> have made and are making an important contribution to American knowledge of the world with which the country must deal . . . most of the programs in the universities are still in rather unstable condition. They are still dependent on short-term outside help. This is due in part to failure to work out an adequate curricular base in undergraduate general education, in part to the failure of universities to delimit their fields and to take adequate responsibility for the fields selected, and in part to the newness of this work and the fact that it probably implies over the next several decades a major rethinking of university policies. . . .
>
> With this situation, fellowship aid is not the answer. Improvement will require basic improvement in the situation of area study programs in the universities.

Fahs felt it would "be undesirable for the Foundation to continue indefinitely as a nursemaid in these fields," but if that was to be avoided a selective program of capital grants—in effect, providing a limited number of area studies programs with endowments in order to put them on a stable financial basis for the long term—might be the best solution. He cited the Near Eastern studies program at Princeton as one possible recipient of a capital grant.[41]

Rockefeller adopted Fahs' proposal and in 1954 gave Princeton a capital grant of half a million dollars for Near Eastern studies and the same amount to Cornell for Southeast Asian studies. These grants were intended, the foundation announced, "to provide greater independence and continuity for two university programs in which the Foundation has previously been interested.

... The universities will need to continue to seek short-term project funds from many sources, but in the meantime it is hoped that these capital grants will provide greater freedom to administrators and scholars both in longterm planning and in meeting immediate needs not readily dealt with through the project approach."[42] The following year Rockefeller gave a capital grant of $510,000 on the same terms to McGill's Institute of Islamic Studies, directed by Wilfred Cantwell Smith, who joined the CNME that same year. Altogether, the Rockefeller Foundation and the Carnegie Corporation of New York are estimated to have spent some nine million dollars on area studies between 1952 and 1963—the equivalent of $70–80 million in 2015.[43]

The Ford Foundation would eventually adopt a similar approach, though it had vastly more money to give away. It was only in 1955–1956, after divesting itself of its Ford Motor Company stock, that the Ford Foundation was able to accurately value its endowment, which came to an astonishing $2.75 billion—about $24 billion in 2015. This realization prompted a rush to reduce its holdings, to avoid Internal Revenue Service scrutiny and to be in a position to disburse enough each year to offset anticipated income. As a result Ford gave away some $550 million in special appropriations in 1955–1956, mainly as grants to nonprofit hospitals and medical schools but also as one-time salary supplements for faculty at 600 colleges and universities across the country. But even after this unprecedented largesse it remained by far the country's richest foundation and continued to need to give away a great deal of money each year.[44]

In a 1959 draft proposal for long-term support for area studies centers, a member of Ford's staff argued that the first "experimental" phase of the introduction of non-Western studies into American education, by means of the creation of a number of interdisciplinary area studies centers, had been more or less completed; what was necessary now was "to develop non-Western studies on a national scale adequate to support American interests and responsibilities as a world leader" through large-scale, long-term support for graduate programs. This task was too vast to be accomplished by the universities alone: they would need help from all three major foundations (but especially Ford) in order to train an adequate supply of manpower for each field, increase participation in area studies by the disciplines, and strengthen the relationship between American and indigenous scholarship. Hence the proposal to allocate some $20 million in ten-year grants "to the best of the existing graduate area studies programs and to a few others of genuine promise."[45]

In planning its new program of long-term support Ford staffers produced assessments of various area studies fields, including one on Near Eastern studies as of 1959. Though it asserted (somewhat surprisingly) that "Near Eastern studies are probably better developed in the United States than those for any of the other non-Western areas," it also found that "there are at present only four well developed university graduate training programs—Columbia, Harvard, Michigan and Princeton—and quality varies considerably among them." Columbia and Harvard were deemed to have the best record of research and publication, while Michigan was said to have "declined in both scope and quality in the past three years" and faculty morale there had fallen. There were in addition seventeen or eighteen other universities where courses on the Middle East and language training were offered. The SSRC Committee on the Near and Middle East was reported to have tackled the field's problems with vigor since its reconstitution in 1955. For its part, the *Middle East Journal*, published by the Middle East Institute, was described as the "principal scholarly journal" in the field and as "an important factor in the development of Near East scholarship in the U.S. and especially so as an outlet for short publications of younger scholars." The survey argued that "national needs for competent manpower" in this field were not yet being met, so there was in fact further room for growth in Near Eastern studies. A major effort would, however, be needed to strengthen the participation of underrepresented disciplines, which included everything except history and political science, and to improve the quality and quantity of research, especially on the modern period. "The collaboration of U.S. and Near Eastern scholars in both training and research poses one of the most important and difficult problems for the field of Near Eastern scholarship," the report went on, pointing to an issue that would haunt the field for years to come. The assessment recommended that in addition to bolstering the strongest of the existing programs, Ford should "during the next two or three years . . . look for opportunities to help develop one or two more genuinely first class Near East graduate training centers," ideally one in the Middle West (perhaps at Indiana University or the University of Chicago) and another on the West Coast (perhaps at UCLA).[46]

As Robert A. McCaughey has discussed, Ford officers ultimately decided not to decide which specific area and international studies programs they should fund. Instead, John Howard, director of Ford's International Training and Research division, "decided to change ITR's strategy from funding relatively short-term individual projects that ITR judged to have merit to one of providing long-term funding to selected universities, each of which would then take it upon itself to decide which among its many international studies proposals and ongoing projects deserved support."[47] In June 1959 Ford's board of trustees endorsed this approach by approving a new program that would give certain universities large "institutional block grants" over multi-year periods, to be used at their discretion to support area and international studies over the long term.

In the program's first year, a total of $9.1 million went to area studies and another $6 million to international studies at just three universities: Harvard (which received $5.6 million altogether), Columbia ($5.5 million) and the University of California ($4 million, divided between Berkeley and UCLA). It was these block grants that, for example, enabled Harvard's Center for Middle Eastern Studies to hire new faculty and expand the range of its activities. In 1961 Ford awarded another $19.2 million in institutional grants for area and international studies to seven other universities: Chicago, Indiana, Michigan, Pennsylvania, Princeton, the University of Washington and Yale; the following year Cornell, Stanford and Wisconsin received a total of $7 million. Subsequent grants to universities totaled many millions more.[48] All told, according to one estimate, between 1959 and 1963 Ford gave $42 million in such long-term block grants to fifteen universities; about 62 percent of that total supported non-Western language and area studies.[49] This massive surge in spending—the equivalent of more than $200 million in 2015—in the space of just a few years far outstripped anything Ford, or any other foundation, had ever committed before.

Federal Funding Arrives at Long Last

The Ford and Rockefeller foundations' unprecedented munificence to area and international studies programs in the 1950s and early 1960s, mainly benefiting a limited number of elite private and public universities, certainly helped accelerate the expansion of Middle East studies and other area studies fields in this period, especially at those institutions on the receiving end of this windfall. But there was another development that fed the boom in area studies in the late 1950s and the early–mid 1960s, one which spread the wealth much more widely and evenly than the foundations had and led to the creation of new centers at universities which most likely would never have established them on their own. This was the creation, at long last, of a large-scale government program to fund area studies and training in non-Western languages.

This was something that the SSRC and others had been hoping for since the end of the Second World War and had worked particularly hard to achieve during the Korean War—all in vain. Now, changing circumstances finally made such a program politically possible. During the Second World War and through the first decade of the Cold War, the government had pumped billions of dollars into institutions of higher education, for contracted military, scientific and medical research (including Cold War-related area studies research projects funded by intelligence agencies or the military) as well as to enable veterans of the Second World War and then the Korean War to attend college (the GI bills). By the mid-1950s there were growing calls for more direct forms of federal aid to colleges and universities, to broaden access to higher education and increase the number of Americans proficient in foreign languages.[50] However, many conservatives, including powerful members of Congress representing southern states, vigorously opposed federal funding for higher education, in large part because they feared that an expanded federal role might undermine racial segregation. Then, in October 1957, at a time when concerns were already being voiced about the purportedly poor state of education in America and a supposed dire shortage of mathematicians and scientists, the Soviet Union launched Sputnik, the first human-made satellite to orbit the earth. This greatly magnified fears that the U.S. was falling behind the communist enemy in science and technology, and strengthened congressional and public support for unprecedented levels of federal spending on education, including higher education.[51]

In September 1958 President Eisenhower signed into law the National Defense Education Act (NDEA) which for the first time provided large-scale government funding directly to educational institutions to "insure trained manpower of sufficient quality and quantity to meet the national defense needs of the United States." The NDEA authorized massive new funding for a range of purposes, including student loans on generous terms to make higher education more widely accessible; expanded science, math and foreign language instruction in secondary schools; a new graduate student fellowship program to support the training of college and university teachers; and research on the effective use of educational media. Title VI of the act created a new program to fund university-based "centers for the teaching of any modern foreign language with respect to which the Commissioner [of Education] determines (1) that individuals trained in such language are needed by the Federal Government or by business, industry, or education in the United States, and (2) that adequate instruction in such language is not readily available in the United States." It also provided funding for the development of improved methods and materials to teach foreign languages, and fellowships for students undergoing training in these languages and in "other fields needed for a full understanding of the area, region, or country in which such language is commonly used. . . ."[52]

Congress initially authorized $8 million a year for Title VI, but the funds actually appropriated only reached that sum in 1962. Annual appropriations rose to $13 million in 1964 and to a high of $15.8 million in 1967, with centers for Middle East studies receiving a proportion that averaged around 13 percent of total Title VI spending.[53] Overall, almost $100 million was appropriated under Title VI in its first decade—the equivalent of approximately $700–800 million in 2015.[54] Universities were quick to secure federal funding to establish or expand centers for Middle East studies, hire faculty and fund graduate students. In 1951 there had been only five Middle East centers or programs, at Columbia, Dropsie College, the University of Michigan, Princeton and the School of Advanced International Studies. Harvard had established its Center for Middle Eastern Studies in 1954, while the University of California at Los Angeles founded its Center for Near Eastern Studies three years later. When Title VI funding became available several of the existing programs quickly applied for and secured federal support, including Harvard, Michigan and Princeton in 1959, and UCLA and SAIS in 1960. They were joined by new Title VI programs at Portland State University, the University of Texas and the University of Utah in 1960; at the University of California, Berkeley, Georgetown University and the University of Pennsylvania in 1965; and at New York University in 1967.[55] Altogether, twelve NDEA-supported Middle East centers were in operation by 1968, with around 300 affiliated faculty and some 8000 students enrolled in language and area courses.

A number of other universities, including Columbia and the University of Chicago, did not in this period have NDEA-funded Middle East centers but did secure Title VI fellowships to support some of their graduate students.[56]

When he signed the NDEA into law, President Eisenhower described it as an emergency measure that would be terminated after four years.[57] But some of its components, including Title VI, would live on for many decades to come, even if the program's survival was sometimes in doubt and the real value of the appropriations made under it fluctuated over time. Title VI provided a very important—and, compared to foundation grants, relatively stable and more widely distributed—stream of resources for area studies at American universities, a stream that helped the field expand dramatically in the late 1950s and early 1960s, and later enabled it to survive the diminution of foundation support.

Yet another channel through which federal dollars began flowing to U.S. area studies was also established in this period. In 1954 Congress had enacted the Agricultural Trade Development and Assistance Act (better known as Public Law 480), envisioned as both a boon to American farmers and a tool of the Cold War. Through what came to be known as the "Food for Peace" program, the law allowed poor countries to pay for food imports from the United States in their own (soft) currencies rather than in (hard) dollars. A 1958 amendment to PL 480, introduced by Representative John Dingell of Michigan, enabled the nonconvertible proceeds from such sales of U.S. agricultural commodities to be used for the acquisition of scientific and cultural goods and services. As Mortimer Graves, who had recently been compelled to step down as executive director of the ACLS but was still circulating memoranda, put it:

> This opens up most exciting prospects: the acquisition of the most significant publications in almost all the languages of Eastern Europe, Asia, Latin America, and Africa; their analysis, evaluation, and cataloguing; their deposit in numerous American research centers geographically dispersed through the United States; and even the integral translation of those most significant for our understanding of the thinking and the phenomena of the affected countries. It is hardly necessary to say that the successful implementation of such a program would mean the dawn of a new day in American understanding of the rest of the world, and American acquisition of knowledge not now available to us.
>
> All educational institutions making any attempt at area studies, research organizations in practically all fields of inquiry, industrial and commercial com-

panies with either research concerns or interests abroad, and the media of communication stand to profit from this measure.[58]

The Library of Congress and university libraries would use PL 480 funds to acquire books and periodicals published abroad, thereby building up their collections at relatively low cost.[59] These funds would also later be used to fund American research centers abroad and enable them to offer research fellowships, as well as to support the Center for Arabic Study Abroad in Cairo, whose establishment is discussed later in this chapter.

The CNME in its Heyday

SSRC officials had long wanted to strengthen the social science component of the CNME's membership, so that it could do more and better work promoting research on the contemporary Middle East, but this proved difficult. For example, it was only in 1958 that the reconstituted CNME finally acquired an economist, in the person of Charles Issawi (1916–2000), in this period one of the very few scholars in the United States conducting research on, and teaching about, the economies and economic history of the Middle East.[60] For a time the SSRC hoped to push things further, by sponsoring an initiative to integrate Middle East studies into its ongoing project to remake political science in the United States. The SSRC's Committee on Comparative Politics, which had been established in 1954 and was playing a central role in elaborating modernization theory, co-sponsored a seminar with the CNME in 1958 to discuss a program of research on political groups in the Middle East and Asia. But there does not seem to have been any follow-up and the initiative soon died. This is not really surprising: the social scientists on the committee were not particularly engaged with comparative politics as it was then taking shape in mainstream U.S. political science, while their humanist colleagues were likely to have been uninterested in such a project.[61] Meanwhile, the weight of the humanities on the CNME had been bolstered by the appointment that same year of the noted Orientalist Gustave von Grunebaum (1909–1972), director of UCLA's new Center for Near Eastern Studies.[62] Reflecting these and other changes, by 1958–1959 the committee consisted of four humanists (Gibb, von Grunebaum, Smith and Young) and three social scientists (Issawi, Khadduri and the archaeologist and ethnographer Louis Dupree).[63]

In late February–early March 1959 the CNME, on the initiative of Dankwart Rustow, for the first time convened a conference in the Middle East itself, attended by twenty-one American social scientists working on the region. Held in Tehran and funded by the CNME's Ford grant, the conference focused on the research climate in the region and on possibilities and prospects for social science research, but it also provided an opportunity for American scholars currently conducting research on the Middle East to share their experiences and knowledge of local resources with one another. According to Dankwart Rustow's report, much of the discussion at the conference "centered on the increasing restrictions placed on social science research in a number of Near Eastern countries, and the consequent need for reconciling the susceptibilities of host countries with the demands of long-range research planning and of scholarship."[64] Strikingly, every one of the conference presenters, discussants and attendees was American; not a single Iranian scholar was invited to participate. According to the minutes of CNME's next meeting, some committee members "expressed regret that local scholars had not been included in the meetings."[65] Cleon Swayzee, who held the CNME's pursestrings at Ford and was an advocate of greater collaboration between American and Middle Eastern scholars, was also concerned by their exclusion and raised the issue with committee chair T. Cuyler Young:

> In the first place, it seems to me fairly clear that most of the representatives to the conference saw themselves as individual research specialists and were not particularly interested in local scholars, except as local individuals or institutions might be of help in the carrying out of a planned project. Even those who were representatives of institutions with area programs or members of the SSRC Committee did not seem to have a deep concern with the problem of local social science research activity. There were frequent references to the undeveloped state of social science research and the difficulties which were encountered because of the unfavorable research climate, but these deficiencies were viewed simply as handicaps to be taken into account in the process of doing research.[66]

In discussing the issue subsequently, CNME members insisted that local scholars' "attendance would have precluded free discussion of research potentialities in the Middle East, a principal conference topic. If indigenous scholars had been included, a quite different sort of conference, with other objectives, would have resulted." They were likely correct in their belief that including Iranian scholars would have made for a "quite different sort of conference"—if not necessarily in the sense the CNME meant. At a some-what later committee meeting Pendleton Herring (probably feeling some heat from Ford) reported that P&P had asked "whether it would be desirable for the [committee] to find ways of stimulating the development of scholar-ship indigenous to the Near and Middle East." But CNME members felt that it would be inadvisable to take on this mission, and another decade would pass before the committee would come to see intellectual collaboration with Middle Eastern scholars as a priority.[67]

The Joint Committee in Action

Though Pendleton Herring had been rebuffed when he first raised the is-sue in 1956, the question of transforming the CNME into a joint ACLS-SSRC committee was not forgotten, and in 1959 the two academic organizations finally decided to proceed with this step. In a sense this change would simply bring the committee's formal status into line with what it was already doing: since its reconstitution in 1955 it had included leading scholars in the hu-manities as well as in the social sciences, and much of its work had concerned issues that had historically been the province of the ACLS. In 1957 Mortimer Graves had been forced to step down as the dominant figure at the ACLS, opening the way for the installation of new leadership and renewed external support for the organization; this likely contributed to smoother collabo-ration between the SSRC and the ACLS. In addition, most if not all of the SSRC's regional committees had been established as, or had become, joint committees, so it seemed appropriate that the CNME adopt this format as well. Last but not least, with the committee's Ford funding set to run out at the end of 1959–1960, there was a feeling that a joint committee would have a better chance of securing a larger grant from Ford.

Various bodies needed to approve the change, which took some months, but in May 1959 Herring formally informed CNME that it was to be re-established as a joint ACLS-SSRC committee. But he hastened to assure its members that, since it already included several humanists, this shift would not entail any sweeping change in its composition or mandate, though the new joint committee would probably need to broaden the temporal scope of its grant programs, hitherto restricted to the modern period. Commit-tee members welcomed this enlargement of its scope, as long as it did not lead to "greatly reduced support for social science research on the Middle East."[68] The first meeting of the Joint Committee on the Near and Middle East of the American Council of Learned Societies and the Social Science Research Council (JCNME) took place in October 1959. But despite the change in the formal sponsorship of the committee, the SSRC remained its primary institutional home: it continued to play the leading role in overseeing and supporting its operations, provided a staffperson for it and took the lead in selecting its members and securing funding for it, though nominally in consultation with the ACLS.

In its new format the JCNME mainly continued to pursue projects already under way, many of which involved developing the infrastructure of U.S. Middle East studies as an academic field. They included preparation of a handbook of anthropological research on the Middle East, similar to handbooks developed for a range of other fields; the development of improved teaching methods and materials for Middle Eastern languages; an annotated bibliography of Arabic publications; the translation from Polish into English of a manual on Ottoman archival materials; and continued collaboration with the Association of Research Libraries to develop library resources on the Middle East.[69] The committee also discussed organizing a summer institute for college teachers offering courses on the Middle East, but this does not seem to have materialized. In April 1960 the Ford Foundation awarded the joint committee a three-year grant of $200,000 for its operations and its research grant program—a significant increase over the previous Ford grant and another manifestation of Ford's largesse toward area studies in this boom period.

In this context, with Middle East studies palpably expanding and its prospects apparently bright, the JCNME began in 1960 to discuss for the first time whether and how scholars in this field might organize themselves. In October of that year H. A. R. Gibb, arguing that "the sheer paucity of scholars working in this field in North America created a need for more regular contact than was now possible," called for a conference that would showcase recent research but would also "bring together scholars actively engaged in teaching and research on the Islamic and modern Near and Middle East."[70] As I discuss in Chapter 7, a main purpose of the proposed conference was to gauge sentiment among scholars in the field about joining one of the existing scholarly associations or forming a new one, and then to determine how to proceed. The scholarly component of this conference was planned mainly by Gibb, Rustow and Schorger, along with the committee's SSRC staffer, Roland Mitchell, who had taught American history at MIT before joining the SSRC and who would work with the JCNME into the 1980s.

Held on October 20–22, 1961, at the Barclay Hotel in New York City, it was the first scholarly event the committee had organized in the United States in almost four and a half years—an indication of the extent to which it had focused on dimensions of field-building other than developing and promoting a research agenda for Middle East studies.[71] Thirty-three men— they were indeed all men—attended the Barclay Hotel conference, mostly university-based scholars. Three papers, circulated in advance but apparently never published, were presented and discussed: "The Self-Image of Islamic Culture," by H. A. R. Gibb; "The Social Community in the Contemporary Near East," by William Schorger (a replacement for Morroe Berger, who declined the invitation to present); and "The Political Community in the Contemporary Near East," by political scientist Leonard Binder.[72] The conference marked a high-point for the JCNME in its original composition: it generated no intellectual agenda or follow-up, and the committee appears to have run out of steam soon thereafter. Though it continued to meet regularly to review applications for, and award, the Ford-funded postdoctoral research grants at its disposal, it now had no major projects on its agenda and spent a great deal of time engaged in fruitless discussions of possible future research activities. In this sense the JCNME replicated the experience of its predecessor the CNME: it experienced an initial burst of energy and then sank into lassitude. In the long run, then, the October 1961 conference's scholarly impact was less important than the quest for professional organization that it helped set in motion.

JCNME members were well aware of the committee's loss of energy and focus. At its May 1962 meeting one member "summed up his impression of the discussion saying that while the joint committee had accomplished a good deal in the past in the services it had performed and projects it had undertaken, it appeared to him that the joint committee had no very clear idea of what it might do in the future other than administer the grants program."[73] At the same time, SSRC leaders began to voice concerns about what they characterized as a need to strengthen the "analytical social science content" of the joint committee's activities, which they saw as too oriented toward the humanities.[74] At the end of the 1961–1962 academic year they decided to shake things up by changing much of the committee's membership, though it may also have been the case that some of the veteran members decided they had given enough time to this endeavor and chose to move on. Thus in the middle of 1962 T. Cuyler Young left the committee he had led since 1955; he was replaced as chair by Egyptologist John A. Wilson (1899–1976), who had run the University of Chicago's Oriental Institute for a decade, had been involved with ACLS committees for the field going back to the late 1930s and had joined the JCNME in 1960. Gibb, Khadduri, Rustow and Smith also stepped down, though Schorger and von Grunebaum remained. Among the new members appointed was Princeton sociologist Morroe Berger. He was by this point the leading American sociologist working on the Middle East, though he did not have much competition for that distinction because there were still very few sociologists in the field.[75] From this point onward, the SSRC and ACLS would rotate people on and off the committee much more regularly, usually retaining a core membership for some years to ensure continuity while replacing or adding other members almost every year.

Since 1955 the CNME/JCNME had devoted itself primarily to securing resources for the field and building its infrastructure; as a result it had largely neglected its mandate to formulate and implement a research agenda for the field. Now that issue surfaced once again: in the late fall of 1962, at the first meeting of the committee in its new composition, Morroe Berger proposed that it seek "to promote, induce, and implement good research on numerous questions that are currently neglected." The examples of research topics he proposed included "the current religious organization of Islamic countries," "Islamic law and the legal systems of the various countries," "the physical and human structure of cities," "the social consequences of the development of the petroleum industry." But as had often been the case, committee members could not agree on a research agenda.[76] Ford renewed the committee's grant for another three years in December 1962, giving it $150,000 for research grants and $30,000 to support its activities—equivalent in total to $1.4 million in 2015. But over the months that followed the JCNME achieved no progress in planning research, and in September 1963 the ACLS and SSRC again intervened, apparently in the hope that shaking up its membership once more and beefing up its social science component would enable it to escape the doldrums.

John Wilson now left the committee, apparently much to his relief; as he wrote to Pendleton Herring, "Although I have enjoyed the associations and derived a great deal of profit from being on the Committee, I fear that the decision to turn the problems over to other people is a wise one. Last year I felt it difficult to keep the discussions on a realistic track and did not myself have the imagination sufficient to combine realism with vision."[77] Morroe Berger took over as chair, and the SSRC added Leonard Binder (who now also joined the SSRC's Committee on Political Behavior, established in 1949); the University of Chicago historian of Islam Marshall G. S. Hodgson (1922–1968); Charles Issawi, who had served on the committee earlier; and political scientist Malcolm H. Kerr (1931–1984) of UCLA.[78] In 1964 they were joined by Bernard Lewis (born 1916) of the School of Oriental and African Studies at the University of London, the first time someone not based at an American or Canadian university had been appointed to the committee. Anxious to prioritize the committee's research mission, Berger proposed that it undertake an inquiry into the state of Middle East studies in the United States with a focus on research and graduate training. This would complement the survey of undergraduate education on the Middle East that J. C. Hurewitz had recently conducted. There was some skepticism about the utility of such an inquiry, but in the end Berger and Issawi were empowered to develop a questionnaire that, it was hoped, could yield useful information. What data this initiative yielded is not clear, but Berger seems to have drawn on it for the (rather gloomy) assessment of the field's prospects that he published in 1967.[79]

In contrast to its inactivity on the research front, the committee's engagement with Middle Eastern language instruction picked up steam again in this period. In 1963 the CNME noted that for Arabic, Persian and Turkish there was no "generally accepted standard in respect to what should be taught in the classical literary, the modern literary, or the modern colloquial forms." The committee subsequently sponsored a small conference of Arabic language teachers to address the issue of standardization. This was a problem with which teachers of Arabic were already grappling, individually but also collectively, at a series of conferences for teachers of Arabic convened since 1958 at several universities, and then at the annual meetings of the Modern Language Association. These efforts, along with the attainment at long last of a critical mass in Arabic instruction in the United States, in terms of numbers of instructors, programs and students, culminated in the formation in 1963 of the American Association of Teachers of Arabic.[80]

Under pressure from the SSRC to show more active leadership in setting the field's scholarly agenda and encouraging exploration of understudied or altogether neglected topics, the JCNME decided in 1963–1964 to adopt a different approach. Still unable to develop its own research agenda, it resolved to instead use the funds at its disposal to support a series of academic conferences on specific themes organized in collaboration with university-based area studies centers. By this means it finally began in the mid-to-late 1960s to have a significant impact on the intellectual life of North American Middle East studies, and the volumes published as a result of at least two of those conferences—on Middle Eastern cities and on economic history—offer a clear indication of how far the field had come over the past decade or so.

The first of this series of conferences was held in May 1965 at New York University, which would not have a Near Eastern studies department until the following year, when R. Bayly Winder arrived from Princeton to found and lead it, followed a year later by a Title VI area studies center. Kemal Karpat, then assistant professor of comparative government and international relations at NYU, organized the conference, which focused on social change and democracy in contemporary Turkey. It brought together a number of U.S.-based scholars of Turkey but also Bülent Ecevit, then a member of Turkey's parliament and later prime minister, whose presentation discussed "labor in Turkey as a new social and political force." The resulting volume, edited by Kemal Karpat and titled *Social Change and Politics in Turkey: A Structural-Historical Analysis*, would be published in 1973.[81]

The committee co-sponsored another conference, on urbanism in the Middle East, held at the University of California, Berkeley, in October 1966, in conjunction with the university's Center for Middle Eastern Studies, founded three years earlier. Ira Lapidus would prepare the conference papers for publication; the volume that resulted appeared in 1969 as *Middle Eastern Cities: A Symposium on Ancient, Islamic, and Contemporary Middle Eastern Urbanism*, including chapters by Janet Abu-Lughod, Oleg Grabar, S. D. Goitein and Ira Lapidus, among others.[82] This was the first edited volume resulting from a scholarly conference sponsored by the SSRC's Committee on the Near and Middle East since the publication of *Social Forces in the Middle East* fourteen years earlier. The JCNME helped fund yet another conference, the plans for which were developed mainly by Bernard Lewis, on the economic history of the Middle East, held at the School of Oriental and African Studies in London in July 1967. The volume that resulted was edited by Michael Cook and published in 1970 as *Studies in the Economic History of the Middle East*. It was in many respects a landmark book for its attention to the hitherto very understudied fields of Middle Eastern economic and social history.

Meanwhile, the committee continued its field-building work. Perhaps most significantly, in 1965–1966 the committee played a leading role in creating a new Arabic-language training program located in the Middle East. There were several antecedents for this initiative. In 1961 the Carnegie Corporation had begun to fund a program, run by Princeton, to send ten to fifteen promising undergraduates annually for a year of language training at the Middle East Centre for Arabic Studies (MECAS) in Shimlan, Lebanon. Established by the British Foreign Office at that location in 1947 to teach Arabic to its staff, Lebanese often called it the "spy school" because a substantial number of its graduates were reputed to work for British or other intelligence agencies. In 1964 Portland State University launched a summer program in Egyptian colloquial Arabic at the American University in Cairo.

In 1966 the JCNME began discussions with officials at the U.S. Office of Education (until 1979 part of the Department of Health, Education and Welfare) about funding for a new program for advanced Arabic-language training, and CNME member William Brinner explored possible sites while on a trip to the region in March–April 1966. He concluded that the American University in Cairo (AUC) offered the best location for the proposed center, federal funding was secured, and a committee of American Arabists representing a consortium of U.S. universities began to work with AUC officials on plans for what would be called the Center for Arabic Study Abroad (CASA), to be administered by an interuniversity committee which Brinner himself would chair. Because of the June 1967 war, the first group of twenty CASA students spent the fall 1967 semester studying in Berkeley rather than Cairo, though the program was established at AUC soon thereafter.[83]

Though neither the CNME nor the JCNME achieved as much as the SSRC had hoped in terms of its mission to guide scholarly research in Middle East studies, it did contribute substantially to the development of the field's infrastructure between the mid-1950s and the mid-1960s. The rapid growth of

U.S. Middle East studies in this period, fueled by an unprecedented surge of both foundation and federal funding, was manifested in a dramatic increase in the number of Middle East studies centers, programs and departments at universities across the country, a growing body of faculty and students, and the availability of a substantial array of sources of financial support for research and training. These included the CNME's own relatively small grant program, various foundation and government fellowships (including the Ford Foundation's Foreign Area Fellowship Program, the Title VI-funded National Defense Foreign Language fellowships as well as the Fulbright and Fulbright-Hays fellowships), and the fellowships now available (thanks to the PL 480 program) from the American Research Center in Egypt (founded in 1948) and the American Research Institute in Turkey (founded in 1964).[84] Along the way there appeared new cohorts of scholars and teachers trained, partially or wholly, within the programs, institutions and networks that the emergence of area studies had created. From the early 1960s they and others were increasingly convinced that Middle East studies now required, and could sustain, a higher level of professional organization, perhaps even a national membership organization of its own. The path toward achieving that goal would, however, be long and complex.

7 "A Need for More Regular Contact"

It is . . . probable that the earlier failures helped ensure the success of MESA: while people became warier, they also felt more and more that it was about time an organization was founded.

—I. William Zartman, 1970

MEMBERS OF THE JCNME began to discuss whether to seek, and how to achieve, a higher level of professional organization for scholars in U.S. Middle East studies as early as 1960, launching a process that, after many twists and turns, culminated in the founding of the Middle East Studies Association (MESA) six years later. But in fact MESA was preceded by another, now largely forgotten, organization that, while not claiming or seeking to be the professional-academic membership association that many in the field were coming to feel was both necessary and feasible, nonetheless for a time played an active role in promoting Middle East studies and connecting scholars, teachers and others with one another. This organization's trajectory, and MESA's, illustrate some of the complexities involved in establishing and sustaining a national organization for this emerging academic field.

Henry Siegman's Big Idea

Established in 1959, the American Association for Middle East Studies (AAMES) played an active role in the field for about five years; it then very quickly faded from memory. Its virtual disappearance from the historical record is due, at least in part, to the fact that most of the space that it sought to occupy was quickly taken over by the much more successful and durable Middle East Studies Association. But it may well also have had something to do with AAMES' actual or alleged political associations and agenda, which probably contributed to its demise and led even academics who had been involved with it to put it out of mind.

AAMES' founder and moving spirit was Henry Siegman, who served as its executive secretary and editor of its newsletter from its inception until its demise in 1964 or 1965. In fact, although Siegman recruited leading scholars in the field to serve on the association's board of trustees and participate in its programs and activities, and although a good many faculty and students from across the country signed up as members, AAMES was throughout its lifespan more or less a one-man show run on a shoe-string budget. Siegman was born in 1930 in Germany, where his father was active in the religious-Zionist movement. When the Nazis came to power his family fled Germany and eventually made its way to the United States. He served as a U.S. Army chaplain during the Korean War and graduated from City College. As Siegman tells the story, in the late 1950s, while he was studying at the New School for Social Research in New York, he was asked by Rabbi Irving Miller, at the time president of the American Zionist Council (AZC), to develop a plan to enhance Israel's standing in the American academic community.[1] Originally founded in 1939 as the Emergency Committee for Zionist Affairs and subsequently renamed several times, the AZC was in the 1950s the main coordinating body for all the Zionist organizations operating in the United States. Its lobbying wing, the American Zionist Committee for Public Relations, which among other things worked to secure U.S. aid to Israel, had been active since 1951; it was renamed the American Israel Public Affairs Committee (AIPAC) in 1959 and by the 1970s would establish itself as one of the country's most powerful and effective lobbying organizations.

According to Siegman, Rabbi Miller was primarily interested in advancing the AZC's pro-Israel public relations work among academics. However, Siegman says he told Miller that, in the long run, a strictly nonpolitical and academic association promoting the growing field of Middle East studies in the United States would most effectively redound to Israel's benefit and enhance its standing in American academic life. Siegman relates that though the AZC had no interest in such an initiative, Miller himself was broad-minded and helped him secure funding from a Philadelphia foundation with which to launch the kind of organization Siegman proposed. (I will have more to say about AAMES' initial funding shortly.) According to Siegman, he then proceeded to consult with acquaintances in the field, especially J. C. Hurewitz at Columbia, and through him got to know other well-known figures, including Charles Issawi (then also at Columbia) and Majid Khadduri of SAIS. Finally, at a 1959 meeting convened by Thomas Clark Pollock, dean of arts and science at NYU from 1947 to 1962, AAMES was officially launched, describing itself as a nonprofit, nonpolitical educational organization seeking to foster public interest in, and the scholarly study of, the Middle East. For most of its existence Pollock would serve as the association's president and the eminent Biblical archaeologist William F. Albright as chair of its board of trustees.[2]

As Hurewitz later described it, AAMES saw its primary mission as fostering "interest in the Middle East at the undergraduate level in colleges and universities across the country."[3] In this sense it can be seen as sharing the emphasis that Mortimer Graves and the ACLS had placed on undergraduate education about the non-Western world in the 1930s, 1940s and early 1950s, rather than the SSRC's focus on social science research and graduate training. Siegman and his associates were particularly interested in enhancing the ability of college faculty with no expertise on the Middle East to offer quality instruction about the region and in making such instruction an established component of the undergraduate curriculum, especially at smaller colleges which lacked significant human and library resources in this field.

Toward that end, soon after its inception AAMES commissioned J. C. Hurewitz to conduct a survey of courses, instructors and resources on the Middle East for undergraduates at colleges and universities in the United States; according to Siegman the Ford Foundation provided funding for the survey. The report that Hurewitz produced, published in 1962, explained that the survey's purposes were "to determine the overall problems to which the rapid spread of Middle East studies has given rise and to establish an order of priority among indicated corrective methods," and to "further guidelines for the Association's future program."[4] Hurewitz detailed the problems that he found to be afflicting undergraduate education on the Middle East, including "the generally low level of library resources on the Middle East," "the even more meager supply of textbooks and related teaching aids, and the prevalence of overtrained and undertrained instructors." (53) He asserted that the

JCNME "functioned in effect as a liaison agency for the centers" established with foundation support at a number of large universities but that it "has shown almost no interest in undergraduate education on the Middle East." Moreover, he argued, "the foundations have patently neglected the development of library resources and textbooks on the Middle East." (61, 63) The *New York Times* published an article summarizing the findings of Hurewitz's survey under the headline "Mid-East Studies Found Ill-Taught."[5]

To address the deficiencies that Hurewitz's survey documented, AAMES launched a series of initiatives. One of its main activities from its inception was organizing summer workshops (called Faculty Institutes) designed to educate college and university faculty about the Middle East so they could teach their students more effectively—a pedagogical model which the ACLS had deployed from the late 1920s and which had even earlier precedents. These began modestly in July 1960 with a two-week workshop held at Thiel College in Pennsylvania in which Majid Khadduri participated. Similar sessions were held in subsequent years at the University of Illinois and Williams College. By 1963 the summertime Faculty Institute that AAMES organized, held at the University of Utah's Middle East Center, stretched over eight weeks, featured lectures by H. A. R. Gibb, Philip Hitti and Charles Issawi, among others, and included faculty from colleges across the country. AAMES also sponsored a Visiting Scholar Program which brought faculty from some of the Title VI centers (among them Gustave von Grunebaum and Dankwart Rustow) to small colleges for lectures, and in 1961 it organized a workshop at Brooklyn College for high school teachers. In the summer of 1963, with partial funding from PL 480 funds provided by the State Department through the Fulbright-Hays program, AAMES organized a faculty seminar which took fourteen college and university faculty on a seven-week trip to Egypt and Israel; there they met with faculty at institutions of higher education, government officials and others.[6] AAMES sought Ford Foundation funding for additional summer faculty trips in 1965 and 1966, but it went out of existence before plans for those trips got very far.[7]

In addition to its effort to strengthen undergraduate teaching about the Middle East, AAMES worked to keep those involved in the field connected and informed, with some degree of success. Its newsletter, eventually titled *Middle East Studies*, ostensibly a quarterly but sometimes published less regularly, disseminated news about language training programs and resources, academic conferences, available research and travel grants, Title VI awards and faculty appointments. It also featured longer articles on issues in the field, for example a discussion of "Arabic Language Instruction in the United States: Instructional Materials" by Aziz S. Atiyah of the University of Utah, an essay on "New Approaches to Oriental Civilizations" by Irene Gendzier of Boston University, and a report on the 25th Congress of Orientalists in Moscow by an anonymous participant. Its board, committees and programs encompassed a range of prominent scholars in the field, including (at various points) Gustave von Grunebaum, Joseph Schacht, Majid Khadduri, Hisham Sharabi and J. C. Hurewitz, along with William F. Albright and Salo Baron.

Last but not least, AAMES launched a rather ambitious program to promote and subsidize the publication of books and bibliographies that college faculty could utilize for more effective teaching and from which the interested general public might benefit as well. The first book published under its auspices was *Government and Politics of the Middle East*, by Maurice Harari, which appeared in 1962 and offered an accessible survey of the politics and history of a number of Middle Eastern countries in the modern and contemporary periods. AAMES set forth the goals of its publishing program in the book's front matter:

> The growth of undergraduate instruction on the Middle East in recent years, part of a mounting interest in non-Western studies in American higher education, has created a number of problems that have gone largely unattended. One of these problems is the lack of teaching materials—textbooks, supplementary readings, and source materials—suitable for instruction on the area. Maurice Harari's book, sponsored by the American Association for Middle East Studies, is intended to help alleviate this problem.
>
> It is hoped that Dr. Harari's book will find an audience among responsible citizens with an adult interest in world affairs.[8]

Under an arrangement with Atherton Press, a division of Prentice-Hall, AAMES' Publications Committee—chaired by Majid Khadduri and composed of George Hourani, J. C. Hurewitz, Daniel Lerner, A. J. Meyer, Richard Nolte and Hisham Sharabi—also subsidized and oversaw the publication of Richard Nolte's edited volume *The Modern Middle East* (1963), I. William Zartman's *Problems of New Power in Morocco* (1964) and Lester G. Seligman's *Leadership in a New Nation: Political Development in Israel* (1964).[9] AAMES awarded an annual prize "for the manuscript that has made the most distinguished contribution to contemporary Middle East scholarship" and worked to get the manuscript published.

It will be noted that many of the scholars who participated in AAMES' activities were also connected with the JCNME. Henry Siegman had in fact contacted the committee in 1960 to inform it of his intention to organize summer workshops for college faculty teaching courses about the Middle East and to ask about the committee's own plans, so as to avoid duplication. The committee was not interested in formal collaboration with AAMES, but clearly many JCNME members and other leading scholars in the field felt that AAMES' professional and curricular development work, and its efforts to boost the standing and visibility of U.S. Middle East studies, were valuable and so were quite willing to sign up as members and to participate actively in its programs.[10]

In his 1962 report Hurewitz had recommended that AAMES reconsider its current dual aims of promoting Middle East studies at the undergraduate level and trying to raise standards, and instead give priority to improving quality: "... area studies must be made academically respectable and must be thoroughly assimilated into the curriculum, if they are to endure. At present far too many schools have undertaken Middle East instruction with untrained teachers, poor libraries, and nonexistent teaching aids. Instead of instructing the students they are simply turning the uninformed into the misinformed." (66) Toward this end Hurewitz urged AAMES to assume an "advisory and coordinating function" for the field, including the organization of conferences on undergraduate pedagogy on the Middle East, the development of library resources, and the expansion of its summer seminars for college faculty and its visiting faculty program. In fact, implementing even some of these recommendations was well beyond the human and material resources available to AAMES. Perpetually short of funds, it had to cancel its 1962 annual meeting owing to financial difficulties, and Siegman's fundraising efforts do not seem to have been very successful. This may well have contributed to the organization's demise sometime in 1964 or early 1965. Its last public manifestation may have been a press release dated December 1964 in which it announced that its Prize Committee, headed by Princeton's T. Cuyler Young and including C. Ernest Dawn, George Hourani, J. C. Hurewitz and A. J. Meyer, had awarded AAMES' annual prize for best manuscript to Rouhollah K. Ramazani of the University of Virginia; it would be published in 1966 by the University Press of Virginia as *The Foreign Policy of Iran: A Developing Nation in World Affairs, 1500–1941.*[11]

The Zionist Connection?

According to Henry Siegman, AAMES folded because he accepted a full-time position on the staff of what was then called the National Jewish Community Relations Advisory Council, founded in 1944 by the Council of Jewish Federations to combat antisemitism, promote tolerance and pluralism in American society and foster good relations between Jews and non-Jews.[12] As Siegman tells it, he had run AAMES more or less on his own: it functioned largely because of the time and energy he put into it, his abilities as an organizer and fundraiser, and his personal relationships with board members. As a result, when he took a full-time job elsewhere there was no one to replace him, and so AAMES ceased to function.[13]

It seems, however, that there may be more to the story. In his unpublished account of the events leading up to the formation of the Middle East Studies Association in 1966, I. William Zartman (who would play important roles both in running that organization and as a member of the JCNME) asserted that AAMES "fell to the Arab-Israel split," "apparently because of an alleged connection with Zionist circles."[14] AAMES does in fact seem to have had covert Zionist connections, a fact which first came to light in 1963 and may well have contributed to its demise.

In the last years of the Eisenhower administration and the early years of the Kennedy administration, U.S. government officials had repeatedly expressed concern about what they regarded as lobbying and other activity on behalf of Israel by entities that were not properly registered as agents of the Israeli government under the Foreign Agents Registration Act (FARA). Those entities included the AZC and AIPAC. In 1963 the Senate Foreign Relations Committee, chaired by Senator J. William Fulbright, took up the issue in the context of a wide-ranging investigation into lobbying on behalf of a number of foreign governments by individuals and organizations not registered as agents of those governments, as required by law. On May 23 and August 1, 1963, the committee held hearings on lobbying and public relations activity on behalf of Israel orchestrated and funded by the Jewish Agency-American Section, Inc., the American affiliate of the Jewish Agency for Israel. When the latter entity was founded in 1929 as the Jewish Agency for Palestine, it was supposed to represent the interests of both Zionist and non-Zionist Jews worldwide in the development of the Jewish "national home" in Palestine. But it soon fell under Zionist control and functioned as the de facto leadership of the Jewish community in Palestine. After 1948, while formally a non-state institution primarily involved in Jewish immigration, settlement and economic development in Israel, it was in reality under the effective control of the Israeli government.

The Fulbright committee hearings demonstrated that the Jewish Agency-American Section, which since 1960 had not been registered as an agent of the Israeli government under FARA, was passing funds from the Jewish Agency for Israel, headquartered in Jerusalem, to American organizations such as the American Zionist Council in order to support their activities on behalf of Israel in the United States.[15] Those activities included paying for subscriptions to AIPAC's publication *Near East Report*, thereby indirectly subsidizing lobbying on Israel's behalf, and funding the Jewish Telegraphic Agency, an ostensibly independent news service. But with the AZC and the Louis M. Rabinowitz Foundation (founded in 1944 by a Jewish clothing manufacturer) serving as conduits, funding was also channeled from Israel to an entity called the Council for Middle Eastern Affairs, established by the predecessor of the American Zionist Council—the same Zionist umbrella organization whose president had supported Siegman's launching of AAMES. From 1950 onward the Council for Middle Eastern Affairs had published a journal called *Middle Eastern Affairs*, edited by the Israeli scholar Benjamin Shwadran (born 1907), formerly director of the American Zionist Emergency Council's research department; in the early 1960s it appeared ten times a year.

As Martin Kramer has put it, "To some extent, *Middle Eastern Affairs* represented a response to the *Middle East Journal*, which had been published by the Middle East Institute since 1947. . . . The two publications propounded alternative and sometimes opposite views of the Middle East, at a time when the United States sought to define its new role as a great power in the region." Kramer apparently meant that while the *Middle East Journal* (funded in part by donations from U.S. oil companies and others doing business in the region) took a "pro-Arab" stance, *Middle Eastern Affairs* was "pro-Israel" in its perspective. Over its lifespan of fourteen years, many senior American scholars of the Middle East published in *Middle Eastern Affairs* or served on its editorial advisory board. We have no evidence as to whether any of them knew that the journal's publisher, the Council for Middle Eastern Affairs, and through it this ostensibly scholarly and independent journal, were actually funded by an organ of the State of Israel to the tune of $48,000 a year in 1958 and 1959 (the equivalent of almost $400,000 in 2015), though by 1963 the annual subsidy seems to have dropped to just under $19,000 (the equivalent of $147,000).[16]

In response to a query from Senator Fulbright, Victor Rabinowitz (1911–2007), a prominent left-wing lawyer who had assumed the presidency of the Rabinowitz Foundation when his father died in 1957, explained that in serving as a conduit for funding to the Council for Middle Eastern Affairs the foundation had simply been continuing a practice that had begun in his father's day and that he had not known that the Jewish Agency was a representative of the Israeli government. However, Rabinowitz informed Fulbright that, "under the circumstances, the foundation no longer cared to receive funds from any source for transmittal to the Council on Middle Eastern Affairs [sic]." *Middle Eastern Affairs* abruptly ceased to appear a few months after it was revealed that it had been secretly subsidized by what Bayly Winder would later delicately refer to as "politically concerned parties," probably because the Jewish Agency-American Section cut off funding once the source of that funding had become public knowledge.[17]

These revelations must have heightened suspicions about covert efforts by Israel and by Zionist organizations to influence scholarship on the Middle East in the United States, suspicions which affected AAMES as well. William F. Albright, chair of AAMES' board of trustees, was in 1963 also a member of both the editorial advisory board of *Middle Eastern Affairs* and the board of directors of its publisher the Council for Middle Eastern Affairs, now revealed to be an Israeli front organization. But the Fulbright hearings also implicated AAMES directly, because they yielded evidence that Henry Siegman's organization had links with Zionist funding sources and public relations efforts. Documents entered as evidence at the hearings showed that Jewish Agency funds channeled through the AZC had provided AAMES with a total of $1700 in 1959 and another $600 in 1960 (equivalent in total to almost $19,000 in 2015)—apparently some or all of the funds which had made it possible for Henry Siegman to convene AAMES' founding conference and get his organization up and running. Asked about these funds by Senator Fulbright, Gottlieb Hammer, executive vice chairman of the Jewish Agency-American

Section, insisted that he had never heard of AAMES and had no idea what the payments to it were for. Fulbright did not pursue the matter by subpoenaing Henry Siegman or anyone else associated with AAMES.[18]

Siegman adamantly denies that he ever wittingly received funds from the AZC and insists that, as far as he knew, the money with which AAMES was launched came from a Philadelphia foundation, through the good offices of Rabbi Miller.[19] Beyond the $2300 in 1959–1960 that we know about, there is no firm evidence that AAMES received additional financial support from or through the AZC or another conduit thereafter. However, the published record of Senator Fulbright's committee hearings included an internal AZC memorandum outlining the plans for the 1962–1963 budget year of that organization's Committee on Information and Public Relations, to be funded by the Jewish Agency-American Section, which listed "Support for the American Association for Middle East Studies" as a component of its work in "Academic Circles." Other AZC activities under this rubric included "Cultivation of leaders in the academic community" and "Cooperation with colleges and universities in setting up of seminars on the Middle East." The AZC thus seems to have regarded support for AAMES as a way to further its mission of "projecting a positive image of Israel on the American scene," though it is not clear what form that support took after 1960.[20]

It is hard to discern any explicitly Zionist tone or content, or propagandizing on behalf of Israel, in AAMES' publications or activities. Nonetheless, it is not impossible that AAMES received funding from the Jewish Agency or some other Israeli source after 1960, directly or indirectly, and that, as with *Middle Eastern Affairs* and its publisher, the termination of that funding after the Fulbright committee's hearings contributed to the organization's demise. In any case, the revelations that AAMES had, at a minimum, received some or all of its initial funding from the country's leading Zionist organization, that it continued to be seen by the AZC as a valuable component of its public relations campaign on behalf of Israel and that some of AAMES' leaders were also associated with another Zionist-funded academic enterprise no doubt went some way toward undermining the organization's credibility and raising suspicions about its real agenda, especially as tensions between Israel and the Arab states intensified from 1964 onward.

Notwithstanding its links with the American Zionist movement and the murky circumstances surrounding its demise, AAMES in its relatively short lifespan kept people informed of what was going on in U.S. Middle East studies and worked assiduously to promote undergraduate education on the region. In so doing, and as a national membership organization, it contributed significantly to fostering a sense of Middle East studies as a distinct, country-wide academic field with common challenges and accomplishments, just as an influx of government and foundation funding was stimulating that field's expansion and its institutional density. It thus for a time filled a gap that neither the JCNME nor the university-based Middle East studies centers nor the Middle East Institute, oriented primarily to Washington policymakers and U.S. business interests in the region, were able, or aspired, to fill. Indeed, though it was not designed as, and never sought to be, an academic-professional organization for Middle East studies, and did not organize scholarly conferences or publish a scholarly journal, AAMES nonetheless performed some of the functions that the Middle East Studies Association would later assume, and its activities no doubt prompted those working in this field to consider more seriously the formation of a professional organization for it.

In Search of a Home

The JCNME had been in contact with AAMES from early in the latter organization's life and does not seem to have perceived it as a threat or a rival. Indeed, a number of committee members (and many others in the field) readily participated in AAMES' activities. Moreover, the committee's encounter with Siegman's outfit helped prompt a discussion in February 1960—apparently the first of its kind—about whether the time had come to move toward establishing a membership association for scholars in the field, similar to the Association for Asian Studies (founded in 1941 as the Far Eastern Association, an outgrowth of the ACLS' efforts in that field over the previous decade, and renamed in 1956), the African Studies Association (founded in 1957) or the American Association for the Advancement of Slavic Studies (established in 1948 but relaunched in 1960 as a national professional membership organization).[21] H. A. R. Gibb also raised the related question of a scholarly journal for the field. These issues would occupy an increasingly important place on the committee's agenda in the years to come.

No one seems to have envisioned AAMES as a possible vehicle for organizing U.S. Middle East studies: it seemed for a time to serve certain useful purposes, but for the longer-term needs of the field something quite different was called for. As a result, at several meetings during 1960 JCNME members discussed whether the American Oriental Society, founded in 1842, might serve as the scholarly association that this growing field now seemed to need. Wilfrid Cantwell Smith vigorously rejected the idea, arguing that the AOS "reflected the European tradition of training in the classics" and "does not include or fully meet the needs of social scientists and humanists with interests outside the ancient period." Dankwart Rustow concurred, noting that "unlike some of his social science colleagues who had resigned from the American Oriental Society in protest several years ago, he had never joined the Society." He added that "he saw no good reason to expect that any organization should be able to meet equally the needs of cuneiform specialists interested in ancient Babylonia and of political scientists interested in the contemporary Near East" and suggested that scholars with interests like his might actually be happiest as members of the Association for Asian Studies. There was also some discussion of whether the *Middle East Journal*, published by the policy- and business-oriented Middle East Institute and at the time experiencing financial difficulties, might serve the needs of scholars; but Young argued that "either by draft or design, the editorial staff had cut itself off from effective contact with the scholarly community."

Gibb's position was that "the sheer paucity of scholars working in this field in North America created a need for more regular contact than was now possible," and so he called for a conference that would "bring together scholars actively engaged in teaching and research on the Islamic and modern Near and Middle East." Committee members were uncertain whether or not there was in fact a "groundswell" of sentiment for a membership organization for American scholars studying the Middle East. But they eventually agreed to organize a conference that would bring together key faculty at the major Middle East centers, and others by invitation, to discuss research on the Middle East but also to gauge sentiment for joining or establishing a scholarly association and address other issues of common interest.[22]

Before that conference convened in October 1961, T. Cuyler Young circulated to participants a preliminary statement explaining that, beyond discussion of the scholarly papers to be presented there (see Chapter 6), the committee saw the conference as an opportunity "to discuss the prospect and attendant problems of continued discourse among members of the scholarly community interested in Islamic and modern Near and Middle Eastern studies," including initiating periodic meetings of such scholars and students as well as their affiliation with an existing scholarly entity or the formation of an entirely new membership organization.[23] The final session of the conference was therefore devoted to a discussion of "Professional Concerns." There seems to have been broad agreement at the session on the need for a higher level of scholarly association in the field, and out of the conference there emerged a "Cooperating Committee on the Development and Organization of Near Eastern Studies," composed of JCNME members Schorger and von Grunebaum along with the historian of Islamic art Oleg Grabar (Michigan), political scientist Manfred Halpern (Princeton), J. C. Hurewitz (Columbia) and Lewis V. Thomas (Princeton). Its mandate, as the JCNME minutes described it, was to "investigate the possibilities of promoting better communication among scholars working on Near and Middle Eastern Studies, through the instrumentalities of publications, annual meetings, or a membership association." The joint committee agreed to provide up to $500 to support the Cooperating Committee's activities, "while taking no responsibility for [its] deliberations or conclusions. . . ."[24]

The new Cooperating Committee held three meetings in 1962–1963 and explored a number of options. Committee members first approached the Association for Asian Studies, proposing an arrangement whereby for a period of three years the AAS would act as an "umbrella" for scholars of the Middle East, accepting them as members and enabling them to organize panels at its annual meetings, after which they would decide whether they were in a position to organize their own association. But the terms for affiliation offered by the AAS board of directors, which seems to have felt that the association already included too many disparate and troublesome elements, proved unacceptable. The Cooperating Committee was then compelled to decide whether to persist in seeking some form of affiliation with the AOS or move toward establishing an independent organization. All but one member (J. C. Hurewitz) voted against trying to launch an independent organization, on the grounds that the field was not yet ready for such a step, though the AOS option (which von Grunebaum favored) did not seem palatable or even feasible either. The possibility of transforming the Middle East Institute in a more scholarly direction was also broached but abandoned. Eventually, by the process of elimination, establishing a new organization came to seem the best option, but it remained unclear how that goal could be achieved; nor did discussion of launching a scholarly journal for the field yield any concrete results.[25]

The Cooperating Committee met for the last time in January 1963, without having made much headway. Before that final meeting, the JCNME's SSRC staffperson Roland Mitchell, clearly frustrated, proposed that the committee simply take the initiative by sending out a call for a national Middle East studies conference at some convenient location and developing a program for it.

> . . . it would be made clear that one of the purposes of the conference would be to ascertain whether the time was ripe for the establishment of a permanent scholarly organization—and, that a solid bit of data for reaching a conclusion would be the number of individuals who would be in attendance. If a sizeable group should appear and the program is a "success" then you should go ahead and get an association organized trusting to Allah, the Centers, and the goodwill and beneficence of individuals willing to give their time gratis to keep the organization going.
>
> How pay [sic] for the initial effort? Donations of time, subsidies from Centers for mailing costs, and registration fees to pay for meeting rooms.[26]

But the Cooperating Committee did not rise to the occasion and soon disbanded. As I. William Zartman would put it some years later:

> Yet there seems to have been no confidence that this group of scholars [in Middle East studies] felt academically lonely enough to band together for company, or that such banding together could be justified in lasting, satisfying terms. One of the [Cooperating] Committee's memoranda expressed the feeling well: "There is, on the part of the 'social scientists' a sense that something should be done but an uncertainty as to *what* should be done, whereas on our more traditional side of things there is a greater assuredness about what we want to do but a forlorn realization that it is perhaps of no great interest to others. . . . it may be wondered whether there is a sufficient concentration of scholarly and intellectual activities in the Near East field to justify such an enterprise."[27]

Launching MESA

Nonetheless, interest in an academic organization for U.S. Middle East studies continued to build. By this point in time, some of the area studies fields had already established a professional membership organization and others were moving in that direction. For example, early in 1965 the ACLS-SSRC Joint Committee on Latin American Studies began exploring the creation of a new national organization for the field, formally established as the Latin American Studies Association in May 1966.[28] These developments, as well as increasingly vigorous calls for action from within U.S. Middle East studies, heightened the pressure on the JCNME—the only national body in the field, and mandated by its sponsors the SSRC and ACLS to promote and lead its development—to at long last do something. In the fall of 1965 the JCNME was reported to be still "unenthusiastic about the organization of an association at this time," but it nonetheless "instructed Mr. Berger to explore the feasibility of such a move, as well as the possibility that some kind of journal might be established, either independently or in conjunction with an association."[29]

Morroe Berger, now chair of the JCNME, played a central role in finally getting a scholarly organization launched. At the committee's March 1966 meeting he put the issue squarely to his colleagues:

> After discussion of the several kinds of journals that might be published in the field and the alternatives of encouraging the Middle East Institute to become a scholarly association, encouraging the establishment of a separate association, or taking no action, Mr. Berger suggested that whether the committee believes there is a need for some more formal organization in Near and Middle East studies is the single most important question. If it thought there was some need for an association, it should take action; otherwise the subject should be dropped.

Berger went on to tell his colleagues that Don Peretz (born 1922), then Associate Director of the Office of Foreign Area Studies of New York State's Department of Education, had written to propose holding a conference of those scholars who desired to create an organization that would help improve teaching and research in the field. As Peretz later put it, "A number of us felt that a similar organization [like the ones for Asian, African and Eastern European studies] would not only be useful but was also needed for the Middle East. In the mid-1960s we persuaded the Social Science Research Council to consider the idea and to convene a meeting in New York to discuss it."[30] There was also a call to establish a membership organization from a group of scholars associated with the Middle East Institute.[31]

Finally, "at the urging of interested persons"—and, one suspects, much hectoring by Morroe Berger—the committee overcame its ambivalence and agreed to convene the meeting Peretz had proposed. It was scheduled for September 29, 1966, the day before the JCNME's upcoming meeting, with a list of invitees developed by Berger and Roland Mitchell, and then reviewed by the committee.[32] Dankwart Rustow later recalled that he had "helped make sure that [the list of invitees for] the association would be well balanced in its composition, including social scientists, as well as linguists and historians, and specialists on Turkey and Israel as well as Arabists."[33] The draft list of invitees (all men) included every member of the JCNME along with many of the better-known scholars in the field, Don Peretz, and representatives of the Ford and Rockefeller foundations, the ACLS and the SSRC.[34]

Morroe Berger, along with a number of other current and former JCNME members, now strongly favored the creation of a new national membership organization for the field and played a very energetic role in its founding and early leadership. But a range of motives and expectations went into the JCNME's decision to sponsor this initiative, despite the skepticism of some of its members. For one, it was hoped that once the new association was firmly established "it could assume responsibility for improving the teaching of Arabic and other languages of the area and also initiate a program of translations of European scholarly research works about the Near and Middle East." In other words, off-loading such activities onto the new association might enable the JCNME to devote itself more fully and effectively to the task of promoting research (especially social science research) and setting a scholarly agenda for the field.

At least some committee members also hoped that the projected association could, as it was put at one meeting, "help to give stability to the field by discouraging the proliferation of centers in universities and colleges before the supply of competent scholars is adequate"—though "whether MESA would be the appropriate agency to undertake such an assignment, and whether such discouragement would be feasible was questioned."[35] Ironically, this concern was prompted by the vigorous growth of the field since the mid-1950s—the very growth that by the mid-1960s that made a national professional organization both possible and widely desired. The proliferation of Middle East centers, programs and departments, including at large state universities which without Title VI funding would probably not have been able to create or sustain them, naturally meant both more graduate programs and larger graduate programs, which in turn meant more graduate students and eventually more newly minted PhDs looking for teaching jobs. The entry into the field of a great many more students, scholars and teachers than would have been imaginable in the mid-1950s could be taken as a sign of its success, but some JCNME members and other leading scholars in Middle East studies were troubled by it. They had long expressed concern about the need to maintain high standards in the field, and they were not convinced that some of the newer programs could train their students to those standards. They therefore worried about what they feared was a looming disparity between the relatively numerous new academic positions at both newly established and older (but expanding) programs, on the one hand, and on the other the available supply of what they deemed to be properly trained scholars and teachers. This led them to conclude that there were now too many Middle East studies centers, though they certainly did not think that their own centers could be dispensed with; it was always other (usually newer) centers whose closing might be a good thing—which might also mean more funding for the remaining centers. This anxiety about the purportedly inferior quality of the newer cohorts of scholars in the field, and of the programs that had produced them, would persist for a long time, mainly among established scholars based at elite universities, though for obvious reasons it could not always be voiced openly.[36]

No minutes are available for the JCNME-sponsored conference that met on September 29, 1966, to lay the foundations of the new national membership association for Middle East studies; all we know is that the attendees elected a committee chaired by Morroe Berger to draft bylaws and plan a second meeting at which the new association for Middle East studies would be formally established. That second meeting, by invitation only, took place at the offices of the SSRC on December 9, 1966, and included thirty-seven men from public and private universities with Middle East studies centers or programs and from other institutions. The official minutes of the meeting at which MESA was founded do not give any hint of conflict or contention.[37] However, political scientist I. William Zartman, who had begun teaching at New York University that same year, would characterize the discussions as "intricate," and Dankwart Rustow would much later offer the following vignette:

One scene I remember vividly from the founding meeting was a seemingly end-less and increasingly contentious debate about some rather trivial passage in the proposed by-laws. For some minutes I agonized, asking myself how I could help the assembled scholars get out of this impasse. If I intervened for or against the proposed bylaws amendment, I would obviously antagonize the other side; if I proposed a third solution—or an indefinite tabling—I might antagonize both; and either way, the debate would be needlessly dragged out. But, suddenly, I had a better idea.

I rose to ask for the floor and, when recognized by the chair, proceeded to say, quietly and firmly, "Mr. Chairman, I propose that we change the name of this organization from Middle East Studies Association to Middle East Studies Soci-ety." As I sat down without further explanation, there was a moment of puzzled silence. Then a few people throughout the room started smiling and whispering to their neighbors the acronym that had been my true intent: *MESS*! Soon there was a wave of laughter—and the previous trivial issue was dropped without further ado as we returned to the more serious part of the agenda.[38]

The meeting formally established the Middle East Studies Association of North America, whose founding statement declared that its purpose was to "promote high standards of scholarship and instruction, to facilitate commu-nication among scholars through meetings and publications, and to foster cooperation among persons and organizations in North America and abroad concerned with the study of the area." The meeting also approved the new association's bylaws and elected Morroe Berger as president. This had appar-ently required extensive prior negotiations by telephone: the eminent Orien-talist Gustave von Grunebaum was older than and clearly senior to Berger, but Berger had been the moving spirit in founding MESA. In the end a com-promise was reached, with Berger chosen as president but von Grunebaum designated honorary president.[39] John S. Badeau (1903–1995), who had been president of the American University in Cairo from 1945 to 1953 and U.S. ambassador to the United Arab Republic from 1961 to 1964, was named vice president, and Charles J. Adams, William M. Brinner, Richard H. Nolte, Wil-liam R. Polk, William D. Schorger and R. Bayly Winder were elected as the other members of MESA's first board of directors. One of the board's first de-cisions was to accept NYU's offer to host the organization and provide office space, secretarial assistance and an annual subvention of $2500.[40] That sub-vention was used to supplement the salary of the person appointed MESA's executive secretary and treasurer, NYU's own I. William Zartman.[41]

When MESA was established fifty-one "founding fellows" (again, all men) were named, including the thirty-seven actual attendees at the December 1966 meeting. This status was reserved for "persons of scholarly attainment in Middle East studies," which meant that they held a doctorate, taught courses relating to the Middle East and had published scholarly work on the region. Fellows were not only deemed the highest category of membership in the new association, they were the only members eligible to vote. It was apparently Gustave von Grunebaum who had insisted on a "quality" category of membership; but restricting the vote to established scholars, and requiring the board to vet and approve all applications for membership, would also help keep control of the association in this group's hands and make a takeover by outsiders (or by the broader membership) more difficult. However, within a few years it became clear that another category of voting members was needed between fellows and students; as a result the category of "regular" members was created in 1972 for those who were not students but did not satisfy all the criteria for fellowship, and the right to vote was extended to student members. In 1980 the categories of fellows and regular members were combined into a new category of "full" members, thereby abolishing the special status within MESA of established scholars.[42] That decision probably reflected the changing character of MESA's leadership, growing confidence in its stability and perhaps also a desire for greater (and more equal) member participation.

A few years after MESA's founding I. William Zartman offered his assessment of what had made that event possible:

> The major ingredient was a group of "modernists" who were no longer interested in joining the Orientalist *zawias* [Arabic for Sufi "lodge"], their "modernism" doubtless enhanced by the growing Third World, comparative, disciplinary attentions that were arising from various post-war sources. Their disaffection with the old school provided a split within Middle East scholarship that was at least as deep, more elitist, but less emotional than the Arab-Israeli split within their midst; in fact, being "modernist" the new group was probably more susceptible to the Arab-Israeli tensions than the old school, which was primarily Arabist in its more contemporary interest but more ecumenical in its roots. One attempt at organization [presumably AAMES] fell to the Arab-Israel split and the shadow remained. It is probably not accidental that the efforts at organization, including the finally successful attempt, took place between the Suez war

and the June war, and it is most likely that the last attempt succeeded in the nick of time, since a year later it would have been seen as an attempt of one side or the other to respond to the June defeat or victory. It is also probable that the earlier failures helped ensure the success of MESA: while people became warier, they also felt more and more that it was about time an organization was founded. Another element that helped was the continued training of new blood. The established "modernists" were not a homogenous age structure and as a group were scarcely old enough to constitute an old guard, and there was enough new production of scholars to ensure growth and continuity.[43]

Commenting on a draft of Zartman's account, Roland Mitchell suggested that "you could stress more than you do the fact that the organization was the result of the great increase of numbers of specialists resulting from the development of centers such as Princeton, Harvard, etc., and the funding of the training of scholars by the major foundations and the federal government. An association in 1956 would have been inconceivable because there were too few modernists. Ten years later was a different story."[44]

In 1987 R. Bayly Winder offered his own perspective on the events that led up to the founding of MESA, in which he had been deeply involved:

But academics are known to be a cantankerous lot; and over time, as the number of Middle Eastern academics grew, discontent set in: The AOS was too ancient and too philological; the MEI was too modern, too government oriented, and too "journalistic." Where could someone publish a study of eighteenth-century Iraq or give a paper on the conservatism of the poetic tradition in Qajar Iran? Various *ad hoc* cabals would complain, but their members were also wary. Wary about offending the AOS which was "sort of" their professional home, wary about bringing down the wrath of the MEI on their heads, and wary that the Arab-Israeli dispute would polarize if not blow up any academic group interested in the modern Middle East. Therefore, for years nothing happened. But pressure for the creation of an organization like the Association of Asian Studies [*sic*] or the Latin American Studies Association continued to build.[45]

That pressure seems to have come disproportionately from academics who specialized in the modern or contemporary periods, had received disciplinary training as social scientists or as historians, and had begun their academic careers in the later 1950s or early 1960s, though of course key figures like Berger, Rustow and Winder had received their doctorates a decade or so earlier. Many members of this cohort had entered the field of Middle East studies when it was already beginning to attain a degree of institutional density and coherence, and for them the absence of a proper, modern professional association was by the mid-1960s increasingly intolerable. Moreover, by that point they had as a group attained sufficient size, status and influence to make things happen, and they would play a central role in the new association for years to come.[46]

MESA: Getting Off the Ground

In its first months of existence MESA's very modest income was derived from membership dues, the subvention from NYU, and small donations from a number of universities. The new association probably could not have survived, much less flourished, with such limited resources. Fortunately for MESA, the Ford Foundation (with which many JCNME members and a number of the association's leaders had longstanding ties) came to the rescue. For Ford, supporting newly established scholarly associations in area studies seemed a good investment. A year or so after the establishment of the Latin American Studies Association in May 1966, Ford gave it a $100,000 grant to support its operation and activities.[47] Similarly, in August 1967 Ford provided MESA with a five-year general support grant of $56,000 (the equivalent of nearly $400,000 in 2015), and it was this grant that allowed the new organization to get up and running, and to begin to plan for the longer term.[48] Ford's expectation was that within five years MESA would become financially self-sustaining, though in reality achieving this goal took much longer.

With this new funding in hand, the association held its first annual meeting at the University of Chicago in December 1967, with some 260 participants; by the end of that meeting it claimed 400 members.[49] Of that very first annual meeting MESA reported to Ford that "more important than numbers was the quality of response evident at the meeting. Members in attendance and papers presented showed that the organization was filling a need among young scholars of Middle East studies specializing in the social sciences. Perhaps as significant was the presence, along with these younger members, of older established figures in Middle East studies, including those in the humanities."[50] There were in fact complaints within the new association that the program of the first annual meeting was too oriented toward the social sciences, but this concern seems to have faded away over time.[51] MESA would experience rapid growth in the years that followed: by its fifth annual meeting in 1971 it had 1,438 members, including 609 fellows, 458 students, 235 "associate" members (who were not academics) and forty-six institutional members, mainly affiliated universities.[52]

MESA moved quickly toward launching a scholarly journal, and the first issue of the new *International Journal of Middle East Studies* (*IJMES*), dated January 1970, appeared soon after the organization's third annual meeting, held in Toronto. The new quarterly's first editor was the Ottomanist Stanford Shaw (1930–2006), who in the late 1960s left Harvard to join the faculty of UCLA. The association also began publishing a bulletin for its members soon after its establishment, featuring news of the association and the field, abstracts of papers presented at its annual meetings, and a number of "state of the art" articles on Middle East studies. Among the latter was an assessment of the Middle East studies field by Morroe Berger, apparently drafted around May 1967, which appeared in the second issue of the *Middle East Studies Association Bulletin* a few months later.

One might have expected Berger, as MESA's first president, to strike an optimistic note. Instead, his characterization of the region on which the new association focused was rather negative and his assessment of his field's prospects quite gloomy. Cautioning against the tendency of scholars to "overestimate the importance of their field of study in relation to others," Berger listed what he regarded as some of the region's "limitations owing to its nature and its political and cultural place in the world today." For one, Berger asserted, its languages were difficult for Americans to master. In addition, "the modern Middle East and North Africa is not a center of great cultural achievement, nor is it likely to become one in the near future. The study of the region or its languages, therefore, does not constitute its own reward so far as modern culture is concerned." Moreover, Berger asserted, the region "is not a center of great political power nor does it have the potential to become one," and "it has been receding in immediate political importance to the U.S. (and even in 'headline' or 'nuisance' value) relative to Africa, Latin America and the Far East." The region thus "has in only small degree the kinds of traits that seem to be important in attracting scholarly attention. This does not diminish the validity and intellectual value of studying the area or affect the quality of the work scholars do on it. It does, however, put limits, of which we should be aware, on the field's capacity for growth in the numbers who study and teach." (15–16) In this we can see an allusion to the concerns discussed earlier about excessive growth in the field and the threat it allegedly posed to quality. Given the crisis that would erupt in the Middle East just weeks after Berger drafted his assessment, and the central role that the region would play in world affairs (and in U.S. foreign policy) in subsequent decades, his prognosis was obviously wide of the mark. One may also wonder what Berger's colleagues, having just launched what they must have hoped would be a successful new organization, felt about his rather depressing assessment. It was nonetheless published as written, though readers of the *Middle East Studies Association Bulletin* were cautioned "to bear in mind that Professor Berger prepared and submitted the report early in May 1967, before the outbreak of war in the Middle East."[53]

Soon after its establishment MESA appointed a Committee on Research and Training (CRT) to "define needs, identify tasks, coordinate work, locate sources of financing and assign projects bearing on research, training and educational materials in Middle East studies," with separate subcommittees working on bibliography, language teaching materials and libraries.[54] Some of these tasks had previously fallen within the purview of the JCNME's mission. CRT members were initially uncertain about whether MESA should get involved in overseeing research projects or seeking funding for them. As an anonymous CRT member put it early on, it was unclear whether or not MESA

> should intervene at all in the pluralistic, competitive confusion by which research projects are devised, proposed, and financed. Might we not be squelching the creativity of individual scholars, favoring group projects over individual projects, or library projects over field projects, or projects utilizing aggregate data over projects utilizing interview data? Contrarily, should the Association undertake to oppose, influence, or compete with the large University Centers of Middle East studies or the staffs of the wealthy foundations, or even government bureaucrats, all of whom now determine who gets what in Middle East (and other area) research funds.[55]

In a move that suggests that its members possessed a sense of humor, CRT soon thereafter renamed itself the Research and Training Committee (RAT) and decided that its top priority should be a comprehensive assessment of the Middle East studies field. With Ford funding MESA convened a small conference at NYU in February 1970 at which leading scholars in the field discussed "institutional and fiscal matters" as well as "problems of academic setting, the broader cultural context of scholarly endeavors and the intellectual and methodological dimensions of Middle East research."[56] Participants pointed to a number of problems that they felt afflicted the field, including (paradoxically) both its newness and its historic roots in Bible studies and Semitics, as a result of which it had supposedly not started with what one participant termed a "clean slate." One may of course doubt whether any academic field or discipline has ever actually begun with a clean slate; all have had to struggle with the complex legacies of the past. Nonetheless, this perception indicated persistent fault lines within the field as well as within its new professional organization. Other participants in the February 1970 conference lamented a possible oversupply of Middle East studies centers, a frequent refrain among scholars associated with the older centers established with foundation funding who were ambivalent about the quality of training offered at the new centers launched in the 1960s with Title VI funding. Zartman, by this time not only MESA's executive secretary but also a member of the JCNME, offered his own list of thirteen problems facing the field, ranging from "the unattractiveness of the area for students seeking a specialization" to "the isolation of area specialists from other areas and disciplines when grouped in a large university and from each other when alone in small college departments" to "the impending scarcity of funding." Various ways of strengthening the field in a period of shrinking resources were discussed, but no agreement was reached on firm plans for action.[57]

Soon thereafter RAT, now chaired by Leonard Binder, decided to spin off its subcommittees and focus exclusively on organizing a major conference on the "state of the art" in Middle East studies, scheduled for 1973, with an edited volume of the conference papers to be published afterward. This project was intended, as MESA described it to the Ford Foundation, "to provide the community of scholars on the Middle East with a broad and intellectually sound overview of knowledge about the Middle East, an understanding of the organization and compartmentalization of that knowledge, an explanation of the current status of the various arts, and sound evaluations of future methods, substantive needs and priorities."[58] There is an echo in that last goal of the longstanding, but never realized, hope of formulating a research agenda for the field rooted in some coherent analysis of its character. Staging such an event was, however, well beyond MESA's still limited resources, as were several other projects the association hoped to launch. It therefore applied for a second Ford grant in 1972, seeking $201,000 over a three-year period—the equivalent of more than $1.1 million in 2015. More than 40 percent of that total would go to Binder's "state of the art" conference project, with two other projects accounting for most of the remainder. One of these, budgeted at a total of $54,000 over three years, would bring scholars from the Middle East to visit North American universities on a regular basis. As I discuss in Chapter 8, the tenuous links between U.S.-based scholars of the Middle East, on the one hand, and on the other scholars and academic institutions in the Middle East had by this time come to be seen as a serious problem for the field. The other project, for which MESA requested $12,000 in Ford funding, had been developed by MESA's Committee on Middle East Images in Secondary School Texts, formed in 1971 and chaired by Farhat J. Ziadeh of the University of Washington. It proposed to produce several studies of the factual errors about, and prejudicial images of, the Middle East in public school textbooks, in order to counter bias and to bring MESA into closer contact with K-12 educators and their students.[59]

Ford approved MESA's three-year funding request, which also included a badly needed $17,000 a year to cover MESA's operating costs. I discuss the 1973 "state of the art" conference that this grant made possible, and the 1976 volume that resulted from it, in Chapter 8. The first Middle Eastern scholar brought to the United States through MESA's new Ford-funded Visiting Scholars Program was the Palestinian poet Salma Khadra al-Jayyusi, who presented a paper at MESA's 1973 annual meeting in Milwaukee and visited Middle East studies centers and departments across the country. The second was the Tunisian sociologist Abdelkader Zghal; he had just been recruited to the JCNME in the context of its own efforts to strengthen connections with scholars and academic institutions in the Middle East. All told, some fifteen scholars, writers and intellectuals from the Middle East would attend a MESA annual meeting and visit colleges and universities in the United States and Canada under the auspices of this program through the 1977–1978 academic year.[60] Meanwhile, the work of the Image Committee initiated by Farhat Ziadeh led to the production of two reports aimed at high-school teachers and school officials. The first, released in 1975, was "The Image of the Middle East in Secondary School Textbooks." Authored by William J. Griswold of Colorado State University, it assessed textbooks currently in use and offered model syllabi on Islam, the Middle East and the Arab-Israeli conflict. In 1977 MESA released "American Images of Middle East Peoples: Impact on the High School," by Michael W. Suleiman of Kansas State University, which was based on a survey of 800 high school teachers; it found them "poorly prepared to teach about the Middle East and largely unaware of their own biases."[61]

The 1972 Ford grant thus enabled MESA to undertake several ambitious projects and fostered a sense of optimism about the association's future, at least among its leaders. One sign of the association's progress was, as Zartman reported to Ford,

> a trend in the association for more and more people other than the "founding fathers" to be brought into active participation in MESA affairs. For instance, none of those who worked on the Program Committee had been active in MESA affairs until the present academic year. The turnover seems to coincide with a shift in intellectual interest as well: in literature from orientalism to a concern with the application of modern literary theories to Near Eastern literatures; in the social sciences from classical structural studies to a concern with the problematics of contemporary societies; in politics to a franker discussion of the problems of the area, such as the Arab-Israeli confrontation, than was believed possible for the association a few years ago.[62]

I discuss later in this chapter the third of the shifts that Zartman noted, the growing range of political issues that were deemed permissible to address. But there was another change that Zartman did not mention at all but that by the early 1970s was already beginning to transform both MESA's composition and its intellectual life: the growing significance in it both of women scholars and of the study of women and gender.

In the early to mid-1970s "second-wave" feminism and women's studies began to have a significant impact on U.S. Middle East studies, and thus on MESA.[63] Anthropologist Amal Rassam of Queens College (City University of New York) had organized a pioneering MESA panel on Middle Eastern women in 1973, and thereafter things moved relatively quickly. In a December 1974 letter, Roxann A. Van Dusen reported on the papers on women that had been presented at that year's annual meeting of MESA and on the informal discussion session she had convened there to discuss "next steps" for research on women in the Middle East:

The appearance of papers on women is as good an indicator as any of this expanding field. From one or two papers gerrymandered into inappropriate panels at the 1970 meetings [*sic*], there were 34 panels devoted exclusively to research on Middle Eastern women at the 1974 meetings. At those meetings I heard of four separate books in preparation on Middle Eastern women: a Nikki Keddie-Lois Beck anthology; Schilling's book, which many people seemed to have heard of; a general review by Lina Hamadi; and an anthology (now dormant, if not moribund, I suspect) by Greer Fox and Kathleen Merriam. In addition, an annotated bibliography on Middle East women (by Ayad al-Qazzaz) is due in 1975. And none of the people responsible for these forthcoming publications seemed aware that the others existed.[64]

Two years later an observer reporting to the Ford Foundation commented on

the large percentage of women scholars actively participating in the [1976] MESA meeting. Not only were women present in relatively large numbers, they participated in several impressive panels dealing with such contemporary topics as the Role of Women in Middle Eastern Societies and the Secular Origins of Muslim-Christian Conflict. More women are thus probably being recruited into the field, introducing into the panels more social science oriented research topics. This inference conforms with our assumption that changes in scholarly orientations most often occur with the recruitment of scholars into a given field. At another level, the affirmative action stance of universities and the SSRC awards program may already be exercising some influence in broadening opportunities for female scholars.[65]

With the number of women scholars in the field growing, and with scholarly work on women and gender advancing both in quantity and in quality, two pioneers in the field, Elizabeth Fernea and Suad Joseph, found it possible in the wake of the 1975 MESA annual meeting to express the hope that "the tide is turning so that soon we may anticipate, not only women's studies, men's studies, or children's studies, but studies of human beings as they relate together in Middle Eastern society."[66]

Women also gradually began to assume leadership positions in MESA, whose founders and early leaders were exclusively male. In 1970 the UCLA historian of modern Iran Nikki Keddie became the first woman elected to MESA's board of directors. Four years later historian Afaf Lutfi al-Sayyid Marsot (born 1933), also of UCLA, was elected MESA's vice president (a position abolished the following year), and in 1979 she became the first woman to serve as the association's president; she replaced Stanford Shaw as editor of *IJMES* in 1980. The ascent in MESA of women scholars and of scholarship on women and gender was of course not as smooth as this account might suggest: getting women into leadership positions in MESA, and making room within the field for women's studies, were not achieved without struggle. Nonetheless, by the end of the 1970s MESA's leadership, and the range of topics addressed at its annual meetings, were unquestionably more diverse, at least in terms of gender, than they had been earlier in the decade.

Fear of (Certain Kinds of) Politics

Many of those who would become MESA's founders and early leaders had witnessed the foundering both of the Council on Middle Eastern Affairs and of AAMES, which they believed could be attributed to their political connections—specifically, their links with Zionist organizations. Moreover, six months after the association was launched the June 1967 war took place, bringing what was then generally referred to as the Arab-Israeli conflict (and soon the broader question of Palestine) to the fore, in the Middle East but also among scholars of the region based in the United States. MESA's leaders also had before their eyes many contemporary examples of academic turmoil and division, at colleges and universities across the country but also within scholarly organizations. Much of this was fueled by new cohorts of graduate students and younger faculty shaped not by the Cold War, as their elders had been, but by struggles for racial and social justice at home and for an end to the bloody war that the United States was waging in Indochina. They also challenged what they perceived to be the silencing within their field or discipline of discussion of current issues, of critical analytical and political perspectives, and of the relationship between knowledge and power.

In Latin American studies, for example, students and scholars opposed to U.S. domination of the continent and supportive of struggles for radical social change began to coalesce in the mid-1960s, some of them around the North American Congress on Latin America (NACLA), founded in 1966. A radical Caucus for a New Political Science emerged within the American Political Science Association in 1967, while the following year witnessed the launching of the Committee of Concerned Asian Scholars by graduate students and faculty unhappy with the refusal of the Association of Asian Scholars to allow discussion of contemporary political issues, especially the Vietnam War. A Black Caucus demanding reform of the largely white-led African Studies Association emerged in 1968, leading to the formation of a separate African Heritage Studies Association the following year.[67] In this fraught context, MESA's founders were anxious lest political disagreements among the new association's members regarding conflicts in the Middle East undermine and perhaps even destroy it. They therefore explicitly defined MESA from the outset as a nonpolitical scholarly organization and sought to avoid open discussion of potentially contentious or divisive issues.

So, for example, in its first years MESA's leadership worked to control or even suppress discussion at its annual meetings of the Arab-Israeli conflict, for fear of endangering the young organization by revealing or exacerbating divisions among its members and embroiling itself in controversy. To judge from the programs published in the *MESA Bulletin*, panels focusing directly on this conflict were entirely absent from the association's first three annual meetings. In a similar vein, I. William Zartman relates that he was told that he had been chosen as MESA's first executive secretary because as a Maghrib specialist he was deemed to have no involvement with or position on the Arab-Israeli conflict or other contentious issues involving the Mashriq. In fact, Zartman would visit the Mashriq, along with Turkey and Israel, for the first time only in 1970.[68]

MESA could not, however, be entirely or easily insulated from the Arab-Israeli conflict, from other conflicts roiling various parts of the Middle East, or from politics more broadly. It took a lot of vigilance and policing to contain or suppress discussion of certain issues deemed threatening or divisive, and over the longer term pressures from both within and without would compel MESA's leadership (itself undergoing significant change as the years passed) to accommodate discussion of issues it had earlier preferred to avoid. But even early on, despite the de facto ban on discussing what was at the time the field's potentially most divisive issue—the Arab-Israeli conflict—it kept surfacing in various ways. At MESA's very first annual meeting, at the University of Chicago in November 1967, the board decided to ask—to compel, actually—one "Mr. Shabtai," a graduate student at the University of Chicago who worked at the Israeli consulate, to withdraw the paper on an aspect of the Arab-Israeli conflict that he had planned to present—"to the disappointment of the contending sides massed in the audience," as Zartman put it. The board subsequently declared that "the program should not contain papers on politically controversial subjects by representatives of diplomatic services of foreign countries" and discussed instituting "a control mechanism or screening device that should be built into the selection of invited and volunteered papers," to "raise the academic level of papers presented" but also, presumably, to prevent this kind of incident from recurring.[69] Zartman also reported that "Arab students have met from time to time to consider various courses of action, ranging from the outright political to simply attempts to be more strongly represented in the program," though they seem to have been successfully contained by the leadership. And before the association's third annual meeting, held in Toronto in November 1969, some MESA members (presumably graduate students) called for the proceedings to be suspended in solidarity with the massive demonstrations against the war in Vietnam taking place at the same time, though apparently nothing came of this.[70]

But it seems that even MESA's own leaders could not resist addressing contentious political issues, especially the Arab-Israeli conflict. Thus the presidential address delivered in November 1968 by George F. Hourani of the University of Michigan, MESA's second president, was titled "Palestine as a Problem of Ethics" and assessed the claims of Arabs and Jews to that land. Hourani concluded that, in moral terms, "the original Zionist movement and the establishment of a [Jewish] national home under the British mandate had no justification" but that on balance "it would be best for the Arabs to accept the Jewish presence and a state of Israel in a part of Palestine."[71] A protest lodged by the Israeli consulate was duly ignored.[72] This experience seems to have led MESA's third president, R. Bayly Winder of NYU, to forewarn the board of directors a few months later that in his upcoming presidential address at Toronto he planned to discuss "the revisions, additions, and omissions to Arabic textbooks made by the Israeli occupation forces" in the West Bank and Gaza. The board discussed the matter and concluded that "although controversial issues should not always be the subject of the Presidential address, the President is free to speak on whatever subject he chooses."[73] In fact, Winder's address only very briefly mentioned this issue.[74] But his self-restraint, or self-censorship, apparently caused him much discomfort: a few months later, in discussing "the pervasive nature of the Arab Israeli dispute as far as it affects these studies" in the off-the-record setting of the February 1970 conference on the state of U.S. Middle East studies mentioned earlier,

Winder talked about that experience:

> I will cite one example. If you look in the presidential speech that I gave in To-
> ronto, reprinted in the Bulletin which we have just received, you will find it—if
> you had the misfortune to hear it, and you wish to read it—that they are quite
> different and, let me say frankly, I was very unhappy with those remarks. The
> reason I was unhappy was not that I had nothing to say, but it was that I really
> lost my nerve at the end. The subject is so touchy, emotions are so deep, that I
> finally ended up sort of saying nothing. In print, I summoned up my courage
> a little bit more and said a little bit more. Even there, the nerve ends were con-
> stantly alert as to what one was going to say. I would submit that if you think of
> the great controversies about United States policy toward China, for example,
> which have beset the East Asian community of scholars over the last couple of
> decades, they were not of the same order of magnitude or intensity and did not
> affect studies and scholarship nearly as much as our political problems do.[75]

By 1970 it had become increasingly clear that MESA could no longer avoid
even scholarly discussion of the Arab-Israeli conflict, and the leadership's
fears seem to have eased. Panels and papers that engaged with the conflict
(and eventually with the question of Palestine broadly defined) soon became
a regular, even prominent, feature of MESA's annual meetings. Hence Zartman's statement to Ford, quoted earlier, that there could now be "a franker
discussion of the problems of the area, such as the Arab-Israeli confrontation, than was believed possible for the association a few years ago."[76] But
MESA's engagement with the issue still had its limits. For example, in May
1976 Elaine C. Hagopian of Simmons College in Boston, at the time president
of the Association of Arab-American University Graduates (AAUG), wrote
to MESA's president L. Carl Brown of Princeton to propose a joint letter to
the New York Times about the deteriorating state of Palestinian education in
the Israeli-occupied West Bank and Gaza. The AAUG had been founded in
1967 to promote discussion and critical analysis of issues involving the Arab
world and the United States; Ibrahim Abu-Lughod, Naseer Aruri and Edward W. Said were among its best-known figures. Brown declined to sign
the letter on the ground that MESA was "barred by its bylaws from taking a
stand on any issue that might be construed as political."[77] It would take many
more years before MESA would begin to advocate consistently and publicly
in defense of academic freedom. In 1988, during the first Palestinian intifada,
the business meeting broke new ground by endorsing a resolution protesting

the closing by the Israeli authorities of Palestinian universities in the West Bank and Gaza. Two years later MESA established a permanent Committee on Academic Freedom—one of the few area studies associations to have such a body—through which it began to speak out vigorously in defense of academic freedom, in North America as well as in the Middle East and North Africa. On this issue as on others, it had come a long way over the previous decade and a half.

The Intelligence Test

There were other, in some ways even more fundamental, issues that MESA's leaders also did not wish to address but which nonetheless came increasingly to the fore by the mid-1970s. These often pertained to the political and ethical dimensions of pursuing the study of the contemporary Middle East in the United States at that historical moment. More threatening even than allowing scholarly discussion of the Arab-Israeli conflict was confronting the easy relationship forged during the Cold War between academia and the American national security state, a relationship that had now come under widespread challenge. For MESA, this involved, among other things, dealing with the question of its stance toward—and, potentially, some of its leading members' links with—various agencies of the United States government, including its intelligence and military apparatuses.

From the 1950s onward, in Middle East studies as in other area studies fields and many disciplines, a number of leading scholars (especially political scientists) had conducted research on contract for, or served as consultants to, an intelligence agency, the armed forces, the State Department or a quasigovernmental entity like RAND.[78] The roster includes T. Cuyler Young, Leonard Binder, J. C. Hurewitz, Manfred Halpern and Nadav Safran, and almost certainly others whose connections and activities in this regard we do not know about.[79] For a long time these kinds of relationships (when publicly known) either passed without comment or were seen as a praiseworthy service that American scholars could and should render to their country. Many of the leading figures in U.S. Middle East studies were no more willing or able than their counterparts in other area studies fields to address whether the connection between the knowledge they produced, on the one hand, and on the other the power and policies of the United States in the region under study, might raise serious ethical and political concerns, or even threaten the integrity and autonomy of the academic enterprise. This silence came under increasing challenge from the late 1960s onward, as the links between what went on in the Middle East and what went on in the United States—including American scholarship on the Middle East—faced heightened scrutiny. As a result MESA would be increasingly compelled to face demands that it at least acknowledge that research and teaching about the Middle East in the United States were related, politically, morally and epistemologically, to what was going on in that region, including the exercise of American power there.

In U.S. Middle East studies these issues did not become the focus of contention until the early or mid-1970s, somewhat later than in some other area studies fields and disciplines. For example, the Middle East Research and Information Project, publisher of *MERIP Reports* (later renamed *Middle East Report*), was founded only in 1971. As elsewhere, political critique when it surfaced was inextricably bound up with intellectual critique. Nineteen seventy-five witnessed the publication in Britain of the first issue of *Review of Middle East Studies*, featuring incisive critiques by a set of younger scholars of key components of the dominant intellectual paradigms of Middle East studies as practiced in the United States and Britain. At almost the same moment *MERIP Reports* published a lengthy article on the "Middle East Studies Network" which offered a critical survey of the field in the United States and for the first time documented some of its leading figures' connections with intelligence agencies and the military.[80]

One of those mentioned in that issue was I. William Zartman, MESA's executive secretary from 1966 to 1977 (and from 1968 to 1975 also a member of the JCNME). In another issue of *MERIP Reports* published a few months later, Jim Paul revealed that back in the fall of 1968 Zartman had played a leading role in a government-funded war game exercise (designated CONEX II) focusing on the Maghrib and organized by MIT's Center for International Studies (CENIS), closely linked to the CIA.[81] CONEX II, with participants and observers drawn from intelligence agencies and the military as well as academia, simulated rising tensions between Algeria and Morocco that culminated in armed conflict. The game's main goal, as Jim Paul put it, was to explore whether "limited war can be used to benefit American power in the region." Paul's exposé appeared at a moment of deepening crisis between Algeria and Morocco over the former Spanish Sahara; it was picked up by the Paris-based journal *Afrique Asie*, which published a version of the story in April 1976 just as Algeria and Morocco were again on the brink of armed conflict.[82]

It is unclear what if anything Zartman's colleagues or the MESA membership at large knew before 1975 of his role in CONEX II, or who else in the MESA leadership of the time had intelligence connections in this period. But by this point there were certainly some in MESA and in the field at large who deemed it unacceptable for scholars, but also academic organizations, to maintain or even permit links with intelligence agencies or their personnel. Their concerns were heightened by media revelations in this period about egregious wrongdoing by government security and intelligence agencies, which led to the appointment in 1975 of a select Senate committee, chaired by Senator Frank Church. The committee held hearings and published detailed reports on the reckless and often illegal activities of the CIA, the National Security Agency and the Federal Bureau of Investigation, including plots to assassinate foreign leaders, the staging of coups d'état, warrantless surveillance of American citizens, covert campaigns to destroy radical, civil rights, black nationalist and antiwar leaders and movements, and much else.

The Church committee's final report of April 1976 also found that "The Central Intelligence Agency has long-developed clandestine relationships with the American academic community, which range from academics making introductions for intelligence purposes to intelligence collection while abroad, to academic research and writing where CIA sponsorship is hidden." Declaring itself "disturbed both by the present practice of operationally using American academics and by the awareness that the restraints on expanding this practice are primarily those of sensitivity to the risks of disclosure and not an appreciation of dangers to the integrity of individuals and institutions," the report concluded that "it is the responsibility of private institutions and particularly the American academic community to set the professional and ethical standards of its members."[83] This prompted William W. Van Alstyne, president of the American Association of University Professors, to write to then CIA Director George H. W. Bush in May 1976 requesting that the agency stop recruiting academics for covert activities that "betray their professional trust." "A government which corrupts its colleges and universities by making political fronts of them," Van Alstyne declared, "has betrayed academic freedom and compromised all who teach."[84] Even the American Political Science Association, no hotbed of radicalism, would adopt a resolution in 1976 criticizing the involvement of academics in covert intelligence operations under the guise of academic research and calling on its members not to participate in government-sponsored intelligence activities unless such sponsorship was disclosed to all those affected by it.[85]

It was in this context that Boston University political scientist Irene Gendzier, who had been elected to the MESA board in the fall of 1974, asked her colleagues to consider whether the association (whose board retained the right to vet all applications for membership) should allow CIA agents to join. In effect, Gendzier argued that MESA's avowedly nonpolitical character required it to bar intelligence agents from membership, since granting them membership was in and of itself a political act. The MESA board rebuffed Gendzier when she first raised the question in March 1975, but she persisted over the subsequent two years, during which time the scope of her concerns broadened. In the spring of 1976 David Steinberg, an official of the U.S. Agency for International Development (AID), an arm of the Department of State, contacted MESA to initiate discussion about the possibility of funding jointly organized workshops and conferences.[86] Gendzier and several other board members were concerned by the prospect of MESA collaborating with a government agency, especially given recent revelations about collaboration between the CIA and AID, including the CIA's extensive use of the development agency to provide cover for its clandestine operatives and operations. But there was also AID's provision of counterinsurgency training to police and security personnel from Latin American dictatorships, not a few of whom tortured and murdered alleged subversives after returning home, and more broadly the alignment of AID's mission with the Cold War foreign policy goals of the United States.[87] Around the same time MESA, chronically short of funds, had launched an effort to solicit donations from a broad range of corporations, including the big oil companies but also military contractors.[88] The only positive response MESA received was from Northrop (known today as Northrop Grumman), one of the country's largest manufacturers of military aircraft. Gendzier argued that a scholarly association should not solicit or accept funds from such companies, whose products had so recently been deployed with massively lethal effect in Indochina.

Citing what she took to be the board's refusal to seriously consider the implications of accepting CIA agents as members of MESA and of a possible relationship with AID, both of which she saw as undermining MESA's claim to be nonpolitical, Gendzier informed president L. Carl Brown in April 1976 that she planned to resign from the board.[89] This prompted Brown (who had been among those expressing concerns about collaboration with AID) to circulate Gendzier's letters among board members and solicit their responses. At its subsequent meeting, in November 1976, the board decided to terminate discussions with AID but by a vote of 6–3 in effect rejected Gendzier's objection to accepting CIA agents as members by resolving that "MESA not stand in the way of the free flow of ideas through discriminatory membership."[90] The Northrop issue appears to have faded away on its own, though into the 1980s MESA did receive modest donations from a number of oil companies, including Esso (later Exxon), Mobil and Gulf.[91]

Gendzier thereupon resigned but was compelled to wage a protracted struggle to ensure that the published (and somewhat sanitized) summary of the minutes of the November 1976 board meeting accurately reflected the discussion that had actually taken place and to secure the right to make her reasons for resigning known to the membership at large.[92] The association's leadership, as always fearful of divisiveness, was reluctant to allow its dirty laundry to be aired in public, but Gendzier persisted and in May 1977 her letter of resignation (redrafted following objections by board members) was finally published in the *MESA Bulletin*. Citing the Church committee's findings and Van Alstyne's letter, she argued that allowing CIA agents to join MESA "represents a serious violation of the nature of MESA as an academic association, a potentially dangerous situation for those American and foreign members of MESA, and a compromising practice on the part of the MESA leadership." Her letter concluded:

> Far from even recognizing that there is a problem, as the Church Committee Report suggested, the resolution passed by the majority of Board members disregards the injunctions of the Church Committee Report and by its terminology indicates a marked indifference to the nature of the CIA itself. It remains for individual MESA members therefore to concern themselves with the establishment of appropriate professional and ethical standards as members of the academic community and of one of its professional associations.[93]

There were certainly some MESA members, and even some board members, who shared Gendzier's concerns, but at the time they seemed to be in the minority and her resignation did not have a major impact on the association. This incident is nonetheless significant. In the 1970s and into the 1980s, a substantial number of the graduate students and younger faculty who had entered the field in the late 1960s and 1970s, and were thus formed, intellectually and politically, within a very different set of contexts than their elders who ran MESA, felt deeply alienated from the association's leadership; some of them would even launch, and for a number of years in the late 1970s and early 1980s sustain, another framework within which to pursue their own vision of Middle East studies: the Alternative Middle East Studies Seminar (AMESS).[94] Over a longer time span, however, generational change coupled with the decline of the paradigms and norms which had earlier dominated the field would do their work. In the 1980s and beyond, new cohorts would infuse MESA with intellectual and political perspectives very different than those of the association's founders and their immediate successors, and eventually they would take center stage and reshape it accordingly.

Opening MESA Up

Even as new kinds of political issues came to the fore in the mid-1970s, MESA experienced contention over what many members had come to see as a lack of democracy, transparency and accountability in the association. For much of its first decade it was largely run in a rather undemocratic manner by a small, self-perpetuating group of men drawn from among its founders; Richard Bulliet would later characterize it as "a very small club."[95] Under its original bylaws, MESA's board of directors itself appointed the nominating committee which selected candidates for the association's officers and board, who were subsequently voted on by the membership. In practice, this seems to have meant that I. William Zartman, the association's executive secretary through its first decade, convened whichever nominating committee members were available to meet at MESA's NYU office and this small group, in informal consultation with the association's officers and other leading figures, more or less determined who would run MESA. In short, as Bulliet put it two decades later, "it was a very strongly guided association that reflected the views of the field held by a fairly small number of people who were more or less the founders."[96]

Unsurprisingly, this led to discontent as MESA grew. As early as 1971 a group of MESA members petitioned for a change in the bylaws that would have the nominating committee elected by the fellows at the annual meeting, but the proposal seems to have been voted down.[97] The issue resurfaced a few years later, at the business meeting held at the November 1975 MESA annual meeting in Louisville, Kentucky, in the context of a broader critique of MESA voiced by the Turkish historian Kemal Karpat of the University of Wisconsin-Madison. The minutes report that Karpat "called for a change from what he perceived to be the current Orientalists [sic] cultural-determinist, patronizing attitude toward the area. He criticized the MESA Board as a closed circle and said that nominations are forced to be made from the same people. He said he had been punished for his attitude in the past and indicated that if something was not done, he would take corrective measures within MESA." A number of other participants supported Karpat's call for more democratic procedures, but MESA president Roderic Davison responded that the nominating committee was always open to receiving suggestions for nominees, which rather missed Karpat's point. According to Bulliet, MESA's founders "were very hurt" by Karpat's accusation "because they didn't think they were a clique; they thought they were concerned and trying to nurture [MESA] into an association."[98] In the end it was agreed that the incoming president (L. Carl Brown of Princeton) would appoint an *ad hoc* committee to look into the question of the association's nominating procedures for officers and board members.[99]

The demand for change was evidently strong enough that this committee, headed by Ernest Dawn and including Kemal Karpat and Fauzi Najjar, recommended that the bylaws be amended such that while the board of directors would propose the names of ten fellows to serve on the nominating committee, additional candidates could be proposed at the business meeting, whereupon the membership would choose among them by mail ballot. Nominations for officers and board members could also be made by petition. In addition, any future executive secretary (i.e., after the incumbent, Zartman) would have to be re-appointed annually by the board, "with due regard for the desirability of periodic changes in the tenure of the office."[100] This language suggests that there were those who felt that future executive secretaries should not hold the position for as long as Zartman had—and perhaps not wield as much power, either. These amendments were approved by the board, the business meeting and the membership at large, with effect from the 1977 annual meeting. In principle these amendments provided for greater membership participation in choosing the association's leadership.

As it happened, Zartman had announced that he would be stepping down as MESA's executive secretary early in 1976. NYU was still the association's institutional host, and in the absence of an alternative it eventually became clear that Zartman's replacement would have to be someone based in or near New York City and therefore able to come on a regular basis to MESA's office, located at NYU's Hagop Kevorkian Center for Near Eastern Studies. Historian Richard Bulliet, who had been teaching at Columbia since 1975, filled the bill and was appointed executive secretary. Bulliet asserts that on assuming the position he discovered that MESA's finances were in a parlous state and so had to devote much of his time to rectifying the situation by cutting costs, increasing revenues and rationalizing procedures. As Bulliet tells it, this included working with Afaf Lutfi al-Sayyid Marsot, who had succeeded Stanford Shaw as editor of *IJMES*, to publish extra issues in order to reduce the journal's substantial backlog of accepted but unpublished submissions; this improved the flow of revenue from membership dues, collected by Cambridge University Press on MESA's behalf. The *Middle East Studies Association Bulletin* was also moved from NYU to Seattle, where Jere Bacharach of the University of Washington became its editor.[101]

Meanwhile, the end of Ford's five-year grant to MESA was approaching. With the association experiencing what it termed "complex budgetary problems" and still in need of external support, Bulliet approached the Ford Foundation for a third grant, applying for $17,000 a year for three years to cover core operating expenses and $25,000 to fund the Visiting Scholars Program (VSP). Foundation staff favored continued support for MESA: it had, they reported, "proved to be a vigorous and lively organization, commanding the respect and participation of its members and providing much needed leadership to an otherwise disjointed collection of scholars, programs and centers. Moreover, while the Foundation has moved away from core support for area studies programs, aside from the interdisciplinary research workshops and conferences sponsored by the Social Science Research Council, assisting MESA would enable the [Middle East and Africa] office to maintain its links to the broader Middle East studies community."[102] Ford granted MESA another $42,000 over three years (the equivalent of about $153,000 in 2015), for the VSP and for what it described as "terminal, phased support of MESA's operating costs."

In August 1980 New York University informed MESA that it was no longer willing to provide free office space or cover half the salary and benefits of the association's administrative assistant.[103] Around the same time Richard Bulliet announced his intention to step down as executive secretary, in circumstances discussed in Chapter 8. After a lengthy search process and protracted negotiations, MESA found both a new home and a new executive secretary. In 1981 its secretariat moved to the University of Arizona at Tucson, where it has remained, and the geographer Michael Bonine (1942–2011), a member of the university's faculty since 1975, became MESA's executive director (as the position was renamed). In the 1980s MESA seems to have finally achieved financial stability and developed an increasingly ramified and effective organizational framework, including standing committees and a growing number of affiliated organizations and institutional members.

Looking back from the vantage point of 1985, Ford staff characterized the foundation's support for MESA as a success story: "Foundation grants to MESA have responded to the needs encountered at pivotal points in the development of Middle East studies. The first grant was intended to enable MESA to establish itself as a viable professional society in Middle East studies, the second to conduct studies of the basic accomplishments and needs in the field, and the third to insure MESA's continuing viability by easing the transition to self-sufficiency. The grants have achieved these purposes and as satisfactory reporting has been received, they may now be closed."[104]

Ford's characterization seems broadly accurate: whatever its travails, shortcomings and internal conflicts, MESA in its first two decades or so certainly succeeded in establishing itself as the preeminent academic association in its field and in winning broad acceptance as its prime venue for scholarly (and social) interaction. But in the process it also underwent significant change, in terms of the demographics of its membership, its openness to a broader range of intellectual and political perspectives, and its willingness and capacity to engage with contentious issues.

Open Season

Ironically, MESA's success in the 1980s and beyond in adapting to, and accommodating, the changing perspectives and interests of its increasingly diverse membership (which along the way probably came to include a growing proportion of people of Middle Eastern origin) would open it up to attack.

In the early twenty-first century critics on the right would contrast the "new" MESA, allegedly politicized and dominated by "mandarins of the left," with the "old" MESA, which had supposedly been a genuine scholarly association run by properly genteel and politically conservative white men.[105] The truth is obviously more complex, though MESA had certainly evolved over the decades, and from the early 1980s onward its leaders felt increasingly willing to take public stands on issues from which their predecessors would likely have shied away.

One set of issues with which MESA now had to contend concerned outside funding of Middle East programs at American universities. Certain institutions in the field—mainly elite private universities—had long received funding from Arab sources (and before the 1979 revolution from Iran), as well as from oil and other U.S. companies doing business in the region. Now, however, universities faced growing criticism, much of it from increasingly vigilant and vocal American Jewish organizations, for accepting donations from Arab individuals and governments. This prompted MESA's board to issue a statement in November 1979 denouncing "vague allegations and unfounded generalizations" to the effect that donations from "Middle Eastern sources" to American institutions of higher education "have compromised established principles of academic freedom and equality of access to education. . . . The scholars and administrators engaged in university programs in Middle East studies are capable of administering these funds in a professionally responsible fashion and are intent upon doing so."[106] Making sure that donors have not attached strings to their donations is a perfectly legitimate concern, though of course the concerns raised about funding from Arab donors were themselves often politically motivated. In any case, in this instance MESA's board can be seen as defending an older way of doing business.

Three years later MESA would revisit the issue of outside funding, but it now did so not to insist that universities could be trusted to ensure that donations from foreign sources did not influence research, teaching or appointments (which they sometimes probably did), but rather to address some of the same concerns that Irene Gendzier had raised six or seven years earlier. In 1981 Nikki Keddie, MESA's president at the time, informed the board of her concerns about "funding coming from defense-related agencies and disagreement with the earlier MESA statement [of 1979] voicing confidence in academic integrity in the face of allegedly corrupting financing." She wanted a new statement that would at a minimum call for disclosing all funding sources.[107] Despite some opposition, in November 1982 the board proposed, and MESA's membership subsequently approved, a resolution declaring that "the continued credibility and trust of the public in academic research on the Middle East rests upon an open and free disclosure of funding sources for such research" and calling upon its members (but also organizations and institutions in the field) to "disclose fully in any written results and also to all persons involved in its conduct (i.e., participants, contributors and subjects) all sources of support—other than personal—for that research."[108] However, the business meeting rejected an additional clause calling on members, as a matter of principle, "to make public their research consultancies, official connections with governmental organizations of all countries, and sources of extramural research support."[109] Apparently that was going a bit too far for those present. Nonetheless, the resolution was a significant departure for MESA, marking its first public break with Cold War norms governing the relationship between academia and the national security state, and signaling how much it had changed even since the mid-1970s—and how the definition of the term "nonpolitical," often invoked by MESA's founders and their successors, and embedded in its bylaws, had evolved over time.

MESA would take things several steps further in 1985. For one, reaffirming its 1982 resolution on disclosure of funding sources, it adopted a resolution criticizing Harvard University's Center for Middle Eastern Studies because its director at the time, political scientist Nadav Safran, had failed to disclose that the CIA had helped fund a conference he had organized on Islamic fundamentalism.[110] That same year MESA also for the first time publicly stated its opposition to certain forms of collaboration by scholars with intelligence agencies. This action was taken in response to the Defense Academic Research Support Program, an initiative launched in 1982 by the Defense Intelligence Agency (DIA) and designed (as the agency informed the SSRC) "to obtain a wide range of scholarly and expert perceptions, viewpoints, appraisals, opinions, and assessments to supplement analyses and policy deliberations within the Defense Department."[111] The program solicited research proposals on topics that included the Islamic clergy in Iran, Syrian-Iraqi relations, water in the Middle East and the West Bank. Military and intelligence agencies had since the late 1940s routinely sought such proposals from area specialists, and they had often gotten them; and some scholars would continue to do work for the CIA and other intelligence agencies on contract.[112] Through the 1970s few among the senior figures in U.S. Middle East studies felt that this was an issue that needed to be addressed.

However, by the early 1980s attitudes had begun to change. The new DIA program raised the hackles of the members of the JCNME, who promptly agreed to write a letter to MESA expressing their concern. Signed by every JCNME member, the letter argued that "by publicly identifying such broad subject areas . . . as of explicit interest to the defense intelligence community, the DIA will have served to jeopardize the research activities of the academic community by raising understandable fears in Middle Eastern countries that American scholars have become handmaidens of the strategic interests of the United States and direct purveyors of information to the defense community." The signers pledged not to bid on any of the proposals and urged MESA to address the issue.[113] It was Nikki Keddie, now no longer an officer of the association, who drafted a resolution and urged the MESA board to take a stand. It took two years, apparently because of contention among board members, but in November 1985 MESA finally adopted a resolution on the question. It stated that scholars should contribute responsibly to government efforts to improve the analysis and discussion of foreign policy and international security issues, but for more or less the same reasons the JCNME had set forth in its letter also urged "university-based international studies programs to refrain from responding to requests for research contract proposals from the Defense Academic Research Support Program or from other intelligence entities and calls upon its members to reflect carefully upon their responsibilities to the academic profession prior to seeking or accepting funding from intelligence sources."[114] Again, MESA had clearly come a long way over the previous decade.[115]

Even as MESA began to speak out more clearly and forcefully on the relationship between academia and the state, it was compelled for the first time to confront assaults of a new kind from groups based outside the academy. In November 1982 MESA adopted a resolution declaring that "teachers, students, administrators, and writers in the field should have freedom to express their views without fear of threats, physical attacks, economic or career reprisals, or other forms of intimidation or attack" and insisting that hiring and promotion "be based on ability to fill the requirements of a position, and not to be influenced by personal or political views, national or religious origins, race or gender." The main impetus behind the resolution seems to have been a desire to defend Stanford J. Shaw of UCLA, who had come under attack for allegedly denying or downplaying the Armenian genocide. The same business meeting endorsed a resolution explicitly defending Shaw drafted by the Turkish Studies Association.[116] This was hardly the end of the story: the Turkish government's endowment of chairs of Ottoman and Turkish studies at several American universities, including the Atatürk chair at Princeton's Department of Near Eastern Studies, its funding of the Institute of Turkish Studies in Washington and its continuing efforts to deter scholars from characterizing the 1915 massacres of Armenians in the Ottoman empire as an instance of genocide resulted in continuing controversy.[117]

However, scrutiny and attacks from a very different source began from the early 1980s onward to play an even more important role in the life of MESA and of Middle East studies as a field. One harbinger of what was to come was a campaign launched in 1981 by the Tucson Jewish Community Council against the Near Eastern Center of the University of Arizona at Tucson—MESA's new home base—accusing it of "anti-Israel bias." The university's president eventually intervened and appointed an independent panel of outside scholars to assess the allegations. While the panel found that there had been deficiencies in supervision of the center's outreach program, it rejected the allegations of bias.[118]

Worse was to come: in the course of the 1980s a number of national Jewish organizations, particularly AIPAC and the Anti-Defamation League of B'nai Brith (ADL), launched apparently concerted attacks on scholars of the Middle East and on Middle East centers and programs, among other things by compiling and circulating lists of scholars accused of being anti-Israel propagandists, pro-Arab apologists and even antisemites.[119] MESA responded in November 1984 with a resolution denouncing AIPAC and the ADL for disseminating unfounded accusations and blacklists, and authorizing its Ethics Committee to receive and report on complaints from members.[120] Unsurprisingly, neither the ADL nor AIPAC was deterred, and scholars and institutions deemed critical of Israel would continue to be targeted by both local and national organizations based outside of academia, a campaign that escalated dramatically after September 11, 2001, and persists to the present day.[121] Notwithstanding MESA's success at providing a stable and expansive organizational framework for U.S. Middle East studies by the 1980s, then, this field would in the decades that followed continue to face external threats and pressures (including politically motivated efforts to cut Title VI funding, or use the threat thereof to silence certain viewpoints) that, in kind and scale, no other area studies field had had to contend with since the end of the anticommunist crusades of the late 1940s and 1950s.

8 "The Lower Parts of Max Weber"

The lower parts of Max Weber can be taken apart and put together in many novel ways; a worthy task to which social science calls us to consecrate our energy and treasure over and over again!
—Muhsin Mahdi, 1972

D ESPITE RAPID GROWTH experienced by Middle East studies from the mid-1950s onward and the establishment in 1966 of a professional association for the field, a sense of malaise and pessimism began to creep into assessments of the field's standing and prospects in the later 1960s. Morroe Berger's gloomy 1967 essay was a manifestation of this, as were the fears expressed about such purported problems as the excessive number of Middle East studies centers, the inferior quality of new graduate students and a looming oversupply of ill-trained PhDs. In part these anxieties reflected the stresses and strains of the historical moment, in particular the conflicts that had exposed profound fault lines in American society. But developments specific to area studies, and to Middle East studies in particular, also played a role in fostering, in certain quarters, a new, less optimistic atmosphere and in exacerbating longstanding anxieties about the field's intellectual standing and prospects.

The Age of Retrenchment

According to Robert A. McCaughey, in the fifteen years following the establishment of Ford's International Training and Research division in 1953 the foundation spent about a quarter of a billion dollars on "the academic international studies enterprise," defined very broadly to include international and area studies in all their manifestations. Deploying a narrower definition, George M. Beckmann estimated in 1964 that over the previous dozen years Ford had spent some $138 million "for grants designed to improve American competence to deal with international problems by narrowing the gap between the needs for and the supply of trained personnel and knowledge," with approximately half of that disbursed "to strengthen non-Western language and area studies in American universities and colleges."[1] Whatever the exact figures, area studies had clearly benefited enormously from the very large sums that Ford and its sister foundations had poured into this field, supplemented by substantial funding from Title VI and from universities.

In the late 1960s and early 1970s, however, the flow of outside funding into area studies dropped off, signaling harder times ahead. Changes at the Ford Foundation, by far the biggest funder on the scene, set the new tone. In 1966 McGeorge Bundy was eased out of his position as National Security Advisor to President Johnson and assumed the foundation's presidency. A key architect of American military intervention in Vietnam and well aware that what were now widely referred to as Third World countries were the main battlegrounds of the Cold War, Bundy pushed Ford to shift its priorities. Soon after taking office he terminated Ford's International Training and Research program; responsibility for making and monitoring grants for international and area studies at universities in the United States and Canada was reassigned to Ford's Overseas Division, whose main concern was economic and social development in underdeveloped countries. Ford officials also seriously considered terminating the Foreign Area Fellowship Program (FAFP), since 1962 administered by the ACLS and SSRC, which made research grants in area and international studies. In March 1969 Pendleton Herring, who had stepped down as president of the SSRC the previous year, explained Ford's thinking to his colleagues: "The new focus of the Foundation's international efforts is on helping in the social and economic growth of societies in Latin America, Africa, the Middle East, and Asia. . . . Officers of the Foundation are uncertain about how support of such activities abroad is to be related to continuing support of area training and research in the United States. The primary interest is in advancing the development of countries rather than area studies."[2] In the end, after some delay, Ford ultimately decided to continue to fund the

FAFP, and international and area studies more broadly, including the joint SSRC-ACLS regional committees, though on a more modest scale. Nonetheless, as McCaughey puts it, "an era in philanthropic enterprise could be said to have ended."[3]

For a time it seemed that the tapering off of Ford support for area studies would be more than compensated for by a huge infusion of new federal funding. The International Education Act of 1966 promised to provide hundreds of millions of additional dollars for international education and area studies. But within a year or so of its passage it was clear that the act would never actually be funded by Congress, which was increasingly preoccupied by the soaring cost of the Vietnam War and the faltering domestic economy.[4] Meanwhile, after slowly but steadily rising through the 1960s, the federal funding that for a decade had flowed to area studies centers and graduate training under the Title VI program peaked in the late 1960s, in current as well as constant dollar terms. Even worse, the Title VI program came under threat of extinction at decade's end. When it came into office in 1969 the Nixon administration sought to defund the program altogether; while Congress rejected this, in the 1971 fiscal year the appropriation for Title VI was reduced from $12.85 million to $7.17 million, leading to a temporary halving of the number of supported centers. By fiscal 1974 funding for the program was back up to $11.3 million and it would increase further during the Carter administration, but during Ronald Reagan's presidency it would drop to lower levels and remain there until the 1990s, when the program's funding began to rise again.[5] Thus by the late 1960s signals from both New York and Washington were making it increasingly clear that the "bonanza years" had come to an end and that a new era of more limited resources and slower growth, no growth at all or even retrenchment had begun for area studies.

In this new atmosphere doubts grew about the proliferation of Middle East area studies centers that Title VI funding had made possible since 1958, especially among leaders of the older programs at elite private and public universities, many of which had benefited from generous foundation support. If retrenchment was necessary, some of them seemed quite ready to throw overboard many of the newer centers, often located at public universities. For example, in 1969 key faculty in Princeton's Near Eastern studies program told a Ford Foundation consultant that "the field could not support all the existing Near East centers."

All assumed that some area study programs must continue if Near East stud-ies are to be maintained. [Morroe] Berger estimated that four to six programs would be the optimum number, but [L. Carl] Brown insisted that any fewer than six would only reinforce the reputation of Near East centers as esoteric ap-pendages—removed from the mainstream of academic life. Princeton, UCLA, Michigan and Berkeley were mentioned by all as strong centers, with Carl Brown including Harvard. There seems to be an awareness at Princeton that the Near East field is in bad shape nationally and will not easily be improved soon.[6]

In a similar vein, T. Cuyler Young told the *Daily Princetonian* in 1969 that there were too many Middle East studies programs: "They're coming so fast that there isn't enough top-quality personnel to man them."[7] It is worth not-ing that if six was deemed the optimal number of Middle East programs, well over half the existing centers would be superfluous.

The rapid expansion of the field in the 1960s, and then the prospect of retrenchment at decade's end, also led to much talk about the supposedly inferior quality of many faculty and students in the field. "Superior talent at the senior level is very rare in this country and attempts by Princeton to lure certain of the best people from Europe to the United States have been no more successful than Harvard's," Princeton faculty told the Ford consultant. In a February 1968 memorandum on possible research topics for the JCNME, Malcolm Kerr of UCLA struck a similarly gloomy tone about "the quality and status of Middle Eastern studies": "I am particularly struck by the dearth of new talent coming into the field, while very gifted graduate students have been entering the various disciplines of African studies in large numbers in recent years. The number of highly promising new faces in the Near Eastern field is very small."[8]

The Endless Quest for a Research Agenda

The establishment of MESA in 1966 had enabled the JCNME to free it-self of a number of the field-building tasks it had performed since its incep-tion. But neither this development nor the atmosphere of pessimism that pervaded the field from the late 1960s made it any easier than it had been in the past for the committee to develop a research agenda of the kind desired by the SSRC and by its prime funder and patron, the Ford Foundation. This remained the one major dimension of its mandate that neither the JCNME nor its predecessor the CNME had successfully fulfilled. This persistent failure strengthened the conviction shared by many senior figures in U.S. Middle East studies that the field was intellectually backward in comparison both with other area studies fields and with what was going on in the disciplines, especially political science. As Kerr told his colleagues in 1968, "evidently and rightly, the Ford Foundation would like the SSRC to exert some positive leadership, rather than just passively distributing funds to individuals who come forward." He continued: "Since the M.E. studies field is so diffuse, interdisciplinary, and spotty in talent we cannot make an impact by sitting around talking about 'general' problems across the board (eg. [sic] bemoaning the lack of talent, difficulty of learning Arabic, lack of communication, the gap between modern social science and classicism, etc.). We can only make an impact by sponsoring particular projects that an identifiable group of individuals can carry out concretely and that will be of wider—though *not* necessarily universal—benefit."

Kerr cited the establishment of MESA and of CASA as examples of successful committee initiatives but rejected the idea of "sponsoring a series of random conferences on one-shot topics"—exactly what the committee had been doing in recent years. Instead, he argued, the JCNME should emulate the example of the SSRC's Committee on Comparative Politics (CCP), which, he explained, had since 1961 "concentrated its resources on a prolonged theoretical and empirical study of political modernization with the result that the whole field of comparative politics was given a tremendous shot in the arm." Kerr proposed that the SSRC choose a topic on which the JCNME would, like the CCP, facilitate concentrated research over a period of years by commissioning a group of senior scholars to work on a common theme, resulting in summer research seminars and eventually conferences and publications. This would, Kerr hoped, advance the field as effectively as the CCP's focused work had supposedly done for political science.[9] There is considerable irony in Kerr's pointing to the CCP as a model to emulate at this historical moment: by the late 1960s that committee's efforts to place modernization theory on secure foundations were running out of steam and the paradigm itself was coming under increasingly heavy fire. Meanwhile, the behavioralism that the SSRC hoped would transform political science into a properly scientific discipline did not seem to be delivering what its advocates had promised, and scholars in international relations and other disciplines were also manifesting considerable anxiety about their apparent lack of a coherent and efficacious theory.[10] In short, despite recurrent lamentations by scholars (especially political scientists) about the supposed intellectual inferiority of area studies, there is little reason to think that their colleagues in the disciplines were faring much better.

In any case, consideration of the suggestions offered by Kerr and others was put on hold owing to uncertainties about the continuation of Ford funding. During 1968 and into 1969 Ford was reconsidering its funding priorities, which led to a long delay in deciding whether or not it would even renew its support of the JCNME and its sister committee on Africa. JCNME member Oleg Grabar was so annoyed by the delay that he drafted a statement of protest and asked Roland Mitchell, the committee's SSRC staffer, what he thought about circulating it:

> It is the sentiment of this Committee that the Ford Foundation has acted in a remarkably cavalier manner with the time of the Committee's members and especially with the hopes and expectations of those scholars who have applied for financial help. While it *could* be argued that the Foundation is free to use its money in any way it wants (part of a debatable point), it is equally true that elementary propriety and courtesy would require that Committees be made aware at a reasonable time whether they will or will not be funded, especially when needs were foreseeable a long time in advance.

Mitchell judiciously convinced Grabar to delay circulating his statement, and the foundation did in fact renew its funding for the committee not long thereafter. However, anxieties persisted about the continuation and size of Ford funding, on which the committee was entirely dependent not merely for its research grants and its other activities but probably for its very existence.[11]

Princeton: The Burden of the Early Adopter

In the late 1960s Princeton was widely regarded as having one of the country's leading Near Eastern studies programs, especially after H. A. R. Gibb's incapacitation in 1964 left Harvard's Middle East studies enterprise without a strong hand at the tiller. Yet despite generous funding from both the university and the big foundations, Princeton Near Eastern studies somehow seemed to have never quite managed to overcome its philological heritage and make itself the center for the study of the modern and contemporary

Middle East that its funders had envisioned from 1946 onward. By 1969, when T. Cuyler Young, who had led both Princeton's Department of Oriental Studies and its Program in Near Eastern Studies for a decade and a half, retired, university officials had come to feel that a shake-up was much needed.

The Department of Oriental Studies was now divided into two new departments, East Asian Studies and Near Eastern Studies, and L. Carl Brown was appointed as chair of the latter and as director of the Program in Near Eastern Studies. Brown had served in the Foreign Service in Beirut and Khartoum in 1953–1958 and then trained under Gibb at Harvard, receiving his PhD in 1962. After a four-year stint teaching at Harvard he joined the Princeton faculty; he was thus not only a member of a different generation than Young but also a relative newcomer to the Princeton Near Eastern studies scene. An outside consultant's report on Near Eastern studies at Princeton at this moment of transition makes it clear that the university hoped that Brown's appointment would achieve two key goals: get things moving forward in this field after what was perceived as a long period of stagnation, and overcome the persistent failure of Princeton Near Eastern studies to really put the social sciences and modern history in the lead.

The report, by Ford Foundation consultant John E. Rielly, was apparently commissioned to help the foundation decide what to do after the block grant of $2.5 million over ten years that Ford had awarded to Princeton in 1961 was finished.[12] As Rielly reported after interviewing Princeton administrators and faculty:

> With the retirement of T. Cuyler Young (who had been Chairman of the Near East Program for the past several years) and the recent death or retirement of several of his senior associates, Near Eastern Studies at Princeton have entered a new phase. . . . The previous emphasis in the Department of Oriental Studies on language, literature and archaeology, rather than on the modern disciplines of economics, political science, sociology and modern history, is due to change. Carl Brown and his associates are determined to focus more attention on the modern period and to give a higher priority to relating Near Eastern studies to the modern academic disciplines. The Oriental Studies scholars—largely generalists, rarely discipline-oriented and oftentimes more men of affairs than serious scholars—are gradually being replaced by younger men trained in modern disciplines. In attempting this shift in emphasis, Princeton officials seem to be aware of the many obstacles to its realization: the dearth of high-quality, trained

talent in the field, the low respect for Near Eastern studies in certain of the modern disciplines (especially economics), and the increasing financial vulnerability of exotic regional studies programs in an era of tight budgets and growing democratic decision-making in allocation of university funds. Brown especially is sensitive to the need to relate what has often been regarded as an esoteric field both to modern academic disciplines and to undergraduate education in non-Western fields.[13]

Though Rielly concluded that "Princeton is unlikely to ever become the outstanding international center that most observers expected Harvard to become under Gibb," he recommended that it should remain one of the universities that continued to receive Ford support because it had "a small solid program, effective leadership and is better integrated into the university than most Near East programs." At the time of his report Princeton provided Near Eastern studies with about $300,000 annually in university support, but each year it also received about one-third of the university's Ford grant ($80,000 a year), $136,300 in Title VI support (including $60,000 for graduate fellowships) and $50,250 in corporate gifts; the total annual intake from external sources alone was thus equivalent to $1.7 million in 2015. In addition, Princeton Near Eastern studies benefited from revenues generated by a $400,000 donation from the Iranian government to create the Pahlavi Endowment for Iranian Studies, originally established to bring Iranian scholars to Princeton; the National Iranian Oil Company had contributed an additional $100,000 to the endowment and U.S. corporations another $66,000, though the total of $1.5 million required for the creation of an endowed chair in Iranian studies had not been reached.[14] Rielly believed that Near Eastern studies could manage on $50,000 a year from Ford once the ITR grant ran out and favored continuing support at that level.

Not long thereafter Princeton submitted its formal request for a new round of Ford Foundation funding for Near Eastern studies. In a letter to Ford, Princeton's president Robert F. Goheen highlighted Princeton's strengths in this field and the university's unusually generous support for it from its own funds, but he also declared himself "haunted by the awareness that the American academic community was poorly prepared to offer needed expertise as this country became increasingly involved in Southeast Asia. Although disinclined to add jeremiads, I feel obliged to observe that comparable difficulties may lie ahead for us in the Near East. The Princeton Program in Near Eastern Studies can contribute by helping us face this bleak prospect with greater knowledge."[15] One might argue that, with regard to Southeast Asia, the problem was not so much academia's lack of preparedness or a dearth of expertise as the character and quality of the expertise that was on offer, generally rooted in highly ideological and deeply flawed premises as well as a profound ignorance of local histories, politics and cultures, coupled with the refusal of government officials and the mainstream media to engage with perspectives outside the official consensus. Be that as it may, Princeton had for almost a quarter of a century been promising foundations that its Near Eastern studies program would give greater priority to the modern and contemporary Middle East, thereby yielding more policy-relevant knowledge, and Goheen now reiterated that commitment.

As with the SSRC and most elite universities, Princeton University officials were in close and regular contact with Ford Foundation staff and had a very good sense of what the latter were interested in funding; so Princeton's grant proposals fit well with Ford's current concerns and priorities. In addition to support for two year-long interdisciplinary research seminars culminating in conferences, for merit fellowships for graduate students and for enhancing Princeton's library resources on the Middle East, about one-third of the funds that Princeton requested from Ford would be used to bring scholars from the Middle East to Princeton on a regular basis (for example, one year in three or one semester out of every four), without severing their connections with their home universities. For Princeton this was, as Ford's assessment of the grant request put it, a matter of "enlightened self-interest: keeping the channels open for research and contact for its own faculty in the countries of the Middle East and North Africa, while enhancing its own research and teaching competence by the use of specially qualified experts from the area itself." But Ford also regarded this proposal as contributing to its efforts to achieve "the closer integration of American scholars and scholarship with Middle Eastern and North African institutions and faculties, a trend we have been able to encourage only peripherally among the more financially constricted centers." This might, Ford believed, help overcome the "resentment and suspicion generated in the Middle Eastern and North African countries" that research in these places was still seen by Americans "as amenable only to Western competence carried out by foreign experts parachuting in to work in isolation and remove data to be shared with Western colleagues."

Enhanced cooperation by American and Middle Eastern scholars was, Ford believed, "going to be a *quid pro quo* for continued field research by foreigners in these countries, [but] it is also apparent that the area is beginning to generate scholars as well trained and better grounded than their Western colleagues who can make and are making strong, quality contributions." Thus Princeton's proposal to bring visiting scholars from the Middle East, to teach but also to participate in seminars and conferences, was perceived as complementing the foundation's commitment to contribute to the development of Middle Eastern societies and stem brain drain. These goals underpinned a Ford initiative approved at the end of 1970 that allocated $350,000 for postgraduate awards to young scholars from Middle Eastern universities and research institutes to conduct research in the social sciences on "problems of contemporary relevance to the region."[16] In this context it was helpful that Princeton had already begun negotiations about a visiting appointment with Şerif Mardin (born 1927), described by Ford as "a leading Turkish social scientist who has, in fact, been the key figure in the creation of the Foundation-supported Turkish Social Science Association" and "an excellent example of the rising young Middle Eastern scholar who is already internationally recognized and whose professional and career needs would be most likely to draw him away from the isolation of his Turkish university to a full-time foreign professorship."[17]

In September 1971 the Ford Foundation awarded Princeton Near Eastern studies a grant of $225,000 over four years—the equivalent of $1.3 million in 2015. With this funding in hand, Princeton Near Eastern Studies organized two year-long seminars that culminated in major conferences. One was on comparative modernization; the other, held in 1974, focused on the agrarian, demographic and socioeconomic history of the Middle East. Though there were hopes early on that the resulting edited volume of conference papers would quickly be published by Princeton University Press, it appeared only in 1981, published by the privately owned Darwin Press as part of its Princeton Series on the Near East.[18] In 1975 Princeton applied for an additional grant from Ford, to fund several more year-long seminars culminating in week-long conferences, at a cost of about $50,000 apiece (about $220,000 in 2015). Now the university proposed to focus on Islamic institutions in Africa, the Ottoman "*millet* system," and guilds and their legacy for the modern Middle East, though this last topic was later dropped. In that same year Princeton's

Department of Near Eastern Studies hired both the economist (and economic historian) Charles Issawi and the historian Bernard Lewis, leading a Ford officer to characterize the university as now possessing "one of the foremost collections of high level talent in this country on the Middle East."[19]

Some at Ford apparently had doubts about Princeton's grant proposal. Robert H. Edwards, the head of Ford's Middle East and Africa program, told his colleagues that he was not sure "why, with the world in a parlous state, the Foundation should spend money on leisurely scholarship and upon these relatively esoteric subjects," nor was he sure that the specific topics proposed by Princeton were well thought out. But he ultimately concluded that "these societies will not be less important to us ten years down the road, and a portion of our money should continue to be used as if the apocalypse were not going to occur."[20] Ford had by this time come to regard limited projects of this kind as not only the kind of thing it wished to support but as what in straitened circumstances it could afford to support; so in the end it agreed to fund two seminar-conferences at Princeton, on the status of minorities in the Middle East under the *millet* system and after its demise, and on aspects of Islam in Africa, with particular attention to slavery. The grant would also help bring scholars to Princeton from the Middle East and Africa and provide research assistantships for Princeton graduate students.[21] It would seem that, despite the acknowledged shortcomings of Near Eastern studies at Princeton and its difficulties over a quarter of a century to deliver what it had promised, the Ford Foundation (like the Carnegie Corporation and Rockefeller Foundation earlier on) insisted on remaining optimistic about the program's prospects and could not bring itself to refuse Princeton's requests for additional funding.

Years of Drift

In the late 1960s several of the scholars who had played key roles on the JCNME over the previous several years, among them Morroe Berger, Bernard Lewis and Malcolm Kerr, rotated off. Leadership of the committee soon passed into the hands of two political scientists, Marvin Zonis of the University of Chicago, an Iran specialist who would become chair in 1970, and I. William Zartman of NYU, still serving as MESA's executive secretary. The two of them now took the lead in the committee's renewed efforts to develop the kind of coherent, long-term research program that Kerr had advocated a few years earlier, but progress was slow. This led to yet another bout of frustration, demoralization and self-recrimination about the JCNME's apparent inability to formulate and implement a research agenda.

A case in point was a meeting that the JCNME organized in February 1970 in the hope of engaging leading scholars who were not in the JCNME's orbit, or not even Middle East specialists, in what was envisioned as the committee's program of "research on economic, political, social, and cultural development in the Near and Middle East, both in the past and the present."[22] Among those invited were two noted University of Chicago anthropologists: Bernard S. Cohn (1928–2003), whose work focused on India, and Clifford Geertz (1926–2006), whose influential *Islam Observed* had been published in 1968 and who was about to move to the Institute for Advanced Study. Zonis, Zartman and Princeton's L. Carl Brown represented the JCNME. The meeting was not a success. Zartman would acknowledge in a letter to Roland Mitchell soon thereafter that he and his JCNME colleagues had made "some serious tactical mistakes" in setting up the meeting, as a result of which "our original idea is dead—as dead as the egg shell that contains the chicken and is disregarded [*sic*] when it is born." Cohn, Geertz and the other invitees already had their own research projects and were not really interested in collaborating with the JCNME. Zartman went on:

> We were far too diffident and we are speaking to the wrong audience. If we are going to set up a project we must do it among ourselves or at least bring in a few people whose situation is not basically competitive, as was Frey's and Geertz'. . . . We must give up the notion that we are going to involve all the best leaders in Middle East studies. We must try rather to involve some of the best middle and lower level scholars and we must provide leadership rather than looking for gifted successful figures to lean on.[23]

Brown also came away from the meeting disheartened: he feared that the ideas Zartman and Zonis had brought to it "are destined to be placed in the same dead file with several other tangible suggestions put forward in the past." A month later Brown expressed his desire to leave the committee at the end of the academic year. Another participant reported that "the indirection of the meeting symbolized to me the present lack of direction and leadership in the field. . . ."[24]

There ensued months of inconclusive discussions and abortive proposals. By October 1970 Zartman was writing to his colleagues that "For a full year the Committee has been turning about the question of a longrange [*sic*] co-ordinated research project on development. It is time we landed."[25] A month later Marvin Zonis, by now chair of the committee, felt compelled to try to raise his colleagues' spirits. "It is time the committee stopped berating itself for its failures. While it may be the case that the Middle East field as a whole shows less intellectual vitality than is true for other area fields, I believe there are a variety of objective reasons to explain these shortcomings." These included the region's great linguistic and cultural diversity and the intractable problems of international relations it manifested; it had also proven difficult to integrate the venerable tradition of scholarship on the region with "more contemporary problems and methods of study." On the other hand, Zonis asserted, the field has demonstrated "remarkable vitality in recent years," as demonstrated by recent MESA annual meetings, the association's successful new journal, and "the very impressive numbers of well-trained and bright young scholars entering the field." In fact, Zonis went on, "it is not at all clear to me that the other area committees sponsored by the SSRC have demonstrated more tangible scholarly results than we have in the past."

Part of the problem, Zonis asserted, was that "our Committee is often compared with the SSRC Committee on Comparative Politics"—the very comparison Malcolm Kerr had made a year and a half earlier. Zonis argued that such a comparison was inequitable; in any case, he accurately noted, "a hard contemporary look at the Comparative Politics Committee would reveal considerable internal intellectual disarray, substantial external intellectual attacks, and a general feeling of lack of purpose and direction, all of which seem uncomfortably familiar." The way to overcome the committee's malaise, Zonis argued, was to seek additional funding in order to expand its grants program while also launching subcommittees to promote research on specific topics, for example political elites, education and social change, and social psychology. Zonis concluded by lamenting that the committee had fallen into a state in which "self-censure and self-pity paralyzes resolve, devalues all undertakings as insufficient or irrelevant, and contributes to a self-perpetuating fantasy of incompetence. There is certainly just cause for concern with our field. Let us, finally, move from concern to productive action."[26]

In trying to get the committee moving, Zonis was well aware that MESA had been grappling with whether it should get involved with seeking funding for, and overseeing, scholarly research. MESA's Research and Training Committee (RAT) had by 1971 decided to focus its energies on organizing a major conference to assess the state of U.S. Middle East studies, to be funded by Ford. In light of that initiative, and given that both foundation and Title VI funding seemed to be under threat, Zonis proposed that it was now up to the JCNME to develop a list of research priorities for the field. But he stressed to his colleagues that "these priorities are intended neither to coerce individual scholars nor to direct sources of funds. Rather, I view such priorities as an attempt to give some shape to the Middle Eastern field at a time when only concerted group action may allow us to preserve our relative intellectual and financial standing vis a vis [sic] other area fields."[27] Thus prodded, the committee eventually endorsed sponsoring two research projects, on urbanism and political elites, as Zonis had proposed. At the same time, the committee also informed Ford that it wished to not merely continue but to expand its grants program, even if the funds at its disposal were often used to supplement grants and fellowships from other sources. Perhaps most significantly, at the end of 1970 the committee embraced a call for a change in its priorities (and eventually composition) that had first surfaced over the past year and a half or so in the course of its largely fruitless discussions of research planning.

Incorporating the Natives (and Women)

Until the late 1960s neither the JCNME nor its predecessor the CNME had ever shown much interest in involving Middle Eastern scholars in its research planning or projects. This attitude was manifested in the decision to exclude local scholars from the one conference that the committee organized in the Middle East, in Tehran in 1959, as well as in its membership and activities up to this point. This began to change at the very end of the 1960s when, for the first time in the committee's history, it began to assert that any research project it sponsored "insofar as possible should involve nationals of the area as coequals of Western participants."[28] By November 1970 the committee was telling Ford that it wanted to support "joint research projects with one of the researchers in each project a middle easterner, [sic] who presumably would need to be provided with total support for the period of the grant." Substantial additional funds would be needed for these collaborative projects, with an international selection committee to review proposals, but "if circumstances warranted the Joint Committee might, however, become international itself at some point and take on these duties."[29]

The committee's sudden commitment to engaging with Middle Eastern scholars must be understood in the context of the Ford Foundation's heightened interest from the mid-1960s onward—and thus that of its grantees, including the SSRC—in encouraging collaboration between American and foreign scholars, and in supporting social science research and training in other parts of the world, as well as of factors specific to U.S. Middle East studies. Cold War concerns to develop closer ties with educated elites in politically crucial non-Western countries no doubt contributed to this development. But it was probably also propelled from below, so to speak, by the burgeoning critiques in the 1960s of many of the paradigms predominant in American academia and of what many had come to see as the intellectual imperialism exercised by American scholars, academic institutions and funders. These critiques were perhaps initially advanced most forcefully with regard to Latin America: for example, advocates of various Marxian approaches and of dependency theory in its multiple variants began assaulting the intellectual underpinnings—but also the political implications and consequences—of the modernization theory paradigm so pervasive among American political scientists studying the non-Western world, and more broadly of American political and economic domination. They also denounced what they perceived as the marginalization or suppression of scholarly and intellectual voices that emanated from outside North American academia, and demanded a more equal sharing of resources.

As noted earlier, foundation support for Latin American studies had languished until the Cuban revolution of 1959 and subsequent aftershocks across the region again made it a high priority, at which point the ACLS-SSRC Joint Committee for Latin American Studies (JCLAS) was revived and foundation support began flowing in. After a 1965 conference in Rio de Janeiro, the JCLAS began for the first time to provide grants for research projects on which a scholar from the United States or Canada would collaborate with a scholar from Latin America, and scholars from that region began to be appointed as full members of the joint committee. In 1973 the JCLAS received another Ford grant of $1.5 million to support research, and between 1969 and 1989 nearly half of its research grants went to Latin American scholars.[30] This new priority manifested a growing sense that it was no longer intellectually or politically tenable to treat the rest of the world as exclusively the object of research conducted by North Americans or to ignore the perspectives of indigenous scholars.

With respect to the Middle East in particular, other factors may also have contributed to the shift in Ford's agenda. As discussed earlier, the centerpiece of Princeton's successful grant application to Ford for Near Eastern studies in 1970–1971 was a plan to bring Middle Eastern scholars to Princeton on a regular basis, in part because it was hoped that strengthening ties with Middle Eastern scholars might give American scholars better research access to the Middle East, where conditions had become significantly less hospitable in recent years. It is also worth noting that Ford had long maintained offices in the Middle East, and its staff there, who were often in close contact with local scholars and institutions of higher education, may well have encouraged their bosses back in New York to at long last address this issue. It may also have been the case that the cohorts of American scholars which began to take center-stage in U.S. Middle East studies from the mid-to-late 1960s had in the course of their sojourns in the region developed different kinds of personal and professional ties with their local counterparts (or with different kinds of people) than had been the case for earlier cohorts, and thereby came to understand the value of bringing the work and experience of Middle Eastern scholars into more active and equal dialogue with those of American scholars and their academic institutions. Some may even have seen such intellectual dialogue as a way to remedy what they perceived as the sorry state of U.S. Middle East studies by infusing it with new perspectives, models and ideas.

Whatever the specific factors at play, by 1970 the Ford Foundation was looking for new ways to support Middle Eastern scholars and their research work, whether by enabling them to spend time at American universities or by providing financial support for training and research at universities in the region itself. MESA included a proposal for a new program that would bring scholars from the Middle East to the United States on a regular basis in its 1972 grant request to Ford. The JCNME also got the message, and by the spring of 1971 it was urging the ACLS and the SSRC to seek foundation funding for a new collaborative research grants program, modeled on that of the JCLAS, which would pair an American with a Middle Eastern scholar. The new program's benefits were described as threefold: "increase of knowledge, fostering of cooperation, and improving the likelihood of acquainting scholars of the U.S. and of the area with the latest scholarly developments." The JCNME was careful to stipulate that a collaborative research program should not encourage brain drain from the Middle East or take the form of a "teacher-pupil relationship" between American and Middle Eastern scholars but be based on "equality among the partners." Soon, it was ready to go even further by urging the councils to "appoint members from the area not only to review applications but to participate fully in all aspects of its work," and it began discussing possible appointees from the region. The committee's watchword was now "internationalization" of its membership and its research program.[31]

By the fall of 1971 the idea of appointing Middle East scholars to the JCNME was under serious discussion at the SSRC. But there was a potential complication: what would happen if Israeli as well as Arab scholars were appointed? Committee staffer Roland Mitchell told P&P that "internationalization of the committee might mean exclusion of Israelis, so as not to destroy possibilities for fostering collaborative research on the area. Presumably Israelis would not be welcome at meetings in Arab countries."[32] The SSRC deferred the appointment of Middle Eastern scholars until it could conclude its consultations and resolve the Israel issue. However, in the fall of 1971, with the Ford Foundation about to approve a grant of $326,000 for the committee over a two-year period, including $125,000 for a new collaborative grants program, the committee decided to invite three Middle Eastern scholars to serve as consultants on that program. They were the sociologist S. M. Eisenstadt (1923–2010) of the Hebrew University of Jerusalem, a key figure in the elaboration of modernization theory; the historian Abdullah Laroui (born 1933) of Université Mohammed V in Rabat; and sociologist Şerif Mardin of Ankara University.[33] The new program was announced, and applications solicited, in December 1971, and in the spring of 1972 the first round of collaborative grants was announced.[34] Later that same year the SSRC proceeded to appoint Eisenstadt, Laroui and Mardin as full members of the JCNME. It is not clear why the appointment to the committee of an Israeli scholar no longer seemed to be of concern to the SSRC.[35]

Within a few years JCNME members would come to feel that applications to the collaborative grants program were weaker than they had hoped, and the last grants made under the program were for 1975–1976, after which it was discontinued. A proposal by the committee to replace the collaborative grants with a new program of grants to be made directly by it to scholars in the Middle East, like the program through which the JCLAS provided grants to scholars in Latin America, was not approved.[36] Nonetheless, the JCNME would henceforth always have at least one member from some Middle Eastern or North African country, and in the years that followed it would not only begin to hold some of its meetings in the region but also actively seek to involve local scholars in them. The committee's effort to internationalize, in terms of its membership and its programs, may not have been as extensive or as successful as that of some of the other SSRC-ACLS committees, but at least by the early 1970s it understood that it had to try.

Even as the JCNME was grappling with how to engage more effectively with scholars from the region it studied, it was also, like MESA, compelled to engage with diversification of another kind. As discussed in Chapter 7, by the early 1970s the histories, social roles and status of women in the Middle East, and more broadly questions of gender, had begun to receive greater scholarly and public attention, and eventually to transform U.S. Middle East studies in significant ways, including broadening the field's composition, leadership and intellectual orientation. One manifestation of this shift was the appointment, in the fall of 1973, of the first woman ever to serve as a member of the JCNME: sociologist Janet Abu-Lughod of Northwestern University (1928–2013), who had for some time been involved with the committee-supported research project on urbanism in the Middle East. Abu-Lughod served for two years, at which point the second woman ever appointed to the committee, anthropologist Amal Rassam of Queens College, took her place. Committee members and scholars connected with it now began to discuss and develop proposals for research on women in the Middle East, and the committee acknowledged that it had ignored gender for too long and began to list research on women as one of its priorities.[37] Actually getting research projects on women and gender funded and launched was another matter, but by the mid-1970s it was clear that women could no longer be ignored either as committee members or as an important focus of research.

One other development in this period which may have stimulated more focused research on the region is worth noting. In the early 1970s the JCNME (like the other ACLS-SSRC regional committees) began for the first time to be able to directly award fellowships for doctoral dissertation research. This was a major departure, since the grants under the joint committee's control since 1957 had been exclusively for postdoctoral research. In effect, the Ford-funded Foreign Area Fellowship Program, which had been overseen by an ACLS-SSRC committee since 1962, was now merged into the SSRC's international program. In theory this would (as an SSRC officer would later put it) enable "the area committees to link their research planning to regionally tailored programs of fellowship support."[38] Whether such linkage actually happened in any systematic way is not clear, but the joint committee now began awarding dissertation research fellowships, with a committee of scholars who were not JCNME members conducting the initial screening of applications and the committee reviewing and approving the final list. Four SSRC fellowships for dissertation research on the Middle East were awarded for 1974–1975 and seven for 1975–1976, along with eighteen postdoctoral grants and two collaborative research grants in the latter year.[39]

"The Lower Parts of Max Weber"

Even as it was engaging with diversification, the JCNME at long last got two of its proposed research projects moving ahead—though the outcome and impact on the field of those projects was not quite what their initiators had hoped for. One project focused on political elites in the Middle East. From the 1950s onward, mainstream American political science devoted a great deal of attention to studying the political elites of the so-called "new states." They were deemed to be the central actors in modernization and especially in "political development," an ill-defined term that denoted the processes whereby non-Western polities would (if all went well) ultimately attain stability, order and legitimacy—and perhaps even liberal democracy, though this was often not regarded as necessary, appropriate or even desirable for them. A focus on elites also seemed to offer a methodological alternative both to Marxian class analysis and to visions of pluralist democracy.[40] As I. William Zartman put it in a 1982 volume on North African political elites to which he contributed:

> Politics can best be understood through a study of those who exercise power— those who make the decisions and rules that run society. Although the institutions through which they act or the issues that challenge and constrain them are important, it is the elites of politics who operate the political system. Elites are

known through their origins, their behavior, their relation to the rest of society, and their ways of entrance and exit. Used separately, these elements provide a comprehensive portrait of those in power; combined, they constitute a dynamic of their own that impels society in explicable directions. Developing countries have fewer elites than developed countries, but the importance of the elites is predominant in both.[41]

This conception spawned a large scholarly literature on the political (and to a lesser extent economic) elites of non-Western countries. Several JCNME members had long argued for what one funding proposal described as "a systematic program to stimulate comparative research on the elites of different countries" of the Middle East which, they hoped, would "generate new insights into the processes of development and the roles of different groups and political systems in development." In 1971 Marvin Zonis, then chair of the JCNME, had published his own contribution in this arena, *The Political Elite of Iran*.[42] In 1972 the committee sponsored the first in a planned series of workshops on the roles of political and economic elites in modernization; this project culminated in *Elites in the Middle* East, edited by Zartman and published in 1980. In his introduction to the volume Zartman expressed the hope that "the preparation behind this collection and its exposition of opportunities for useful analysis in the Middle East, combined with the current public attention given to the area, will promote further advances in the study of elites and will contribute to making the Middle East an academically more attractive place to study."[43] Things did not turn out as Zartman had imagined: the emergence of new forms of mass politics in the Middle East, including Islamist sociopolitical movements and the Iranian revolution of 1978–1979, along with the intellectual collapse of modernization theory in American academia, led to declining interest in elite studies and relegated much of the scholarly work done in this vein to the margins.

The second project launched by the committee in the early 1970s also engaged with modernization, though from a historical rather than synchronic perspective. Responding to a memorandum from S. M. Eisenstadt that challenged "the accepted assumptions underlying most models of development," the JCNME began planning a large conference (to be held in Turkey) comparing historical patterns of social change in the Maghrib and Turkey, with Abdullah Laroui and Şerif Mardin in charge of conference planning and research.[44] Not everyone was convinced that the committee was on the right track: in a December 1972 memorandum to his fellow committee members, the Harvard Islamicist Muhsin Mahdi (1926–2007) offered what he described as some "stray thoughts" about the proposed conference on polity, economy and society in the Maghrib and Turkey:

> As an outsider, I cannot help noticing that the proposals remain somewhat narrow in their focus, and some of them betray a business as usual attitude concerning issues and men despite the apparent interest in re-evaluation and new approaches. The lower parts of Max Weber can be taken apart and put together in many novel ways; a worthy task to which social science calls us to consecrate our energy and treasure over and over again!
>
> Western scholars do not encounter Middle Eastern scholars. They select their "external proletariat" whom they have formed in their own image to hear from them echoes of outdated hypotheses and to spring on them their latest products.
>
> Could both groups get together and ask what kind of development, industrialization, reform, urbanization, education, and for what? Could they get together and discuss what they have been doing to each other for a change?
>
> ... A conference can be an opportunity to come out of professional isolation, talk and listen to others who speak a different language, and wonder about what one has been doing. It can also intensify this isolation by satisfying oneself that the social science machine is basically sound and that all it needs is a minor lubrication job.[45]

Mahdi's plea was not heeded and planning for the conference proceeded. It finally took place in May 1975 on the resort island of Buyukada, near Istanbul. However, turning the conference papers into a manuscript suitable for publication as an edited volume, and finding a publisher for it, proceeded very slowly. Princeton University Press apparently rejected the manuscript, and by early 1981 Peter von Sivers, the JCNME member at that point charged with preparing the manuscript for publication, was describing it as an "albatross." Current committee members had expressed strong reservations about seven of the projected twenty chapters and saw problems with many of the others that would require extensive editorial work. Von Sivers noted that the proposed volume was now "nearly six years old. The tightened focus [that he had proposed in order to render it coherent] was novel in 1975, but is now in the middle of the pack at best. There are no startling overall proposals for a better treatment of the question of historical continuity than are already available in recent literature published after 1975."[46] Two years later the manuscript was still proving recalcitrant and no publisher could be found for it; the effort to get it published was eventually abandoned.[47] So like the committee-sponsored research project on elites, this project too thus failed to have any significant, long-term theoretical or methodological impact on Middle East studies. Both were by this time largely irrelevant, relics of modernization theory's heyday which had long since passed.

The anxiety induced by the JCNME's ongoing struggle to identify productive new approaches and foster cutting-edge research that would advance the field was exacerbated by growing evidence that, over the longer term, Ford Foundation support for area studies was likely to decline further. In an address to the annual meeting of the African Studies Association in the fall of 1975, David R. Smock, deputy head of the Ford Foundation's Middle East and Africa program, surveyed Ford's history of support for area studies and outlined what lay ahead; two years later Anne Lesch, who had just joined the staff of Smock's program, would convey almost exactly the same message to MESA members at that association's annual meeting. Over the previous two decades, Smock reported, Ford had spent more than $15 million on U.S.-based research and training relating to the Middle East and Africa, including grants to Middle East studies centers at Harvard, the University of Chicago, Berkeley, Princeton, Columbia, NYU, the University of Pennsylvania and UCLA. Now, despite "heightened public awareness of the impact events in these regions will have on the world," Ford was ceasing to make grants to support the operating costs of Middle East and African area studies centers; more broadly, "with the prospect of drastically reduced budgetary resources, the Foundation staff has had to confront the question of which of its activities should survive or be reshaped in the face of competing claims on scarcer resources." Smock reassured his audience that Ford would continue to support SSRC-sponsored research workshops and conferences as well as the predoctoral and postdoctoral fellowships it awarded, and that funding for the African Studies Association and for MESA would also continue, "although at steadily declining levels." Beyond that, Smock declared, "The most that the Ford Foundation can hope to do is to support particularly promising research projects or research seminars," for which it had budgeted $310,000 a year for the next three years, enough to fund between three and six projects per year. As an example of such projects Smock cited the grant that, as I discussed earlier, Princeton had recently received for two year-long seminars followed by conferences on the status of minorities in the Middle East under the *millet* system and on aspects of Islam in Africa.[48]

Given this situation, and the prospect of further cutbacks, the JCNME felt obliged not long thereafter to consider whether, if Ford funding declined further, it should abandon either the dissertation research fellowship program or its longstanding postdoctoral grant program. Members expressed a preference for keeping the latter going, "since the predoctoral fellowships were assisting young people to acquire training for which there was no job demand."[49] As things turned out, the committee would not actually have to make this choice. Meanwhile, planning for various other committee projects continued; the modest hope was, as one discussion put it, that despite the committee's limited resources it could at least help advance the field by "identifying research areas that are near a takeoff point and giving a boost by a conference, a workshop, or by a research grant."[50]

State of the Art

Middle East studies began to experience challenges to, and contention about, dominant intellectual and political paradigms somewhat later than at least some of the other area studies fields. But by the early 1970s we can discern evidence that the critiques of Orientalism and modernization theory being advanced in Britain and the United States, mainly by younger scholars and graduate students, were beginning to reach even those in the upper strata of the field. For example, in November 1973 JCNME chair Marvin Zonis circulated to his fellow committee members Roger Owen's recently published critical review of *The Cambridge History of Islam*, describing it as raising "a number of issues about the study of Middle Eastern history which the Committee has discussed in the past and which frequently have influenced our decisions about Committee activities."[51] It is in fact not at all evident that the issues Owen raised in this landmark intervention had actually been discussed by the committee or had influenced its thinking; but henceforth it, and Middle East studies as a whole, would be increasingly compelled to engage with, or at least acknowledge, the rising tide of criticism that challenged both Orientalism and modernization theory. Critiques of Orientalism (mainly from a broadly Marxian direction) had already been elaborated, and had begun to have an impact, well before Edward W. Said's landmark book *Orientalism*, published in 1978, landed like a bombshell in the fields of Middle East and Islamic studies.[52] Modernization theory, central to much social science and historical research and writing in the United States on the Middle East as on many other regions of the Third World, had been subjected to increasingly devastating criticism from the late 1960s onward. Nils Gilman has argued that by the early 1970s efforts to "defend the paradigm" of modernization theory from its critics "were no longer working," and he dates the intellectual collapse of modernization theory to the early part of that decade: ". . . in 1973, the [SSRC's Committee on Comparative Politics] would disband, its Princeton University Press series on political development a volume short of the ten originally envisioned, with the last volume presenting not the anticipated metahistorical crescendo of theory, but rather a dirge to the intellectual cadaver of modernization theory."[53]

Among senior scholars in Middle East studies, especially but not exclusively the political scientists among them, a sense of theoretical and methodological uncertainty, anxiety and drift, coupled with persistent fears about declining funding and concerns about the abilities of current graduate students and younger faculty, prompted both soul-searching and a desire to find new ways to advance the field. This was the context in which MESA's Research and Training Committee had in the early 1970s declared its intention of conducting what it regarded as a thorough assessment of U.S. Middle East studies that could help move the field forward. As RAT's chair Leonard Binder put it with reference to the volume that this project eventually yielded, the goal was to "provide a review of recent research and a guide for younger scholars . . . to provide some intellectual justification for the selection of research topics and for the allocation of research and program support funds."[54] With funding from the Ford Foundation, RAT commissioned a number of leading scholars to provide critical surveys of their fields, which they presented at a "State of the Art" conference held at the Center for Advanced Study in the Behavioral Sciences in Palo Alto. The conference stretched through most of August 1973, with separate sessions devoted to each discipline. The papers were discussed again at the 1973 MESA annual meeting in Milwaukee and, after revision, published in 1976 as *The Study of the Middle East: Research and Scholarship in the Humanities and Social Sciences*, edited by Leonard Binder. Each chapter of the book sought to assess and situate the scholarly work on the Middle East produced in the West within a particular discipline or field, attending to what had been accomplished but also to problems, gaps and deficiencies.[55]

In his introduction to *The Study of the Middle East* Binder asserted that "when examined in the light of the disciplines, it seems to me that our recent achievements are not unimpressive" and that "Middle East studies have come of age." (19) But he also offered a rather harsh assessment of the field as a whole:

> The fact is that Middle Eastern studies are beset by subjective projections, displacements of affect, ideological distortion, romantic mystification, and religious bias, as well as by a great deal of incompetent scholarship. To my mind the greatest problem is that of incompetent scholarship, but incompetence can often be disguised or even defended as the application of a subjective, nonquantitative, phenomenological, or anti-positivist approach. . . . The area specialist, basing his arguments on his own long residence in the area or on his knowledge of the languages of the area asserts an arbitrary authority. This authority can be countered by the equally arbitrary authority of another specialist who has as much experience. (16)

Here Binder seemed to be criticizing, from the standpoint of contemporary mainstream U.S. social science, the persistent influence of Orientalism, whose practitioners Binder characterized as "having achieved immense works of scholarship" but who were "all too often content to sum up the meaning of a civilization on the basis of a few manuscripts." (9–10) Binder also asserted that "it appears that the standing of most [Middle East] specialists in the eyes of their disciplinary colleagues is not very high."

> It also appears to be the case that many of those who are most accepted by their disciplinary colleagues are least qualified (in terms of language and area residence) in the eyes of their area colleagues. Moreover, Middle East studies seem to have more than their share of nonspecialized scholars and of non scholarly specialists [*sic*]. Part of the reason for this sorry state of affairs is the failure to apply firm academic standards during the recent period of rapidly induced growth of area specialists. (6–7)

To support his generally pessimistic assessment, which echoed longstanding concerns about the quality of scholarship in the field, Binder cited data which he argued showed that relatively few "so-called Middle East specialists" had achieved competence in one or more Middle Eastern languages or had spent substantial periods actually living in the region.[56] But the real problem with the area studies fields, as Binder assessed them in *The Study of the Middle East,* was that they "were fostered for political reasons . . . as instrumentalities and not ends," "as accumulations of knowledge rather than areas of inquiry and interpretation." These new fields therefore lacked "widely accepted standards of excellence. We have still not decided which are the things worth knowing, which problems require additional research, how the various subjects are to be defined, and all of the rest of the limitations that determine the ways in which the more traditional studies are organized and standards of scholarship are set." Binder went on to explicitly draw on Thomas Kuhn's enormously influential writing on the rise and decline of scientific paradigms, which (Kuhn argued) while ascendant defined what questions could be asked and thus shaped scientists' findings and how they were understood.[57] As Binder put it, "the paradigms of area studies, and of Middle East studies in particular, have not yet been fixed." (2)

Binder hoped that the volume whose production he had orchestrated would elucidate how these paradigms had been and were being forged for Middle East studies, by scholarly communities, universities, foundations, government, corporations and other entities, though he also hoped that it would "enhance the influence and the autonomy of the scholars themselves by means of setting the criteria by which scholarship is to be judged. Many will argue that scholarship is too important to be left to the scholars themselves, but in our system if it is not left to the scholars, then it must be left to those who pay the scholars." (2) Binder seems to have expected that in the not too distant future scholars would at long last successfully forge a productive and generally accepted paradigm for area studies in general and Middle East studies in particular, and thereby finally put these fields on a proper scientific basis—just like what Binder had termed "the more traditional studies," i.e., the disciplines, for which such basic questions as "which are the things worth knowing" and "how the various subjects are to be defined" had supposedly been definitively settled.

In fact, despite Binder's hopes, *The Study of the Middle East* did not do much to help produce or define a proper paradigm for Middle East studies, in terms of object, theory or method—thereby yielding at long last something approaching the interdisciplinary theory and method of area studies that Robert Hall had envisioned some three decades earlier. As Talal Asad noted in a 1977 review of *The Study of the Middle East*, Binder's introduction "hovers between total despair and bland assurance," while "some of the individual contributors are clearly uneasy with the state of their discipline. . . . Yet even these contributors are unable to articulate cogently in this book the reasons for such theoretical poverty." Asad added that the volume as a whole had failed to engage with the question of what constitutes "the theoretical object of Middle East studies," instead evoking "the authority of persons and institutions where sustained intellectual argument is called for."[58] Moreover, in the years that followed not only was a paradigm of the kind Binder envisioned not realized, but the very need for, and even the possibility of, such a thing would be powerfully challenged, taking Middle East studies (along with many other fields and disciplines) in a very different direction. *The Study of the Middle East* thus constitutes something of a snapshot of the mainstream consensus in the field at the time, a survey by leading scholars of a set of scholarly literatures at a moment just preceding the onset of dramatic intellectual shifts. It manifests little engagement with the diverse Marxian or political economy approaches on which, in the early and mid-1970s, most critiques of Orientalism and modernization theory relied; it had relatively little to say about women and gender; and it could not anticipate the Foucault-inspired critique of Orientalism launched soon thereafter by Edward W. Said, much less the broader "cultural turn" which would so dramatically affect the humanities (including Middle East studies) in the 1980s.

In his introduction to *The Study of the Middle East* Binder also addressed the relationship between area studies and the disciplines; given the fact that the volume was organized along disciplinary lines, this issue could hardly have been avoided. However, his effort to stake out an epistemological position that would avoid what he saw as extreme or defective positions on both sides of the divide seems to have been directed mainly at his fellow social (especially political) scientists and was unlikely to have been deemed relevant to the day-to-day work of many in Middle East studies. As we have seen, many early advocates of area studies had expected the new field to facilitate interdisciplinary research or even yield a new kind of interdisciplinary knowledge. This did not happen, and as the institutional development of area studies proceeded there ensued what the noted political scientist Lucian W. Pye described in 1975 as "a quiet but fundamental struggle between the conventional disciplines and area studies which has affected the self-identities of aspiring scholars, the designing, funding, and execution of research, and even the organizing and hiring of faculties." Pye acknowledged that "the structure of knowledge and training organized around separate academic disciplines has not been altered by the establishment of innumerable area studies and training programs" but claimed that nonetheless "the emergence of area specialization has changed perspectives and raised questions which go to the foundations of the social sciences."[59] This claim seems overblown, at least with respect to the preoccupations of mainstream U.S. social science from the 1950s through the 1970s. For example, neither the CNME nor its successor the JCNME devoted much time or energy to grappling with such questions. Moreover, while elucidation of the proper relationship between area studies and the disciplines continued to attract sporadic attention, the main arena in which tensions between them manifested themselves was probably (as Pye suggested) institutional rather than intellectual, over such things as hiring decisions, the allocation of funding and curricula. One suspects that, despite such tensions, in practice most scholars whose work focused on the Middle East found ways of navigating this fault line that enabled them to go about their business.

The Intrusion of Politics

Even as challenges to the dominant paradigms in the field gathered momentum in the 1970s, the politics of the contemporary Middle East and the wider world also began to impinge in unprecedented ways. Neither the CNME nor the JCNME had strayed very far from the theoretical and methodological mainstream of the day, and they rarely if ever engaged in any self-aware or self-critical way with broader questions about what they were doing, why or how. Nor was there much if any attention to the relationship between the knowledge they were seeking to produce and disseminate, on the one hand, and on the other the power and policies of the United States in the region under study. As was the case with MESA, this stance became increasingly untenable for the JCNME in the course of the 1970s as the U.S. became more deeply involved in the Middle East and as new cohorts of graduate students and younger faculty began criticizing what they perceived as the silencing of discussion both of current political issues and of the fraught linkages within the field between knowledge and power. The public exposure in 1975–1976 of the role played by longtime JCNME stalwart I. William Zartman in a 1968 war game exercise involving Algeria and Morocco, discussed in Chapter 7, is a case in point. One suspects that Zartman was infuriated by the revelation; but it must also have put Abdelkader Zghal, the one JCNME member from the Maghrib, in an embarrassing position.

In the years that followed the JCNME would be increasingly compelled to engage with the political implications of its activities and projects. One instance of this involved a conference comparing the historical trajectories of the Ottoman empire and Iran that the committee began to plan as a follow-up to its 1975 conference on Turkey and the Maghrib. Marvin Zonis, who had left the committee at the end of the 1975–1976 academic year after a long stretch as a member and as chair, played the leading role in planning this conference, originally scheduled for September 1977. Among other things, early in 1976 he secured a commitment from Nader Afshar Naderi, the dean of the School of Social Science of the University of Tehran, to host the conference and help cover its costs, though subsequent communication with Naderi proved difficult. No one on the joint committee seems to have given any thought to what holding such a conference in an Iran subject to the autocratic regime of the Shah might mean. However, one of the participants in a May 1976 planning meeting for the conference, the NYU anthropologist Alan Dubetsky, wrote to Marvin Zonis soon thereafter to express his concerns about "the implications of accepting money from the Iranian government, and of holding the conference in Iran."

> It appeared to me that the general consensus [at the planning meeting in New York] was that we should be pragmatic and realistic in regard to this problem. I too think we should be realistic, but I am terribly disturbed by the implications of the kind of pragmatism which was advocated.
>
> The argument, I believe, goes something like this. Iran is giving the Social Science Research Council $15,000 toward the conference. Without that money, it could not be held, since SSRC doesn't have the funds. We all recognize that taking the money and in particular holding the conference in Iran will impose certain constraints on our freedom of expression. However, it is better to do this than to refuse to take the money, and not hold the conference at all. What we must do is be clever about the way we phrase the issues and we can have a modicum of freedom to speak our minds. (And, after all, those of us, Iranians and Americans, who plan to continue to maintain contact with Iran inevitably do a certain amount of self-censorship in our writings anyway).
>
> The more I think about this logic the more I feel shocked at how easily we

are willing to sell our freedom for a mere $15,000. When a particularly oppressive government is the source of that money, then I think we have to be either incredibly naïve or hopelessly cynical not to realize that they are attempting to co-opt us, to undermine any possible attempt on our part at critical thinking, and as a result, to make our conference more palatable to them. I think that any compromise in the expression of our ideas, no matter how small, is a grave issue.

It seems to me that both taking the money and holding the conference in Iran is not only morally and intellectually bankrupt, but will also in the long run undermine any efforts on our part to develop a new, meaningful, and independent perspective on the Middle East. Given the nature of repression and censorship in Iran, it is impossible to think that we will not be influenced by accepting money from that government, and especially by holding the conference on Iranian territory.

Dubetsky went on to note that the impact of the development of capitalism in Iran and Turkey was slated to receive only peripheral attention at the conference, "yet it seems so fundamental to understanding both the social structure of those countries and their relations with Europe and the U.S., both in the earlier turn of the century period, and at present." He proposed holding the conference in some less repressive country and finding alternative sources of funding; if they could not be found then it would be better "not to hold the conference at all, than to do so in such an unprincipled way."[60]

In his response, Zonis claimed that the issues Dubetsky had raised had troubled him for years and acknowledged that "there are some topics which cannot be raised for free discussion within Iran," including more or less "all materials related to Iranian society, economy, and polity, since the inception of the Pahlavis, which is to say around 1921." But the conference was focusing on the nineteenth and early twentieth centuries, concerning which he had been assured there could be unfettered discussion. He also doubted that holding the conference in Iran would contribute to the legitimacy of the regime; this would be a purely scholarly conference, Zonis insisted.[61] When the JCNME discussed the issue, with William Quandt in the chair's seat, it was acknowledged that the participants, "particularly the Iranians, would feel constrained not to criticize, or appear to criticize, the regime," though it was pointed out that this would be the case, for Iranians at least, even if the conference were held outside Iran. Sociologist Ali Banuazizi, who was then a visiting professor at Princeton and had just joined the committee, also noted that the regime was neutral with regard to Iran's history before the Pahlavi period, so that scholars could express their views on that period more freely.[62]

In the end, both the committee and P&P decided in favor of moving ahead with the conference, provided that there would be no government interference in selecting participants and paper topics. Given poor communications with Nader Naderi at the University of Tehran, however, they began exploring alternative sites; eventually an agreement was reached with Reza Shah Kabir University on the Caspian Sea coast (now the University of Mazandaran), whose chancellor had offered assurances that the SSRC deemed satisfactory. This turned out to be a fortunate choice, because by June 1978, when the conference convened, Tehran and most of Iran's other big cities were increasingly engulfed by massive popular protests against the Shah's regime, whereas the town in which this university was located was still calm. No edited volume of conference papers was ever published.[63]

In the mid-1970s the JCNME was also for the first time compelled to grapple with the question of whether it should accept funding for its activities directly from an agency of the U.S. government that was deeply engaged in what was then widely referred to as the Third World. In 1976 David Steinberg, the Agency for International Development official who contacted MESA to propose collaboration (see Chapter 7), also contacted the JCNME to offer funding for conferences and workshops relating to development. As with MESA, Steinberg hoped that AID personnel could benefit from "the knowledge generated by the scholarly community, since too often discussions about A.I.D. assistance have been made with insufficient information about the cultures of the countries being assisted." He expressed particular interest in a conference on "Hierarchy, Inequality, and the State in the Middle East" that the committee had been discussing.[64] Steinberg assured the SSRC that AID would not exercise any influence or control over conference planning, participants, publications or spending, though two or three AID staff members would be invited as observers to any conference the agency helped fund.

A decade or so earlier, this kind of collaboration would probably have passed without challenge or even question. Now, however, in the immediate aftermath of the Vietnam war, and in light of recent revelations by the Church committee and others about U.S. government malfeasance at home and abroad, difficult questions could not be avoided. Though MESA's board of directors decided not to pursue collaboration with AID, only one JCNME member consistently objected to accepting AID funding as a matter of principle. This was Edmund Burke III, a historian of the modern Maghrib at the University of California, Santa Cruz, who had received his PhD from Princeton in 1970 and been appointed to the committee in the fall of 1975. Burke, who was considerably younger than his colleagues on the committee and whose intellectual and political formation was very different from theirs, expressed "concern about the possible misinterpretation of the meaning of A.I.D. support in the eyes of foreign observers, and in the context of its past actions in Southeast Asia and Latin America."[65] At a subsequent committee meeting one member from the region—probably Abdelkader Zghal—noted "the impossibility of his countrymen attending a scholarly conference in his country if a U.S. government representative were present as an observer" but felt that "there would be no such problem . . . if a conference were held in the United States."[66]

The issue was referred to the SSRC's Committee on Problems and Policy and its Council, both of which endorsed the idea of soliciting AID funds as long as specified safeguards were respected.[67] But JCNME members would soon have second thoughts, and the matter was reopened at subsequent committee meetings. The committee now insisted that, at conferences held outside the United States, "the presence of U.S. governmental officials as observers would not be acceptable. . . . The staff was urged to try to persuade A.I.D. to act like a foundation in the granting of its funds and eliminate the provision about observers, instead trusting the committee members to use the funds wisely and accepting published results as a sufficient product for its investment."[68] Eventually, it was agreed that while AID personnel would be notified about all meetings the agency funded, they would only be specifically invited to those meetings "where their presence might be desired because of their expertise or because they might become better informed about the area."[69]

Edmund Burke, who was openly critical of the kind of relationship with the national security state that l'affaire Zartman typified and strongly supported Irene Gendzier in the battle that she was waging with MESA's leadership over the CIA in this same period, left the committee at the end of 1975–1976 because he had research leave from his university the following academic year. He was never re-appointed: it seems clear that he was not deemed a good fit, because of his political views and because he did not conceal his belief that the committee was not adequately engaging with what was actually going on in the region and with the new critical approaches that were emerging at the time.[70] Yet over time, as the JCNME came to include more scholars shaped or at least influenced by the political, social and intellectual transformations of the late 1960s and 1970s, as well as scholars based in the region itself, the committee's attitude toward the propriety of links with intelligence agencies as well as its tolerance for approaches hitherto deemed outlandish also changed. A good example of this is the JCNME's prompt, vigorous and unanimous rejection in 1982 of the Defense Intelligence Agency's initiative to recruit scholars for research projects.[71] This incident marked a turning point for the JCNME as well as for MESA: both were now willing to take public stances critical of certain forms of collaboration with the state, something that would have been unimaginable a decade earlier.

The Struggle Continues

In the end, the JCNME did accept AID funding for one of its research projects—one of the very few that before the 1980s yielded scholarly work of wide impact and lasting value. The committee's project on Hierarchy, Inequality, and the State in the Middle East, soon recast as "Hierarchy, Authority and Justice" (HAJ), was eventually divided into separate components, one of which focused on law and social structure in the Middle East and generated a series of small workshops on aspects of "law as it functions in contemporary Islamic societies." In 1978 the SSRC submitted to AID a proposal developed by a subcommittee of the JCNME for a grant of $1.25 million that would support an expansive four-year program of workshops, conferences, summer training institutes, fellowships and grants focusing on law and social structure in the region, though concerns continued to be expressed about whether, as one SSRC Council member put it, "the Council's reputation in the Third World might be compromised by AID support."[72] In June 1979 AID finally approved a two-year grant to fund part of what was now formally called the Project on Law and Social Structure in the Contemporary Near and Middle East (PLSS), including five workshops, two conferences and one summer institute.[73] Charles Butterworth of the University of Maryland, whose scholarly work focused mainly on Islamic political philosophy, was hired as a consultant to help identify scholars in the Middle East working on related topics and plan PLSS activities; his work and the project as a whole were overseen by a subcommittee of the JCNME that included scholars who were not committee members.

In the years that followed PLSS would engage a broad array of scholars in workshops and conferences on themes relating to law and society, including the role of *waqf* as a legal and social institution, property and property law in the region, taxation and much else. In an April 1980 statement to the Ford Foundation, the JCNME asserted that

> prior to PLSS, scholarly research on law in the Near and Middle East was almost entirely the preserve of the Orientalists whose primary focus was on the *shari'a*, the Muslim law derived from the Koran. PLSS is concerned with all law in the area, including tribal law, customary law, legislation, codes and constitutions imported from the West, as well as the *shari'a*. For PLSS, law is not static rules to be learned by rote, but dynamic prescriptions, determining the structures of societies and at the same time being determined by those structures. In its application of social science to the study of law and society, it is exploring an intellectual frontier that has significance beyond the bounds of Islam.[74]

The first stage of the project yielded a 1985 volume titled *Property, Social Structure and Law in the Modern Middle East*, edited by Ann Elizabeth Mayer and consisting of papers originally presented at a November 1980 conference held at the Rockefeller Foundation Conference Center in Bellagio, Italy. PLSS may be reckoned one of the JCNME's most successful and productive scholarly endeavors, because over time it had a significant intellectual impact on U.S. Middle East and Islamic studies but also because, in the period this study covers, it was the only committee-sponsored research project ever to be developed from scratch, secure substantial external funding, function autonomously over an extended period and involve expansive networks of scholars in many countries. In 1981 Roland Mitchell, the committee's SSRC staffperson, accurately called it "the best piece of work the Joint Committee on the Near and Middle East has undertaken."[75]

Even as PLSS got under way, the JCNME continued to strive to develop a coherent research agenda for U.S. Middle East studies that would address lacunae in the field and open up new directions for research. In a submission to the Ford Foundation drafted in the spring of 1980, the committee explained why it believed that it was finally in a position to take on these tasks and achieve success. "The committee's leading members initially were Orientalists, philologists, and historians with a thorough command of at least one and sometimes all four of the area's basic languages—classical Arabic, Persian, Ottoman Turkish, and Hebrew—acquired in long residence in the countries of the area. . . . Numerically, traditional modes of scholarship—particularly in history, languages, and literature still dominate the field." However, the leading role once played on the committee by Orientalists had now been assumed by social scientists, and since 1970 it had focused its research initiatives on the modern world, with PLSS its most promising long-term project. Moreover, the SSRC and the ACLS had recently committed to appointing to the JCNME only scholars working on the contemporary Middle East; a separate committee would henceforth be responsible for selecting recipients of postdoctoral grants and doctoral dissertation fellowships. As a result, the JCNME insisted, it could now focus exclusively on developing and implementing a research agenda: "Because the committee will no longer need to be representative of all parts of the area, of all major disciplines, and knowledgeable about many centuries of history, new members can be selected on the basis of demonstrated research strength in respect to the on-going interests of the committee or because of their promise to bring to the committee different perspectives and fresh points of view."[76]

In fact, though in this period the committee sponsored a number of projects (most notably PLSS) that spawned workshops, conferences and/or edited volumes, fulfillment of what it regarded as its key intellectual mission would continue to elude it, as it had since its inception in the early 1950s. For example, in the spring of 1980, with the SSRC drafting a new funding proposal for Ford and the National Endowment for the Humanities, the JCNME was asked to prepare a statement on its historical trajectory and future plans, so it decided to invite a small number of scholars to a one-day conference at which a "full and frank discussion of problems and needs of the field of Near and Middle East Studies in the 1980s" could take place.[77] This conference, yet another in a series of anxiety-ridden self-examinations, was held in May 1980 and included the six JCNME members and six nonmembers.[78] The dominant tone at the event was considerably gloomier than the rather optimistic statement that the committee would ultimately submit to the Ford Foundation.

The Columbia historian of Islam Richard Bulliet, who had been appointed to the JCNME in 1978 and was at the time also serving as MESA's executive secretary, offered a particularly pessimistic assessment of the field. Elaborating on his perspective in written form, Bulliet echoed longstanding concerns when he lamented what he saw as the mediocrity of many scholars in the field and the "national interest agenda embodied in the area studies concept," as a result of which many graduate students were inadequately trained. By the late 1960s, he argued, "quantity was rapidly increasing, but low quality was built into the staffing and structure of the Middle East field. . . . The strong orientalists of European formation [like Gibb and von Grunebaum] faded or passed away, and the new luminaries were modernists of indifferent orientalist talents and scarcely more impressive disciplinary talents. They were to be the new leaders of a Middle East studies field that was coming unstuck, but they themselves carried little weight in their nominal social science disciplines."

> This crisis hit other area studies fields in the late sixties, as well, and there it exploded into loud and painful debates as to the intellectual validity and ethical propriety of having major academic enterprises determined in their scholarly pursuits by the national interest agenda. The Vietnamese war tore apart East Asian studies; decolonization and the civil rights movement did the same for African studies. The Middle East field seemed immune and prided itself upon its gentlemanliness. Yet the immunity was not real. In actuality, confrontation within the field was suppressed by the unspoken understanding that the keystone of national interest was Israel, a subject about which it was forbidden to speak. Instead of going through catharsis in the late sixties and coming out with sharpened minds and reexamined priorities, Middle East specialists stuck to business as usual and managed their consciences through other academic and non-academic outlets. The June War of 1967, a major event in American intellectual history, had less effect within the field of Middle East studies than it did outside it.

As a result, Bulliet argued, the 1970s were a period of drift and disarray in the field, and he was very pessimistic about the prospects for remedying the field's defects. "What is not in question," Bulliet warned, "is that if these questions are not addressed, existing divisions will become exacerbated, new funding will reinvigorate and revalidate outgrown concepts of Middle East studies as a creature of the national (and business) interest, the penetration of Middle East scholarship in the disciplines and overall university communities will remain stagnant, mediocrity will continue unabated, and we will all find ourselves in one hell of a mess ten years hence."[79]

In May 1981 Bulliet would request that he not be reappointed to the JCNME for the coming academic year; he cited competing demands on his time but also a lack of enthusiasm about the direction in which the committee seemed to be heading. "My own feeling," Bulliet declared, "which I have frequently expressed, is that the problems of the field are large in scale and structural in nature. Pinpointed research sponsorship does not seem to meet these problems."[80] Bulliet was also unhappy because the JCNME had recently rejected his request for funds with which to conduct an analysis of MESA's membership by age, discipline, training, ethnicity, and so on. Bulliet thought that such an analysis might shed light on the evolution of Middle East studies, but other committee members questioned "whether the scope of the proposal was broad enough or the methodology sufficiently sophisticated to yield significant results." Bulliet suspected that his colleagues were in fact concerned that such a survey might show not only that the proportion of MESA members born in the Middle East was growing but also that their outlook was different from that of U.S.-born members. That same year Bulliet also stepped down as MESA's executive secretary.[81]

Not everyone was quite as pessimistic about the state of the field as Bulliet, but there seems to have been a consensus among conference participants that something urgently needed to be done to strengthen and advance Middle East studies in the United States. Those present raised a broad range of concerns but largely agreed that "the quality of students attracted to the field was the most pressing problem," with language training described as "the major hurdle." "If the problem of language acquisition could be solved," participants concluded, "the focus of graduate training could be disciplinary, thus producing more highly competent specialists. That would not answer the question of the relevance of the training to the job market, but would ensure that research done would be more likely to be of high quality and answer important rather than trivial questions."

The conference participants did not, however, agree on what if anything the committee could do to help strengthen the field, and the "basic question of whether it should define theoretically coherent themes to use in development of the field or whether it should be eclectic, responding to individual initiatives from its members or from the outside," remained unanswered.

In his handwritten record of the discussion Roland Mitchell, the JCNME's longtime staffperson, noted that participants wanted "to address root causes of mediocrity." The field's "dilemma," as he summed it up, was the "ineffectiveness of 20 years of work from an area studies approach in producing quality research," yielding a need to "deliberate on question of how to pursue better & more productive relationship between disciplinary approaches & area."[82] This was obviously not a new set of issues: they had surfaced repeatedly since the early days of Middle East studies, leading to a great deal of anxiety and pessimism among the field's leaders, and over that time span this committee, and other bodies like MESA's Research and Training Committee, had repeatedly struggled to address them effectively. The magic formula, something like Binder's still missing paradigm for the field that would supposedly delineate "theoretically coherent themes" and distinguish the important questions from the trivial, nonetheless remained into the 1980s where it had been for the previous three decades: just out of sight over the horizon, an elusive goal that was pursued but never attained.

Reviewing the conference proceedings a day later, committee members also noted that "both the discussion and the committee's activities in past years had omitted consideration of two fundamental aspects of the present Near and Middle East: the Arab-Israeli conflict, which was a reality of central importance in the Arab world; the existence of oil in the Arab states and its influential role in the internal activities of the wealthy states and in their relations with the rest of the world. There was general agreement that these two realities should not be treated as if they did not exist, but no formula emerged to integrate them into the research planning activities of the committee."[83] These too were hardly new issues, though it was true that the committee had never devoted serious attention to either of them.

Three of the scholars who participated in the May 1980 conference were soon thereafter invited to join the JCNME. They were the scholar of Islamic political philosophy Charles Butterworth; Peter von Sivers, who had begun publishing on nineteenth-century North African history in the mid-1970s; and Eric Davis, by discipline a political scientist and the youngest of the three. Davis' first book, *Colonialism: Bank Misr and Egyptian Industrialization, 1920–1941*, would be published in 1983; it manifested Davis' commitment not to the elite-focused approach still central to U.S. political science research on the Middle East at the time (and to much of the committee's work) but rather to the loosely Marxian approach politely termed "political economy" which many younger scholars and students in Britain and the United States had embraced in the 1970s as offering a theoretical and methodological alternative to both modernization theory and Orientalism. Davis, along with Peter Gran and a few others, were part of an emerging cohort of young American scholars whose intellectual and political formation had been powerfully shaped by the radicalism of the late 1960s and 1970s; Davis and Gran were among the first two in this cohort to secure tenure-track positions at U.S. universities. Both of them were also involved in the loose-knit network of dissident graduate students and faculty known as the American Middle East Studies Seminar (AMESS) that emerged in the late 1970s. Davis sought to reassure his new JCNME colleagues, explaining that AMESS, "which some MESA members believe was undermining MESA, is not intended to replace or compete with MESA but is a group of scholars more interested in theory than in characteristics of the MESA membership."[84] Concerns about AMESS seem to have faded over time, and in 1983 the committee actually allocated $1800 to the AMESS chapter at the University of Texas at Austin to help defray travel and other costs for an AMESS regional seminar planned for that spring.[85]

Despite this infusion of new blood, the committee continued to find it difficult to develop a clear assessment of the field's needs and priorities; and though its members agreed that the field urgently needed new intellectual directions and leadership, they remained uncertain about where these might come from or what form they might take. In the fall of 1980, still anxious for new ideas, the committee asked a number of scholars to submit short statements on the needs of the field but then deemed the submissions "concerned with infrastructure needs, and research gaps. They did not present a coherent whole, however, and the discussion ranged from specific critiques of some proposals to approval of others in principle. No consensus was achieved and it was agreed to reconsider the topic at the next meeting."[86] Discussion of how to effectively advance the field of Middle East studies continued inconclusively over the years that followed. For example, in 1981 the committee compiled a list of twelve topics, ranging from "Political Cleavages and the State" to "Household Economy and Family Relations" to "Recent Demographic Trends" and for a time contemplated emulating the SSRC-ACLS Joint Committee on African Studies by commissioning (for an honorarium) state of the art papers on some of them.[87] Three years later the committee (whose membership had of course changed in the meantime) was still struggling to formulate a research agenda that could push the field forward, or at a minimum (as it was put in one inconclusive discussion in August 1984) come up with "a broad topic which could then be analyzed and studied from different angles using a number of complementary as well as contrasting approaches that together would enhance our understanding of the complex identity of the region."[88] But attaining even that kind of rather watered-down "umbrella project" proved impossible, and as had so often been the case in the past nothing concrete emerged from these discussions.

However, when the committee undertook more modestly conceived projects that focused on field-building, results were sometimes forthcoming. For example, in the course of 1982 the committee formulated a plan for a new international graduate student paper competition described as an expression of the committee's "continuing interest in encouraging younger scholars and in developing new and critical lines of scholarly inquiry." The Ibn Khaldun Prize (and $500) would be awarded annually to up to three papers by graduate students that offered a critique of paradigms or models in the field, proposed new research questions or strategies, presented a synthetic analysis of important research findings, schools or methodologies, or made a substantive contribution to the committee's priority research topics. The competition got off to a slow start: there were few submissions the first year and the committee decided not to make any awards, but the situation gradually improved over time.[89]

In this period the JCNME also supported several smaller-scale research initiatives which led to publications. For example, in 1981 it set up a task force on social stratification in the Middle East and North Africa, led by Ali Banuazizi, which oversaw the compilation and publication of a bibliography on this topic; a year later, in collaboration with the Joint Committee on South Asia, the JCNME sponsored a conference on the state, religion and ethnic politics in Afghanistan, Iran and Pakistan, resulting in an edited volume some years later.[90] The joint committee also secured SSRC funding and logistical support for a conference on "Social Movements and Political Culture in the Contemporary Near and Middle East," held in May 1981. This led to a 1984 published volume edited by Said Amir Arjomand and titled *From Nationalism to Revolutionary Islam*, one of the earlier efforts to engage seriously with Islamism and Islamist movements.[91] Interest in social movements, especially avowedly Islamic social movements, was for obvious reasons very much in the air at this time: another conference held at the University of California at Berkeley a month after the SSRC-sponsored one and addressing overlapping themes (if from somewhat different angles) led to the publication in 1988 of *Islam, Politics, and Social Movements*, edited by Edmund Burke III and Ira M. Lapidus.

Another new JCNME-sponsored research initiative was launched at the suggestion of Eric Davis, who soon after joining the committee proposed an investigation of the impact of oil wealth on societies in the Middle East, a new direction for the committee.[92] Davis and a group of colleagues that included Peter Gran, Samira Haj, Rifaat Abou-El-Haj, Nicolas Gavrielides and others formulated the project and, with SSRC support, took an extended trip to Europe and the Middle East in December 1982 to develop contacts with local scholars. Alarmed by the project's more or less Marxian conceptual framework, some committee members complained that it had "too belligerent a tone" and called for "a greater representation of pluralism," a concern the committee had never before expressed. Despite this, the JCNME allocated additional funding for the project, since Davis and his task force actually seemed to be accomplishing something.[93] In the months that followed, however, a rancorous conflict erupted among the members of the task force. The JCNME ultimately affirmed Davis' authority as task force chair, leading to the embittered departure of those who had opposed him.[94] The task force organized a small SSRC-funded conference in November 1984 and a larger conference at Rutgers in August 1985, funded by the National Endowment for the Humanities and the Ford Foundation. The upshot of its work was the publication in 1991 of *Statecraft in the Middle East: Oil, Historical Memory, and Popular Culture*, edited by Eric Davis and Nicolas Gavrielides.

Meanwhile, in light of the rise of Islamist currents and movements in various parts of the Muslim world, other regional committees and the SSRC staff began in the early 1980s to discuss some kind of transregional comparative research project on "Islam, Islamic movements, and their social and political roles." Some JCNME members were dubious about this idea from the start, instead arguing for "the desirability of focusing on quite discrete topics such as the comparative analysis of fundamentalist movements, Islamic education today in comparative context, different patterns of relationship between Islam and the West, and Islam as the religion of minority populations."[95] In addition to intellectual issues, institutional turf was clearly at stake, and the committee's misgivings grew as plans for an SSRC committee on the comparative study of Islamic societies became more concrete.[96] The JCNME rejected the creation of this new committee as "inopportune," citing "the 'bandwagon effect' of current concerns with the rise of Islamic fundamentalism, the problems related to singling out a particular religion for analysis and the failure sufficiently to explain how Islam is likely to improve the analytical ability of social and political inquiry. . . ."[97] The SSRC ignored these objections and in 1985 established a Joint Committee on the Comparative Study of Muslim Societies "to develop area studies research along thematic rather than regional lines." This generated a series of workshops and, eventually, edited volumes, beginning with *Islam and the Political Economy of Meaning*, edited by William R. Roff and published in 1987.[98] We can perhaps see in this initiative a harbinger of the SSRC's decision a decade later to restructure its international program along transregional and thematic lines in the name of globalization. I will have more to say about this in the Epilogue.

A history of the SSRC produced by a member of its staff sums up the thirty-seven-year lifespan of the JCNME by declaring that it had "focused on consolidating the standing of the Middle East in the social sciences and the humanities as an area for the development and testing of theory, and to move [*sic*] Middle East studies beyond its emphasis on the raw accumulation of knowledge about the region." The account presented here supports neither the passage's (rather vacuous) claim about the committee's purported role in "the development and testing of theory" nor its assertion that Middle East studies emphasized the "raw accumulation of knowledge" about the region, whatever that might mean. There is a bit more substance in what follows: "During the 1980s-90s committee projects converged around the contingent nature of the Middle East as a region, and the extent to which the Middle East was embedded within cultural, economic and political flows that transcend regional boundaries."[99] In fact, from the first half of the 1980s some of what the JCNME did seemed to be moving in that direction, though not very quickly.

This is not to say that the JCNME was without accomplishments after the launching of MESA. But it was in this period no more successful in achieving its avowed goal of developing a coherent (much less interdisciplinary) research agenda for Middle East studies rooted in some clearly defined theoretical paradigm than it had been in its first decade and a half. Meanwhile, new intellectual winds were beginning to blow from unexpected directions, with unanticipated consequences. By the 1980s the contours of the humanities, and to an extent of the social sciences as well, were beginning to change in ways that would render that goal even less attainable—and in the eyes of many, entirely illusory.

Epilogue

N MARCH 1996, after lengthy deliberations, the Social Science Research Council announced that it was radically revamping its international program. To explain this decision SSRC President Kenneth Prewitt invoked the discourse of globalization, declaring that such factors as recent shifts in the global economy and the spread of new information technologies had created "a world shaken loose from its familiar moorings." While Prewitt asserted that area studies, "which holds area constant and invites the participation of multiple disciplines," had been "the most successful, large-scale interdisciplinary project ever in the humanities and the social sciences," he argued that now, from the United Nations to multinational corporations to nongovernmental organizations, "the traditional region-by-region organization [central to area studies] is found to be poorly aligned with the tasks and opportunities of the contemporary world." Moreover, what had once been an "American near-monopoly on studying foreign places" had given way to a situation in which "scholarship of the kind practiced by American area studies is now internationally produced."

As a result, Prewitt declared, "a number of discrete and separated 'area committees,' each focused on a single world region, is not the optimum structure for providing new insights and theories suitable for a world in which the geographic units of analysis are neither static nor straightforward."[1] Soon thereafter Prewitt framed the issue more starkly:

Now free from the bi-polar perspective of the cold war and increasingly aware of the multiple migrations and intersections of peoples, ideas, institutions, technologies and commodities, scholars are confronting the inadequacy of conventional notions of world "areas" as bounded systems of social relations and cultural categories. Critical problems and critical research issues appear in forms that overwhelm conventional definitions of area and region—from the quality of economic, political, and environmental life around the globe to conditions for ensuring the security and well-being of all people. These contemporary issues inspire new and urgent questions about history, religion, and artistic expression that highlight the contingent way in which people have interpreted the conditions of their lives. It therefore follows that we need new intellectual concepts and new ways to organize scholarship.[2]

The SSRC had therefore decided to abandon the structural relationship it had forged with area studies over the previous half-century and adopt a very different approach. All eleven of the regional committees that it co-sponsored with the ACLS, including the Joint Committee on the Near and Middle East, were to be disbanded.[3] The SSRC would henceforth foster international research mainly through a new set of "collaborative research networks" that would focus on problems and themes of broad, transregional, cross-cultural and comparative significance, rather than on specific geographic areas. "Regional advisory panels" with multinational memberships would be established to provide feedback on research and training initiatives from a regional perspective and strengthen links with regional scholars and institutions, but unlike the old regional committees the new panels would not make programmatic or funding decisions. Instead, funding would be channeled through the new research networks as well as through new fellowship programs that were not regionally based, for example what is today known as the International Dissertation Research Fellowship.[4]

The SSRC had long harbored concerns about the intellectual vitality and productivity of area studies. Among other things, as a 1994 internal staff memo put it, the regional committees had failed to "generate adequate cross-regional or thematic research development initiatives on a regular and sustained basis."[5] Moreover, though longstanding concerns about the fraught relationship of area studies with the disciplines, especially the social sciences, had often put aside so as not to hinder field-building, they nonetheless persisted. In the early 1980s Prewitt, then in his first stint as SSRC president

(1979–1985), had observed that "few difficulties have nagged at area studies so persistently as their uneasy relationship to the traditional disciplines in the humanities and social sciences."[6] A decade and so later the SSRC concluded that these chronic concerns, along with changed historical circumstances, had fatally undermined its rationale for fostering area studies as it had for the previous half-century.

The termination of the regional committees, and more broadly the post-Cold War embrace of globalization as a lens through which to make sense of the world, generated a great deal of anxious discussion and debate about the future of area studies, the relationship between the global and the local, and related issues.[7] There were also efforts to reconceive and revitalize area studies, most notably the Ford Foundation-funded "Crossing Borders" project, launched in 1999 to encourage re-examination of "some of the basic premises and procedures" of area studies while avoiding "the facile rhetoric of globalization as homogenization."[8] All this certainly had an impact on the area studies fields: for example, the termination of the regionally based research funding programs meant that graduate students and faculty in each regional field now had to compete for research support with applicants from other fields, which often required them to reframe their projects in terms that seemed less regionally focused, and more thematic, transregional and broadly comparative.

Nonetheless, we should be cautious about assuming that the institutional shifts of the 1990s and all the anxious talk about the future of area studies that ensued had a very profound or lasting impact on the trajectories of the area studies fields—or at least of Middle East studies among them. Since the later 1970s this field had already been experiencing dramatic transformations of various kinds that reshaped it in ways that its first generation or two of leaders could not have envisioned. For example, on the intellectual front the disabling critiques to which both modernization theory and Orientalism had been subjected since the late 1960s helped open up new intellectual terrain in Middle East studies (and of course beyond); this process dramatically accelerated after the publication in 1978 of Edward W. Said's *Orientalism* and the debates it engendered. In roughly the same period, the emergence of women's studies and gender studies challenged conventional intellectual categories and had the same enormous impact on this field as it did across the humanities. Overlapping and interacting with these developments was the so-called "cultural turn" or "linguistic turn" of the 1980s. This meant, of course, many different things to different people but often included a widespread (if highly uneven) engagement with poststructuralist and postmodernist theory in various forms that powerfully affected many humanities disciplines and fields, and to an extent the social sciences as well, along with the rise or growth of fields new to American academia such as postcolonial studies and cultural studies, though the latter had other roots as well.[9]

In addition, this period witnessed a reconfiguration of what had for decades been seen as the troubled relationship between the disciplines and area studies. The latter had long been suspected, or accused, of lacking the "hard core" that each of the disciplines (or the subdisciplines into which many of them were in reality divided) supposedly possessed: an accepted body of theory specifying a distinct object on which the discipline should focus, from which flowed a definition of its boundaries as well as a set of appropriate methods and questions. In fact, there had always been considerable contention within most if not all of the disciplines about these things, and many of the acclaimed theoretical and methodological breakthroughs in the U.S. social sciences during the 1950s and 1960s had by the 1970s come to seem dead ends. As both Immanuel Wallerstein and Timothy Mitchell have usefully argued (if in different ways), the epistemological shifts of the 1980s intensified questioning of what had conventionally been accepted as the conceptual and methodological underpinnings of the disciplines, including their self-definition and presumed objects, and thus of the kinds of questions they asked and how they asked them.[10] So, for example, historians could no longer take the "social" in social history for granted, because the new interest in representation, in the construction of discourses and their imbrication with power, now required grappling with how the concepts of "society" and "the social" themselves came into being and had been deployed to produce certain narratives; anthropologists increasingly unpacked and questioned the concept of "culture" that had been so central to their discipline; feminists and others challenged and redefined conventional notions of the "political"; and so on. In the process many would come to feel that if area studies lacked a hard core, so did the disciplines, even as scholarly attention shifted to how different forms and fields of knowledge had been constructed and naturalized. Hence the utility of Mitchell's argument that "the genealogy of area studies must be understood in relation to the wider structuring of academic knowledge and to the struggles not of the Cold War but of science—and social science in particular—as a twentieth-century political project."[11]

Naturally, questioning the coherence of the traditional disciplines also meant questioning the boundaries conventionally assumed to separate them, leading to much discussion of interdisciplinarity. The founders of area studies had argued that it offered a way to finally transcend disciplinary boundaries and produce truly interdisciplinary knowledge. This is not what actually happened: while scholars from different disciplines collaborated at times—for example, on the JCNME—with few exceptions the research they conducted or sponsored did not significantly challenge or cross disciplinary boundaries; at best it was in some loose sense multidisciplinary. On the other hand, some of the new fields that came to the fore in the long 1980s, for example cultural studies, advanced new kinds of claims to interdisciplinarity, though they continued to operate in academic settings still largely structured along disciplinary lines, which made for persistent tensions.[12]

Beyond changes in the intellectual topography of American academia, Middle East studies was in roughly the same period also reshaped by generational and demographic changes, though without much useful data it is difficult to avoid relying on subjective impressions. One manifestation of this was the way in which, in the 1980s, MESA gradually made room for intellectual and political perspectives which had earlier been largely suppressed or excluded—and for the (generally younger) cohorts whose members espoused those perspectives and who would eventually make the transition from opposition to positions of leadership. The almost frantic efforts of the JCNME in the early 1980s to identify fresh intellectual perspectives, and its strong opposition to having the Defense Intelligence Agency set scholarly research agendas, also indicate how much had changed even since the mid-1970s. In the same period the field also grew more diverse in terms both of gender and of ethnic and regional origin, which brought to it a wider range of perspectives and new kinds of networks. Moreover, it turned out that, despite the fears of their elders, those who entered the field in the 1970s and after were neither poorly trained nor incapable of making important scholarly contributions and taking the field in intellectually exciting new directions. Last but not least, the growing utilization of new sources—for example, the vast Ottoman archives and the records of the so-called "Islamic courts"—opened up new vistas for research and analysis, as well as for productive comparison.

These and other interacting transformations created new possibilities for those involved in Middle East studies, as in other area studies fields, to stop worrying too much about their relationship with the disciplines and instead forge new kinds of connections, and map common intellectual terrain, with scholars and currents across fields and disciplines. In the process the basis was laid for new scholarly languages, exchanges and debates, and new avenues of research, shared by many (though not all) practitioners of the humanities disciplines and of area studies, and even by some social scientists.[13] In this context Middle East studies was increasingly able to at long last free itself from the chronic sense of intellectual backwardness, exceptionalism, inferiority and isolation that had once been so widespread among its senior figures. These transformations also set the stage for what I regard as the field's increasingly self-confident intellectual flourishing over the past three decades, including the production of a broad array of work that engages productively and interactively with scholarship across many fields and disciplines, and that is widely recognized as both theoretically sophisticated and empirically rich.

One key consequence of these changes was the abandonment of the notion that Middle East studies should or could have a distinct paradigm that would define for it a theoretical object, and by extension a set of methods by which the study of that object could be pursued. Just as the Orientalism which posited as its object an essentialized Islamic civilization manifesting cultural uniformity and continuity across time and space had fallen by the wayside, so eventually did the expectation that a theory and method would, somehow, eventually emerge to specify the parameters of Middle East studies and shape its practice. In 1976 Leonard Binder still seemed to be anticipating such a development, and in the early 1980s the JCNME was still struggling to formulate a coherent research program that would guide the field's development. Over the course of the following decade, however, there would be growing recognition—at least in practice—that what gives this field its coherence is essentially the fact that those engaged in it, while doing a great many different things in intellectual terms, all relate to more or less the same region of the world, share the experience of teaching about it, and are engaged with a common set of institutions and networks. The latter include regionally focused departments, centers or programs at various universities, and on the national level the Middle East Studies Association (especially its annual meetings), certain academic journals and fellowship programs, language programs in the United States and abroad, and so on.

In other words, beyond its common geographic focus, the field has an essentially institutional, pedagogical and social rather than an intellectual basis.[14] This does not mean that those who operate in this field, or at least subsets among them, cannot engage in a common intellectual conversation. They can and do, because despite differences of discipline and intellectual orientation they often share substantial specific and general knowledge, linguistic competence, interests and experiences, and the boundaries that once separated disciplines have faded considerably. But even if they have things to talk about and can learn from one another, they do not assume or expect that a historian of ninth-century Baghdad will deploy the same conceptual and methodological apparatus, or pursue the same research questions, as a specialist in contemporary Iranian literature, a student of Moroccan politics or an anthropologist working in Yemen. This development was probably inevitable, and I think that it is also a good thing—but it is not what was initially envisioned by many of the founders of area studies or of Middle East studies, or by their successors through the 1970s.[15] The eminent China scholar John K. Fairbank (1907–1991) captured this transition nicely in his memoirs. "For a time," he noted, "there was a mystique attached to area studies, an assumption that a combining of disciplines would somehow produce a super-discipline, a new intellectual grasp. . . . In the end one had to agree, area study was not a new discipline of organized principles. It was only an activity, something one did."[16]

One might go further and argue that the very imperative to develop Middle East studies research from the top down, or the center out, through the formulation and implementation of a coherent research agenda for the field rooted in some common paradigm was in fact always mission impossible—that this task was not so much difficult or elusive as altogether unrealizable. For those in the SSRC's orbit this vision of field-building had roots in a certain understanding of Second World War research practices and was bolstered by the scientism that engulfed the postwar social sciences in the United States; and it was seemingly validated by (among other things) the apparent success of the Committee on Political Behavior and the Committee on Comparative Politics in elaborating powerful new models (behavioralism and modernization theory) for political science. In the longer term, of course, the projects of those two committees ended in failure, at least with respect to providing better (and properly "scientific") ways of understanding what was going on in the Third World. In any case, this top-down model of intellectual field-building was not well-suited to academic area studies: it is, for example, difficult to see how the intellectual development of a field as diverse, dispersed and complex as Middle East studies could have been successfully guided by a single committee. Like other fields, and even the disciplines for that matter, it tended to grow in much more complicated ways, often haphazardly and unevenly. Moreover, college- and university-based scholars are unlikely to embrace some committee's research agenda unless they see it as relevant to their own interests and work, and they usually do not like being told what the cutting-edge of their field is, unless it happens to be what they are working on; getting them to conform is akin to trying to herd cats.

How then does the interpretation of the history of Middle East studies, and of area studies more broadly, that I have offered here square with other accounts? In the Preface I mentioned Timothy Mitchell's 2004 essay on U.S. Middle East studies, which merits a fuller discussion. Some elements of Mitchell's rich and stimulating essay prefigure my own findings here: for example, he does not assume that this field emerged *ex nihilo* after the Second World War or that it was simply a product of the Cold War, and he notes the widespread perception of inferiority and failure among senior Middle East scholars, a phenomenon addressed at some length in this book. This study has also been enriched by his insistence on relating the trajectory of area studies to the construction of social-scientific knowledge in the twentieth-century United States. On the other hand, my research does not support a number of Mitchell's assertions about the history of U.S. Middle East studies or the genealogy of the field that he seems to be proposing.

Mitchell usefully notes some of the prewar roots of Middle East studies in the United States but goes on to argue that the field's postwar development was actually retarded by the wartime "rupture with the centers of research in the Arab world and the colonial ethnographers and other scholars who moved between Europe and the Middle East," as well as by the established power of social science departments in American academic life; as a result, "the European practice of turning those trained in Oriental Studies into authorities on the modern period could not produce scholarship that qualified in the United States as social science."[17] As my account in this book suggests, however, no academic institution in the prewar United States possessed the kind of deep Orientalist tradition to be found in Britain and on the continent, so it is difficult to see how such authorities could have been produced even had American social science departments had been less powerful. I also do not see evidence of significant prewar linkages between American academia and such research as was under way in the Arab world in the interwar years, by colonial ethnographers or by others, such that the Second World War could have ruptured them. While Philip Hitti was certainly interested in promoting both the teaching of Arabic as a living language and the study of Middle East after the rise of Islam, and while he maintained connections with the Arab world, he was a philologist by training, and I do not think that it is plausible to argue that either he or his Princeton colleagues served before the Second World War as an actual or potential transmission belt for European or Middle Eastern research on the region.

More broadly, and more importantly, I believe that it is inaccurate to assert, as Mitchell does, that Gibb and Bowen's *Islamic Society and the West*, initially commissioned in the 1930s by Arnold Toynbee, Director of Studies at the Royal Institute of International Affairs (RIAA, often referred to as Chatham House), as one of a series of studies of the impact of the West on other civilizations, served as the "blueprint," "framework" or "program" for the development of U.S. Middle East studies that the SSRC strove to implement after the war.[18] As this study shows, neither the SSRC's vision of area studies in general and of Middle East studies in particular, nor the actual trajectory of U.S. Middle East studies, originated in or was in any significant way shaped by the RIAA's Toynbeesque conception of world history.[19] In my judgment, even if H. A. R. Gibb espoused some version of that conception, he never had much real influence on charting this field's course, and the SSRC's vision of area studies had very different roots.

Later in his essay Mitchell asserts that "the customary approach to the analysis of area studies proceeds as a discussion of questions of theory. Questions about the construction of the object of knowledge, or the relationship of U.S. based scholars to the politics of the region, if they are discussed at all, tend to be subsidiary to the story of the theoretical development of the field." But wasn't the critique of Orientalism, by Said but even earlier from a broadly Marxian perspective, centrally about the construction of this field's object of knowledge? And didn't early critics of mainstream Middle East studies (for example, at MERIP or in AMESS) regard "the relationship of U.S. based scholars to the politics of the region" as directly implicated in its theoretical development, rather than as subsidiary to it? Be that as it may, Mitchell, citing Robert Vitalis' critique of the way in which a certain understanding of dependency theory was deployed within Middle East studies, mainly in the study of modern Egyptian history and politics, concludes that "it was not rival theories [like dependency theory] that drove the development of Middle Eastern studies. Theory was a language used to authorize rival strategies and commitments in the competing intellectual politics of the field."[20] Mitchell (and Vitalis) here make a valid and important point about the role of theoretical critique as such in driving change in this field; that is one reason this book focuses on factors and dynamics beyond the realm of ideas, narrowly defined.[21]

Mitchell concludes his 2004 essay by suggesting that if area studies has a future, it is not to provide data or case studies for the social sciences but rather to help "provincialize" them: "Area studies offers a place from which to rewrite the history of the social sciences, and to examine how their categories are implicated in a certain history of Europe and, in the twentieth century, an unachieved American project of universal social science."[22] To that aspiration one can only say "Amen," or perhaps more aptly *in sha' Allah*. But whatever role area studies comes to play, and however it evolves, I see the thrust of Mitchell's assessment of the field as supportive of an argument that I have been at pains to make in this book: it is not particularly useful to treat area studies as essentially a product or epiphenomenon of the Cold War, or as little more than a handmaiden of the postwar national security state.

This has in fact been a recurrent theme in critical writing on the field. For example, in a 1998 essay the historian of East Asia Bruce Cumings depicts area studies as the product of U.S.-Soviet confrontation and (at least in its early years) as the site of "astonishing levels of collaboration between the universities, the foundations, and the intelligence arms of the American state."[23] Following Foucault, Cumings usefully calls our attention to the sites where the most interesting effects of economic and political power—"the ultimate force shaping scholarly studies of what used to be called 'the non-Western world'"—becomes capillary, including universities, departments, centers and academic associations. This perspective makes sense to me, and in this book I have focused on a number of key sites in one area studies field. But as Cumings proceeds he seems to suggest that the Cold War offers an adequate explanation for everything that went on at those sites and that they did not change over time. In a substantially revised version of his essay published in 2004, Cumings offers a more complex assessment of area studies but still insists that "the American state and especially the intelligence elements in it shaped the entire field of postwar area studies. . . ."[24]

In fact, as we have seen, the envisioning of area studies as a new way of producing and disseminating knowledge began well before the Cold War was imaginable, much less under way, and it was foundation, SSRC and ACLS leaders, not government officials, who during and immediately after the war were primarily responsible for turning those visions into reality. Moreover, while the launching of area studies certainly had a great deal to do with the conviction of foundation, government and academic leaders that the United States would attain the status of a global superpower by war's end and that Americans therefore needed to know a lot more about the rest of the world, that is not the same as depicting this whole intellectual and institutional enterprise as if it were nothing but an adjunct of the U.S.-Soviet confrontation, essentially unchanged over the span of almost half a century. It is also worth noting that area studies is still around, a quarter-century or so after the end of the Cold War, buttressed by new rationales and galvanized by new intellectual currents. This fact too suggests that it cannot usefully be treated as a mere byproduct or vestige; its history needs to be studied on its own terms.

Cumings is of course right to remind us that during the Cold War there was a great deal of collaboration between academic area studies and the national security state. But I suspect that such collaboration tended to be concentrated in a limited number of centers for area studies and international studies (Cumings tends to conflate the two), like the Russian research centers at Columbia and Harvard, and the notoriously CIA-funded Center for International Studies at MIT. The great bulk of area studies centers were supported not by intelligence or military contracts but by university and sometimes foundation funds as well as Title VI money; the research pursued by the vast majority of scholars in the postwar area studies fields was neither shaped by nor served the needs of the state, in intent or in outcome; and while some of the graduates of area studies programs entered government service, the great majority did not.[25] There is no doubt that some in area studies saw it as their mission to produce knowledge (and students) to serve the state; but others would develop radical critiques of what that state was doing and denounce their colleagues for collaborating with it. Nor can we overlook the differences among, and the specificities of, the various area studies fields. To make these points is not to diminish the reality of university and foundation complicity with the American national security state during the Cold War (and after), or to absolve anyone of political and moral responsibility for their actions. It is simply to insist that we approach area studies as we would any other object of historical inquiry, by attending to nuance, complexity and contradiction, and by recognizing that this field had no fixed essence but was a multifaceted phenomenon which changed over time.[26]

In the later version of his essay Bruce Cumings offers a colorful assessment of the postwar development of East Asian studies:

> ... the idea [of area studies] was to bring contemporary social science theory to bear on the non-Western world, rather than continue to pursue the classic themes of Oriental studies, often examined through philology. Political scientists were often the carriers of the new "theory" (modernization), and they would begin talking to Orientalists. In return for their sufferance, the Orientalists would get vastly enhanced academic resources (positions, libraries, language studies)—and soon, a certain degree of separation which came from the social scientists inhabiting institutes of East Asian studies, whereas the Orientalists occupied departments of East Asian languages and cultures. This implicit Faustian bargain sealed the postwar academic deal—and meant that the Orientalists didn't necessarily have to talk to the social scientists, after all. If they often looked upon the latter as unlettered barbarians, the social scientists looked upon the Orientalists as spelunkers in the cave of exotic information, chipping away at the wall of ore until a vein could be tapped and brought to the surface, to be shaped into useful knowledge by the carriers of theory.[27]

There is obviously some truth in Cumings' portrait: in Middle East studies as elsewhere, the "languages and cultures," "languages and civilizations" or "languages and literatures" departments tended, at least for a time, to be largely the province of Orientalists, philologists and literature specialists of a rather old-fashioned kind, often alongside scholars of the ancient Near East—and sometimes of Hebrew and Judaic studies as well. But in this regard as well, Cumings' invocation of a capillary perspective is relevant. For example, for a good part of its life the JCNME included both social scientists and Orientalists, and while they were not particularly successful at fostering the kind of research the founders of area studies had anticipated, they did get a lot of field-building done. Moreover, the Middle East studies centers were not exclusively dominated by social scientists, while the intellectual complexion of even the initially philological departments changed over time. So in this respect as well, there is no substitute for fine-grained, historically grounded analysis of specific fields, sites, practices, networks and institutions, which is what I have sought to pursue in this study.

Immanuel Wallerstein offered his assessment of the trajectory of area studies in the United States in an important essay published in 1997.[28] In tracing the emergence and early development of the field Wallerstein certainly notes Cold War concerns and influences but offers a more nuanced account than Cumings, with a focus on what he sees as the unintended consequences of area studies for American academia. He argues that, despite the hopes of Gibb and others that Orientalists could shape area studies in their own image, their bid for dominance ultimately failed. Over the long run, however, the social sciences (and the discipline of history) were also transformed ("corroded," as Wallerstein puts it, but in a good way) by their encounter with area studies, because they were compelled to gradually abandon their exclusive focus on the West, open up to the wider world and begin to question whether the claims of Western social science were truly universal. Wallerstein further argues that the new academic fields that emerged in the 1970s—women's studies, African American studies, Latino studies, Judaic studies, and so on—can be seen as variants of (or at least similar to) area studies, because they were multidisciplinary, historically grounded and stressed specific local knowledges. I am not sure that I find all aspects of Wallerstein's account equally convincing, but he is certainly right to highlight the unintended (and unanticipated) consequences of area studies. Neither area studies writ large nor Middle East studies in particular developed as the founders and early leaders of these fields expected and hoped, they underwent important transformations over time, and they eventually produced and disseminated knowledge—in scholarly venues, in the classroom and for wider publics—of a kind that could not have been anticipated from the vantage point of 1943 or 1951 or even 1966.

A stimulating recent intervention by David Engerman also bears on the relationship between intention and outcome in the historical trajectory of area studies. Engerman argues that those who have criticized area studies for failing to produce much scholarship that was either intellectually valuable or policy-relevant have missed the point, because "area studies was, first and foremost, a pedagogical enterprise, not a research one." Engerman is correct to point out that, over the decades, area studies served as an important vehicle for making instruction in foreign languages and the study of the non-Western world key elements of the undergraduate curriculum in American higher education. But I think that Engerman's assessment of area studies conflates outcome and original intention. As this study shows, for Middle East studies at least (though I suspect the same holds for other regional fields as well), the ACLS' strongly pedagogical conception of the purpose of area studies lost out in the late 1940s to the SSRC's vision for the field, widely embraced by area studies' key funders, founders and academic leaders, which defined its primary purpose as the production of "useful" scholarship and properly trained scholars; hence their focus on scholarly research and on graduate training, seen as the main missions of the new university-based area studies centers. It is certainly possible to argue that, in the long run, the pedagogical achievements of area studies have been at least as important as its intellectual accomplishments, which would make for yet another unanticipated consequence. Yet it remains the case that, into the 1980s, it was the SSRC's vision and program that, whatever its actual results, set the tone and shaped expectations for much of area studies—and justified the inflow of most of the outside funding that the field received.[29]

There remains the question of how useful the knowledge that area studies produced actually was to government officials and the national security state. This is not an easy question to answer, in part because we lack much of the information we would need for a proper assessment. But I would venture to say that, overall, it was probably not very useful. T. Cuyler Young and his Princeton Consultants colleagues may have offered the CIA intelligent feedback on the agency's National Intelligence Estimates in the 1950s and 1960s; perhaps I. William Zartman's role in the CONEX II war game exercise in 1968 helped intelligence and Pentagon officials make better sense of the relationship between Algeria and Morocco at that moment; and it is conceivable that Nadav Safran's CIA-funded research on Saudi Arabia gave policymakers a better understanding of that country in the 1980s. But I am not convinced that, by and large, the government officials responsible for formulating and implementing U.S. policy in the Middle East and North Africa were much influenced by (or even read) work on modernization or political elites or the role of the military produced even by that minority of scholars in Middle East studies who strove to be policy-relevant. I tend to think that the conclusions Bruce Kuklick reaches in his study of the influence of U.S. foreign policy intellectuals in the three decades after the Second World War also apply to those in Middle East studies who hoped their work would inform policymaking:

> While they professed deep understanding, they actually groped in the dark. Much of the time fashion was more important than validity. At the same time, irrespective of the quality of their knowledge, in the usual case the ideas of the cerebral strategists had little causal impact. They served to legitimate but not to energize policies. Intellectuals were most effective when they showed, after the fact, that some endeavors had been desirable. Or they articulated schema that exculpated policymakers—or themselves—from responsibility for action later identified as bad. The basic though not the only function of strategic ideas was to provide politicians with the fictions used to give meaning to policies for the public.[30]

In any case, from the later 1960s growing numbers of academics (and future academics) became increasingly critical not only of specific government policies but of the propriety and morality of using their knowledge to serve the ends of the state. I suspect that both the perceived inutility of much supposedly policy-relevant work by college- and university-based scholars, and the reluctance of many of them to do such work, contributed to opening up the space within which the foreign-policy "think tanks" proliferated in the 1970s and after. Though these institutions sometimes recruited people trained in area studies programs, they explicitly focused on the production of policy-relevant knowledge about contemporary issues and embedded themselves deeply in the world of Washington DC in ways that relatively few college- and university-based scholars wished or were able to do. This left the great bulk of those in area studies and many other fields even further from the halls of power. We cannot know whether the latter scholars' deep knowledge of the Middle East and the wider Muslim world might have helped the United States adopt less disastrous and counterproductive policies in those regions, policies that for decades have caused much pain to this country but have often had catastrophic consequences for those on the receiving end of American power. But as Kuklick suggests, there is little reason to think that those in power have had much interest in hearing perspectives that do not justify what they already intended to do and that do not conform to the narrow consensus that tends to prevail in Washington.

Meanwhile, area studies persists as a distinct academic enterprise within the American research university and as a set of well-developed and institutionalized national scholarly fields and associated organizations and programs, and it seems likely to survive into the foreseeable future. The initial intellectual rationale for area studies may have fallen by the wayside long ago, and Middle East studies obviously did not turn out as its founders and early leaders intended and anticipated. Nonetheless, over the decades an apparently durable academic field of some value to the world of scholarship, to higher education and to the common weal was built, and it still seems to be doing something useful by bringing scholarly attention, institutional resources and pedagogical energies to bear on regions of the world that would otherwise probably be neglected, by ensuring that "less commonly taught" languages actually get taught, by producing much excellent scholarship that has at times challenged both the parochial biases and the universalist pretensions of certain disciplines, by training a great many students, scholars and teachers, and by trying to reach and inform a wider public about vital places and issues.

Ironically, notwithstanding Middle East studies' accomplishments, scholars, teachers and institutions in the field have been subject to often vicious threats and assaults from highly organized and well-funded groups based outside academia, especially since September 11, 2001. For the most part, the campaigns waged by these groups have sought to silence views with which they disagree, mainly about Israel (including scholarship that challenges their preferred historical narrative) but also about the role of the United States in the Middle East. This seems to be a cost of doing business for a field focused on a region in which the United States has for the last half-century and more been so deeply and often painfully involved, and about which many Americans have powerful sentiments that can be mobilized for political ends.

Despite such challenges, and despite budget-cutting by financially strapped universities as well as recurrent threats to reduce or eliminate the Title VI funding on which many centers and programs depend, Middle East studies has endured, as have the other area studies fields. They have all changed a great deal over the past seven decades, of course, sometimes along similar lines and sometimes in disparate ways, and there is no reason to think that they will not continue to evolve further in the years ahead. The historical trajectory of Middle East studies has had its own specificities and today remains unhappily distinctive among its sister area studies fields because of the external pressures to which it continues to be subjected. Nonetheless, it continues to function, even to thrive, and to accomplish useful things, and we must hope that this will be sustained into the future.

Notes

Preface

1. Tamar L. Gutner, *The Story of SAIS* (Washington DC: School of Advanced International Studies, 1987), 1.

2. Bundy's two successors as National Security Advisor—Walt W. Rostow and Henry Kissinger—also spoke at SAIS that year. The next time Kissinger came to SAIS for a lecture was in 1970, soon after the U.S. sent ground forces into Cambodia. A student posed the very first question: "Mr. Kissinger, do you consider yourself to be a war criminal?" Kissinger walked out, never to return (at least as of 1987). Gutner, *SAIS*, 69–70. For a devastating portrait of Bundy and his colleagues, see David Halberstam, *The Best and the Brightest* (New York: Random House, 1972).

3. McGeorge Bundy, "The Battlefields of Power and the Searchlights of the Academy," in *The Dimensions of Diplomacy*, ed. E. A. J. Johnson (Baltimore: Johns Hopkins University Press, 1964), 1, 2–3.

4. Ibid., 3.

5. Ibid., 8–9.

6. For consistency's sake this book generally uses the term "Middle East studies" to denote this academic field, because this is how it is commonly referred to today. This usage is of course anachronistic for some of the periods I discuss, and so I sometimes use the term "Near Eastern studies" when that seems more appropriate. On how the region has been denoted in the West see Zachary Lockman, *Contending Visions of the Middle East: The History and Politics of Orientalism*, 2nd edition (Cambridge: Cambridge University Press, 2010), 97–99, and Michael E. Bonine,

Abbas Amanat and Michael Ezekial Gasper, eds., *Is There a Middle East?: The Evolution of a Geographical Concept* (Stanford: Stanford University Press, 2012).

7. See for example an essay by Bruce Cumings which has been published in several versions, two of which I discuss more fully in the Epilogue: "Boundary Displacement: Area Studies and International Studies during and after the Cold War," in *Universities and Empire: Money and Politics in the Social Sciences during the Cold War*, ed. Christopher Simpson (New York: The New Press, 1998), 159–188, and the revised version published six years later as "Boundary Displacement: The State, the Foundations, and Area Studies during and after the Cold War," in *Learning Places: The Afterlives of Area Studies*, eds. Masao Miyoshi and H. D. Harootunian (Durham: Duke University Press, 2002), 261–302. On Cold War-era scholarship and its links with policymaking more broadly, see Irene L. Gendzier, *Managing Political Change: Social Scientists and the Third World* (Boulder: Westview Press, 1985); Michael E. Latham, *Modernization as Ideology: American Social Science and "Nation Building" in the Kennedy Era* (Chapel Hill: University of North Carolina Press, 2000); and Nils Gilman, *Mandarins of the Future: Modernization Theory in Cold War America* (Baltimore: Johns Hopkins University Press, 2003).

8. Matthew F. Jacobs, *Imagining the Middle East: The Building of an American Foreign Policy, 1918–1967* (Chapel Hill: University of North Carolina Press, 2011), which focuses on the informal networks of scholars and other experts which helped shape U.S. Middle East policy, and Osamah F. Khalil, "America's Dream Palace: The Rise of the U.S. National Security State and Middle East Expertise, 1902–2012" (unpublished manuscript under review), whose focus is well described by its subtitle. Khalil explores some of the same terrain that I cover in this book, but his perspective, interests, research questions and sources are quite different from mine. I cite here chapter and page numbers from the version of his manuscript that he graciously shared with me in November 2014.

9. On this question, to which I return in the Epilogue, see also David Engerman, "Social Science in the Cold War," *Isis* 101 no. 2 (June 2010): 393–400, which discusses work that questions the assumption made by many intellectual and political historians that "social science in the Cold War . . . equals Cold War social science."

10. Emily Hauptmann, "The Ford Foundation and the Rise of Behavioralism in Political Science," *Journal of the History of the Behavioral Sciences* 48 no. 2 (Spring 2012): 155. See too Mark Solovey, *Shaky Foundations: The Politics-Patronage-Social Science Nexus in Cold War America* (New Brunswick: Rutgers University Press, 2013), who suggests that "as the literature on the social sciences in Cold War America has acquired increasing depth, interest in 'following the money' has emerged as a central theme." (2)

11.   Zachary Lockman, "Challenges and Responsibilities in a Time of Crisis," *Middle East Studies Association Bulletin* 42 nos. 1/2 (Summer/Winter 2008): 5–15 (hereafter cited as *MESA Bulletin*).

12.   Timothy Mitchell, "The Middle East in the Past and Future of Social Science," in *The Politics of Knowledge: Area Studies and the Disciplines*, ed. David Szanton (Berkeley: University of California Press, 2004), 74–118. Another essay by Mitchell, published a year earlier, covers much of the same ground; see "Deterritorialization and the Crisis of Social Science," in *Localizing Knowledge in a Globalizing World: Recasting the Area Studies Debate*, eds. Ali Mirsepassi, Amrita Basu and Frederick Weaver (Syracuse: Syracuse University Press, 2003), 148–170.

13.   Robert A. McCaughey, *International Studies and Academic Enterprise: A Chapter in the Enclosure of American Learning* (New York: Columbia University Press, 1984), xi.

14.   I also do not find McCaughey's evidence of enclosure entirely convincing: for example, it seems to me that he ignores sites through which academics seek to engage with nonacademic constituencies, including policymakers but also the wider public interested in international affairs.

15.   Some exciting new research is already on the way: for example, Robert Vitalis, *White World Order, Black Power Politics* (Ithaca: Cornell University Press, 2015), on the history of the field of international relations in the United States and its largely unacknowledged (or suppressed) imbrication with race and empire.

Chapter 1

1.   This is the clear implication of, for example, Bundy, "Battlefields of Power," as well as of much of the scholarly literature framing area studies as in essence a Cold War phenomenon.

2.   Ferdinand Lundberg, *America's 60 Families* (New York: Vanguard Press, 1937), 325, 326. Throughout this book I use the online CPI Inflation Calculator of the Bureau of Labor Statistics (http://data.bls.gov/cgi-bin/cpicalc.pl), which uses the average Consumer Price Index for a given calendar year to determine its 2015 equivalent.

3.   Edward H. Berman, *The Influence of the Carnegie, Ford, and Rockefeller Foundations on American Foreign Policy: The Ideology of Philanthropy* (Albany: SUNY Press, 1983), 15. The brutal response of Carnegie and Rockefeller to their own workers' demands for justice and equity had of course helped fuel the anticapitalist sentiment and the demands for fundamental social change that their philanthropic work now sought to combat. Examples include the violent suppression of the strike at Carnegie Steel's Homestead, Pennsylvania, plant in 1892 and the 1914 massacre

by National Guard soldiers of striking coal miners and their families evicted from the Rockefeller-owned company town of Ludlow, Colorado. Like all great fortunes, those that funded the new foundations were stained by blood.

4. In so doing they built on several decades of scholarly and public discourse about race and empire—discourse which, as Robert Vitalis has shown, was later written out of the story that the academic field of international relations told of its origins. See Robert Vitalis, "The Noble American Science of Imperial Relations and its Laws of Race Development," *Comparative Studies in Society and History* 52 no. 4 (October 2010): 909–938, and more fully his *White World Order*. As Vitalis notes, *Foreign Affairs*, published by the Council on Foreign Relations, began life in 1910 as the *Journal of Race Development*.

5. See Inderjeet Parmar, *Foundations of the American Century: The Ford, Carnegie, and Rockefeller Foundations in the Rise of American Power* (New York: Columbia University Press, 2012)

6. The Institute of Pacific Relations is particularly noteworthy, since like the post-Second World War area studies centers it focused on a specific (if extremely expansive) geographic region and sought to produce interdisciplinary, policy-relevant knowledge. However, unlike the postwar area studies centers, it was not university-based but a freestanding institution supported entirely by foundation funding, and its scope explicitly encompassed the United States as well as all the countries of what would much later come to be called the "Pacific Rim" (and beyond). See Paul F. Hooper, "The Institute of Pacific Relations and the Origins of Asian and Pacific Studies," *Pacific Affairs* 61 no. 1 (Spring 1988): 98–121, and Vitalis, *White World Order*, ch. 4.

7. See Walter Metzger, "The Academic Profession in the United States," in *The Academic Profession: National, Disciplinary, and Institutional Settings*, ed. Burton R. Clark (Berkeley: University of California Press, 1987), 123–208.

8. Alfred De, "International Understanding and World Peace: The American Council of Learned Societies, 1919–1957" (PhD diss., City University of New York, 2004), 33.

9. For a "company history" of the General Education Board, which closed its doors in 1964, see "General Education Board," accessed June 20, 2014, http://rockefeller100.org/exhibits/show/education/general_education_board.

10. Frank A. Ninkovich has argued that, early on, the ACLS "languished for want of funds because of its competition with the Social Science Research Council for overall domestic leadership in the intellectual arena. The SSRC proved more attractive to the philanthropic community (especially the Rockefeller philanthropies) because it promised practical use for the tools of social science, especially reform uses, whereas the ACLS could suggest only vague benefits to be derived from

its humanistic stewardship." *The Diplomacy of Ideas: U.S. Foreign Policy and Cultural Relations, 1938–1950* (Cambridge: Cambridge University Press, 1981), 17. On the history of the SSRC see the overlapping studies commissioned by that organization: Elbridge Sibley, *Social Science Research Council: The First Fifty Years* (New York: Social Science Research Council, 1974) and Kenton W. Worcester, *Social Science R7esearch Council, 1923–1998* (New York: Social Science Research Council, 2001); both are available at http://www.ssrc.org/about/history/. On the SSRC in the interwar period, and more broadly on the central role of the Rockefeller Foundation in the development of the social sciences in the United States, see Donald Fisher, *Fundamental Development of the Social Sciences: Rockefeller Philanthropy and the United States Social Science Research Council* (Ann Arbor: University of Michigan Press, 1993).

11.   De, "International Understanding," 52. The University of Chicago as an institution, founded in 1890, was a pet project of, and massively funded by, John D. Rockefeller Sr. and his associates.

12.   On Leland see Peter J. Wosh, ed., *Waldo Gifford Leland and the Origins of the American Archival Profession* (Chicago: Society of American Archivists, 2011).

13.   De, "International Understanding," 66, 68. On the prewar period see too Stephen Marshall Arum, "Early Stages of Foreign Language and Area Studies in the U.S.: 1915–1941" (PhD diss., Teachers College of Columbia University, 1975), which includes a survey of courses offered in this period at a sample of universities.

14.   De, "International Understanding," 52, 56–58; *American Council of Learned Societies Bulletin* 10 (April 1929), hereafter cited as *ACLS Bulletin*. On the Rockefeller Foundation's early engagement in China see David Ekbladh, *The Great American Mission: Modernization and the Construction of an American World Order* (Princeton: Princeton University Press, 2010), 25–37.

15.   Summer institutes that brought scholars together for focused intellectual exchange and/or training were common in many fields from at least the 1920s onward. Examples include the Institute of Politics held annually at Williams College in Williamstown, Massachusetts, between 1921 and 1930, which focused on a different geographical region and set of issues each year, and the Linguistic Institutes run (with ACLS support) by the Linguistic Society of America from 1928 onward. See Vitalis, *White World Order*, ch. 4, and Julia S. Falk, "The LSA Linguistic Institutes" (unpublished paper), accessed February 22, 2015, www.linguisticsociety.org/files/LSA-90%20 Institutes.docx.

16.   Rockefeller Foundation, *Annual Report 1933* (New York: Rockefeller Foundation, 1934), 321–322; *ACLS Bulletin* 20 (December 1933).

17.   Meeting of the ACLS executive committee, March 17, 1934, box B40, American Council of Learned Societies records, Library of Congress (hereafter cited as ACLS); De, "International Understanding," 73ff.

18. McCaughey, *International Studies*, 108.

19. *Daily Princetonian*, April 29, 1936. Reischauer, older brother of the noted Japan scholar and ambassador Edwin O. Reischauer, would be killed in Shanghai by a Japanese bomb in August 1937. His friends would later call him the first American to be killed in the Second World War, though that distinction may rightfully belong to the American volunteers killed fighting fascism in Spain earlier that same year.

20. Helen Delpar, *Looking South: The Evolution of Latin Americanist Scholarship in the United States, 1850–1975* (Tuscaloosa: University of Alabama Press, 2008), 111–116; see too Howard F. Cline, ed., *Latin American History: Essays on its Study and Teaching, 1898–1965* (Austin: University of Texas Press, 1967), 251–264.

21. Proceedings, Committee on Mediterranean Antiquities, April 10, 1931, box B83, ACLS; meeting of the ACLS executive committee, March 17, 1934, box B40, ACLS; Rosane Rocher, "W. Norman Brown, 1892–1975," *Journal of the American Oriental Society* 96 no. 1 (January–March 1976): 3–6.

22. On the history of the study of the ancient Near East in the United States see Bruce Kuklick, *Puritans in Babylon: The Ancient Near East and American Intellectual Life, 1880–1930* (Princeton: Princeton University Press, 1996).

23. See Jeffrey Abt, *American Egyptologist: The Life of James Henry Breasted and the Creation of His Oriental Institute* (Chicago: University of Chicago Press, 2011). As Bruce Kuklick notes, in the early decades of the twentieth century "the sense educated Americans had of the pre-classical era came from [Breasted]." *Puritans*, 112.

24. McCaughey, *International Studies*, 100–101.

25. Kuklick, *Puritans*, 183–184.

26. Quoted in Willem A. Bijlefeld, "A Century of Arabic and Islamic Studies at Hartford Seminary," *The Muslim World* 83 no. 2 (April 1993): 105.

27. *The Moslem World* 1 no. 1 (January 1911): 2; Lockman, *Contending Visions*, 102. The journal was renamed *The Muslim World* in 1947, at which time its subtitle was also revised; see Bijlefeld, "A Century," 107. Samuel M. Zwemer (1867–1952), the founder and longtime editor of *The Moslem World*, was nicknamed the "Apostle to Islam" by his missionary colleagues.

28. See for example D. S. Margoliouth, "The Caliphate Historically Considered," *The Moslem World* 11 no. 4 (October 1921): 332–343. Margoliouth's father had converted from Judaism to Anglicanism.

29. J. C. Hurewitz, *Undergraduate Instruction on the Middle East in American Colleges and Universities* (New York: American Association for Middle East Studies, 1962), 5–6. Lybyer (1876–1949) was educated at Princeton and Princeton Theological Seminary and then taught mathematics at Robert College in Istanbul before pursuing his doctorate at Harvard; after a stint at Oberlin he taught at the University of

Illinois from 1913 to 1944. On Lybyer's conception of Ottoman history, and Gibb and Bowen's, see Lockman, *Contending Visions*, 104–108.

30.   My thanks to Linda Stahnke Stepp of the University Archives of the University of Illinois at Urbana-Champaign for providing this information, in an email message to author, June 17, 2014.

31.   Philip K. Hitti, "Arabic and Islamic Studies in Princeton University," *The Moslem World* 31 no. 3 (July 1941): 292–294; James Kritzeck and R. Bayly Winder, eds., *The World of Islam: Studies in Honour of Philip K. Hitti* (London: MacMillan, 1960); and "A Talk with Philip Hitti," *Aramco World* 22 no. 4 (July–August 1971). For an interesting exploration of Hitti's links with American University of Beirut graduates in Brazil, see John Tofik Karam, "Philip Hitti, Brazil, and the Diasporic Histories of Area Studies," *International Journal of Middle East Studies* 46 no. 3 (August 2014): 451–471.

32.   Report of the Committee on Near Eastern Studies, box B65, ACLS. See too Hitti, "Arabic and Islamic Studies," 292–294.

33.   For example, as early as 1933 the ACLS gave a grant of $1000 to the American Institute for Persian Art and Archaeology to subsidize a catalog of Persian Islamic architecture; see Leonard Outhwaite to Mortimer Graves, September 25, 1933, and "Requisition upon the ACLS," September 30, 1933, box B65, ACLS. This institute, later renamed the Asia Institute, had been founded by Arthur Upham Pope (1881–1969) who with his wife Phyllis Ackerman pioneered the study and collection of Iranian Islamic art in the United States. In 1940 Pope founded the Committee for National Morale, which mobilized leading psychologists, anthropologists and others to combat fascism, in part by promoting a "democratic personality" that could resist fascist propaganda and the "authoritarian personality" it supposedly inculcated. See Fred Turner, *The Democratic Surround: Multimedia and American Liberalism from World War II to the Psychedelic Sixties* (Chicago: University of Chicago Press, 2013), and Jamie Cohen-Cole, *The Open Mind: Cold War Politics and the Sciences of Human Nature* (Chicago: University of Chicago Press, 2014).

34.   Graves to Hitti, April 10 and April 19, 1934, box B65, ACLS.

35.   Graves to Mehmet Aga-Oglu, March 24, 1935, box B65, ACLS; *ACLS Bulletin* 23 (June 1935): 51.

36.   Summer Seminar in Arabic and Islamic Studies, 1935, box B9, ACLS; R. Bayly Winder, "Four Decades of Middle Eastern Study," *Middle East Journal* 41 no. 1 (Winter 1987): 41–42; *Princeton Alumni Weekly* 35 no. 23 (March 29, 1935); *ACLS Bulletin* 25 (July 1936): 79–81; Nabih A. Faris, "Islamic and Arabic at Princeton Again," *The American Scholar* 7 no. 3 (Summer 1938): 373–374. A Princeton graduate, Wright taught history at the American University of Beirut for several years while earning his master's degree and then returned to Princeton, from which he received a PhD

in 1928. After several years studying Turkish he returned to Princeton to teach; then, from 1935 to 1943, he served as president of Robert College and its sister institution, the American College for Girls, later merged into what is now Boğaziçi University. After OSS and other government service during the war, Wright would (as we will see in Chapter 4) return to Princeton and for a time play a leading role in the ACLS' effort to promote Near Eastern studies.

37. Mortimer Graves, "Relation to institutional development," 1936 or 1937, box B9, ACLS.

38. Mortimer Graves, "A Note on what I take to be the Council's Interest in Arabic-Islamic and in Indic-Iranian Studies," 1936 or 1937, box B9, ACLS.

39. Graves, "Relation to institutional development," box B9, ACLS.

40. Faris, "Islamic and Arabic at Princeton." See too Leland to Hitti, November 5, 1936, box B9, and Graves to Hitti, November 9, 1937, box B53, ACLS.

41. *Daily Princetonian*, May 9, 16, 1939.

42. Matthew Jacobs says that in 1939 ten American universities "offered training in Middle Eastern languages." See Jacobs, *Imagining*, 40. But the sources he cites actually seem to refer only to Arabic, and one suspects that at most of those universities Arabic was taught as an adjunct to Hebrew and/or Aramaic.

43. Leland to the members of the committees on Mediterranean Antiquities and Byzantine Studies, February 15, 1937, box B83; Wilson to Leland, February 18, 1937, box B83; Sturtevant to Leland, April 7, 1937, box B87; Sturtevant to Robert P. Blake, June 5, 1937, box B83; Blake to Sturtevant, June 10, 1937, box B83; Sturtevant to Cross, June 11, 1937, box B83; Graves to CNMES, October 22, 1937, box B83, ACLS.

44. Ibid.; Mortimer Graves, "A Note on what I take to be the Council's Interest in Arabic-Islamic and in Indic-Iranian Studies," 1936 or 1937, box B9, and Graves to Karl Reuning, February 17, 1936, box B9, ACLS; *ACLS Bulletin* 27 (November 1938).

45. "Luncheon of the Islamic Group," *Journal of the American Oriental Society* 58 no. 2 (June 1938): 399–400.

46. Shaw would also serve as chief of the State Department's Division of Near Eastern Affairs and, in 1941–1944, as Assistant Secretary of State. In 1933 he had submitted to the State Department a pioneering study of social change in contemporary Turkish society titled "Family Life in Modern Turkey," but it was not published until long after his death; see Rifat N. Bali, ed., *Family Life in the Turkish Republic of the 1930's: A Study by G. Howland Shaw* (Istanbul: Isis Press, 2007).

47. *ACLS Bulletin* 31 (June 1940); "Background: Proposed Center for Islamic Studies in the LC," December 23, 1940, box E16, ACLS.

48. See Committee on Islamic Culture, "Brief Statement of Purpose and Method of Operation of the Islamic Archives," 1950, box E16, and "Proposed Center for Islamic Studies in the LC," December 19, 1940, box E16, ACLS. The campaign

by the ACLS to make the Library of Congress a center for Islamic scholarship was initially bound up with a plan to get the Austrian scholar of the Ottoman empire Paul Wittek (1894–1978), who among other accomplishments helped prevent the sale of the vast Ottoman archives to Bulgaria as scrap paper, out of Nazi-occupied Belgium and into the United States, where he could be installed as director of the Library's proposed Center for Islamic Studies. As things developed, Wittek managed to escape to Britain and after the war began teaching at the School of Oriental and African Studies.

49. MacLeish to Leland, October 3, 1941, box E16, ACLS. On MacLeish just before and during the war see Brett Gary, *The Nervous Liberals: Propaganda Anxieties from World War I to the Cold War* (New York: Columbia University Press, 1999), ch. 4.

50. For a description of Smith's collection, formally named the Archive for Islamic Art and Culture, see http://siris-archives.si.edu/ipac20/ipac.jsp?uri=full=3100001~!283688!0. A donation of $9000 from Professor James R. Jewett of Harvard, channeled through the ACLS, made it possible to begin cataloging the archive, managed from 1949 by a Committee on Islamic Culture established by Smith.

51. *ACLS Bulletin* 33 (October 1941): 25; 36 (December 1944): 19–20; 38 (December 1945): 79.

52. See George M. Beckmann, "The Role of the Foundations," *Annals of the American Academy of Political and Social Science* 356 (November 1964): 13–14.

53. Ellen Condliffe Lagemann, *The Politics of Knowledge: The Carnegie Corporation, Philanthropy, and Public Policy* (Middletown CT: Wesleyan University Press, 1989), 154–155, 159. On the foundations' promotion of interdisciplinarity see too Cohen-Cole, *Open Mind*, ch. 3; David L. Seim, *Rockefeller Philanthropy and Modern Social Science* (London: Pickering & Chatto, 2013), 119ff; and David C. Engerman, "The Pedagogical Purposes of Interdisciplinary Social Science: A View from Area Studies in the United States," *Journal of the History of the Behavioral Sciences* 51 no. 1 (Winter 2015): 78–92. On the role of the foundations and the SSRC in promoting behavioralism in political science after the war, see Emily Hauptmann, "The Ford Foundation," and "The Development of Philanthropic Interest in the Scientific Study of Political Behavior," Rockefeller Archive Center Research Reports Online, accessed June 17, 2013, www.rockarch.org/publications/resrep/hauptmann.pdf.

54. Engerman, "Social Science," 394.

Chapter 2

1. "Preliminary Proposals for the organization of a School of Modern Oriental Languages and Civilizations in Washington," 1941, box E5, ACLS.

2. Waldo G. Leland to Walter A. Jessup, January 15, 1942, folder 11, box 327, Series

III.A.8, Carnegie Corporation of New York Records, Rare Book and Manuscript Library, Columbia University Libraries (hereafter cited as CCNY).

3. Robert T. Crane to Walter A. Jessup, April 2, 1942, folder 9–17, box 327, Series III.A.8, CCNY.

4. Redfield was one of the intellectual authors of the concept of modernization, beginning with his 1930 book *Tepotzlán, a Mexican Village: A Study of Folk Life*, based on doctoral dissertation research partially funded by the SSRC. As Clifford Wilcox puts it, Redfield was "arguably the first to use the word 'modernization' in the specialized sense that it came to acquire in post-World War II social science, and he proved highly original in the modernization project through his grounding of his empirical studies of change in nineteenth-century European social theory." *Robert Redfield and the Development of American Anthropology* (Lanham MD: Lexington Books, 2004), 5.

5. Quoted in De, "International Understanding," 120.

6. On the ILP see David H. Price, *Anthropological Intelligence: The Deployment and Neglect of American Anthropology in the Second World War* (Durham: Duke University Press, 2008), 74ff, and David C. Engerman, *Know Your Enemy: The Rise and Fall of America's Soviet Experts* (New York: Oxford University Press, 2009), 16.

7. Mortimer Graves, memorandum, 1942, box E5, ACLS.

8. Engerman, *Know Your Enemy*, 16.

9. On the ASTP see Louis E. Keefer, *Scholars in Foxholes: The Story of the Army Specialized Training Program in World War II* (Jefferson NC: McFarland & Co., 1988). For a discussion of the impact of the crash wartime language programs on the development of Arabic instruction in the United States, see Ernest McCarus, "History of Arabic Study in the United States," in Aleya Rouchdy, ed., *The Arabic Language in America* (Detroit: Wayne State University Press, 1992), 208. See too James Vachel Dougherty, "A History of Federal Policy Concerning College or University-Based Foreign Language and Area Studies Centers, 1941–1980" (PhD diss., University of Maryland, 1993), ch. 3. For an early description of the CATP see Charles S. Hyneman, "The Army's Civil Affairs Training Program," *American Political Science Review* 38 no. 2 (April 1944): 342–353.

10. Quoted in George Q. Flynn, *Conscription and Democracy: The Draft in France, Great Britain, and the United States* (Westport CT: Greenwood Press, 2002), 128.

11. See William Nelson Fenton, *Area Studies in American Universities* (Washington DC: American Council on Education, 1947). The survey of ASTP programs and the reports on them were commissioned by the Ethnogeographic Board, discussed below.

12. Wayland J. Hayes and Werner J. Cahnman, "Foreign Area Study (ASTP) as

an Educational Experiment in the Social Sciences," *Social Forces* 23 no. 1 (1944): 164. In 1943 Columbia University's Joint Committee on Graduate Instruction appointed a Committee on Area Studies to discuss the pedagogical implications of the new approach; see Immanuel Wallerstein, "The Unintended Consequences of Cold War Area Studies," in Noam Chomsky et al., *The Cold War and the University: Toward an Intellectual History of the Postwar Years* (New York: New Press, 1997), 197.

13. Neil Smith, *American Empire: Roosevelt's Geographer and the Prelude to Globalization* (Berkeley: University of California Press, 2003), 253.

14. Ethnogeographic Board, minutes, August 3, 1942, folder 3939, box 331, series 200S, record group (hereafter RG) 1.1, Rockefeller Foundation archives, Rockefeller Archive Center (hereafter cited as RF). On the Ethnogeographic Board see Matthew Farish, "Archiving Areas: The Ethnogeographic Board and the Second World War," *Annals of the Association of American Geographers* 95 no. 3 (2005): 663–679, and *The Contours of America's Cold War* (Minneapolis: University of Minnesota Press, 2010); Price, *Anthropological Intelligence*, 97ff; and Martin W. Lewis and Kären E. Wigen, *The Myth of Continents: A Critique of Metageography* (Berkeley: University of California Press, 1997), 162–166.

15. January 15, 1943, folder 3939, box 331, series 200S, RG 1.1, RF.

16. Conference on Bolivian Indians, September 20, 1942, with cover letter from the board's director, William Duncan Strong, to Waldo Leland of the ACLS, November 12, 1942, folder 3939, box 331, series 200S, RG 1.1, RF.

17. On the history of the OSS see Bradley F. Smith, *The Shadow Warriors: O.S.S. and the Origins of the C.I.A.* (New York: Basic Books, 1983).

18. Robin W. Winks, *Cloak and Gown: Scholars in the Secret War, 1939–1961* (New York: William Morrow and Company, 1987), 80; on R&A specifically, see Barry M. Katz, *Foreign Intelligence: Research and Analysis in the Office of Strategic Services, 1942–1945* (Cambridge: Harvard University Press, 1989).

19. Bundy, "Battlefields of Power," 2.

20. Katz, *Foreign Intelligence*, 22. See too *War Report of the OSS* (New York: Walker and Company, 1976), a redacted version of the original classified 1947 report.

21. Oral History Interview with Edwin M. Wright, Harry S. Truman Library and Museum, accessed June 24, 2014, http://www.trumanlibrary.org/oralhist/wright.htm. During the war Wright served in intelligence in Iran, Egypt and Palestine.

22. Winks, *Cloak and Gown*, 85–86.

23. Founded in 1907 as a nonsectarian and largely secular graduate institution, Dropsie became an important center for training in Judaic studies and in ancient Near Eastern languages and literatures. It stopped granting degrees in 1986 and became the Annenberg Research Institute; in 1993 it was absorbed into the University of Pennsylvania as its Center for Judaic Studies.

24. E. A. Speiser, "Near Eastern Studies in America, 1939–45," *Archiv Orientální* 16 no. 1 (December 1, 1947): 87. See too E. A. Speiser, "Oriental Studies and Society," *Journal of the American Oriental Society* 66 no. 3 (July–September 1946): 193–197. A copy of Speiser's certificate of merit from William Langer, head of the OSS Research and Analysis branch, can be found in folder 5211, box 443, series 1, subseries 75, RG 2, Social Science Research Council Archives, Rockefeller Archive Center (hereafter cited as SSRC). Note that what I cite here as RG 2 is also sometimes referred to in the finding aid for the SSRC archives as Record Group 1, Accession 2.

25. On Hurewitz see Jacobs, *Imagining*, 39–40. Carleton Coon's account of his wartime exploits can be found in *A North Africa Story: The Anthropologist as OSS Agent, 1941–1943* (Ipswich MA: Gambit, 1980); but see too Price, *Anthropological Intelligence*, 248–259, which provides the previously unpublished postscript of *A North Africa Story*. Frye related his wartime adventures in his autobiography, *Greater Iran: A 20th-Century Odyssey* (Costa Mesa CA: Mazda Publishers, 2005). On the role of Middle East scholars in the OSS see too Khalil, "America's Dream Palace," ch. 2.

26. See Katz, *Foreign Intelligence*, 138–164.

27. P&P minutes, January 17, 1943, folder 1785, box 315, series 2, RG 1, SSRC. Note that what I cite here as RG 1 is sometimes referred to in the finding aid for the SSRC records as Record Group 1, Accession 1.

28. William L. Langer, *In and Out of the Ivory Tower* (New York: Neale Watson Academic Publications, 1977), 231. One of the two Carnegie staffers who visited Langer was John W. Gardner, who would play a central role in launching area studies.

29. Engerman, *Know Your Enemy*, 18.

30. President Roosevelt's disdain for European colonialism was no secret, and foundation, SSRC and ACLS officials were likely to have been well aware of wartime planning for a postwar global "open door" order overseen by the United States. See Smith, *American Empire,* chs. 13–14.

31. Committee on World Regions, draft of Hamilton's report, February 25, 1943, folder 1386, box 229, subseries 19, series 1, RG 1, SSRC; Social Science Research Council, *World Regions in the Social Sciences* (New York: Social Science Research Council, June 1943), mimeographed.

32. CWR meeting minutes, February 25, 1943, folder 1386, box 229, subseries 19, series 1, RG 1, SSRC.

33. Council minutes, April 1–2, 1944, folder 2097, box 356, series 9, RG 1, SSRC.

34. Council minutes, September 11–12, 1943, folder 2097, box 356, series 9, RG 1, SSRC.

35. Committee on War Service of Anthropologists, Division of Anthropology

and Psychology, National Research Council, "Anthropology During the War and After," March 10, 1943, box B89, ACLS.

36. P&P minutes, March 31, July 28–29, 1944, folder 1785, box 315, series 2, RG 1, SSRC; Council minutes, September 11–12, 1943 and April 1–2, 1944, folder 2097, box 356, series 9, RG 1, SSRC.

37. Graves to John Marshall, February 22, 1944, folder 2506, box 209, series 200, RG 1.1, RF. In the 1930s and early 1940s Marshall (1903–1980) played a critical role in channeling Rockefeller Foundation funding into research on propaganda and mass communications; see Gary, *Nervous Liberals*, ch. 3.

38. See for example the minutes of the CWR meeting of February 25, 1943 (folder 1386, box 229, subseries 19, series 1, RG 1, SSRC), at which Graves and Pendleton Herring argued whether undergraduate or graduate education should receive priority, and also Graves to David H. Stevens, February 1, 1944, folder 2506, box 209, series 200, RG 1.1, RF.

39. John Marshall, "Area Studies," interoffice memo, February 21, 1944, folder 2506, box 209, series 200, RG 1.1, RF.

40. Ibid.

41. "Notes on a discussion of the future of Area Studies in post-war education," February 28, 1944, *100 Years: The Rockefeller Foundation*, accessed April 10, 2013, http://www.rockefeller100.org/items/show/1786; Graves to Marshall, February 22, 1944, folder 2506, box 209, series 200, RG 1.1, RF.

42. The Rockefeller Foundation, *Conference on Area and Language Programs in American Universities*, March 15–16, 1944, mimeographed transcript, 35, folder 2506, box 209, series 200, RG 1.1, RF.

43. Mortimer Graves, "The Future of Area Studies," March 1, 1944, folder 2506, box 209, series 200, RG 1.1, RF. See too Graves' memorandum to a joint meeting of the ACLS executive committee and advisory board, March 30–31, 1944, box D2, ACLS.

44. Donald Young and Paul Webbink, "Social Science Considerations in the Planning of Regional Specialization in Higher Education and Research," March 1944, folder 165, box 31, series 900, RG 3.2, RF.

45. P&P minutes, March 31, July 28–29, 1944, folder 1785, box 315, series 2, RG 1, SSRC; Council minutes, September 11–12, 1943 and April 1–2, 1944, folder 2097, box 356, series 9, RG 1, SSRC.

46. David Harrison Stevens, "Proposal for a national plan of work on foreign languages, institutions, and customs," June 7, 1944, *100 Years: The Rockefeller Foundation*, accessed April 10, 2013, http://www.rockefeller100.org/items/show/1788, and Joseph H. Willits, "Memo from Joseph H. Willits to David H. Stevens regarding area studies," July 26, 1944, *100 Years: The Rockefeller Foundation*, accessed April 10, 2013, http://www.rockefeller100.org/items/show/1789. See also Darwin H. Staple-

ton, "Joseph Willits and the Rockefeller's European Programme in the Social Sciences," accessed April 10, 2013, http://link.springer.com/content/pdf/10.1023%2FA%3A1023602713292.

47. This total includes about half a million dollars granted by the Laura Spelman Research Memorial before it was merged into the foundation in 1929. See folder 2529, box 375, series 200, RG 2, RF.

48. P&P minutes, October 27, 1945, folder 1786, box 316, series 2, RG 1, SSRC.

49. Robert John Matthew, *Language and Area Studies in the Armed Service: Their Future Significance* (Washington: American Council on Education, 1947).

50. P&P minutes, October 27, 1945, folder 1786, box 316, series 2, RG 1, SSRC.

51. Ibid.

52. P&P minutes, December 8, 1945 and February 16, 1946, folder 1786, box 316, series 2, RG 1, SSRC.

53. See for example Hall to Leland, March 10, 1937, and Hall to Graves, November 30, 1937, box B50, ACLS. On the 1937 institute see J. R. Hayden, "The Institute of Far Eastern Studies," *American Political Science Review* 32 no. 1 (February 1938), 114–116.

54. On Hall's life and career see http://um2017.org/faculty-history/faculty/robert-b-hall/memoir and http://um2017.org/faculty-history/faculty/robert-b-hall/memorial.

55. *American Anthropologist* 56 no. 2, accessed July 21, 2014, http://onlinelibrary.wiley.com/doi/10.1525/aa.1954.56.2.02a00090/pdf.

56. In the late 1940s, after leaving government service, Halperin was recruited to head Boston University's fledgling interdisciplinary Department of Latin American Regional Studies, one of the early postwar area studies initiatives. In 1953, at the height of the "Red Scare," he was summoned to testify before the Senate Internal Security Subcommittee about allegations that he had been a member of the Communist Party before the war and part of a Soviet spy ring during it. Though Halperin denied under oath that he had engaged in espionage, he refused to answer the committee's specific questions by invoking his Fifth Amendment right to avoid self-incrimination and was suspended from his academic position pending an investigation. He then fled the country with his family and spent the next decade and a half in Mexico, the Soviet Union and Cuba before accepting a position at Simon Fraser University in Vancouver, Canada, where he taught until his retirement. See Don S. Kirschner, *Cold War Exile: The Unclosed Case of Maurice Halperin* (Columbia MO: University of Missouri Press, 1995), and "Maurice Halperin, 88, a Scholar Who Chronicled Castro's Career," *The New York Times*, February 12, 1995.

57. Scheme of Discussion, first meeting of the JECWAR, February 23, 1946, folder 1386, box 229, subseries 19, series 1, RG 1, SSRC.

58. JECWAR, second meeting, April 27, 1946, folder 1386, box 229, subseries 19, series 1, RG 1, SSRC.

59. Delpar, *Looking South*, 129–130; Cline, *Latin American History*, 289–316.

60. JECWAR, annual report for 1945–46, Appendix 4, Council and P&P minutes, folders 1786 and 1787, box 316, series 2, RG 1, SSRC; Smith, *Shadow Warriors*, passim.

61. Robert B. Hall, *Area Studies: With Special Reference to their Implications for Research in the Social Sciences* (New York: Social Science Research Council, 1947).

62. On the history of American studies/American civilization as an academic field see for example Gene Wise, "'Paradigm Dramas' in American Studies: A Cultural and Institutional History of the Movement," *American Quarterly* 31 no. 3 (1979): 293–337, and Matthias Oppermann, *American Studies in Dialogue: Radical Reconstructions between Curriculum and Cultural Critique* (Frankfurt/New York: Campus Verlag, 2010).

63. Robin Winks has argued that postwar "area studies programs in American universities came to reflect the relative strengths of the area-related staffs in the OSS. The weakest, most troubled area for R & A was Latin America, and as an area of study Latin America continues to receive less attention in American universities than it deserves. The OSS was slow in moving into Near and Middle Eastern studies, and even slower in South Asian studies, and these two focuses for area studies programs remain less well endowed in money, number of scholars, in students studying the relevant languages, than other area programs." *Cloak and Gown*, 115. It seems to me that this formulation draws too direct and simple a connection between the OSS and postwar area studies.

Chapter 3

1. The scholarly literature on the history of the Cold War is vast. For a start see Melvyn P. Leffler and David S. Painter, eds., *Origins of the Cold War: An International History* (London: Routledge, 1994); Odd Arne Westad, *The Global Cold War: Third World Interventions and the Making of Our Times* (Cambridge: Cambridge University Press, 2006); and Melvyn P. Leffler and Odd Arne Westad, eds., *The Cambridge History of the Cold War*, 3 vols. (Cambridge: Cambridge University Press, 2010).

2. As Tim Weiner points out, 5 percent of the funds appropriated by Congress for the Marshall Plan for its first five years—up to $685 million—were made available to the new CIA. "Secret funds were the heart of secret operations. The CIA now had an unfailing source of untraceable cash." *Legacy of Ashes: The History of the CIA* (New York: Doubleday, 2007), 28.

3. Sigmund Diamond, *Compromised Campus: The Collaboration of Universi-*

ties with the Intelligence Community, 1945–1955 (New York: Oxford University Press, 1992), passim.

4. Bundy, "Battlefields of Power," 3. See too Cumings, "Boundary Displacement: Area Studies" and "Boundary Displacement: The State."

5. Gilman, *Mandarins of the Future*, 117. Herring graduated from Johns Hopkins University in 1925, received his doctorate in political science from the same university three years later, and then began teaching at Harvard; his most influential scholarly work was *The Politics of Democracy: American Parties in Action*, published in 1940. During the war he served as an advisor to a number of government agencies, and in 1946 he left Harvard and joined the staff of the Carnegie Corporation, only to take a leave of absence soon thereafter to serve as director of the United Nations Atomic Energy Commission. He then returned to the Carnegie Corporation where he helped design the new national security infrastructure embodied in the National Security Act of 1947, after which he assumed the presidency of the SSRC.

6. Quoted in Farish, *Contours*, 118.

7. Council minutes, April 3–4, 1948, folder 2100, box 358, series 9, RG 1, SSRC.

8. Ibid.

9. Claude DeVane, *Higher Education in Twentieth-Century America* (Cambridge: Harvard University Press, 1965), 58–59; National Center for Education Statistics, *120 Years of American Education: A Statistical Portrait*, accessed November 5, 2014, www.nces.ed.gov/pubs93/93442.pdf. Of course, enrollment rates varied greatly along racial, class and gender lines.

10. Thomas Bender, "Politics, Intellect, and the American University, 1945–1995," in *American Academic Culture in Transformation: Fifty Years, Four Disciplines*, eds. Thomas Bender and Carl E. Schorske (Princeton: Princeton University Press, 1997), 24–25.

11. See W. H. Cowley and Don Williams, *International and Historical Roots of American Higher Education* (New York: Garland Publishing, 1991).

12. Bender, "Politics," 17–18, 24–25.

13. Clark Kerr, *The Uses of the University* (Cambridge: Harvard University Press, 1963), 7.

14. Robert Nisbet, *The Degradation of the Academic Dogma: The University in America, 1945–1970* (New York: Basic Books, 1971), 13, 72, 87.

15. Mario Savio, "Sit-In Address on the Steps of Sproul Hall," *American Rhetoric Top 100 Speeches*, accessed December 17, 2014, http://www.americanrhetoric.com/speeches/mariosaviosproulhallsitin.htm. The Berkeley students were fighting the administration's ban on political activity on campus, including fundraising for the civil rights movement; see Robert Cohen, *The Free Speech Movement: Reflections on Berkeley in the 1960s* (Berkeley: University of California Press, 2002).

16. See for example Theodore Roszak, ed., *The Dissenting Academy* (New York: Pantheon Books, 1967); Noam Chomsky et al., *The Cold War & the University: Toward an Intellectual History of the Postwar Years* (New York: The New Press, 1997); and Christopher Simpson, ed., *Universities and Empire: Money and Politics in the Social Sciences during the Cold War* (New York: The New Press, 1998). For Chomsky's indictment of American scholars and intellectuals for their complicity with a state waging what he regarded as a criminal war in Vietnam, see his classic *American Power and the New Mandarins* (New York: Pantheon, 1967). The term "military-industrial-academic complex" appeared in early drafts of President Dwight Eisenhower's January 1961 farewell address, but "academic" dropped out by the final version.

17. Rockefeller Foundation, *Annual Report 1944* (New York: Rockefeller Foundation, 1945), accessed February 22, 2015, http://www.rockefellerfoundation.org/about-us/annual-reports/1940–1949.

18. Charles B. Fahs, "Area Studies: An Outline of Humanities Concern," December 3, 1946, folder 165, box 31, series 900, RG 2, RF; also available at http://rockefeller100.org/items/show/1791.

19. Charles B. Fahs, "Brief on Language and Area Studies in the U.S.," December 3, 1946, folder 165, box 31, series 900, RG 3.2, RF.

20. Rockefeller Foundation, *Annual Report 1945* (New York: Rockefeller Foundation, 1946), 13–14, accessed February 22, 2015, http://www.rockefellerfoundation.org/about-us/annual-reports/1940–1949.

21. See Geroid Tanquary Robinson, "The Russian institute," *100 Years: The Rockefeller Foundation*, accessed April 10, 2013, http://www.rockefeller100.org/items/show/5195. On the history of the Russian Institute (now the Harriman Institute) see Philip E. Mosely, "The Russian Institute of Columbia University," *Proceedings of the American Philosophical Society* 99 no. 1 (Jan. 27, 1955): 36–38. The richest account of the development of Russian and Soviet studies in the United States is Engerman, *Know Your Enemy.*

22. Carnegie Corporation board of trustees meeting, October 1945, box 37, series I.A.3, CCNY.

23. "Memorandum on International Education and Carnegie Corporation," April 18, 1946, submitted to the Carnegie Corporation executive committee, and Carnegie Corporation board of trustees meeting, May 16, 1945, box 38, series I.A.3, CCNY.

24. Carnegie Corporation board of trustees meeting, January 16, 1947, box 38, series I.A.3, CCNY; Carnegie Corporation of New York, *Annual Report 1947* (New York: Carnegie Corporation of New York, 1947), 28; "For the Information of the Trustees," Carnegie Corporation board of trustees meeting, January 19, 1950, box 39, series I.A.3, CCNY.

25. John W. Gardner, "Are We Doing Our Homework in Foreign Affairs?," *The Yale Review* 37 no. 3 (March 1948): 404.

26. Carnegie Corporation board of trustees meeting, March 20, 1947, box 38, series I.A.3, CCNY.

27. Carnegie Corporation board of trustees meeting, May 15, 1947, box 38, series I.A.3, CCNY.

28. On the Carnegie Corporation, Harvard's Russian Research Center, the FBI and the intelligence establishment, see Diamond, *Compromised Campus,* chs. 3–4.

29. Carnegie Corporation executive committee meeting, September 25, 1947, and Carnegie Corporation board of trustees meeting, March 18, 1948, box 38, series I.A.3, CCNY.

30. John Gardner and Donald Young, Record of Interview, February 13, 1947, folder 14, box 327, series III.A.8, CCNY.

31. P&P minutes, February 15, 1947, folder 1788, box 316, series 2, RG 1, SSRC.

32. CWAR minutes, March 2, 1947, in folder 12, box 328, series III.A.8, CCNY; John Gardner to Robert Hall, May 14, 1947, folder 2, box 329, series III.A.8, CCNY; "A Tentative Fellowship Program to be sponsored by the Committee on World Area Research of the Social Science Research Council," draft, October 9, 1947, in folder 5, box 328, series III.A.8, CCNY; executive committee minutes, March 17, folder 1847, box 326, series 3, SSRC; P&P minutes, November 1, 1947, folder 1788, box 316, series 2, RG 1, SSRC; Council minutes, September 8–11, 1947, folder 2099, box 357, series 9, RG 1, SSRC.

33. Young to Gardner, November 14, 1947, and Gardner to Young, November 28, 1947, folder 5, box 328, series III.A.8, CCNY.

34. Charles Wagley, *Area Research and Training: A Conference Report on the Study of World Areas,* Social Science Research Council Pamphlet 6 (New York: Social Science Research Council, June 1948), iii.

35. E. A. Speiser, *The United States and the Near East* (Cambridge: Harvard University Press, 1947). Speiser's book was published as part of the "American Foreign Policy Library," a series edited by former Under Secretary of State Sumner Welles (1892–1961).

36. On Talcott Parsons, Harvard's Department of Social Relations (generously funded by Carnegie) and the vision of a unified social science they promoted, see Gilman, *Mandarins of the Future,* ch. 3; Lagemann, *Politics of Knowledge,* 166–171; Cohen-Cole, *Open Mind,* ch. 3; and Joel Isaac, *Working Knowledge: Making the Human Sciences from Parsons to Kuhn* (Cambridge: Harvard University Press, 2012), ch. 5. As David C. Engerman notes, many at Harvard's Russian Research center also embraced the vision of behavioralism as a path toward a unified social science; see *Know Your Enemy,* ch. 2.

37. As I discuss later, this joint committee had actually been disbanded in 1947 and replaced by a short-lived advisory body; see Delpar, *Looking South*, 148. In this light Kenton Worcester's mention of a Committee on Latin American Studies organized by the SSRC in 1947–1948 in his history of the SSRC may be misleading: this committee was a pale substitute for the disbanded joint committee and was soon dissolved, with no immediate successor. See Worcester, *Social Science Research Council*, 44.

38. Council minutes, September 11–14, 1950, folder 2101, box 358, series 9, RG 1, SSRC.

39. On the contexts within which this "search for a method" took shape see Solovey, *Shaky Foundations*, and Mark Solovey and Hamilton Cravens, eds., *Cold War Social Science: Knowledge Production, Liberal Democracy, and Human Nature* (New York: Palgrave Macmillan, 2012).

40. Solovey, *Shaky Foundations*, 111–112.

41. P&P minutes, April 2, 1948, folder 1789, box 316, series 2, RG 1, SSRC.

42. On Steward's life and work see Virginia Kerns, *Scenes from the High Desert* (Urbana: University of Illinois Press, 2003), and Richard O. Clemmer, L. Daniel Myers and Mary Elizabeth Rudden, eds., *Julian Steward and the Great Basin: The Making of an Anthropologist* (Salt Lake City: University of Utah Press, 1999).

43. Guide to the Records of the Puerto Rico Project 1943–1951, New York University, accessed June 20, 2013, http://dlib.nyu.edu/findingaids/html/rism/puertorico/bioghist.html. The project's findings would be published in 1956 as Julian H. Steward et al., *The People of Puerto Rico: A Study in Social Anthropology* (Urbana: University of Illinois Press, 1956). See Eric Wolf's thoughtful appraisal, "Remarks on The People of Puerto Rico," in *Pathways of Power: Building an Anthropology of the Modern World* (Berkeley: University of California Press, 2001), as well as Antonio Lauria-Perricelli, "Materialist Scholarship and The People of Puerto Rico," *Identities: Global Studies in Culture and Power* 18 no. 3 (published online January 3, 2012): 194–202, accessed July 16, 2013, doi: http://dx.doi.org/10.1080/1070289X.2011.635281, and Howard Brick, "Neo-Evolutionist Anthropology, the Cold War, and the Beginnings of the World Turn in U.S. Scholarship," in Solovey and Cravens, *Cold War Social Science*, 161ff. On Operation Bootstrap see Richard Weisskoff, *Factories and Food Stamps: The Puerto Rico Model of Development* (Baltimore: Johns Hopkins University Press, 1985).

44. Kerns, *Scenes*, 251.

45. Ibid.; see too Lauria-Perricelli, "Materialist Scholarship."

46. John Gardner and Pendleton Herring, Record of Interview, July 12, 1948, folder 12, box 328, series III.A.8, CCNY; P&P minutes, April 2, 1948, folder 1789, box 316, series 2, RG 1, SSRC.

47. See Wagley, *Area Research and Training*, 10.

48. Isaac, *Working Knowledge*, 171–172.

49. Harvard historian William Langer, wartime head of the OSS Research and Analysis branch, asserted that it had broken "'the artificial barriers separating one approach from another' to produce a strategic intelligence research method. This accomplishment not only made R. and A. more influential but helped pave the way for the area studies and interdisciplinary projects so popular at American universities in the postwar era." Smith, *Shadow Warriors*, 363.

50. See Cohen-Cole, *Open Mind*, passim.

51. Steward would in fact explicitly criticize the Tarascan project for involving only anthropologists and (to a lesser extent) geographers, and also for failing to explore how the communities it studied were part of larger units. See Julian Steward, *Area Research: Theory and Practice* (New York: Social Science Research Council, 1950), published as SSRC Council Bulletin 63.

52. See Wolf, "Remarks," for a discussion of Steward's theoretical insights and limitations as manifested by the Puerto Rico Project.

53. Steward received $4000 from the Rockefeller Foundation for producing this essay; see Grant-in-Aid, June 24, 1948, and Albert C. Jacobs to Joseph H. Willits, July 6, 1948, folder 4169, box 487, series 200, RG 1.2, RF.

54. Gardner and Herring, Record of Interview, July 12, 1948, folder 12, box 328, series III.A.8, CCNY.

55. Circular from Elbridge Sibley, March 1, 1949, folder 12, box 328, series III.A.8, CCNY.

56. Council minutes, September 11–14, 1950, folder 2101, box 358, series 9, RG 1, SSRC.

57. See Center for Japanese Studies, University of Michigan, "Okayama Field Station," accessed July 16, 2013, http://www.ii.umich.edu/cjs/aboutus/historyofcjs, and Richard H. Heindel, *The Present Position of Foreign Area Studies in the United States: A Post-Conference Report* (New York: Social Science Research Council, 1950), 45–46.

Chapter 4

1. Charles B. Fahs, "Brief on Language and Area Studies in the U.S.," December 3, 1946, folder 165, box 31, series 900, RG 3.2, RF.

2. Rockefeller Foundation, *Annual Report 1946* (New York: Rockefeller Foundation, 1947), 228–229.

3. See Farhat Ziadeh, "Winds Blow Where Ships Do Not Wish To Go," in *Paths to the Middle East: Ten Scholars Look Back*, ed. Thomas Naff (Albany: State University of New York Press, 1993), 312.

4. On the Dodges and AUB, see Robert Kaplan, *The Arabists: The Romance of an American Elite* (New York: The Free Press, 1993), passim; Jacobs, *Imagining*, 19–20; Brian VanDeMark, *American Sheikhs: Two Families, Four Generations, and the Story of America's Influence in the Middle East* (Amherst NY: Prometheus Books, 2012); and Robert Vitalis, *America's Kingdom: Mythmaking on the Saudi Oil Frontier* (Stanford: Stanford University Press, 2007), passim.

5. Rockefeller Foundation, *Annual Report 1946*, 229–230.

6. Winder, "Four Decades," 53–54.

7. Dodds to Josephs, May 22, 1947, folder 15, box 299, series III.A.7, CCNY.

8. Ibid.

9. Josephs to Dodds, May 26, 1947, folder 15, box 299, series III.A.7, CCNY.

10. Dodds to Josephs, May 29, 1947, folder 15, box 299, series III.A.7, CCNY.

11. See "Present Status and Future Needs—Program in Near Eastern Studies, Princeton University," c. 1951, folder 15, box 299, series III.A.7, CCNY. As Osamah Khalil notes, State Department officials, particularly at the department's Foreign Service Institute which trained many of its personnel, welcomed the establishment of Princeton's new program because they expected it to produce a substantial number of well-trained graduates who would join the Foreign Service. "America's Dream Palace," ch. 3, 118ff.

12. *The Daily Princetonian*, November 8, 1943, January 17, 1947, November 23, 1949.

13. See "Meeting to Treat Near East Culture," *The Daily Princetonian*, March 24, 1947, and "Scholars Divided on Future of East," *The New York Times*, March 28, 1947. The twelve-day "Colloquium on Islamic Culture in its Relation to the Contemporary World" in September 1953, which brought together some seventy delegates, half of them from Muslim communities and countries and the other half American scholars, foundation officials and others, was probably the largest such event; see *The Daily Princetonian*, September 16, 1953. Not all Princeton events made the same kind of splash: a Carnegie Corporation staffer who observed the sixth annual Near East conference at Princeton in 1954 declared that the "organization and actual conduct of the discussions corresponded to the type of program one would expect to find sponsored by a world affairs council" and added that the identity and tone of some of the speakers "conformed to the pro-Arab (and anti-Israeli) orientation of most of Near Eastern people [sic] at Princeton." William Marvel, May 21, 1954, folder 15, box 299, series III.A.7, CCNY.

14. William Marvel, "Princeton University—Program in Near Eastern Studies," January 20, 1953, folder 15, box 299, series III.A.7, CCNY.

15. See Berger's Princeton University personnel record, Faculty 1951–1965, Department of Near Eastern Studies Records, Princeton University Archives,

Department of Rare Books and Special Collections, Princeton University Library (hereafter cited as PU).

16. Rockefeller Foundation, *Annual Report 1952* (New York: Rockefeller Foundation, 1953), 275, and Department of Oriental Languages and Literatures, "Report to the President for the Academic Year July 1, 1951 to June 30, 1952," folder 15, box 299, series III.A.7, CCNY.

17. "CPH's Visit to Program in Near Eastern Studies (Princeton)," November 16, 1951, folder 15, box 299, series III.A.7, CCNY.

18. Rockefeller Foundation, *Annual Report 1954* (New York: Rockefeller Foundation, 1955), 238–239. Rockefeller would make grants of the same size to Cornell for Southeast Asian studies that same year and the following year to McGill University's Institute of Islamic Studies, founded in 1951 thanks to an earlier grant from the Rockefeller Foundation. I discuss these grants more fully in Chapter 6.

19. Ford Foundation Information Bulletin no. 53, April 18, 1956, Grants PA 56–136 (microfilm reel 295), Ford Foundation Archives, Rockefeller Archive Center (hereafter cited as FF); "Ford Foundation Grants for Research Projects in Near Eastern Studies," October 15, 1959, RG FA 610 (Cleon Swayzee office files), FF.

20. "Near Eastern Studies and the ACLS," June 4, 1947, box E21, ACLS. It is worth noting that this was a moment of turmoil for the ACLS. As Alfred De discusses, the organization's veteran leaders (especially Waldo Leland and Mortimer Graves) faced growing criticism for their allegedly antiquated notion of the humanities, their personal domination of the organization and its failure to assure representation of scholars and others not drawn from a small number of elite universities in the Northeastern United States. Pressure for reform from the Rockefeller Foundation forced Waldo Leland to retire in 1946 and the ACLS was restructured the following year. Graves remained in place, but in the years that followed the ACLS was hampered by limited resources. See De, "International Studies," 181ff.

21. Gibb had apparently last visited the United States in June 1942 in order to deliver two lectures, on "Social Change in the Near East" and "The Future for Arab Unity," at the University of Chicago, as part of a conference on "The Near East: Problems and Prospects" funded by the Harris Foundation. See Philip W. Ireland, ed., *The Near East: Problems and Prospects* (Chicago: University of Chicago Press, 1942).

22. The relevant correspondence, and a transcript of the conference, can be found in folders 3090–3091, box 259, series 200R, RG 1.1, RF. On Coon and the CIA see Price, *Anthropological Intelligence,* 254–255.

23. Hall, *Area Studies,* 50.

24. Gardner, "Are We Doing Our Homework?," 407.

25. Rockefeller Foundation staff produced a summary of the Scarbrough report after its release for internal consumption: see Inter-Office Correspondence, December 11, 1947, folder 165, box 31, series 900, RG 3.2, RF. In the wake of his visit to the United States Gibb proposed to his American interlocutors possible avenues of cooperation, including joint translation projects and eventually a conference that would bring together British and American Orientalists; but in the end nothing came of these ideas, owing mainly to lack of funds. See for example Gibb to Calverley, August 23, 1947, Calverley to ACLS executive director Cornelius Krusé, July 14, 1948, and Fahs to Stafford, December 16, 1948, box E21, ACLS.

26. Rockefeller Foundation, *Annual Report 1947* (New York: Rockefeller Foundation, 1948), 226–227.

27. Winder, "Four Decades," 45.

28. Hoskins' "defection" from the Fletcher School to SAIS, and the fact that he took hundreds of books from Fletcher's collection along with him, made for some years of bad blood between the two institutions; see Gutner, *SAIS*, 9–10. On Hoskins see too Jacobs, *Imagining*, 38–39.

29. Minutes of the first meeting of CNES, October 10–11, 1947, box E21, ACLS; *The Daily Princetonian*, May 17, 1949. Like many of his State Department colleagues Wright was highly critical of President Truman's decision to support the establishment of Israel and of what he regarded as undue Zionist influence on American policy, and he would be denounced by Zionists as an enemy of Israel or even an antisemite.

30. Rockefeller Foundation, *Annual Report 1947*, 227.

31. Rockefeller Foundation, *Annual Report 1948* (New York: Rockefeller Foundation, 1949), 279–280.

32. Gardner to Hall, May 14, 1947, in CCNY, folder 2, box 329, series III.A.8, CCNY. Gardner added that "Louis Prechtling [he meant Frechtling] and William Eddy from the State Department might be useful additions to the group." William Eddy (1896–1962), born in Lebanon to missionary parents, served in the OSS during the war and was then appointed U.S. Minister to Saudi Arabia; he translated at the historic shipboard meeting on the Suez Canal between President Roosevelt and King Abd al-Aziz ibn Sa'ud in February 1945. In 1946 Eddy was appointed Special Assistant to the Secretary of State for Research and Intelligence; a key figure in U.S. intelligence circles, he helped establish the CIA and later worked as a consultant to Aramco while continuing to assist the CIA. On Eddy, Aramco and Saudi Arabia, see Vitalis, *America's Kingdom*, passim. Louis E. Frechtling was associated with the Foreign Policy Association before the war and in 1947 was apparently employed at the Department of State's Office of Intelligence Research, successor to the OSS R&A branch; he went

on to a long career in the State Department. Eddy would have no role in postwar U.S. Middle East studies, but Frechtling participated in the January 1951 meeting that prepared the way for the launching of the SSRC's committee for the region.

33. Wagley, *Area Research and Training*, 29–32.

34. See the minutes of the second, third and fourth meetings of CNES, January 23–24, April 1 and June 26, 1948, box E21, ACLS.

35. Frye, *Greater Iran*, 98–99.

36. Graves to Odegaard (excerpt), January 3, 1949, box E22, ACLS; see too annex no. 15 to the agenda of the ACLS board of directors meeting, January 26–27, 1949, box E22, ACLS.

37. Speiser to Odegaard, February 22, 1949, box E22, ACLS.

38. CWAR minutes, November 13, 1948, folder 1386, box 229 1, subseries 19, series 1, RG 1, SSRC.

39. Wright to Calverley, July 15, 1948, box E21, ACLS. For examples of the resentment felt by "ancientists" about the perceived domination of the "modernists," see Speiser to Calverley, September 5, 1947, box E21, ACLS, as well as Speiser's complaints at the committee's third meeting about how new members were chosen.

40. Krusé to Wright, July 31, 1948, box E21, ACLS.

41. Report, April 20, 1949, and minutes of the sixth meeting of the CNES, June 25–26, 1949, box E22, ACLS.

42. American Council of Learned Societies, *A Program for Near Eastern Studies in the United States* (Washington DC: American Council of Learned Societies, 1949).

43. See too Heindel, *The Present Position*, 7–9, and Winder, "Four Decades," 45–46.

44. *ACLS Bulletin* 44 (September 1951): 37–38.

45. Smith to Odegaard, July 16, 1949, box E22. ACLS.

46. Annex 6-I to the agenda of the ACLS Board of Directors meeting, July 10–11, 1950, box E22, ACLS.

47. For a biographical sketch see K. Allin Luther, "In Memoriam: T. Cuyler Young, 16 August 1900–31 August 1976," *International Journal of Middle East Studies* 8 no. 2 (April 1977): 267–269.

48. Rockefeller Foundation, *Annual Report 1951* (New York: Rockefeller Foundation, 1952), 394ff. The other committee members were the Biblical scholar Carl Kraeling (1897–1966), then at the University of Chicago; Harold W. Glidden, who had received his doctorate from Princeton, worked in the Near East section of R&A and was now at the State Department; and John Kingsley Birge (1888–1952) of Hartford Seminary. Birge had spent thirty years in Turkey working for the American Board of Commissioners for Foreign Missions, which since 1810 had overseen American Prot-

estant missionary work in many parts of the world, ran its Redhouse Press, and had published on the Bektashi order as well as *A Guide to Turkish Area Study*.

49.   Other Arabic titles selected for translation early on included Mirit Butrus Ghali's *Siyasat al-Ghad*, Ahmad Amin's *Hayati*, Taha Husayn's *Mustaqbal al-Thaqafa fi Misr* and Fakhr al-Din al-Zawahiri's *al-Siyasa w'al-Azhar*. See "Near Eastern Translation Program," 1952, box E21, ACLS, and *ACLS Bulletin* 46 (May 1953): 35–37.

50.   "T. Cuyler Young Will Visit Iran to Aid Embassy," *The Daily Princetonian* (February 12, 1951).

51.   ACLS board of directors minutes, May 16–17, 1952, and "A Proposed Summer Session on Near Eastern language and civilization, 1952," box E21, ACLS; *ACLS Bulletin* 47 (May 1954): 2–3, 36–37.

52.   On this chapter in the history of the ACLS see De, "International Relations," 202ff.

Chapter 5

1.   Charles Fahs, "Area Studies: A Reexamination," September 22, 1948, and "Area Studies," June 10, 1949, folder 165, box 31, series 900, RG 3.2, RF.

2.   Travel grants were awarded to Carleton Coon, to visit the Near East "for the purpose of appraising the facilities available to American research workers," and to Richard N. Frye (at the time a Junior Fellow at Harvard's Society of Fellows) for travel to Iran. Two Princeton men received research grants: C. Ernest Dawn for doctoral dissertation research on "Greater Syria and its Implication for Arab Unity," and Willard E. Beling, a postdoctoral fellow, "for study of the development, growth, and present trend of the social, political, and economic life of the Arabic Near East"—arguably the most vaguely defined project on the list that year. SSRC Committee on Area Research Fellowships, folder 5, box 328, series III.A.8, CCNY; Council minutes, April 3–4, 1948, folder 2100, box 358, series 9, RG 1, SSRC. Beling (1919–2009) would soon go to work for Aramco, though in 1958 he returned to academia and spent most of the remainder of his career teaching international relations at the University of Southern California. In 1976 the Saudi government provided funding for a new King Faisal Chair of Islamic and Arab Studies at USC and designated Beling as its first incumbent, generating considerable controversy. See http://www.legacy.com/obituaries/latimes/obituary.aspx?n=willard-a-bill-beling&pid=129309240 and http://www.danielpipes.org/161/the-politics-of-muslim-anti-semitism. On Beling's career at Aramco see Robert Vitalis, "Aramco World: Business and Culture on the Arabian Oil Frontier," in *Counter-Narratives: History, Contemporary Society, and Politics in Saudi*

Arabia and Yemen, eds. Madawi Al-Rasheed and Robert Vitalis (New York: Palgrave MacMillan, 2004), 163.

3. Carnegie Corporation board of trustees meeting, October 21, 1948, folder 5, box 328, series III.A.8, CCNY.

4. "Summary of Actions Taken by the Meeting of University Representatives Called by the Carnegie Foundation for the Advancement of Teaching," March 25, 1949, folder 3, box 328, series III.A.8, CCNY; John Gardner and Paul Webbink, Record of Interview, October 10, 1949, folder 4, box 329, series III.A.8, CCNY; CWAR, annual report for 1948–49, folder 1386, box 229, subseries 19, series 1, RG 1, SSRC.

5. On the latter see Joint Committee on Southern Asia, *Southern Asia Studies in the United States: A Survey and Plan* (Philadelphia: Joint Committee on Southern Asia, 1951). A new Joint Committee on South Asia would be established in 1976.

6. See Wendell Bennett, *Area Studies in American Universities* (New York: Social Science Research Council, 1951), passim.

7. Delpar, *Looking South*, 147–149.

8. Paul Webbinck to Robert M. Lester, August 3, 1950, folder 4, box 329, series III.A.8, CCNY.

9. Richard H. Heindel, *The Present Position of Foreign Area Studies in the United States: A Post-Conference Report* (New York: Social Science Research Council, 1950), 1.

10. David Engerman notes that, with the decline of group research projects even in Russian/Soviet studies, "area studies centers, even those established to promote interdisciplinary research, had become . . . 'places where research was done' rather than 'places that did research.'" "Pedagogical Purposes," 87.

11. J. C. Hurewitz, "The Education of J. C. Hurewitz," in Naff, *Paths to the Middle East*, 102.

12. Conference on Study of World Areas at Columbia University, Record of Interview, May 5–6, 1950, and Gardner and Taylor, Record of Interview, May 8, 1950, folder 4, box 329, series III.A.8, CCNY; John W. Gardner and Pendleton Herring, Record of Interview, November 2, 1950, folder 16, box 327, series III.A.8, CCNY. Taylor, who during the war had served in the Office of War Information, would (along with Wittfogel and others) testify before the Senate Internal Security Subcommittee (the infamous "McCarran Committee") that China scholar Owen Lattimore had failed to recognize the danger of Soviet expansionism and had thereby abetted communism; he later became a strong supporter of U.S. military intervention in Vietnam.

13. Council minutes, September 11–14, 1950, folder 2101, box 358, series 9, RG 1, SSRC.

14. Conference on Study of World Areas at Columbia University, Record of Interview, May 5–6, 1950, folder 4, box 329, series III.A.8, CCNY.

15. Richard Heindel to CWAR, September 25, 1950, "Some Suggestions from the 2nd National Conference," folder 1386, box 229, subseries 19, series 1, RG 1, SSRC.

16. "For the Information of the Trustees," box 39, series I.A.3, 6, CCNY.

17. Jacobs, *Imagining*, 42–43; Khalil, "America's Dream Palace," ch. 3, 137f.

18. P&P minutes, February 10, 1951, folder 1792, box 317, series 2, RG 1, SSRC; CWAR annual report for 1950–51, folder 1386, box 229, subseries 19, series 1, RG 1, SSRC.

19. Council minutes, September 11–14, 1950, folder 2101, box 358, series 9, RG 1, SSRC.

20. Charles Dollard and Pendleton Herring, Record of Interview, April 15, 1951, folder 15, box 327, series III.A.8, CCNY.

21. JP (?) and Pendleton Herring, Record of Interview, April 16, 1951, folder 15, box 327, series III.A.8, CCNY. See too Khalil, "America's Dream Palace," ch. 3, 138ff.

22. Ibid., ch. 3, 144ff. Khalil also notes that the published version of Bennett's survey did not include all the data he had collected. For an example of press coverage see "Colleges Found Lacking in Courses to Teach Understanding of the World's Major Areas," *The New York Times*, August 19, 1951, which drew heavily on Bennett's survey.

23. In this period there were a few others, like Charles Fahs of Rockefeller, who sporadically argued that "studies of regions both in the United States and in foreign countries can be considered 'area studies.'" See Charles Fahs, "Area Studies," June 10, 1949, folder 165, box 31, series 900, RG 3.2, RF. As late as 1959 Cleon Swayzee of the Ford Foundation would claim, much like Hall in 1947, that prewar "classical programs in Greek and Latin were area studies programs; they were even multidisciplinary with course offerings in history, geography, politics, fine arts, literature and, of course, language," though he added that "For the most part, however, language competence became the principal goal of classical learning." "Proposal for Long-Term Support for Foreign Area Study Centers," 1959, folder titled "Long-Term Support: Background material, working papers," box 1, FA610, FF. Such alternative framings of area studies eventually faded away.

24. Richard Ettinghausen, ed., *A Selected and Annotated Bibliography of Books and Periodicals in Western Languages Dealing with the Near and Middle East With Special Emphasis on Medieval and Modern Times* (Washington DC: Middle East Institute, 1952). A supplement appeared in 1954.

25. Dankwart A. Rustow, "The Middle East," in *Political Science and Area Studies: Rivals or Partners?*, ed. Lucien W. Pye (Bloomington: Indiana University Press, 1975), 172. In 1956–1958 the Middle East Institute published at least three annual surveys, titled *Current Research on the Middle East*, to enable scholars to find out who was currently working on what but also to help overcome what the editors described

as the "cleavage" between Orientalists and social scientists by listing their ongoing research projects in a single volume. See Harvey Hall and Ann W. Noyes, eds., *Current Research on the Middle East 1955* (Washington DC: Middle East Institute, 1956), preface. These surveys list a great many research projects on the ancient, Islamic or modern Middle East under way; but of course many of these were long-term and would not be published until years later. In the interim, indeed until the late 1950s or early 1960s, the scholarly literature on the modern and contemporary Middle East remained sparse.

26. CWAR meeting, October 6–7, 1950, folder 1386, box 229, subseries 19, series 1, RG 1, SSRC.

27. Cleland had been caught outside Egypt when the Second World War began and spent several years in Washington DC working for the Office of War Information. He returned to AUC later in the war but resigned in 1947 after he was passed over for the post of president of the university; he then accepted a position in Washington as head of Middle East research at the Department of State's Office of Intelligence Research, which had inherited much of the personnel of the OSS Research and Analysis branch, and later taught at American University in Washington DC. On Cleland's work on Egypt's population see Omnia El Shakry, *The Great Social Laboratory: Subjects of Knowledge in Colonial and Postcolonial Egypt* (Stanford: Stanford University Press, 2007), 153–164; on his career at AUC see Lawrence R. Murphy, *The American University in Cairo: 1919–1987* (Cairo: American University in Cairo Press, 1987), passim.

Peter G. Franck (1913–1989), listed as the working committee's secretary, was born in Berlin and came to the United States in the late 1930s. In the early 1950s he was apparently teaching as an adjunct professor at American University while pursuing a doctorate in economics at the University of California, Berkeley. After working as a consultant in Egypt, Iran, Pakistan and Afghanistan, Franck took up a teaching position at Syracuse University. For a short biography of Franck see http://archives.syr.edu/collections/faculty/sua_franck_pg.htm. Franck was a friend of the noted economist Albert O. Hirschman in Berlin before the Nazi rise to power; on their relationship then and after, see Jeremy Adelman, *Worldly Philosopher: The Odyssey of Albert O. Hirschman* (Princeton: Princeton University Press, 2013), passim.

28. CWAR meeting, October 6–7, 1950, folder 1386, box 229, subseries 19, series 1, RG 1, SSRC.

29. Philip Baram, *The Department of State in the Middle East, 1919–1945* (Philadelphia: University of Pennsylvania Press, 1978), 67.

30. Gardner and Herring, Record of Interview, November 2, 1950, folder 16, box 327, series III.A.8, CCNY; Richard Heindel to Pendleton Herring and Paul Webbinck, November 8, 1950, and Herring to Fred Eggan, November 14, 1950, folder 5311, box 443, subseries 75, series 1, RG 2, SSRC.

31.   Herring to Wood, November 29, 1950, folder 5311, box 443, subseries 75, series 1, RG 2, SSRC. Bryce Wood received his doctorate in political science from Columbia in 1940 and then worked at the State Department during the war before joining the SSRC staff.

32.   "Suggestions for Members of Proposed Near East Committee of SSRC," December 6, 1950, folder 5311, box 443, subseries 75, series 1, RG 2, SSRC.

33.   For Hurewitz's account of his career see Naff, *Paths*, ch. 3. On Tannous see Afif I. Tannous, *Village Roots and Beyond: Memoirs of Afif I. Tannous* (Beirut: Dar Nelson, 2004), and Nathan J. Citino, "The Ottoman Legacy in Cold War Modernization," *International Journal of Middle East Studies* 40 no. 4 (November 2008): 582–585.

34.   Gardner to Dollard, January 3, 1951, folder 9, box 328, series III.A.8, CCNY; emphasis in the original. See too John Gardner and Pendleton Herring, Record of Interview—Luncheon, January 3, 1951, folder 17, box 327, series III.A.8, CCNY.

35.   "Summary Minutes of Conference on Near Eastern Studies," January 11, 1951, folder 1449, box 241, series 20, RG 1, SSRC.

36.   Louis L. Orlin, ed., *Michigan Oriental Studies in Honor of George C. Cameron* (Ann Arbor: Department of Near Eastern Studies, University of Michigan, 1967). See too "Cameron, George Glenn," *Encyclopedia Iranica*, accessed August 5, 2013, http://www.iranicaonline.org/articles/cameron-george-glenn-philologist-and-historian-b, and Matthew W. Stolper, "George G. Cameron, 1905–1979," *The Biblical Archaeologist* 43 no. 3 (Summer 1980): 183–189.

37.   Though appointed in 1948, Cameron did not actually take up his new position at Michigan until 1949 because he spent the 1948–1949 academic year as Annual Professor of the Baghdad School of the American Schools of Oriental Research. For Cameron's own vision of his program as of 1950 see Cameron to John Gardner, October 16, 1950, folder 7, box 227, series III.A.5, CCNY. See too see Ernest McCarus, "A Lust for Language," in Naff, *Paths*, ch. 6.

38.   Frye, *Greater Iran*, 99.

39.   See University of Michigan President Harlan Hatcher to John W. Gardner, February 21, 1952, "FA" of Carnegie to Hatcher, February 26, 1952, and George Cameron, "1952 Summer Session" (report on grant), December 12, 1952, in folder 7, box 221, series III.A.5, CCNY. Carnegie would later push Cameron to find ways to make his summer program attractive to people from government, business and the armed forces, rather than mainly to graduate students already studying the region; see William Marvel and George Cameron, Record of Interview, December 28, 1954 and February 18, 1955, folder 7, box 221, series III.A.5, CCNY. For a Carnegie staffer's very positive assessment of Near Eastern studies at Michigan as of August 1952, see "WM's Visit to the Program in Near Eastern Studies," August 4–5, 1952, folder 7, box 221, series III.A.5, CCNY.

40. Orlin, *Michigan Oriental Studies*, xvi.

41. George G. Cameron, "The University of Michigan Field Project in the Near East, 1951," draft submitted September 1950, and Gardner to Cameron, November 16, 1950, folder 7, box 221, series III.A.5, CCNY.

42. In Naff, *Paths*, 185, where McCarus offers a brief account of the "expedition."

43. "CPH's Visit to the Department of Near Eastern Studies (University of Michigan)," November 15, 1951, folder 7, box 221, series III.A.5, CCNY. In 1953 Michigan would request an additional grant of $35,000 from Ford "for a project under which graduate students were taken to the Near and Middle East for field training under faculty supervision." Ford Foundation, *Annual Report for 1953* (New York: Ford Foundation, 1954), 32.

44. Coon's intellectual formation had taken place in the 1920s, and much of his scholarly work as a physical anthropologist focused on the origins and classification of human racial groups. As his son Carleton S. Coon Jr., would later put it, "My father got into racial theory at a time when race theory was respectable. Those were the days when anthropologists ran off to Africa and the Middle East armed with skin color charts and calipers for taking skull measurements." Quoted in Kaplan, *The Arabists*, 104. In fact, Coon Sr. never stopped believing in race theory: his 1962 book *The Origin of Races* would evoke a firestorm of criticism from cultural anthropologists, and the extent of Coon's own racism (including his secret collaboration with vociferous opponents of desegregation and the civil rights movement in the United States in the early 1960s) has since become public knowledge. See John P. Jackson Jr., "'In Ways Unacademical': The Reception of Carleton S. Coon's *The Origin of Races*," *Journal of the History of Biology* 34 no. 2 (Summer 2001): 247–285, and *Science for Segregation: Race, Law, and the Case against Brown v. Board of Education* (New York: New York University Press, 2005); Susan Slyomovics, "State of the State of the Art Studies: An Introduction to the Anthropology of the Middle East and North Africa," in *Anthropology of the Middle East and North Africa: Into the New Millenium*, eds. Sherine Hafez and Susan Slyomovics (Bloomington: Indiana University Press, 2013), 6–8; and Jonathan Marks, "Race Across the Physical-Cultural Divide in American Anthropology," in *A New History of Anthropology*, ed. Henrika Kuklick (Malden MA: Blackwell Publishing, 2008).

45. Nicholas B. Dirks, "South Asian Studies: Futures Past," in Szanton, *The Politics of Knowledge*, 351.

46. John W. Gardner and Philip K. Hitti, Record of Interview, April 6, 1948, folder 15, box 299, series III.A.7, and Gardner to Dollard, January 3, 1951, folder 9, box 328, series III.A.8, CCNY.

47. Pendleton Herring to John W. Gardner, January 22, 1951, and Gardner to Herring, January 29, 1951, folder 5311, box 443, subseries 75, series 1, RG 2, SSRC.

48. See "Over-all support for area studies," January 1955, *100 Years: The Rock-efeller Foundation*, accessed May 22, 2013, http://rockefeller100.org/items/show/1803.

49. "For the Information of Trustees," Carnegie board of trustees meeting, March 15, 1951, 3–4, and agenda, 21–22, box 39, series I.A.3, CCNY. In January 1951, citing the distinguished reputation established by Harvard's Russian Research Center in its three years of existence, Carnegie gave it a grant of $750,000 (equivalent to almost $6.9 million in 2015), to be disbursed over five years. Among other things Carnegie officers noted that the RRC was "currently engaged in an important classified research project under Air Force sponsorship." See agenda, Carnegie board of trustees meeting of January 18, 1951, Ibid. See also Russian Research Center, *Ten-Year Report and Current Projects, 1948–1958* (Cambridge: Russian Research Center, Harvard University, 1958).

50. See the "Gaither Report," whose recommendations were endorsed by the foundation's board in 1949; it can be found at http://www.fordfoundation.org/pdfs/about/Gaither-Report.pdf. On the guidance which Carnegie Corporation leaders, including John Gardner, provided to Ford early on, see Lagemann, *Politics of Knowledge*, 178–179. As Stanley Diamond points out, however, in her work on Carnegie Lagemann has nothing to say about the foundation's extensive links with the intelligence community or about the fact that its funding of area studies in the mid- and late 1940s was at least in part motivated by its desire to address that community's needs. Diamond, *Compromised Campus*, 302 n.13.

51. McCaughey, *International Studies*, 147.

52. On the CIA-Ford Foundation relationship see *inter alia* Jason Epstein, "The CIA and the Intellectuals," *The New York Review of Books,* April 20, 1967; Frances Stonor Saunders, *The Cultural Cold War: The CIA and the World of Arts and Letters* (New York: New Press, 1999); Cumings, "Boundary Displacement: Area Studies," 272–275; and Oliver Zunz, *Philanthropy in America: A History* (Princeton: Princeton University Press, 2012), ch. 5. Despite their links with the national security state, and despite their complicity in purging colleges and universities of alleged communists and communist sympathizers, Ford and the other big foundations were themselves attacked by the right during the "Red Scare" ("McCarthy") period of the early 1950s. Yet as Zunz notes, "The communists were more accurate in their denunciation of liberal foundations for funding CIA spies . . . than the McCarthyites were in their claims that tax-exempt institutions harbored and funded communists." *Philanthropy*, 193.

53. Gardner and Herring, Record of Interview (telephone), March 1, 1951, and John W. Gardner and Stanley Gordon, Record of Interview (telephone), March 22, 1951, folder 15, box 327, series III.A.8, CCNY.

54. Joseph B. Casagrande and Elbridge Sibley, "Area Research Training Fellowships and Travel Grants for Area Research: An Epilogue," *Items* 7 no. 4 (December 1953).

55. See for example William W. Marvel and Morris Opler, Record of Interview, March 20, 1953, folder 4, box 328, series III.A.8, CCNY.

56. On Carnegie's withdrawal from funding area studies, see for example William W. Marvel to George G. Cameron, December 9, 1955 and November 12, 1958, folder 7, box 221, III.A.5, CCNY.

57. "The Ford Foundation Presents Middle East Fellowship Offers," *The Vassar Chronicle*, December 6, 1952, 5.

58. Ford Foundation, *Annual Report for 1952* (New York: Ford Foundation, 1953), 22.

59. Berman, *Influence*, 103; McCaughey, *International Studies*, 153–154.

60. McCaughey, *International Studies*, ch. 7. See too Berman, *Influence*, 102.

61. Schuyler C. Wallace to Cleon Swayzee, December 18, 1952, and the BOTR staff's early 1953 assessment of the field and of Columbia's proposal, in Grants, grant 53–64, microfilm reel 0405, FF. Ford staff noted that the "principal part of [Columbia's Near Eastern] program is currently financed by foreign governments [including Iran, Israel, Pakistan and Turkey] which wish to enlarge the number of American experts and raise the level of American public opinion on the Near and Middle East."

62. CNME minutes, February 7, 1951, folder 1449, box 241, series 20, RG 1, SSRC.

63. "A Social Science Research Program on the Near East," June 7, 1951, folder, 1449, box 241, series 20, RG 1, SSRC.

64. "Draft Outline of Research Program Based on Discussion at the Meeting of April 28, 1951 (1st Revision, May 16, 1951)," folder, 1449, box 241, series 20, RG 1, SSRC.

65. For different versions see CNME, "The Social Sciences and the Near East: Proposals for Research and Development," February 12, 1952, and "The Development of Near Eastern Studies in the United States," March 14, 1952, folder 1449, box 241, series 20, RG 1, SSRC.

66. Stanley T. Gordon to Carl Spaeth, January 29, 1952, General Correspondence 1952, microfilm reel C-1155, FF.

67. CNME annual report for 1951–52, folder 1446, box 244, series 20, RG 1, SSRC.

68. Bryce Wood to CNME, Memorandum, February 21, 1952, folder 1449, box 241, series 20, RG 1, SSRC; Gardner and Herring, Record of Interview (telephone), March 3, 1952, folder 17, box 327, series III.A.8, CCNY. See too the letter CNME sent to the authors of the conference papers, June 16, 1952, General Correspondence 1952, microfilm reel C-1155, FF.

69. See Summary Minutes, folder 1449, box 241, series 20, RG 1, SSRC; punctuation in the original.

70. Timothy Mitchell, who as I discuss sees the SSRC as having embraced H. A. R. Gibb's conceptual framework for Middle East studies, has commented that "the titles of the papers read like the table of contents of Gibb and Bowen's study" *Islamic*

Society and the West, the first segment of which had been published in 1950. I am not convinced that Gibb and Bowen's conception of social categories and relations in what they depicted as the premodern Ottoman-Islamic empire served as the model for those who commissioned or wrote these papers. Mitchell, "The Middle East," 80. See too Lockman, *Contending Visions*, 106–108, 150–151, 165–166.

71. In Naff, *Paths*, 99.

72. "Near Eastern Studies," 87.

73. Summary Minutes, folder 1449, box 241, series 20, RG 1, SSRC; emphasis in the original.

74. William Marvel, October 24–25, 1952, folder 9, box 328, series III.A.8, CCNY.

75. Cameron to CNME, September 25, 1953, folder 5314, box 443, subseries 75, series 1, RG 2, SSRC; see too folder 1450, box 241, series 20, RG 1, SSRC.

76. Unpublished Reports, March 1953, BOTR Activities Report (016857), FF.

77. Cleon Swayzee to John Gardner, February 5, 1953, folder 9, box 328, III.A.8, CCNY; External Research Staff and Psychological Intelligence and Research Staff, Department of State, Topic List no. 3, "Suggested Topics for Social Science Research on Near East," December 15, 1953, in folder 5314, box 443, subseries 75, series 1, RG 2, SSRC. On the CIA's relationship with the External Research Service see Khalil, "America's Dream Palace," ch. 3, 126ff, who also notes that FAFP fellows were often debriefed by CIA or State Department officers after their return (160).

78. Bryce Wood to Pendleton Herring, October 2, 1953, folder 5314, box 443, subseries 75, series 1, RG 2, SSRC, and Cumings, "Boundary Displacements," 272–273.

79. See box 18, FA 608 (John Howard office files), FF. On Ford in Iran see Victor V. Nemchenok, "'That so Fair a Thing Should Be so Frail': The Ford Foundation and the Failure of Rural Development in Iran, 1953–1964," *Middle East Journal* 63 no. 2 (Spring 2009): 261–284.

80. Jerome S. Rauch, "Area Institute Programs and African Studies," *Journal of Negro Education* 24 no. 4 (Autumn 1955): 423, 424–425.

81. David H. Price, *Threatening Anthropology: McCarthyism and the FBI's Surveillance of Activist Anthropologists* (Durham: Duke University Press, 2004), 346–347.

82. Cameron to CNME, September 25, 1953, folder 5314, box 443, subseries 75, series 1, RG 2, SSRC.

83. William Marvel, Pendleton Herring and Bryce Wood, Record of Interview, November 5, 1953, folder 17, box 327, series III.A.8, CCNY.

84. Cameron to Wood, October 28, 1954, folder 5314, box 443, subseries 75, series 1, RG 2, SSRC.

85. John Ervin, Jr., to Pendleton Herrington, October 15, 1954, with enclosed readers' reports, folder 5314, box 443, subseries 75, series 1, RG 2, SSRC.

86. Cameron to Herring, November 1, 1954, folder 5314, box 443, subseries 75, series 1, RG 2, SSRC; emphasis in the original.

87. CNME, "Final Report to the Carnegie Corporation of New York on the Work of the Committee, 1951–1955," August 16, 1955, folder 9, box 328, series III.A.8, and William Marvel and Pendleton Herring, Record of Interview, August 22, 1955, folder 17, box 327, series III.A.8, CCNY.

88. John B. Howard to Don K. Price, May 20, 1955, Grants, PA 56–136, microfilm reel 295, FF.

Chapter 6

1. Herring to Young, June 14, 1955, folder 5315, box 443, subseries 75, series 1, RG 2, SSRC.

2. For Young's take on Iran before the oil issue erupted, see his essay "The Race between Russia and Reform in Iran," *Foreign Affairs* 28 no. 2 (January 1950): 278–289.

3. Henry F. Grady, *The Memoirs of Ambassador Henry F. Grady from the Great War to the Cold War*, ed. John T. McNay (Columbia: University of Missouri Press, 2009); but see also Ervand Abrahamian, *The Coup: 1953, the CIA, and the Roots of Modern U.S.-Iranian Relations* (New York: The New Press, 2013), 95–97, 112.

4. T. Cuyler Young, "The Social Support of Current Iranian Policy," *Middle East Journal* 6 no. 2 (Spring 1952): 125–143.

5. Kermit Roosevelt, *Countercoup: The Struggle for the Control of Iran* (New York: McGraw-Hill, 1979), 79.

6. Ervand Abrahamian, email message to author, July 15, 2013. See too Richard W. Cottam's review of *Countercoup*, in which he states that Roger Black was "a pseudonym for an easily identified academic specialist on Iran." *Iranian Studies* 14 nos. 3/4 (Summer-Autumn 1981): 269–272.

7. T. Cuyler Young, "Iran in Continuing Crisis," *Foreign Affairs* 40 no. 2 (January 1962): 275–292.

8. See James Goode, "Reforming Iran during the Kennedy Years," *Diplomatic History* 15 no. 1 (January 1991): 21.

9. On the Princeton Consultants see John Cavanagh, "Dulles Papers Reveal CIA Consulting Network," *Forerunner*, April 29, 1980, accessed July 15, 2013, http://www.cia-on-campus.org/Princeton.edu/consult.html. As CIA director George Tenet (like Dulles a Princeton alumnus) put it in March 2001, in remarks at the opening of a Princeton conference on the CIA's analyses of the Soviet Union during the Cold War, "from the early 1950s to the early 1970s, CIA's Office of National Estimates benefited from the counsel of its 'Princeton consultants'—a group of schol-

ars who met at Princeton and exchanged ideas with CIA's top analysts." Accessed July 13, 2013, https://www.cia.gov/news-information/speeches-testimony/2001/dci_speech_03082001.html. Young's relationship with the CIA goes unmentioned in most accounts of his life; but, curiously, the *Daily Princetonian* article on Young's retirement (May 25, 1969) noted that Young "has continued to advise several government agencies, including the CIA and the National Board of Estimates, which prepares intelligence reports for the National Security Council, about two weeks each year." See too Khalil, "America's Dream Palace," ch. 5, 215ff.

10. For more information on Young's career see the press release issued by Princeton University on his retirement, May 10, 1969, Young, T. Cuyler, 1962–1970, Office of the President Records: Robert F. Goheen Subgroup, Box 350, Folder 17, PU.

11. T. Cuyler Young, CNME report to the SSRC Council, March 24–25, 1956, folder 1466, box 244, subseries 20, series 1, RG 1, SSRC.

12. On Gibb's life and thought see Albert Hourani, *Europe and the Middle East* (Berkeley: University of California Press, 1980), ch. 6.

13. See Khalil, "America's Dream Palace," ch. 5, 211.

14. Langer, *Ivory Tower*, 231–232.

15. From the original March 1953 proposal for a Middle Eastern studies program at Harvard, quoted in Don Babai, ed. *Reflections on the Past, Visions for the Future* (Cambridge: Center for Middle Eastern Studies, 2004), 3.

16. Rockefeller Foundation, *Annual Report 1956* (New York: Rockefeller Foundation, 1957), 220–221.

17. Hamilton A. R. Gibb, "Problems of Modern Middle Eastern History," in *Studies on the Civilization of Islam*, eds. Stanford J. Shaw and William R. Polk (Boston: Beacon Press, 1962), 336, 343. This essay was originally published in the spring 1956 issue of the Middle East Institute's *Report on Current Research*.

18. See Babai, *Reflections*, 8. ARAMCO also provided grants to Harvard's center (as well as others) for many years.

19. Gibb to Herring, October 13, 1955, folder 5315, box 443, subseries 75, series 1, RG 2, SSRC.

20. Gibb to Young, February 27, 1956, folder 5315, box 443, subseries 75, series 1, RG 2, SSRC. Lockard (died 1977) served in the OSS in Kenya and Beirut during the war and then joined the CIA; he returned to Harvard, where he had taught before the war, and later served as associate director of its Center for Middle Eastern Studies until he retired in 1973. See *Anthropology News* 18 issue 7 (September 1977): 3.

21. Smith to Herring, October 13, 1955, folder 5315, box 443, subseries 75, series 1, RG 2, SSRC.

22. His address was published as Wilfred Cantwell Smith, "The Place of Oriental Studies in a Western University," *Diogenes* 4 no. 16 (December 1956): 107, 108.

23. Smith to Herring, October 13, 1955, folder 5315, box 443, subseries 75, series 1, RG 2, SSRC.

24. Dankwart A. Rustow, "Connections," in Naff, *Paths*, 278. As Nathan Citino notes, in 1954–1955 Young and Hurewitz had been among the members of a Council on Foreign Relations group coordinated by Rustow to study the "Defense of the Middle East." "Ottoman Legacy," 587.

25. On Rustow's complex engagement with modernization theory see Begüm Adalet, "Mirrors of Modernization: The American Reflection in Turkey" (PhD diss., University of Pennsylvania, 2014), ch. 1.

26. In Naff, *Paths*, 99.

27. P&P minutes, January 9 and March 23, 1956, folder 1466, box 244, subseries 20, series 1, RG 1, SSRC.

28. Herring to Young, December 2, 1955, folder 5315, box 443, subseries 75, series 1, RG 2, SSRC.

29. Howard A. Reed, who had received his doctorate from Princeton in 1951 and in 1955–1957 served on the staff of Ford's office in Beirut, sent the foundation's New York office detailed comments on CNME's work, based on a close and critical reading of its minutes, but they do not seem to have elicited much interest on the New York end. See for example Howard A. Reed, "Comments on Minutes of SSRC-NE Committee's 4th Meetings, May 4, 1956," folder titled "Near East—General Information through 1960," box 2, FA 610, FF.

30. McCarus, "History," in Naff, *Paths*, 210–211; "Near Eastern Studies Summer Session 1960," folder 1452, box 241, subseries 20, series 1, RG 1, SSRC. U.S. government agencies would also establish their own language-training programs, for example the army program at Monterey, California, that was eventually known as the Defense Language Institute, as well as programs run by the CIA, the National Security Agency, the State Department (through the Foreign Service Institute) and the Peace Corps.

31. Naff, *Paths*, 278.

32. "Recommendations of the Subcommittee on Transliteration," September 20, 1957, folder 1452, box 241, subseries 20, series 1, RG 1, SSRC.

33. T. Cuyler Young, "The Social Science Research Council Committee on the Near and Middle East: A Progress Report to June 1, 1957," folder 1451, box 241, subseries 20, series 1, RG 1, SSRC.

34. Among the early recipients of these grants were Nikki R. Keddie (born 1930), then an instructor in history at Scripps College, who was awarded $7,800 in 1958 to spend thirteen months in Britain and Iran studying the transformation of Iranian intellectual life in the 1890–1914 period, and Richard W. Cottam (1924–1997), then teaching at the University of Pittsburgh, who received $1500 for research on the

development of Iranian nationalism. See "Supplement to the Minutes of the 14th Meeting of the Committee on the Near and Middle East," December 19, 1958, folder 1452, box 241, subseries 20, series 1, RG 1, SSRC. The CNME initially rejected Leonard Binder of the University of California for funding in 1957 (a year after he had completed his dissertation at Harvard) because it felt he was not yet prepared, in terms of his knowledge of Persian and of Iran, to successfully implement his proposed project on "The Politics of the Ulama in Iran." But after an appeal from the SSRC Committee on Political Behavior, which had approved a research grant for Binder, the committee reversed itself and awarded him funding. "Supplement to the Minutes of the 11th Meeting of the Committee on the Near and Middle East," March 18, 1958, folder 1452, box 241, subseries 20, series 1, RG 1, SSRC.

35. JCNME annual report for 1959–60, folder 1466, box 244, subseries 20, series 1, RG 1, SSRC.

36. P&P minutes, January 18, 1957, folder 1466, box 244, subseries 20, series 1, RG 1, SSRC.

37. CNME, annual report for 1956–57, folder 1466, box 244, subseries 20, series 1, RG 1, SSRC.

38. CNME, folder 1411, box 233, subseries 20, series 1, RG 1, SSRC.

39. Worcester, *Social Science Research Council*, 63.

40. Beckmann, "The Role of Foundations," 17.

41. Charles B. Fahs, "Long-Range Policy with Regard to Area Studies," April 5, 1954, folder 165, box 31, series 900, RG 3.2, RF.

42. Rockefeller Foundation, *Annual Report, 1954*, 230.

43. Beckmann, "The Role of Foundations," 15.

44. McCaughey, *International Studies*, 168–170.

45. "Proposal for Long Term Support for Foreign Area Study Centers," 1959, folder titled "Long-Term Support—Background materials, working papers," box 1, FA 610, FF. This proposal may well have been drafted by Ford staffer Melvin J. Fox, as its language is quite similar to a memo sent by Fox to Cleon O. Swayzee, April 20, 1959, folder titled "Long-Term Support—Background Material, Working Papers Re: International Training and Foreign Area Studies, 1959–1963," box 1, FA 610, FF. See too Cleon Swayzee to John Howard, "Problems in the Foreign Area Field which Require Attention at the National Level," October 26, 1959, folder titled "National Agencies," box 2, FA 610, FF. Swayzee's desire to strengthen the links between U.S. and Middle Eastern scholars may have been heightened by the exclusion of Iranian scholars from the CNME's conference in Tehran in February–March 1959, discussed later in this chapter.

46. "The Near East," with a cover note by Cleon Swayzee, October 14, 1959, folder titled "Long-Term Support—Area papers," box 1, FA 610, FF.

47. *International Studies*, 184–185.

48. Ibid, 191–194; John B. Howard, "Budgetary Information Concerning the Long-Term Support Program," November 9, 1960, box 1, FA 610, FF.

49. Beckmann, "The Role of Foundations," 16.

50. See for example William Riley Parker, *The National Interest and Foreign Languages* (Washington DC: U.S. Government Printing Office, 1954). Parker, a professor of English at New York University, was executive secretary of the Modern Language Association, secretary of the board of directors of the ACLS and a member of the U.S. National Commission for UNESCO.

51. On the origins and passage of the NDEA see Barbara Barksdale Clowse, *Brainpower for the Cold War: The Sputnik Crisis and National Defense Education Act of 1958* (Westport CT: Greenwood Press, 1981); Nancy Ruther, *Barely There, Powerfully Present: Thirty Years of U.S. Policy on International Higher Education* (New York: Routledge, 2002), ch. 3; Wayne J. Urban, *More than Science and Sputnik: The National Defense Education Act of 1958* (Tuscaloosa: University of Alabama Press, 2010); and Dougherty, "A History of Federal Policy," ch. 4.

52. The full text of the act can be found at http://www.gpo.gov/fdsys/pkg/STATUTE-72/pdf/STATUTE-72-Pg1580.pdf, accessed September 12, 2014. In the spirit of the times, section 1001(f) of the act required that each recipient of a loan or other funding sign "an affidavit that he does not believe in, and is not a member of and does not support any organization that believes in or teaches, the overthrow of the United States Government by force or violence or by any illegal or unconstitutional methods," and also that he or she swear allegiance to the United States and promise to defend its constitution and laws "against all enemies, foreign and domestic." Many college and university faculty, and even some administrators, objected to this requirement, and after much protest it was removed from the law in 1962. See Urban, *More than Science and Sputnik*, 184–189.

53. Ruther, *Barely There*, 66ff.

54. K. Forbis Johnson et al., *Reauthorization of the Higher Education Act: Program Descriptions, Issues, and Options*. Report prepared by the Congressional Research Service for the Committee on Labor and Human Resources, 99th Cong., 1st sess., Feb. 1985. Senate print, 404. Accessed January 27, 2015, http://congressional.proquest.com/congressional/docview/t21.d22.crs-1985-crs-0011?accountid=12768.

55. Berkeley established a Committee for Middle Eastern Studies in 1963; it was designated a center several years later.

56. Middle East Institute, *Middle East Area Study Programs at American Universities and Colleges, 1970*, 5th edition (mimeographed, 1970). In the decades that followed, centers at the University of Washington, the University of Arizona, Ohio State

University, Indiana University and Yale would at various points secure Title VI funding as well.

57. See President Eisenhower's signing statement at http://www.presidency.ucsb.edu/ws/?pid=11211, accessed September 14, 2014. Title VI would be incorporated into the Higher Education Act of 1965 and its subsequent reauthorizations.

58. "A Communication from Mortimer Graves," April 20, 1958, folder 1452, box 241, subseries 20, series 1, RG 1, SSRC.

59. See Alex Boodrookas, "Food for Books: Grain Aid, Cold War Scholarship, and the Weaponization of American Research Libraries" (MA thesis, Hagop Kevorkian Center for Near Eastern Studies, New York University, 2014).

60. Born in Egypt and trained in economics at Oxford, Issawi worked for the Egyptian government, taught at the American University of Beirut and then did a stint with the United Nations in New York before joining the faculty of Columbia University in 1951. See Naff, *Paths*, ch. 5.

61. See CNME, annual report for 1957–1958, folder 1466, box 244, subseries 20, series 1, RG 1, SSRC, and Gilman, *Mandarins*, passim.

62. Born and educated in Vienna, von Grunebaum came to the United States in 1938, at the time of the *anschluss*. An authority on medieval Islamic history and culture, he taught at the Asia Institute in New York and at the University of Chicago, and then moved to UCLA in 1957. For a biographical sketch see http://texts.cdlib.org/view?docId=hb9t1nb5rm&doc.view=frames&chunk.id=div00068&toc.depth=1&toc.id=. For a critique of von Grunebaum's intellectual approach see Abdallah Laroui, *The Crisis of the Arab Intellectual: Traditionalism or Historicism?* (Berkeley: University of California Press, 1976).

63. Dupree (1925–1989) spent much of his career as the Afghanistan and Pakistan specialist at the American Universities Field Staff, established in 1951 to provide American colleges with specialized teaching personnel in international affairs. See Jon W. Anderson, "Anthropology's Middle Eastern Prehistory: An Archaeology of Knowledge," in Hafez and Slyomovics, *Anthropology of the Middle East and North Africa*, 51–52.

64. CNME minutes, October 16, 1959, folder 1452, box 241, subseries 20, series 1, RG 1, SSRC.

65. CNME minutes, May 1, 1959, folder 1452, box 241, subseries 20, series 1, RG 1, SSRC.

66. Cleon Swayzee (quoting from a letter he had received) to T. Cuyler Young, April 8, 1959, Grants, PA56–136 (microfilm reel 295), FF.

67. At one point there had apparently been a plan to have some or all of the American social scientists interact with a conference of Iranian scholars sponsored by

UNESCO, but the UNESCO conference was postponed and no alternative arrangement for a joint meeting was made. CNME minutes, May 1, 1959, and JCNME minutes, October 16, 1959, October 14–15, 1960, folder 1452, box 241, subseries 20, series 1, RG 1, SSRC.

68. P&P minutes, June 12, 1959, folder 1801, box 318, series 2, RG 1, SSRC; CNME minutes, May 1, 1959, folder 1452, box 241, subseries 20, series 1, RG 1, SSRC.

69. The handbook appeared in 1968 as a bound photocopy and three years later as a published book: Louise E. Sweet, ed., *The Central Middle East: A Handbook of Anthropology and Published Research on the Nile Valley, the Arab Levant, Southern Mesopotamia, the Arabian Peninsula, and Israel* (New Haven: HRAF Press, 1971).

70. JCNME minutes, February 13, 1960, April 20, 1960, October 14–15, 1960, folder 1452, box 241, subseries 20, series 1, RG 1, SSRC. See too I. William Zartman, untitled typewritten draft of notes on MESA's formation and early history (hereafter cited as "Draft History of MESA"), and Zartman to Mitchell, July 21, 1970, and Mitchell to Zartman, July 27, 1970, in folder 5326, box 445, subseries 75, series 1, RG 2, SSRC. Zartman's account was drafted in the summer of 1970 as one of several "case histories" to be provided to the Language and Area Studies Review run by Richard D. Lambert, whose 1973 survey I discuss in Chapter 8; see Margaret Gardiner to I. William Zartman, February 23, 1970, folder labeled "Correspondence, 1970," Middle East Studies Association records (hereafter cited as MESA). The revised version of Zartman's account, dated September 1970, was titled "History of MESA" and circulated in mimeograph; see folder labeled "History of MESA," MESA.

71. Dankwart Rustow's report to JCNME on plans for the conference and list of proposed invitees, January 5, 1961; "Plans for Conference on Near and Middle Eastern Studies," February 10, 1961; and T. Cuyler Young, "Preliminary Statement for serious discussion at the Dobbs Ferry Conference," October 11, 1961, in folder 1453, box 241, subseries 20, series 1, RG 1, SSRC. The conference was initially to be held at Dobbs Ferry but was later moved to New York City.

72. Binder had just begun teaching at the University of Chicago; his first book, *Religion and Politics in Pakistan*, had recently been published, to be followed in 1962 by *Iran: Political Development in a Changing Society*. The concept of "political community" was much in vogue at the time: for example, in his 1961 book *Egypt in Search of Political Community: An Analysis of the Intellectual and Political Evolution of Egypt, 1804–1952* (Cambridge: Harvard University Press, 1961), Nadav Safran acknowledged his intellectual debt to the political philosopher Sebastian De Grazia, author of *The Political Community: A Study of Anomie* (Chicago: University of Chicago Press, 1948), which combined elements of Durkheimian sociology and Freudian psychology.

73. JCNME minutes, May 12, 1962, folder 1454, box 241, subseries 20, series 1, RG 1, SSRC.

74. See for example P&P minutes, September 10–11, 1960, folder 1802, box 318, and November 6, 1961, folder 1803, box 318, in series 2, RG 1, SSRC.

75. JCNME minutes, February 16, 1962, May 12, 1962, November 19, 1962, folder 1454, box 241, subseries 20, series 1, RG 1, SSRC. Like many American liberal intellectuals in this period, Morroe Berger was active in the Congress for Cultural Freedom (CCF), founded in 1950 to mobilize American intellectuals, writers and scholars for the Cold War anticommunist crusade. Citing a personal communication from the late Palestinian political scientist and activist Ibrahim Abu-Lughod (1929–2001), Timothy Mitchell reports that in this period Berger sought on behalf of the CCF to recruit an editor for the organization's planned Arabic-language organ *Hiwar*. Mitchell relates that in seeking to recruit an editor Berger insisted that *Hiwar* publish articles dealing with the situation of Muslim communities in the Soviet Union—a stipulation very much in keeping with the CCF's anti-Soviet mission and its mode of operation. The Palestinian poet Tawfiq Sayyigh (1923–1971) was eventually hired as the journal's founding editor and *Hiwar* began to appear in Beirut in 1962. We do not know whether or not Berger knew that the Congress for Cultural Freedom was established, funded and largely controlled by the CIA as an instrument of its global anticommunist and anti-Soviet campaign, meaning that *Hiwar*, like the CCF's other publications, was covertly financed by the intelligence agency; it seems clear, however, that Tawfiq Sayyigh had no knowledge of who was indirectly bankrolling his journal. In any case, as Frances Stonor Saunders has argued, many more of those involved with the CCF likely knew that it was a CIA front (or at least had strong suspicions) than were willing to admit it after its true character was exposed in the American press in 1966–1967. *Hiwar*, like the CCF itself, went out of business soon thereafter. See Mitchell, "The Middle East," 91, 115 n. 6; Saunders, *Cultural Cold War*, 334; Denys Johnson-Davies, *Memories in Translation: A Life between the Lines of Arabic Literature* (Cairo: American University in Cairo Press, 2006), 70–72; Peter Coleman, *The Liberal Conspiracy: The Congress for Cultural Freedom and the Struggle for the Mind of Postwar Europe* (New York: the Free Press, 1989), 189–190; Hugh Wilford, *The Mighty Wurlitzer: How the CIA Played America* (Cambridge: Harvard University Press, 2008), chs. 4–5; and Khalil, "America's Dream Palace," ch. 5, 249ff.

76. JCNME, November 19, 1962, folder 1454, box 241, subseries 20, series 1, RG 1, SSRC.

77. Wilson to Herring, September 16, 1963, folder 5322, box 444, subseries 75, series 1, RG 2, SSRC.

78. JCNME minutes, October 18, 1963, folder 1454, box 241, subseries 20, series 1, RG 1, SSRC. On the origins and early history of the SSRC Committee on Political Behavior see Hauptmann, "The Development of Philanthropic Interest" and "The Ford Foundation."

79. I discuss both Hurewitz's survey and Berger's assessment in Chapter 7.

80. JCNME minutes, October 18, 1963, folder 1454, box 241, subseries 20, series 1, RG 1, SSRC; Ernest N. McCarus, "A Lust for Language," in Naff, *Paths*, 190; McCarus, "History," 211ff; Center for Applied Linguistics of the Modern Language Association, "Nine Reports on Conferences Concerning the Teaching of Middle Eastern Languages, 1958–1963," in folder 1455, box 241, subseries 20, series 1, RG 1, SSRC.

81. JCNME annual report for 1964–1965, folder 1466, box 244, subseries 20, series 1, RG 1, SSRC.

82. In his thoughtful review of the volume R. Stephen Humphreys suggested that "the net impression given by the book is one of a series of inchoate working hypotheses, supported by a partial and tentative documentation," but he hastened to add that "at this point in our studies, no more can be expected" and that "the reader will nevertheless find his efforts rewarded by an insight into the kinds of problems which are beginning to be defined and the techniques which are being evolved to deal with them." *Journal of the American Oriental Society* 92 no. 1 (January–March 1972): 119–122. Berkeley's Center for Planning and Development Research and its Department of City and Regional Planning were co-sponsors of the conference.

83. CASA incorporated the existing Portland State University summer program at AUC. JCNME, annual report for 1965–66, folder 1466, box 244, subseries 20, series 1, RG 1, SSRC; McCarus, "History," 214–215; *Middle East Studies Association Bulletin* 1 no. 2 (November 15, 1967): 28–29 (hereafter cited as *MESA Bulletin*).

84. ARCE had initially been an exclusively Egyptological institution but, according to its website, in 1962, with the involvement of the U.S. Department of State, it "entered into an expanded and more structured consortium, and was charged with managing and distributing over $500,000 yearly in Public Law 480 (Food for Peace) funds." Accessed July 9, 2013, http://www.arce.org/main/about/historyandmission. The scope of ARCE's mandate was eventually expanded to encompass research on Egypt after the rise of Islam as well. In this connection see Cleon Swayzee, "Some Notes on the Proposed Use of Public Law 480 Funds for the Establishment of an American Research Center in the Near East," May 22, 1961, folder titled "American Centers in the Near East," box 1, FA 610, FF.

Chapter 7

1. Henry Siegman, telephone interviews with author, August 19, 2014, and February 25, 2015; see too interview with Henry Siegman, July 30, 2014, *Democracy Now*, accessed July 30, 2014, http://www.democracynow.org/.

2. On Albright's early career see Kuklick, *Puritans*, ch. 9. As I note in Chapter 4, Albright was involved with the ACLS' efforts in the late 1940s to organize Near Eastern studies.

3. In Naff, *Paths*, 90.

4. Hurewitz, *Undergraduate Instruction*, 1–2, 3.

5. *New York Times*, July 16, 1962.

6. Kenneth W. Mildenberger, "The Federal Government and the Universities," *Annals of the American Academy of Political and Social Science* 356 (November 1964): 26.

7. See AAMES' proposal for Ford funding, box 1, FA 610, FF.

8. Maurice Harari, *Government and Politics of the Middle East* (Englewood Cliffs NJ: Prentice-Hall, 1962). Born in Egypt, Harari (1923–2011) received his PhD in international relations from Columbia in 1953, taught at several universities, held various positions at the Ford Foundation and later served as a dean at California State University, Long Beach.

9. President's Report to the Annual Meeting of the Board of Trustees of AAMES, May 26, 1963, American Association for Middle East Studies, 1962–1963, Folder 38, Box 9, Department of Near Eastern Studies Records, PU.

10. See for example JCNME minutes, October 14–15, 1960, folder 1452, box 241, subseries 20, series 1, RG 1, 1960, SSRC.

11. AAMES press release, December 14, 1964, American Association for Middle East Studies, 1962–1963, Department of Near Eastern Studies Records, folder 38, box 9, PU.

12. It is known today as the Jewish Council for Public Affairs, which declares itself "the representative voice of the organized American Jewish community in addressing the principal mandate of the Jewish community relations field," including "the safety and security of the state of Israel." Accessed August 20, 2014, http://engage.jewishpublicaffairs.org/p/salsa/web/common/public/content?content_item_KEY=4147#History.

13. Henry Siegman, telephone interviews with author, August 19, 2014, and February 25, 2015. After leaving AAMES Henry Siegman would become an increasingly important player in American Jewish public affairs. In November 1965, following his stint at the National Jewish Community Relations Advisory Council, he became executive vice-president of the Synagogue Council of America, which coordinated

the three main religious movements in American Judaism. In 1978 he became executive director of the American Jewish Congress, among the most prominent American Jewish organizations, a post he would hold until 1994; he then became a Senior Fellow of the Council on Foreign Relations. However, from the early 1970s onward his thinking about the Israeli-Palestinian conflict evolved considerably, and he is probably best known today as a highly outspoken critic of Israel's policies toward the Palestinians. See http://www.jta.org/1965/11/15/archive/rabbi-henry-siegman-chosen-top-executive-of-synagogue-council, accessed July 30, 2014, and http://www.fpa.org/events/index.cfm?act=show_event&event_id=343, accessed August 11, 2013.

14.   Zartman, "History of MESA," 4, 5.

15.   On the hearings see for example *The New York Times*, August 2, 1963.

16.   Martin Kramer's introduction to "An Index to the Shwadran Collection," which includes the research files of the American Zionist Emergency Council and the Council for Middle Eastern Affairs, held at the Moshe Dayan Center of Tel Aviv University, accessed September 24, 2014, http://www.martinkramer.org/sandbox/reader/archives/the-shwadran-collection-in-context/; Senate Foreign Relations Committee, "Activities of Nondiplomatic Representatives of Foreign Principals in the U.S.," May 23 and August 1, 1963 (Washington DC: Government Printing Office, 1963), 1408; Isadore Hamlin (Executive Director of the Jewish Agency-American Section) to Victor Rabinowitz, February 6, 1963, folder labeled "Correspondence, Jan-June 1963," box 25, Victor Rabinowitz Papers, Tamiment Library and Robert F. Wagner Labor Archive, Elmer Holmes Bobst Library, New York University. See too Victor Rabinowitz, *Unrepentant Leftist: A Lawyer's Memoir* (Urbana IL: University of Illinois Press, 1996). It is worth noting that in 1951 the CIA helped found the American Friends of the Middle East, which worked to promote positive attitudes toward the Arab world and counter lobbying on behalf of Israel, and for years provided it with funding and guidance. *Ramparts* magazine exposed the organization's CIA connection in 1967. See Hugh Wilford, *America's Great Game: The CIA's Secret Arabists and the Shaping of the Modern Middle East* (New York: Basic Books, 2013), passim.

17.   Senate Foreign Relations Committee, "Activities," 1709–1710; Winder, "Four Decades," 59–60.

18.   Senate Foreign Relations Committee, "Activities," 1278–1280. Fulbright did, however, write Siegman to ask for more information about AAMES and its connection with the AZC and funding from Israel. In his July 1963 response, Siegman promised that the matters Fulbright had raised would be brought to the attention of AAMES' president, chairman of the board and treasurer when they returned to New York after the summer; but it does not seem that anyone at AAMES had any subsequent communication with Fulbright. Ibid., 1773.

19. Henry Siegman, telephone interview with author, February 25, 2015.

20. Senate Foreign Relations Committee, "Activities," 1339–1340, 1351.

21. In 2010 it renamed itself the Association for Slavic, East European, and Eurasian Studies.

22. JCNME minutes, February 13, 1960, April 20, 1960, October 14–15, 1960, folder 1452, box 241, subseries 20, series 1, RG 1, SSRC. See too Zartman, "History of MESA," 1–2.

23. Dankwart Rustow, report to JCNME on plans for the conference and list of proposed invitees, January 5, 1961; "Plans for Conference on Near and Middle Eastern Studies," February 10, 1961; and T. Cuyler Young, "Preliminary Statement for serious discussion at the Dobbs Ferry Conference," October 11, 1961, in folder 1453, box 241, subseries 20, series 1, RG 1 SSRC. The conference was initially to be held at Dobbs Ferry, a favorite site for SSRC-sponsored conferences, but was later moved to New York City.

24. JCNME minutes, October 19, 20, 22, 1961, Ibid.

25. JCNME minutes, May 12, 1962, Ibid; Cooperating Committee minutes, November 19, 1962, folder 1454, box 241, subseries 20, series 1, RG 1, SSRC.

26. Quoted in Schorger to the Cooperating Committee, January 16, 1963, folder 1454, box 241, subseries 20, series 1, RG 1, SSRC.

27. Zartman, "History of MESA," 3.

28. Delpar, *Looking South*, 162–163.

29. JCNME minutes, October 1965, folder 1456, box 241, subseries 20, series 1, RG 1, SSRC.

30. Peretz (born 1922) had worked in Palestine for the American Friends Service Committee and as a journalist before obtaining a PhD at Columbia under J. C. Hurewitz. In 1962 he began working at the New York State Department of Education, which had received a Ford Foundation grant of several hundred thousand dollars to provide a range of in-service programs on foreign, especially non-Western, area studies for teachers across the state, including training seminars, model courses, summer institutes, and study trips. See Don Peretz, "Vignettes—Bits and Pieces," in Naff, *Paths*, ch. 8, especially 248–253. In 1967 Peretz would begin teaching at the State University of New York at Binghamton, where he spent the rest of his academic career.

31. Zartman, "Draft History of MESA," 6.

32. JCNME minutes, March 20, 1966, folder 1456, box 242, subseries 20, series 1, RG 1, SSRC, and JCNME annual report 1965–1966, folder 1466, box 244, subseries 20, series 1, RG 1, SSRC.

33. In Naff, *Paths*, 279.

34. See Berger to JCNME, May 26, 1966, the attached list of invitees and the draft

"master list," folder 1456, box 242, subseries 20, series 1, RG 1, SSRC, and Berger's letter of invitation on behalf of the JCNME, June 15, 1966, in folder labeled "Establishment of MESA—Correspondence," MESA.

35.   JCNME minutes, January 27, 1967, folder 1456, box 242, subseries 20, series 1, RG 1, SSRC.

36.   JCNME, annual reports for 1966–1967 and 1967–1968, folder 1466, box 244, subseries 20, series 1, RG 1, SSRC.

37.   "Minutes of Meeting Establishing the Middle East Studies Association, New York City, December 9, 1966," dated January 3, 1967, in folder labeled "Establishment of MESA—First Nominating Committee, 1967," MESA.

38.   In Naff, *Paths*, 279.

39.   See Alan W. Horton to Anne H. Betteridge, March 5, 1994, in folder labeled "Establishment of First MESA Nominating Committee—1967," MESA.

40.   Roland Mitchell, December 12, 1966, memo on the formation of MESA and list of participants in its founding meeting, folder 4974, box 409, subseries 74, series 1, RG 2, SSRC; on NYU support for MESA, see R. Bayly Winder to Morroe Berger, November 17, 1966, PA 67–520 (microfilm reel 4900), FF.

41.   MESA board of directors minutes, December 10, 1966, in binder titled "Board Meeting Minutes 1966–1980," MESA. After receiving his PhD in international relations from Yale in 1956, Zartman was drafted and spent some four years in the armed services (including two years stationed in Morocco), where much of his time was devoted to training or service in various branches of military intelligence. It was this experience, as Zartman tells it, that enabled him to re-enter the academic world as an expert on Africa and the Middle East. Like others in his cohort in Middle East studies, an SSRC postdoctoral grant enabled him to complete the research on post-independence Moroccan politics on which his first two books drew. He taught at the University of South Carolina and then, from 1966, at NYU. Much of his early work was on the politics of North Africa, especially Morocco, but he would go on to publish extensively on conflict resolution, negotiations, game theory and the study of political elites. I discuss his intelligence connections later in this chapter. I. William Zartman, telephone interview with author, August 28, 2014.

42.   Zartman to the board of directors, "Agenda of February 26 Meeting of the Board," and MESA board of directors minutes, February 26, 1971, in binder titled "Board Meeting Minutes 1966–1980," MESA; *MESA Bulletin* 6 no. 2 (May 1, 1972): 84.

43.   Zartman, "History of MESA," 5.

44.   Mitchell to Zartman, July 27, 1970, folder 5326, box 445, subseries 75, series 1, RG 2, SSRC.

45.   Winder, "Four Decades," 52.

46.   In this connection see Zartman, "History of MESA," 5, who asserts that

"Almost all of the founding fifty, while not necessarily venerable, had at least made a significant contribution to the field by the *beginning* of the decade, and many of them were at the Berkeley conference in 1961; by 1967 the Young Turks had become established in institutional positions, and their demarche had weight." Emphasis in the original. Zartman was apparently referring to the JCNME-sponsored conference that I discuss in Chapter 6, held not in Berkeley but at the Barclay Hotel in New York.

47. Delpar, *Looking South*, 163.

48. Howard R. Dressner to Morroe Berger, August 22, 1967, PA 67–520 (microfilm reel 4900), Grants, FF.

49. According to a participant, one memorable feature of that first annual meeting was the lecture on dreams in Islamic culture delivered at the formal banquet by Gustave von Grunebaum; as a result of the heavy dinner, and perhaps also the topic and the speaker's delivery, many of those present dozed off. See the transcribed interview with William Ochsenwald conducted by Nancy Dishaw of MESA's staff in the mid-2000s as part of the unpublished "People's History of MESA" (hereafter PHM), MESA.

50. "Narrative Report," August 9, 1968, PA 67–520 (microfilm reel 4900), Grants, FF.

51. See *MESA Bulletin* 2 no. 1 (March 1, 1968): 15.

52. *MESA Bulletin* 6 no. 1 (February 1, 1972): 39.

53. *MESA Bulletin* 1 no. 2 (Nov. 15, 1967): 1–18. When published Berger's report was characterized as one of a series of reports on world regions requested by the Department of Health, Education and Welfare in connection with the implementation of the International Education Act, which I discuss in Chapter 8. On Berger's assessment of the field see too Edward W. Said, *Orientalism* (New York: Pantheon, 1978), 288–290.

54. *MESA Bulletin* 1 no. 2 (Nov. 15, 1967).

55. Untitled, c. 1969 or 1970, folder 5327, box 445, subseries 75, series 1 RG 2, SSRC. See too "Priorities in Middle East Studies," drawn up by MESA's Government Support Committee after the 1971 annual meeting, folder 1458, box 242, subseries 20, series 1, RG 1, SSRC.

56. Minutes of the February 1970 conference, PA 67–520 (microfilm reel 4900), Grants, FF. A report on this conference was presented at a plenary session of MESA's 1970 annual meeting.

57. Ibid.

58. MESA request for Ford funding, 1972, PA 67–520 (microfilm reel 4900), Grants, FF.

59. Ibid.

60. Anne Nagle to William Carmichael, "Close-out of Grant 67–520 to the Middle East Studies Association of North America," July 24, 1985, grant 67–520 (microfilm reel 4900), Grants, FF. MESA also received several grants in the $1000-$1500 range from ESSO Middle East; see *MESA Bulletin* 7 no. 3 (October 15, 1973): 90.

61. Ford Foundation staff report on MESA's request for a Ford Foundation grant, 1978, PA 67–520 (microfilm reel 4900), Grants, FF; *MESA Bulletin*, passim. In 1975–1976 MESA also served as the contractor for an Office of Education-funded study assessing the depiction of Egypt in American primary and secondary school literature, with Farhat Ziadeh serving as principal investigator. In this same period, during which Egyptian President Anwar al-Sadat developed close ties with the United States, there were other efforts to get MESA involved in State Department-run cultural and educational exchange programs with Egypt as well as with other Arab countries and with Iran. See the contract between MESA and the Office of Education, signed June 1975; Afaf Lutfi al-Sayyid Marsot to Robert Fernea, Malcolm Kerr, R. Bayly Winder and I. William Zartman, January 17, 1975, in the folder labeled "1975," MESA; and MESA board of director minutes, November 9, 1974, personal papers of Irene Gendzier (hereafter IG).

62. "Report to the Ford Foundation on the Activities of the Middle East Studies Association of North America during the Academic Year 1973–1974," PA 67–520 (microfilm reel 4900), Grants, FF.

63. See Lockman, *Contending Visions*, 170–171.

64. Roxann A. Van Dusen to Janet Abu-Lughod, December 11, 1974, folder 5362, box 448, subseries 75, series 1, RG 2, SSRC. Van Dusen attended and reported on the MESA meeting at the request of Janet Abu-Lughod, the first woman to serve on the JCNME (see Chapter 8), in order to help formulate a proposal for JCNME research support.

65. Dr. Wilbert J. Le Malla (spelling unclear), November 16, 1976, 67–520, Grants, FF.

66. "A Brief Commentary and Report on the Roundtable and Panels on Women's Roles Held at the 1975 MESA Meeting," *MESA Bulletin* 10 no. 2 (May 1, 1976): 20–23.

67. According to one assessment of African studies, "Diaspora Blacks accused white scholars of controlling access to knowledge about their African homeland. Progressives faulted the ASA for its policy of political neutrality. Together, critics accused the African Studies establishment of cozying up to colonial governments, remaining silent about the injustices of apartheid, and condoning a whole host of abuses that weighed heavily against the welfare of Africans." Pearl T. Robinson, "Area Studies in Search of Africa," in Szanton, *Politics of Knowledge*, 146. See too Delpar, *Looking South*, 168ff; Nathan Karnovsky, "The Other Cultural Revolution:

The Academic Uprising of the American China Scholar" (BA thesis, Haverford College, 2012); and Cumings, "Boundary Displacement: The State," passim.

68. I. William Zartman, telephone interview with author, August 28, 2014. Frank Tachau reported that at MESA's second annual meeting Manfred Halpern, introducing George Hourani's presidential address (on which more later), declared openly that the Arab-Israeli conflict "was a problem that the founders of the organization had decided to avoid at all costs." PHM, MESA.

69. MESA board of directors minutes, December 9, 1967, March 18, 1968, in binder titled "Board Meeting Minutes 1966–1980," MESA; Zartman, "History of MESA," 23; *MESA Bulletin* 2 no. 1 (March 1, 1968): 19.

70. Zartman, "History of MESA," 23–24.

71. George F. Hourani, "Palestine as a Problem of Ethics," *MESA Bulletin* 3 no. 1 (February 15, 1969): 15–25.

72. Zartman, "History of MESA," 23.

73. MESA board of director minutes, April 11, 1969, in binder titled "Board Meeting Minutes 1966–1980," MESA.

74. R. Bayly Winder, "Adghath Ahlam," *MESA Bulletin* 4 no. 1 (February 15, 1970): 15–22.

75. Minutes of the February 1970 conference, PA 67–520 (microfilm reel 4900), Grants, FF.

76. "Report to the Ford Foundation on the Activities of the Middle East Studies Association of North America during the Academic Year 1973–1974," PA 67–520 (microfilm reel 4900), Grants, FF.

77. Hagopian to Brown, May 13, 1976, and Brown to Hagopian, June 9, 1976, in folder labeled "Board of Directors, 1976," MESA. On the AAUG see too Lockman, *Contending Visions*, 172–173. I erroneously state there that the AAUG was founded in "the late 1970s"; I should have said "the late 1960s."

78. Originally established by the Air Force to explore long-term weapons development, RAND (from "R and D," research and development) was constituted in 1948 as an independent, nonprofit consulting firm that largely served government agencies. There is a large scholarly literature on RAND; see for example Alex Abella, *Soldiers of Reason: The Rand Corporation and the Rise of the American Empire* (Orlando FL: Harcourt, 2008).

79. Lockman, *Contending Visions*, 141–148.

80. *MERIP Reports* no. 38 (June 1975).

81. See Jim Paul, "Games Imperialists Play," *MERIP Reports* 45 (March 1976), 17–20. Paul was in the late 1960s and early 1970s one of Zartman's doctoral students in political science at NYU and participated in the exercise. However, to avoid committing academic suicide (as Paul puts it), he deferred going public with the story

until he had completed his doctorate. Jim Paul, email message to author, July 26, 2013. After a stint teaching political science, Paul became a central figure in MERIP and in 1993 was founding executive director of the Global Policy Forum, an organization that monitors policymaking at the United Nations.

CENIS had been founded in 1951 with CIA funding. As Jamie Cohen-Cole puts it, "CENIS provided a critical function for Cambridge intellectuals. Since CIA funding was covert, CENIS allowed members such as Walt Rostow and visitors such as McGeorge Bundy to wear the mantle of apolitical objectivity while simultaneously conducting intelligence work. Although CENIS scholars were convinced of their own objectivity, they were nevertheless concerned not to allow the source of their funds to become known to the public lest they no longer appeared objective." *Open Mind*, 128. CENIS' formal relationship with the CIA was only terminated in 1966, owing in large part to protests by MIT faculty who felt that the connection compromised the university's integrity. Not long thereafter it became a prime target for protestors who denounced its deep involvement in research related to the Vietnam war. On the history of CENIS see Donald L. M. Blackmer, *The MIT Center for International Studies: The Founding Years, 1951–1969* (Cambridge: MIT Center for International Studies, 2002); for a more critical perspective see Gilman, *Mandarins*, ch. 5, and Cumings, "Boundary Displacements," 278–280. On conflict simulation at CENIS see Christopher Simpson, "U.S. Mass Communication Research, Counterinsurgency, and Scientific 'Reality'," in *Communication Researchers and Policy-making*, ed. Sandra Braman (Cambridge: MIT Press, 2003), 157.

82. "L'Operation Conex II," *Afrique Asie* no. 107 (April 19, 1976). In 1963 the two countries' armies had fought a brief but intense "War of the Sands" over a disputed border region.

83. U.S. Senate, *The Final Report of the Select Committee To Study Governmental Operations With Respect To Intelligence Activities* ("Church Committee"), Book I, "Foreign and Military Intelligence," April 26, 1976, 189–190, accessed September 20, 2014, http://www.intelligence.senate.gov/churchcommittee.html. This was of course not the first time that collaboration between scholars and intelligence agencies had surfaced in public: witness the uproar caused by the U.S. Army's Project Camelot, launched in 1964 to recruit scholars for research on the causes of "social breakdown" in Third World countries that might be exploited by the communists. See Lockman, *Contending Visions*, 144.

84. Noel Epstein, "Professors Decry Recruiting by CIA," *Washington Post*, May 6, 1976.

85. *PS* 10 no. 1 (Winter, 1977): 55.

86. See for example Steinberg to Zartman, April 30, 1976, in folder labeled

"Board of Directors, 1976," MESA. As I discuss in Chapter 8, Steinberg simultaneously contacted the JCNME to propose similar kinds of collaboration.

87. See William Blum, *The CIA: A Forgotten History—US Global Interventions since World War 2* (London: Zed Books, 1986) and Jeremy Kuzmarov, *Modernizing Repression: Police Training and Nation Building in the American Century* (Amherst MA: University of Massachusetts Press, 2012).

88. See for example Zartman to Charles Issawi, October 24, 1975, in folder labeled "1975," and MESA board of directors minutes, November 10, 1976, IG.

89. MESA board of directors minutes, March 16, 1975, and Irene L. Gendzier to L. Carl Brown, April 7 and September 14, 1976, IG.

90. MESA board of directors minutes, November 10, 1976, IG.

91. See for example "Cash Receipts and Disbursement Reports, October 31, 1981," and "Statement of Cash Receipts for Nine Months Ending September 30, 1983," in folders labeled "1981" and "1983," respectively, MESA.

92. See for example Gendzier to Zartman, January 17 and February 22, 1977, and Gendzier to George Makdisi, February 22, 1977, IG.

93. *MESA Bulletin* 11 no. 1 (February 1, 1977): 61, and 11 no. 2 (May 1, 1977): 120–121; Irene Gendzier, telephone interview with author, September 14, 2014.

94. Lockman, *Contending Visions*, 171. AMESS held its first national conference, attended by some 150 people, in November 1979 but faded away in the early 1980s as the energies that had initially propelled it waned and as MESA began to offer a more hospitable intellectual and political environment. See the plaintive but humorous editorial "Is AMESS a Mess?," published in one of the last issues of its newsletter *New Directions in Middle East Studies*, c. 1981: "Is it a matter of the petering out of the energy of a few active firebrands who may have managed to generate much of the early excitement? Have a few years of satisfying pursuit of revisionist critiques of orientalism succeeded in routing our more radical inclinations and breeding complacency? Has the irony of the acronym, originally conspired as an indictment against the establishment, become unraveled at our own doorstep?"

95. Interview with Richard Bulliet, PHM, MESA; see too Richard Bulliet, "Pages from a Memoir—The Middle East Studies Association," accessed March 30, 2015, https://www.academia.edu/8302705/PAGES_FROM_A_MEMOIR_THE_MIDDLE_EAST_STUDIES_ASSOCIATION.

96. Ibid.

97. *MESA Bulletin* 5 no. 3 (October 1, 1971): 74, and 6 no. 1 (February 1, 1972): 42; see too MESA board of directors minutes, November 6, 1974, 7, IG.

98. Interview with Richard Bulliet, PHM, MESA.

99. Richard Bulliet, email message to author, August 2, 2014; *MESA Bulletin* 10 no. 1 (February 1, 1976): 71.

100. *MESA Bulletin* 11 no. 1 (February 1, 1977): 64.

101. Richard Bulliet, email message to author, August 2, 2014, and "Report of the Executive Secretary," November 1980, in folder labeled "Board of Directors, 1980," MESA.

102. Ford Foundation staff report on MESA's request for a Ford Foundation grant, 1978, PA 67–520 (microfilm reel 4900), Grants, FF.

103. Norman Cantor to Farhat Ziadeh, August 21, 1980, in folder labeled "Establishment of MESA—UofA Bid," MESA.

104. Anne Nagle to William B. Carmichael, July 24, 1985, PA 67–520 (microfilm reel 4900), Grants, FF.

105. See Lockman, *Contending Visions*, ch. 7.

106. MESA board of directors, "Statement on Foreign Financing of Middle East Studies, November 7, 1979, in binder titled "Board Meeting Minutes 1966–1980," MESA.

107. MESA board of directors minutes, March 21, 1981, in binder titled "Board Meeting Minutes 1966–1980," MESA.

108. *MESA Bulletin* 17 no. 1 (July 1983): 114, 119.

109. Ibid., 114.

110. MESA board of directors minutes, November 21, 1985, in binder titled "Board Meeting Minutes 1981–1989," MESA.

111. Walter R. Longanecker, Jr., to Kenneth Prewitt, May 4, 1983, folder 1464, box 244, subseries 20, series 1, RG 1, SSRC.

112. For example, Harvard's Nadav Safran received a $107,430 grant from the CIA for the research project that led to his 1985 book *Saudi Arabia: The Ceaseless Quest for Security*. Safran's contract with the CIA stipulated that the agency had the right to review and approve the manuscript before publication and that its role in funding the book not be disclosed. See Lockman, *Contending Visions*, 246.

113. JCNME minutes, meeting of May 13–14, 1983, and JCNME members to Michael Bonine, May 26, 1983, folder 1464, box 244, subseries 20, series 1, RG 1, SSRC.

114. Cited in the text of a 1993 resolution on the National Security Education Program, accessed September 1, 2014, http://www.mesa.arizona.edu/about/resolutions.html. See too MESA board of directors minutes, November 2, 1983, in binder titled "Board Meeting Minutes 1981–1989," MESA.

115. In November 1990 MESA's business meeting endorsed a "sense of the meeting" resolution submitted by the board of directors condemning the Iraqi occupation of Kuwait and calling for a peaceful, negotiated solution of the crisis based on UN resolutions. This seems to have been the only occasion on which MESA took an explicit position on a current conflict in the region.

116.   The texts of these two resolutions can be found in the binder titled "Board Statements & Resolutions," MESA.

117.   See for example Amy M. Rubin, "Critics Accuse Turkish Government of Manipulating Scholarship," *Chronicle of Higher Education* 42 no. 9 (October 27, 1995); William H. Honan, "Princeton is Accused of Fronting for the Turkish Government," *New York Times*, May 22, 1996; and Susan Kinzie, "Board Members Resign to Protest Chair's Ousting," *Washington Post*, July 5, 2008.

118.   Adamec to center directors, June 3, 1983, and Bonine to Koffler and Koffler to Bonine, September 23, 1983, in folder labeled "1983," MESA; Amy Newhall, email message to author, May 3, 2015.

119.   On this campaign and its context see Lockman, *Contending Visions*, 253–255.

120.   *MESA Bulletin* 19 no. 1 (July 1985): 126–127. The Ethics Committee had been established some years earlier to deal with both conflicts among members and relations with outside entities.

121.   See Lockman, *Contending Visions*, 255ff, and the website of MESA's Committee on Academic Freedom, at http://mesana.org/committees/academic-freedom/intervention/index.html.

Chapter 8

1.   McCaughey, *International Studies*, 195; Beckmann, "The Role of Foundations," 15.

2.   P&P minutes, March 20, 1969, folder 1466, box 244, subseries 20, series 1, RG 1, SSRC.

3.   McCaughy, *International Studies*, 242; Francis X. Sutton and David R. Smock, "The Ford Foundation and Area Studies," *Issue: A Journal of Opinion* 6 nos. 2–3 (Summer-Autumn 1976): 69.

4.   McCaughey, *International Studies*, 239–240.

5.   See Dougherty, "A History of Federal Policy," ch. 6, and the very useful "HEA-Title VI Funding History, FY 1959-FY 2014," accessed November 14, 2014, http://kurzman.unc.edu/international-education/crippling-international-education-sources/.

6.   John E. Rielly, "Near Eastern Studies at Princeton," September 10, 1969, PA 71–508 (microfilm reel 4445), Grants, FF. That there was disagreement about whether Harvard's Center for Middle Eastern Studies qualified as strong reflected the sense of drift, even paralysis, that afflicted that center after H. A. R. Gibb suffered an incapacitating stroke in 1964, leaving it without an effective leader for many years to come. On this period at Harvard see Babai, *Reflections on the Past*, 11–15.

7. *Daily Princetonian*, May 25, 1969.

8. John E. Rielly, "Near Eastern Studies at Princeton," September 10, 1969, PA 71–508 (microfilm reel 4445), Grants, FF; Malcolm Kerr, memo to JCNME, February 19, 1968, folder 5325, box 444, subseries 75, series 1, RG 2, SSRC.

9. Ibid., emphasis in the original; JCNME annual report for 1968–1969, folder 1466, box 244, subseries 20, series 1, RG 1, SSRC.

10. See Charles Lindblom, "Political Science in the 1940s and 1950s," and Rogers M. Smith, "Still Blowing in the Wind: The American Quest for a Democratic, Scientific Political Science," in *American Academic Culture*, eds. Bender and Schorske, 243–305; Gilman, *Mandarins*, chs. 4, 6; and Nicolas Guilhot, ed., *The Invention of International Relations Theory: Realism, the Rockefeller Foundation, and the 1954 Conference on Theory* (New York: Columbia University Press, 2011).

11. Oleg Grabbar, with cover note to Roland Mitchell, January 9, 1969, and Mitchell to Grabar, January 10, 1969, folder 5325, box 444, subseries 75, series 1, RG 2, SSRC; Henry W. Riecken, president of the SSRC, to the joint ACLS-SSRC area studies committees, January 1970, folder 5326, box 445, subseries 75, series 1, RG 2, SSRC.

12. From 1962 to 1969 John Rielly worked as a foreign policy assistant to senator and then vice president Hubert Humphrey, and subsequently served as a full-time consultant for the Ford Foundation's Office of European and International Affairs. From 1971 to 2001 he was president of what was then called the Chicago Council on Foreign Relations.

13. John E. Rielly, "Near Eastern Studies at Princeton," September 10, 1969, PA 71–508 (microfilm reel 4445), Grants, FF.

14. "Projected Budget: 1969–70," PA 71–508 (microfilm reel 4445), Grants, FF, and *The Daily Princetonian*, September 6, 1974, February 28, 1979, March 15, 1979. These donations to Princeton were part of a broader effort by the Shah's regime to bolster its connections with American academic institutions and enhance its reputation, especially after the sharp rise in oil prices in 1973 put much greater resources at the Shah's disposal.

15. Robert F. Goheen to J. Wayne Fredericks, June 3, 1970, PA 71–508 (microfilm reel 4445), Grants, FF.

16. Ford Foundation, *Annual Report October 1, 1970 to September 30, 1971* (New York: Ford Foundation, 1971), 80–81.

17. "Background and Justification," Request No. ID-1118, PA 71–508 (microfilm reel 4445), Grants, FF.

18. See A. L. Udovitch, ed., *The Islamic Middle East, 700–1900: Studies in Economic and Social History* (Princeton: Darwin Press, 1981); "Proposal to the Ford Foundation for Two Seminar-Conferences," February 1975, PA 71–508 (microfilm reel 4445) Grants, FF.

19. David R. Smock (deputy head of the Middle East and Africa program at Ford) to Benedict, Cottingham, Gubser and Hrik, May 2, 1975, PA 71–508 (microfilm reel 4445), Grants, FF.

20. Robert H. Edwards to David R. Smock, May 5, 1975, PA 71–508 (microfilm reel 4445), Grants, FF.

21. David R. Smock, "Ford Foundation Support for Middle Eastern and African Studies in the U.S.," *MESA Bulletin* 10 no. 1 (February 1, 1976): 20–25.

22. See Mitchell to Geertz, November 26, 1969, folder 5325, box 444, subseries 75, series 1, RG 2, SSRC.

23. Zartman to Mitchell, March 2, 1970, folder 5326, box 445, subseries 75, series 1, RG 2, SSRC.

24. Brown to Mitchell, February 12, 1970, March 14, 1970, and John L. Simmons, February 19, 1970, folder 5326, box 445, subseries 75, series 1, RG 2, SSRC.

25. Zartman to JCNME, October 5, 1970, folder 5327, box 445, subseries 75, series 1, RG 2, SSRC, and JCNME minutes, meetings of April 13, 1970, November 20, 1970, folders 5326 and 5327, box 445, subseries 75, series 1, RG 2, SSRC.

26. Zonis to JCNME, November 20, 1970, folder 5327, box 445, subseries 75, series 1, RG 2, SSRC. On the Committee on Comparative Politics in this period see Gilman, *Mandarins*, ch. 6.

27. Zonis to JCNME, November 20, 1970, folder 5327, box 445, subseries 75, series 1, RG 2, SSRC.

28. JCNME, annual report for 1969–1970, folder 1466, box 244, subseries 20, series 1, RG 1, SSRC. Around the same time Zartman wrote Mitchell to propose a new program that would bring younger and mid-level professors, teachers and university administrators from the Middle East to the United States for a year of training in research methods, pedagogy, etc., though nothing seems to have come of this. Zartman to Mitchell, January 19, 1969, folder 5325, box 444, subseries 75, series 1, RG 2, SSRC.

29. JCNME minutes, November 20, 1970, folder 5327, box 445, subseries 75, series 1, RG 2, SSRC.

30. On Latin American studies in this period see Delpar, *Looking South,* 157–174; Paul W. Drake and Lisa Hilbink, "Latin American Studies: Theory and Practice," in Szanton, *Politics of Knowledge,* 36; and Adelman, *Worldly Philosopher,* 469. Albert Hirschman became chair of the Joint Committee on Latin American Studies in the fall of 1973.

31. JCNME minutes, April 23, 1971, folder 5327, box 445, subseries 75, series 1, RG 2, SSRC; JCNME annual report for 1970–1971, folder 1466, box 244, subseries 20, series 1, RG 1, SSRC.

32. P&P minutes, March 25, 1971, folder 1801, box 319, series 2, RG 1, SSRC; P&P

minutes, September 11–12, 1971, folder 1466, box 244, subseries 20, series 1, RG 1, SSRC; See too Sutton and Smock, "Ford Foundation," 71.

33.   JCNME minutes, October 24, 1971, folder 1457, box 242, subseries 20, series 1, RG 1, SSRC; P&P minutes, November 13, 1971, and Executive Committee meeting, December 22, 1971, folder 1466, box 244, subseries 20, series 1, RG 1, SSRC.

34.   Five grants were made that year: to Daniel Crecelius and Abdul-Karim Rafeq for a comparative study of the *'ulama* of Cairo in the eighteenth century; to William Gamson and Ephraim Yuchtman for a study of the police in Israeli society; to Harvey Goldberg and Haim Blanc for research in Israel on the language and culture of Libyan Jews in Israel; to Clement Henry Moore and A. K. Abu-Akeel for research in engineering education in Egypt; and to Nicholas Hopkins and Abdelkader Zghal for a comparative study of modernization in two Tunisian villages. JCNME annual report for 1971–1972, folder 1466, box 244, subseries 20, series 1, RG 1, SSRC.

35.   JCNME annual report for 1971–72, and Council minutes, September 10–12, 1972, folder 1466, box 244, subseries 20, series 1, RG 1, SSRC.

36.   See for example JCNME minutes, meeting of March 29–30, 1974, folder 1459, box 242, subseries 20, series 1, RG 1, SSRC, and "Proposal to Extend Eligibility for Postdoctoral Grants to Local Scholars in the Middle East," undated but probably 1974–75, folder 1460, box 243, subseries 20, series 1, RG 1, SSRC.

37.   Roxann A. Van Dusen to the JCNME, March 17, 1975, folder 1459, box 242, subseries 20, series 1, RG 1, SSRC; and "The Study of Women in the Middle East: Some Thoughts" and "The Program of the Joint Committee on the Near and Middle East," July 1975, presumably produced for potential funders, in folder 1460, box 243, subseries 20, series 1, RG 1, SSRC. In this same period Nancy A. Shilling, who was then teaching political science at Hunter College of the City University of New York, submitted a proposal for funding for a planning meeting that would lay the groundwork for a training seminar on Arab women to be held in Cairo or Beirut in 1976. See Nancy A. Shilling, "Grant Application," 1974–75, folder 1459, box 242, subseries 20, series 1, RG 1, SSRC.

38.   Worcester, *Social Science Research Council*, 63.

39.   JCNME, annual report for 1974–1975, folder 1467, box 244, subseries 20, series 1, RG 1, SSRC. In this period the committee also provided support for efforts to improve library resources on the Middle East.

40.   See Gendzier, *Managing Social Change*, 178–181 and passim.

41.   I. William Zartman et al., *Political Elites in Arab North Africa: Morocco, Algeria, Tunisia, Libya, and Egypt* (New York: Longman, 1982), 1.

42.   "Proposed Program of the Joint Committee on the Near and Middle East, 1971–73," folder 5327, box 445, subseries 75, series 1, RG 2, SSRC.

43. I. William Zartman, ed., *Elites in the Middle East* (New York: Praeger Publishers, 1980), 8.

44. See S. M. Eisenstadt, "Some Possibilities for Seminars or Workshops on Various Areas of Middle East Studies—Especially as Related to Problems of 'Development' or Modernization," undated, folder 1458, box 242, subseries 20, series 1, RG 1, SSRC.

45. Muhsin Mahdi to JCNME, December 27, 1972, folder 1458, box 242, subseries 20, series 1, RG 1, SSRC.

46. Von Sivers to Mitchell, January 4, 1981, folder 5395, box 451, subseries 75, series 1, RG 2, SSRC.

47. JCNME minutes, May 13–14, 1981, folder 1464, box 244, subseries 20, series 1, RG 1, SSRC; Peter von Sivers, email message to author, September 5, 2014.

48. Smock, "Ford Foundation Support"; Anne Lesch, "Funding and Middle East Area Studies," November 12, 1977, PA 67–520 (microfilm reel 4900), Grants, FF.

49. JCNME minutes, January 28–29, 1977, folder 1461, box 243, subseries 20, series 1, RG 1, SSRC.

50. JCNME, minutes of December 1–2, 1973, folder 1459, box 242, subseries 20, series 1, RG 1, SSRC. Zonis advocated for a new working group on "psychological processes in the Middle East . . . in their social, economic, and political settings," but like many other research projects discussed by the JCNME over the years, nothing seems to have come of this. See Marvin Zonis to JCNME, May 29, 1974, folder 5349, box 448, subseries 75, series 1, RG 2, SSRC, and Zonis to JCNME, October 3, 1974, folder 1459, box 242, subseries 20, series 1, RG 1, SSRC. Two decades later Zonis would publish *Majestic Failure: The Fall of the Shah* (Chicago: University of Chicago Press, 1991), his own foray into psychobiography.

51. Marvin Zonis to JCNME, November 20, 1973, folder 5345, box 447, subseries 75, series 1, RG 2, SSRC; Roger Owen, "Studying Islamic History," *Journal of Interdisciplinary History* 4 no. 2 (Autumn 1973): 287–298.

52. For a fuller discussion see Lockman, *Contending Visions*, chs. 5–6.

53. Gilman, *Mandarins*, 217.

54. Leonard Binder, ed., *The Study of the Middle East: Research and Scholarship in the Humanities and Social Sciences* (New York: John Wiley & Sons, 1976), 7.

55. The topics covered were the Islamic religious tradition (Charles Adams), history (Albert Hourani), anthropology (Richard T. Antoun, with David M. Hart and Charles L. Redman), Islamic art and archaeology (Oleg Grabar), political science (I. William Zartman), philosophy (Seyyed Hossein Nasr), linguistics (Gernot L. Windfuhr), literature (Roger Allen, with William L. Hanaway and Walter Andrews), sociology (Georges Sabagh) and economics (John Simmons).

56. Binder drew on a survey by Richard D. Lambert, *Language and Area Studies Review* (Philadelphia: American Academy of Political and Social Science, 1973), funded by the federal Office of Education and sponsored by the SSRC. The *Middle East Studies Association Bulletin* explained the context for Lambert's survey: "After 20 years of growth and development, non-Western area studies have come upon a time of trouble, particularly since the mid-sixties. The result has been a concern for the present role and the future usefulness of area studies within the academic community and beyond. There is, therefore, a need for empirical data on which government, foundations, and universities can base their planning. Against this requirement has emerged a nation-wide project to survey language and area studies in the United States." *MESA Bulletin* 3 no. 3 (October 15, 1969). In his preface to Lambert's survey former SSRC president Pendleton Herring acknowledged fears that funding for area studies might be drying up but struck a much more positive note than had Binder: "Despite uncertainties of support and in the face of considerable indifference and resistance, dedicated scholars and determined administrators brought into being area programs diverse in quality, but many highly distinguished. Area studies have been innovative, experimental, and resilient. They have met a challenge, and they fulfill a need." (xvii) A decade later, in another study funded by a Department of Defense contract and a grant from the National Endowment for the Humanities, Lambert would present a much more celebratory portrait of area studies: foundation and Title VI support had led to "the creation of a network of institutions unmatched anywhere in the world, a national resource whose loss would immediately impoverish the capacity of our democratic society and our government to understand the complex, interrelated world in which we live. . . . The language and area studies efforts have built an ample and complex infrastructure of skills and information, one that yields, as economists would put it, rich externalities to consumers of this information and expertise in both the public and private sectors." Richard D. Lambert et al., *Beyond Growth: The Next Stage in Language and Area Studies* (Washington DC: Association of American Universities, 1984), 9–10.

57. For an interesting perspective on Kuhn's work and the contexts within which it developed, see Isaac, *Working Knowledge*, passim.

58. *MESA Bulletin* 11 no. 3 (October 1, 1977): 36–37.

59. Lucien W. Pye, "The Confrontation between Disciplines and Area Studies," in Pye, *Political Science and Area Studies*, 3. Interestingly, Dankwart Rustow's contribution to this volume did not really focus on the relationship between Middle East studies and political science; instead it offered a survey of work on Middle East politics and expressed the hope that, somehow, the study of this field would eventually contribute to the advancement of comparative politics. See too Adalet, "Mirrors of Modernization."

60. Alan Dubetsky to Marvin Zonis, May 13, 1976, folder 1461, box 243, subseries 20, series 1, RG 1, SSRC.

61. Marvin Zonis to Dubetsky, May 28, 1976, folder 1461, box 243, subseries 20, series 1, RG 1, SSRC.

62. Political scientist William B. Quandt (1941–) taught at the University of Pennsylvania and then worked at the RAND Corporation in 1968–1972; he served on the staff of the National Security Council in 1972–1974 and again in 1977–1979, after which he would for many years be a Senior Fellow at the Brookings Institution. Quandt's two years on JCNME, which he joined in 1975 and chaired the following year, marked the first time someone who had just left full-time government service (and would soon return to it) had ever been a member.

63. P&P minutes, September 10, 1977, and SSRC and JCNME annual reports for 1976–77, folder 1476, box 244, subseries 20, series 1, RG 1, SSRC; JCNME minutes, meeting of October 1–2, 1976, folder 1461, box 243, subseries 20, series 1, RG 1, SSRC; Ali Banuazizi, email message to author, April 9, 2015.

64. Early formulations of this topic occasioned lively discussions among committee members, some of whom demanded (and received) "assurances that the project would not purposely or accidentally result in imposing Western concepts on Islamic society." JCNME minutes, meeting of February 20–21, 1976, folder 1460, box 243, subseries 20, series 1, RG 1, SSRC.

65. JCNME minutes, meeting of February 20–21, 1976, folder 1460, box 243, subseries 20, series 1, RG 1, SSRC. See too Edmund Burke III to Rowland Mitchell, March 10, 1976, IG, in which Burke laid out his objections to JCNME collaboration with AID at length.

66. JCNME minutes, meeting of February 20–21, 1976, folder 1460, box 243, subseries 20, series 1, RG 1, SSRC.

67. Roland Mitchell to P&P, March 10–11, 1976; P&P minutes, March 10–11, 1976; Council minutes, March 12–13, 1976, in folder 1476, box 244, subseries 20, series 1, RG 1, SSRC.

68. JCNME minutes, meeting of April 30, 1976, folder 1461, box 243, subseries 20, series 1, RG 1, SSRC.

69. JCNME minutes, meeting of October 1–2, 1976, folder 1461, box 243, subseries 20, series 1, RG 1, SSRC.

70. For example, Burke recalls bringing Fred Halliday's 1974 book *Arabia Without Sultans* to his colleagues' attention as an example of recent work that addressed developments in the region that were entirely off the committee's radar. Halliday's radical analysis of the autocratic and pro-Western regimes of the Arabian peninsula and of the societies over which they ruled must have seemed utterly alien to most of Burke's fellow committee members. Edmund Burke III, telephone interview with author, July 26, 2013.

71. JCNME minutes, meeting of May 13–14, 1983, and JCNME members to Michael Bonine, May 26, 1983, folder 1464, box 244, subseries 20, series 1, RG 1, SSRC.

72. JCNME, annual report for 1977–1978, folder 1467, box 244, subseries 20, series 1, RG 1, SSRC; SSRC Executive Committee minutes, June 16, 1978; and P&P minutes, October 6, 1978, folder 1467, box 244, subseries 20, series 1, RG 1, SSRC.

73. JCNME, annual report for 1978–1979, folder 1467, box 244, subseries 20, series 1, RG 1, SSRC.

74. JCNME, "Statement to the Ford Foundation," folder 1462, box 243, subseries 20, series 1, RG 1, SSRC.

75. Roland Mitchell to Richard C. Robarts of the Ford Foundation, June 3, 1981, folder 5401, box 452, subseries 75, series 1, RG 2, SSRC. For an early report on the PLSS' activities, see Charles E. Butterworth, "Project on Law and Social Structure," *MESA Bulletin* 15 no. 1 (July 1981): 7–10.

76. JCNME, "Statement to the Ford Foundation," April 1980, folder 5394, box 451, subseries 75, series 1, RG 2, SSRC.

77. Conference letter of invitation, folder 4393, box 451, subseries 75, series 1, RG 2, SSRC; JCNME minutes, meeting of March 15–16, 1980, folder 1462, box 243, subseries 20, series 1, RG 1, SSRC.

78. The latter were sociologist Said Amir Arjomand, who had just completed his PhD; Charles Butterworth; the young political scientist Eric Davis of Rutgers University; the Oxford anthropologist Michael Gilsenan; the University of Pennsylvania historian Thomas Naff; and historian Peter von Sivers of the University of Utah. For the minutes of the conference see Ibid.

79. Richard W. Bulliet, "Reflections on the Study of the Middle East in America," May 11, 1980, folder 1462, box 243, subseries 20, series 1, RG 1, SSRC.

80. Bulliet to JCNME chair Robert J. Lapham, May 3, 1981, folder 5396, box 452, subseries 75, series 1, RG 2, SSRC.

81. JCNME minutes, meeting of January 23–24, 1981, folder 1462, box 243, subseries 20, series 1, RG 1, SSRC; Richard Bulliet, email message to author, August 2, 2014; interview with Richard Bulliet, PHM, MESA.

82. See folder 5393, box 451, subseries 75, series 1, RG 2, SSRC.

83. JCNME minutes, meeting of May 9–10, 1980, folder 1462, box 243, subseries 20, series 1, RG 1, SSRC.

84. JCNME minutes, meeting of September 12–13, 1980, folder 1462, box 243, subseries 20, series 1, RG 1, SSRC.

85. JCNME minutes, meeting of February 25–26, 1983, folder 1464, box 244, subseries 20, series 1, RG 1, SSRC.

86. JCNME minutes, meeting of January 23–24, 1981, folder 1462, box 243, sub-

series 20, series 1, RG 1, SSRC. Many of the submitted statements can be found in folder 5395, box 451, subseries 75, series 1, RG 2, SSRC.

87. JCNME minutes, meetings of October 9–10, 1981, February 5–6, 1982, folder 1462, box 243, subseries 20, series 1, RG 1, SSRC.

88. JCNME minutes, meeting of August 5–7, 1984, folder 1465, box 244, subseries 20, series 1, RG 1, SSRC.

89. Announcement of the Ibn Khaldun Prize, folder 1463, box 243, subseries 20, series 1, RG 1, SSRC; JCNME minutes, February 24–25, 1984, folder 1465, box 244, subseries 20, series 1, RG 1, SSRC.

90. Ali Banuazizi, ed., *Social Stratification in the Middle East and North Africa: A Bibliographic Survey* (London: Mansell Publishing, 1984); Ali Banuazizi and Myron Weiner, eds., *The State, Religion, and Ethnic Politics: Afghanistan, Iran, and Pakistan* (Syracuse: Syracuse University Press, 1986). For a contemporary perspective from the left on some of the same issues, see Fred Halliday and Hamza Alavi, eds., *State and Ideology in the Middle East and Pakistan* (New York: Monthly Review Press, 1988).

91. See for example JCNME minutes, meeting of January 25–26, 1981, folder 5395, box 451, subseries 75, series 1, RG 2, SSRC.

92. JCNME minutes, meeting of January 23–24, 1981, folder 1462, box 243, subseries 20, series 1, RG 1, SSRC.

93. JCNME minutes, February 25–26, 1983, folder 1464, box 244, subseries 20, series 1, RG 1, SSRC.

94. JCNME minutes, September 30-October 1, 1983, August 5–7, 1984, folder 1465, box 244, subseries 20, series 1, RG 1, SSRC.

95. JCNME minutes, October 9–10, 1981, folder 1462, box 243, subseries 20, series 1, RG 1, SSRC.

96. See for example David L. Szanton, "Toward a Committee on the Islamic World," February 22, 1984, folder 1465, box 244, subseries 20, series 1, RG 1, SSRC.

97. JCNME minutes, August 5–7, 1984, folder 1465, box 244, subseries 20, series 1, RG 1, SSRC.

98. Worcester, *Social Science Research Council*, 123.

99. Worcester, *Social Science Research Council*, 121.

Epilogue

1. Kenneth Prewitt, "Presidential Items," *Items* 50 no. 1 (March 1996): 15–17.

2. Kenneth Prewitt, "Presidential Items," *Items* 50 nos. 2–3 (June–September 1996): 31.

3. The eleven committees were: African Studies (established in 1960), Chinese Studies (established in 1981 but successor to two earlier committees dating back to the late 1950s and mid-1960s), Eastern Europe (1971, successor to a committee dating back to 1948), Japanese Studies (1967), Korean Studies (1967), Latin America (1959, with a predecessor in 1942–1947), Near and Middle East (1951), South Asia (1976, with a predecessor in the late 1940s and early 1950s), Southeast Asia (1976), Soviet studies (1986, successor to the Slavic and East European committee first established in 1948) and Western Europe (1975); see Worcester, *Social Science Research Council*, 115–127.

4. Prewitt, "Presidential Items," *Items* 50 nos. 2–3 (June–September 1996): 37–40.

5. From a June 1994 SSRC staff memo, quoted in Worcester, *Social Science Research Council*, 129.

6. Quoted in Ibid., 112.

7. See for example Vicente L. Rafael, "The Cultures of Area Studies in the United States," *Social Text* 41 (Winter 1994), 91–111; Masao Miyoshi and Harry D. Harootunian, eds. *Learning Places: The Afterlives of Area Studies* (Durham: Duke University Press, 2002); Ali Mirsepassi, Amritu Basu and Frederick Weaver, eds., *Localizing Knowledge in a Globalizing World: Recasting the Area Studies Debate* (Syracuse: Syracuse University Press, 2003); and David Szanton, ed., *The Politics of Knowledge: Area Studies and the Disciplines* (Berkeley: University of California Press, 2004).

8. See Ford Foundation, *Crossing Borders: Revitalizing Area Studies* (1999), xi, accessed January 31, 2015, www.pacitaabad.com/PDF/Crossing%20Borders.pdf.

9. For a discussion of the critiques of modernization theory and Orientalism, and of developments in the 1980s, see Lockman, *Contending Visions*, chs. 5–6. On the cultural turn see, *inter alia*, Geoff Eley, *A Crooked Line: From Cultural History to the History of Society* (Ann Arbor: University of Michigan Press, 2005) and William H. Sewell Jr., *Logics of History: Social Theory and Social Transformation* (Chicago: University of Chicago Press, 2005).

10. Wallerstein, "Unintended Consequences," 195–231, and Mitchell, "The Middle East." See too Immanuel Wallerstein et al., *Open the Social Sciences: Report of the Gulbenkian Commission on the Restructuring of the Social Sciences* (Stanford: Stanford University Press, 1996).

11. Mitchell, "The Middle East," 76.

12. For an interesting take on the question of interdisciplinarity see Louis Menand, *The Marketplace of Ideas* (New York: W. W. Norton, 2010), ch. 3.

13. Some of the social science disciplines recoiled from these transformations; as Nicholas Dirks put it in 2004, they criticized area studies "from within autonomous and confined disciplinary spaces, spaces that have been increasingly isolated in terms of theory. . . . In the leading departments of political science and economics it is becoming almost impossible to think of hiring someone whose primary

research interests are locatable in a particular area of the 'third' world, despite the rhetoric about the need for comparison." Dirks, "South Asian Studies," 369.

14.   As we have seen, achieving a coherent definition of the space on which Middle East studies focused never seems to have been a priority for the field's founders and their successors. In any case, as with other area studies fields, this region's engagements with transregional and global flows and networks, and its relationship with its diasporas, have begun to receive heightened scholarly attention, making for increasingly fuzzy boundaries.

15.   Two political scientists surveying Latin American studies offer a somewhat similar perspective: in the 1980s, they assert, many scholars abandoned "grand theorizing and structural determinism," especially "the totalizing logic of both modernization and dependency theories," and embraced "healthy eclecticism" and "boundary-crossing." Drake and Hilbink, "Latin American Studies," passim.

16.   John King Fairbank, *Chinabound: A Fifty-Year Memoir* (New York: Harper & Row, 1982), 324.

17.   Mitchell, "The Middle East," 81–82.

18.   Ibid., 79–81.

19.   On Toynbee's vision of history and its influence on Gibb and on Islamic and Middle East studies, see Hourani, *Europe and the Middle East*, chs. 6–7; Owen, "Studying Islamic History"; and Roger Owen, "The Middle East in the Eighteenth Century: An 'Islamic Society' in Decline?," *Review of Middle East Studies* 1 (1975): 101–112.

20.   Mitchell, "The Middle East," 92, 95; Robert Vitalis, "The End of Third-Worldism in Egyptian Studies," *Arab Studies Journal* 4 no. 1 (Spring 1996): 13–32.

21.   But then it is not clear why in this context Mitchell seems to suggest that Samir Amin's work can usefully complicate the conventional narrative of U.S. Middle East studies. It is true that Amin formulated an analysis of capital accumulation as a global process before Immanuel Wallerstein's world-systems theory. But it was mainly dependency theory and world-systems theory on which many of those looking for an alternative to the paradigms dominant in U.S. Middle East studies actually drew most heavily, in part because they only became fully aware of Amin's work relatively late in the game. As Mitchell notes, Samir Amin's *Accumulation on a World Scale: A Critique of the Theory of Underdevelopment* was published in English translation only in 1974.

22.   Mitchell, "The Middle East," 109. Mitchell's implicit reference here is to Dipesh Chakrabarty, *Provincializing Europe: Postcolonial Thought and Historical Difference* (Princeton: Princeton University Press, 2000); for a critical engagement with Chakrabarty see Frederick Cooper, *Colonialism in Question: Theory, Knowledge, History* (Berkeley: University of California Press, 2005). Mitchell's rather posi-

tive and optimistic vision of area studies at the beginning of the twenty-first century stands in sharp contrast to that offered by Harry D. Harootunian and Masao Miyoshi, which I find overblown and unconvincing: "More than fifty years after the war's end, American scholars are still organizing knowledge as if confronted by an implacable enemy and thus driven by the desire to either destroy it or marry it." Moreover, unlike cultural studies, area studies "has today become the beleaguered fortress housing the traditional disciplines as if nothing had changed in the last fifty years, a Maginot Line already obsolete before its completion yet determined to protect its domains from infiltration and appropriation. Although quite antiquated now, the strategy of trench warfare is deployed by scholars of area studies as they try to mount an attack on an enemy they scarcely understand. Their obsession has been so intense over the long duration that we must seriously question the psychological as well as political-economic energy driving it." H. D. Harootunian and Masao Miyoshi, "Introduction: The 'Afterlife' of Area Studies," in Miyoshi and Harootunian, *Learning Places*, 5–6, 8.

23. Bruce Cumings, "Boundary Displacement: Area Studies," 159. More recently, Osamah F. Khalil has asserted that "area studies represented the intersection of the Cold War University and the American national security state." *America's Dream Palace*, Introduction, 11.

24. Bruce Cumings, "Boundary Displacement: The State," 261.

25. Gilbert W. Mercx estimated in 2010 that since 1958 Title VI-funded area studies centers had produced some 300,000 students with MAs and 100,000 with PhDs. I cannot vouch for his numbers, but obviously only a small fraction of these totals can have gone to work for an intelligence agency or the like. See Gilbert Mercx, "Gulliver's Travels: The History and Consequences of Title VI," in David S. Wiley and Robert S. Glew, eds., *International and Language Education for a Global Future: Fifty Years of U.S. Title VI and Fulbright-Hays Programs* (East Lansing MI: Michigan State University Press, 2010), 28.

26. See Engerman, "Social Science," who makes what I take to be a similar set of arguments about U.S. social science in the Cold War era.

27. Cumings, "Boundary Displacement: The State," 264–265.

28. Immanuel Wallerstein, "Unintended Consequences."

29. Engerman, "The Pedagogical Purposes."

30. Bruce Kuklick, *Blind Oracles: Intellectuals and War from Kennan to Kissinger* (Princeton: Princeton University Press, 2006), 15.

Bibliography

Archival Sources

American Council of Learned Societies records, Library of Congress (ACLS)

Carnegie Corporation of New York records, Rare Book and Manuscript Library, Columbia University Libraries (CCNY)

Ford Foundation archives, Rockefeller Archive Center (FF)

Middle East Studies Association records, Middle East Studies Association of North America, Secretariat, Tucson AZ (MESA)

Department of Near Eastern Studies records, Princeton University Archives, Department of Rare Books and Special Collections, Princeton University Library (PU)

Rockefeller Foundation archives, Rockefeller Archive Center (RF)

Social Science Research Council archives, Rockefeller Archive Center (SSRC)

Victor Rabinowitz Papers, Tamiment Library and Robert F. Wagner Labor Archive, Elmer Holmes Bobst Library, New York University

Personal papers of Professor Irene Gendzier (IG)

Books, Articles and Unpublished Papers

Abella, Alex. *Soldiers of Reason: The Rand Corporation and the Rise of the American Empire*. Orlando FL: Harcourt, 2008.

Abrahamian, Ervand. *The Coup: 1953, the CIA, and the Roots of Modern U.S.-Iranian Relations*. New York: The New Press, 2013.

Abt, Jeffrey. *American Egyptologist: The Life of James Henry Breasted and the Creation of His Oriental Institute*. Chicago: University of Chicago Press, 2011.

Adalet, Begüm. "Mirrors of Modernization: The American Reflection in Turkey." PhD diss., University of Pennsylvania, 2014.

Adelman, Jeremy. *Worldly Philosopher: The Odyssey of Albert O. Hirschman.* Princeton: Princeton University Press, 2013.

American Council of Learned Societies. *A Program for Near Eastern Studies in the United States.* Washington DC: American Council of Learned Societies, 1949.

Arum, Stephen Marshall. "Early Stages of Foreign Language and Area Studies in the U.S.: 1915–1941." PhD diss., Teachers College of Columbia University, 1975.

Babai, Don, ed. *Reflections on the Past, Visions for the Future.* Cambridge: Center for Middle Eastern Studies, 2004.

Bali, Rifat N., ed. *Family Life in the Turkish Republic of the 1930's: A Study by G. Howland Shaw.* Istanbul: Isis Press, 2007.

Baram, Philip. *The Department of State in the Middle East, 1919–1945.* Philadelphia: University of Pennsylvania Press, 1978.

Beckmann, George M. "The Role of the Foundations." *Annals of the American Academy of Political and Social Science* 356 (November 1964): 12–22.

Beit-Hallahmi, Benjamin. "National Character and National Behavior in the Middle East Conflict: The Case of the 'Arab Personality.'" *International Journal of Group Tensions* 2 no. 3 (1972): 19–28.

Bender, Thomas, and Carl E. Schorske, eds. *American Academic Culture in Transformation: Fifty Years, Four Disciplines.* Princeton: Princeton University Press, 1997.

Bennett, Wendell. *Area Studies in American Universities.* New York: Social Science Research Council, 1951.

Berman, Edward H. *The Influence of the Carnegie, Ford, and Rockefeller Foundations on American Foreign Policy: The Ideology of Philanthropy.* Albany: State University of New York Press, 1983.

Bijlefeld, Willem A. "A Century of Arabic and Islamic Studies at Hartford Seminary." *The Muslim World* 83 no. 2 (April 1993): 103–117.

Binder, Leonard, ed. *The Study of the Middle East: Research and Scholarship in the Humanities and Social Sciences.* New York: John Wiley & Sons, 1976.

Blackmer, Donald L. M. *The MIT Center for International Studies: The Founding Years, 1951–1969.* Cambridge: MIT Center for International Studies, 2002.

Blum, William. *The CIA: A Forgotten History—US Global Interventions since World War 2.* London: Zed Books, 1986.

Bonine, Michael E., Abbas Amanat and Michael Ezekial Gasper, eds. *Is There a Middle East?: The Evolution of a Geographical Concept.* Stanford: Stanford University Press, 2012.

Boodrookas, Alex. "Food for Books: Grain Aid, Cold War Scholarship, and the Weaponization of American Research Libraries." MA thesis, Hagop Kevorkian Center for Near Eastern Studies, New York University, 2014.

Bundy, McGeorge. "The Battlefields of Power and the Searchlights of the Academy." In *The Dimensions of Diplomacy*, edited by E. A. J. Johnson, 1–15. Baltimore: Johns Hopkins University Press, 1964.

Casagrande, Joseph B., and Elbridge Sibley. "Area Research Training Fellowships and Travel Grants for Area Research: An Epilogue." *Items* 7 no. 4 (December 1953): 37–42.

Chakrabarty, Dipesh. *Provincializing Europe: Postcolonial Thought and Historical Difference*. Princeton: Princeton University Press, 2000.

Chomsky, Noam. *American Power and the New Mandarins*. New York: Pantheon, 1967.

Chomsky, Noam, et al. *The Cold War & the University: Toward an Intellectual History of the Postwar Years*. New York: The New Press, 1997.

Citino, Nathan J. "The Ottoman Legacy in Cold War Modernization." *International Journal of Middle East Studies* 40 no. 4 (November 2008): 579–597.

Clark, Burton R., ed. *The Academic Profession: National, Disciplinary, and Institutional Settings*. Berkeley: University of California Press, 1987.

Clemmer, Richard O., L. Daniel Myers and Mary Elizabeth Rudden, eds. *Julian Steward and the Great Basin: The Making of an Anthropologist*. Salt Lake City: University of Utah Press, 1999.

Cline, Howard F., ed. *Latin American History: Essays on its Study and Teaching, 1898–1965*. Austin: University of Texas Press, 1967.

Clowse, Barbara Barksdale. *Brainpower for the Cold War: The Sputnik Crisis and National Defense Education Act of 1958*. Westport CT: Greenwood Press, 1981.

Cohen, Robert. *The Free Speech Movement: Reflections on Berkeley in the 1960s*. Berkeley: University of California Press, 2002.

Cohen-Cole, Jamie. *The Open Mind: Cold War Politics and the Sciences of Human Nature*. Chicago: University of Chicago Press, 2014.

Coleman, Peter. *The Liberal Conspiracy: The Congress for Cultural Freedom and the Struggle for the Mind of Postwar Europe*. New York: The Free Press, 1989.

Coon, Carleton. *A North Africa Story: The Anthropologist as OSS Agent, 1941–1943*. Ipswich MA: Gambit, 1980.

Cooper, Frederick. *Colonialism in Question: Theory, Knowledge, History*. Berkeley: University of California Press, 2005.

———— and Randall Packard, eds. *International Development and the Social Sciences: Essays on the History and Politics of Knowledge*. Berkeley: University of California Press, 1997.

Cowley, W. H., and Don Williams. *International and Historical Roots of American Higher Education*. New York: Garland Publishing, 1991.

Cumings, Bruce. "Boundary Displacement: Area Studies and International Studies during and after the Cold War." In *Universities and Empire: Money and Politics in the Social Sciences during the Cold War*, edited by Christopher Simpson, 159–188. New York: The New Press, 1998.

——— "Boundary Displacement: The State, the Foundations, and Area Studies during and after the Cold War." In *Learning Places: The Afterlives of Area Studies*, edited by Masao Miyoshi and H. D. Harootunian, 261–302. Durham: Duke University Press, 2002.

De, Alfred. "International Understanding and World Peace: The American Council of Learned Societies, 1919–1957." PhD diss., City University of New York, 2004.

Delpar, Helen. *Looking South: The Evolution of Latin Americanist Scholarship in the United States, 1850–1975.* Tuscaloosa: University of Alabama Press, 2008.

DeVane, Claude. *Higher Education in Twentieth-Century America.* Cambridge: Harvard University Press, 1965.

Diamond, Sigmund. *Compromised Campus: The Collaboration of Universities with the Intelligence Community, 1945–1955.* New York: Oxford University Press, 1992.

Dirks, Nicholas B. "South Asian Studies: Futures Past." In *The Politics of Knowledge: Area Studies and the Disciplines*, edited by David Szanton, 341–385. Berkeley: University of California, 2004.

Dougherty, James Vachel. "A History of Federal Policy Concerning College or University-Based Foreign Language and Area Studies Centers, 1941–1980." PhD diss., University of Maryland, 1993.

Ekbladh, David. *The Great American Mission: Modernization and the Construction of an American World Order.* Princeton: Princeton University Press, 2010.

Eley, Geoff. *A Crooked Line: From Cultural History to the History of Society.* Ann Arbor: University of Michigan Press, 2005.

El Shakry, Omnia. *The Great Social Laboratory: Subjects of Knowledge in Colonial and Postcolonial Egypt.* Stanford: Stanford University Press, 2007.

Engerman, David C. *Know Your Enemy: The Rise and Fall of America's Soviet Experts.* New York: Oxford University Press, 2009.

——— "The Pedagogical Purposes of Interdisciplinary Social Science: A View from Area Studies in the United States." *Journal of the History of the Behavioral Sciences* 51 no. 1 (Winter 2015): 78–92.

——— "Social Science in the Cold War." *Isis* 101 no. 2 (June 2010): 393–400.

Epstein, Jason. "The CIA and the Intellectuals." *The New York Review of Books,* April 20, 1967.

Ettinghausen, Richard, ed. *A Selected and Annotated Bibliography of Books and Periodicals in Western Languages Dealing with the Near and Middle East With Special Emphasis on Medieval and Modern Times.* Washington DC: Middle East Institute, 1952.

Fairbank, John King. *Chinabound: A Fifty-Year Memoir.* New York: Harper & Row, 1982.

Falk, Julia S. "The LSA Linguistic Institutes" (unpublished paper). Accessed February 22, 2015. www.linguisticsociety.org/files/LSA-90%20Institutes.docx.

Faris, Nabih A. "Islamic and Arabic at Princeton Again." *The American Scholar* 7 no. 3 (Summer 1938): 373–374.

Farish, Matthew. "Archiving Areas: The Ethnogeographic Board and the Second World War." *Annals of the Association of American Geographers* 95 no. 3 (2005): 663–679.

———— *The Contours of America's Cold War.* Minneapolis: University of Minnesota Press, 2010.

Fenton, William Nelson. *Area Studies in American Universities.* Washington DC: American Council on Education, 1947.

Fisher, Donald. *Fundamental Development of the Social Sciences: Rockefeller Philanthropy and the United States Social Science Research Council.* Ann Arbor: University of Michigan Press, 1993.

Fleck, Christian. *A Transatlantinc History of the Social Sciences: Robber Barons, the Third Reich and the Invention of Empirical Social Science Research.* London: Bloomsbury Academic, 2011.

Flynn, George Q. *Conscription and Democracy: The Draft in France, Great Britain, and the United States.* Westport CT: Greenwood Press, 2002.

Frye, Richard. *Greater Iran: A 20th-Century Odyssey.* Costa Mesa CA: Mazda Publishers, 2005.

Gallagher, Nancy E., ed. *Approaches to the History of the Middle East: Interviews with Leading Historians of the Middle East.* Reading: Ithaca Press, 1994.

Gardner, John W. "Are We Doing Our Homework in Foreign Affairs?" *The Yale Review* 37 no. 3 (March 1948): 400–408.

Gary, Brett. *The Nervous Liberals: Propaganda Anxieties from World War I to the Cold War.* New York: Columbia University Press, 1999.

Gendzier, Irene L. *Managing Political Change: Social Scientists and the Third World.* Boulder: Westview Press, 1985.

Gibb, Hamilton A. R. *Studies on the Civilization of Islam,* edited by Stanford J. Shaw and William R. Polk. Boston: Beacon Press, 1962.

Gilman, Nils. *Mandarins of the Future: Modernization Theory in Cold War America.* Baltimore: Johns Hopkins University Press, 2003.

Goode, James. "Reforming Iran during the Kennedy Years." *Diplomatic History* 15 no. 1 (January 1991): 13–29.

Grady, Henry F. *The Memoirs of Ambassador Henry F. Grady from the Great War to the Cold War.* Edited by John T. McNay. Columbia: University of Missouri Press, 2009.

Gutner, Tamar L. *The Story of SAIS*. Washington DC: School of Advanced International Studies, 1987.

Hafez, Sherine, and Susan Slyomovics, eds. *Anthropology of the Middle East and North Africa: Into the New Millenium*. Bloomington: Indiana University Press, 2013.

Hall, Harvey, and Ann W. Noyes, eds. *Current Research on the Middle East 1955*. Washington DC: Middle East Institute, 1956.

Hall, Robert B. *Area Studies: With Special Reference to their Implications for Research in the Social Sciences* (Social Science Research Council Pamphlet 3). New York: Social Science Research Council, 1947.

Hallo, William W. *Essays in Memory of E. A. Speiser*. New Haven CT: American Oriental Society, 1968.

Halpern, Manfred. "Middle Eastern Studies: A Review of the State of the Field with a Few Examples." *World Politics* 15 no. 1 (October 1962): 108–122.

Harari, Maurice. *Government and Politics of the Middle East*. Englewood Cliffs NJ: Prentice-Hall, 1962.

Hauptmann, Emily. "The Development of Philanthropic Interest in the Scientific Study of Political Behavior." Rockefeller Archive Center Research Reports Online. Accessed June 17, 2013. www.rockarch.org/publications/resrep/hauptmann.pdf.

——— "The Ford Foundation and the Rise of Behavioralism in Political Science." *Journal of the History of the Behavioral Sciences* 48 no. 2 (Spring 2012): 154–173.

Hawkins, John N. *International Education in the New Global Era: Proceedings of a National Policy Conference on the Higher Education Act, Title VI, and Fulbright-Hays Programs*. Los Angeles: International Studies and Overseas Programs, University of California, Los Angeles, 1998.

Hayden, J. R. "The Institute of Far Eastern Studies." *American Political Science Review* 32 no. 1 (February 1938): 114–116.

Hayes, Wayland J., and Werner J. Cahnman. "Foreign Area Study (ASTP) as an Educational Experiment in the Social Sciences." *Social Forces* 23 no. 1 (1944): 160–164.

Heindel, Richard H. *The Present Position of Foreign Area Studies in the United States: A Post-Conference Report*. New York: Social Science Research Council, 1950.

Heydemann, Steven, with Rebecca Kinsey. "The State and International Philanthropy: The Contribution of American Foundations, 1919–1991." In *American Foundations: Roles and Contributions*, edited by Helmut K. Anheier and David C. Hammack, 205–236. Washington DC: Brookings Institution Press, 2010.

Hirschman, Charles, Charles F. Keyes and Karl Hutterer, eds. *Southeast Asian Studies in the Balance: Reflections from America*. Ann Arbor MI: Association for Asian Studies, 1992.

Hitti, Philip K. "Arabic and Islamic Studies in Princeton University." *The Moslem World* 31 no. 3 (July 1941): 292–294.

Hooper, Paul F. "The Institute of Pacific Relations and the Origins of Asian and Pacific Studies." *Pacific Affairs* 61 no. 1 (spring 1988): 98–121.

Hourani, Albert. *Europe and the Middle East.* Berkeley: University of California Press, 1980.

Hourani, George F. "Palestine as a Problem of Ethics." *Middle East Studies Association Bulletin* 3 no. 1 (February 15, 1969): 15–25.

Huntington, Samuel. "The Clash of Civilizations?" *Foreign Affairs* 72 no. 3 (Summer 1993): 22–49.

Hurewitz, J. C. *Undergraduate Instruction on the Middle East in American Colleges and Universities.* New York: American Association for Middle East Studies, 1962.

Hyneman, Charles S. "The Army's Civil Affairs Training Program." *The American Political Science Review* 38 no. 2 (April 1944): 342–353.

Ikenberry, G. John. *Liberal Leviathan: The Origins, Crisis, and Transformation of the American World Order.* Princeton: Princeton University Press, 2011.

Ireland, Philip W., ed. *The Near East: Problems and Prospects.* Chicago: University of Chicago Press, 1942.

Isaac, Joel. *Working Knowledge: Making the Human Sciences from Parsons to Kuhn.* Cambridge: Harvard University Press, 2012.

Jackson, Jr., John P. "'In Ways Unacademical': The Reception of Carleton S. Coon's *The Origin of Races.*" *Journal of the History of Biology* 34 no. 2 (Summer 2001): 247–285.

———— *Science for Segregation: Race, Law, and the Case against Brown v. Board of Education.* New York: New York University Press, 2005.

Jacobs, Matthew F. *Imagining the Middle East: The Building of an American Foreign Policy, 1918–1967.* Chapel Hill: University of North Carolina Press, 2011.

Johnson-Davies, Denys. *Memories in Translation: A Life between the Lines of Arabic Literature.* Cairo: American University in Cairo Press, 2006.

Joint Committee on Southern Asia. *Southern Asia Studies in the United States: A Survey and Plan.* Philadelphia: Joint Committee on Southern Asia, 1951.

Kaplan, Robert. *The Arabists: The Romance of an American Elite.* New York: The Free Press, 1993.

Karam, John Tofik. "Philip Hitti, Brazil, and the Diasporic Histories of Area Studies." *International Journal of Middle East Studies* 46 no. 3 (August 2014): 451–471.

Karnovsky, Nathan. "The Other Cultural Revolution: The Academic Uprising of the American China Scholar." BA thesis, Haverford College, 2012.

Katz, Barry M. *Foreign Intelligence: Research and Analysis in the Office of Strategic Services, 1942–1945.* Cambridge: Harvard University Press, 1989.

Keefer, Louis E. *Scholars in Foxholes: The Story of the Army Specialized Training Program in World War II.* Jefferson NC: McFarland & Co., 1988.

Kerns, Virginia. *Scenes from the High Desert.* Urbana: University of Illinois Press, 2003.

Kerr, Clark. *The Uses of the University.* Cambridge: Harvard University Press, 1963.

Khalil, Osamah F. "America's Dream Palace: The Rise of the US National Security State and Middle East Expertise, 1902–2012." Unpublished manuscript under review, November 2014.

Kirschner, Don S. *Cold War Exile: The Unclosed Case of Maurice Halperin.* Columbia MO: University of Missouri Press, 1995.

Krige, John, and Helke Rausch, eds. *American Foundations and the Coproduction of World Order in the Twentieth Century.* Gottingen: Vanderhoeck & Ruprecht, 2012.

Kritzeck, James, and R. Bayly Winder, eds. *The World of Islam: Studies in Honour of Philip K. Hitti.* London: MacMillan, 1960.

Kuklick, Bruce. *Blind Oracles: Intellectuals and War from Kennan to Kissinger.* Princeton: Princeton University Press, 2006.

——— *Puritans in Babylon: The Ancient Near East and American Intellectual Life, 1880–1930.* Princeton: Princeton University Press, 1996.

Kuklick, Henrika, ed. *A New History of Anthropology.* Malden MA: Blackwell Publishing, 2008.

Kuzmarov, Jeremy. *Modernizing Repression: Police Training and Nation Building in the American Century.* Amherst MA: University of Massachusetts Press, 2012.

Lagemann, Ellen Condliffe. *The Politics of Knowledge: The Carnegie Corporation, Philanthropy, and Public Policy.* Middletown, CT: Wesleyan University Press, 1989.

Lambert, Richard D., Elinor G. Barber, Eleanor Jorden, Margaret B. Merrill and Leon I. Twarog. *Beyond Growth: The Next Stage in Language and Area Studies.* Washington DC: Association of American Universities, 1984.

——— "Blurring the Disciplinary Boundaries: Area Studies in the United States." In *Divided Knowledge: Across Disciplines, Across Cultures*, edited by David Easton and Corinne S. Schelling, 171–194. Newbury Park CA: Sage Publications, 1991.

——— *Language and Area Studies Review.* Philadelphia: American Academy of Political and Social Science, 1973.

Langer, William L. *In and Out of the Ivory Tower.* New York: Neale Watson Academic Publications, 1977.

Laroui, Abdallah. *The Crisis of the Arab Intellectual: Traditionalism or Historicism?* Berkeley: University of California Press, 1976.

Latham, Michael E. *Modernization as Ideology: American Social Science and "Nation Building" in the Kennedy Era.* Chapel Hill: University of North Carolina Press, 2000.

Lauria-Perricelli, Antonio. "Materialist Scholarship and The People of Puerto Rico." *Identities: Global Studies in Culture and Power* 18 no. 3 (January 3, 2012): 194–202. Accessed July 16, 2013. doi: http://dx.doi.org/10.1080/1070289X.2011.635281.

Leffler, Melvyn P., and David S. Painter, eds. *Origins of the Cold War: An International History.* London: Routledge, 1994.

Leffler, Melvyn P., and Odd Arne Westad, eds. *The Cambridge History of the Cold War.* 3 vols. Cambridge: Cambridge University Press, 2010.

Lewis, Martin W., and Kären E. Wigen, *The Myth of Continents: A Critique of Metageography.* Berkeley: University of California Press, 1997.

Lockman, Zachary. "Challenges and Responsibilities in a Time of Crisis." *Middle East Studies Association Bulletin* 42 nos. 1/2 (Summer/Winter 2008): 5–15.

———— *Contending Visions of the Middle East: The History and Politics of Orientalism*, 2nd edition. Cambridge: Cambridge University Press, 2010.

Lundberg, Ferdinand. *America's 60 Families.* New York: Vanguard Press, 1937.

Luther, K. Allin. "In Memoriam: T. Cuyler Young, 16 August 1900–31 August 1976." *International Journal of Middle East Studies* 8 no. 2 (April 1977): 267–269.

Matthew, Robert John. *Language and Area Studies in the Armed Service: Their Future Significance.* Washington: American Council on Education, 1947.

McCarus, Ernest. "History of Arabic Study in the United States." In *The Arabic Language in America*, edited by Aleya Rouchdy. Detroit: Wayne State University Press, 1992.

McCaughey, Robert A. *International Studies and Academic Enterprise: A Chapter in the Enclosure of American Learning.* New York: Columbia University Press, 1984.

Mead, Margaret, and Rhoda Métraux, eds. *The Study of Culture at a Distance.* Chicago: University of Chicago Press, 1953.

Menand, Louis. *The Marketplace of Ideas.* New York: W. W. Norton, 2010.

Middle East Research and Information Project. "Middle East Studies Network in the United States." *MERIP Reports* 38 (June 1975): 3–20.

Mikesell, Raymond F., and Hollis B. Chenery. *Arabian Oil: America's Stake in the Middle East.* Chapel Hill: University of North Carolina Press, 1949.

Mildenberger, Kenneth W. "The Federal Government and the Universities." *Annals of the American Academy of Political and Social Science* 356 (November 1964): 23–29.

Mirsepassi, Ali, Amritu Basu and Frederick Weaver, eds. *Localizing Knowledge in a Globalizing World: Recasting the Area Studies Debate.* Syracuse: Syracuse University Press, 2003.

Mitchell, Timothy. "Deterritorialization and the Crisis of Social Science." In *Localizing Knowledge in a Globalizing World: Recasting the Area Studies Debate*, edited by Ali Mirsepassi, Amrita Basu and Frederick Weaver, 148–170. Syracuse: Syracuse University Press, 2003.

———— "The Middle East in the Past and Future of Social Science." In *The Politics of Knowledge: Area Studies and the Disciplines*, edited by David Szanton, 74–118. Berkeley: University of California Press, 2004.

Miyoshi, Masao, and Harry D. Harootunian, eds. *Learning Places: The Afterlives of Area Studies*. Durham: Duke University Press, 2002.

Mosely, Philip E. "The Russian Institute of Columbia University." *Proceedings of the American Philosophical Society* 99 no. 1 (Jan. 27, 1955): 36–38.

Murphy, Lawrence R. *The American University in Cairo: 1919–1987*. Cairo: American University in Cairo Press, 1987.

Naff, Thomas, ed. *Paths to the Middle East: Ten Scholars Look Back*. Albany: State University of New York Press, 1993.

Nemchenok, Victor V. "'That so Fair a Thing Should Be so Frail': The Ford Foundation and the Failure of Rural Development in Iran, 1953–1964." *Middle East Journal* 63 no. 2 (Spring 2009): 261–284.

Newhall, Amy. "The Unraveling of the Devil's Bargain: The History and Politics of Language Acquisition." In *Academic Freedom after September 11*, edited by Beshara Doumani, 203–236. New York: Zone Books, 2006.

Ninkovich, Frank A. *The Diplomacy of Ideas: U.S. Foreign Policy and Cultural Relations, 1938–1950*. Cambridge: Cambridge University Press, 1981.

Nisbet, Robert. *The Degradation of the Academic Dogma: The University in America, 1945–1970*. New York: Basic Books, 1971.

Oppermann, Matthias. *American Studies in Dialogue: Radical Reconstructions between Curriculum and Cultural Critique*. Frankfurt and New York: Campus Verlag, 2010.

Orlin, Louis L., ed. *Michigan Oriental Studies in Honor of George C. Cameron*. Ann Arbor: Department of Near Eastern Studies, University of Michigan, 1967.

Owen, Roger. "Studying Islamic History." *Journal of Interdisciplinary History* 4 no. 2 (Autumn 1973): 287–298.

——— "The Middle East in the Eighteenth Century: An 'Islamic Society' in Decline?" *Review of Middle East Studies* 1 (1975): 101–112.

Parker, William Riley. *The National Interest and Foreign Languages*. Washington DC: U.S. Government Printing Office, 1954.

Parmar, Inderjeet. *Foundations of the American Century: The Ford, Carnegie, and Rockefeller Foundations in the Rise of American Power*. New York: Columbia University Press, 2012.

Paul, Jim. "Games Imperialists Play." *MERIP Reports* 45 (March 1976): 17–20.

Price, David H. *Anthropological Intelligence: The Deployment and Neglect of American Anthropology in the Second World War*. Durham: Duke University Press, 2008.

——— *Threatening Anthropology: McCarthyism and the FBI's Surveillance of Activist Anthropologists*. Durham: Duke University Press, 2004.

Pye, Lucien W., ed. *Political Science and Area Studies: Rivals or Partners?* Bloomington: Indiana University Press, 1975.

Rabinowitz, Victor. *Unrepentant Leftist: A Lawyer's Memoir.* Urbana: University of Illinois Press, 1996.

Rafael, Vicente L. "The Cultures of Area Studies in the United States." *Social Text* 41 (Winter 1994): 91–111.

Rauch, Jerome S. "Area Institute Programs and African Studies." *Journal of Negro Education* 24 no. 4 (Autumn 1955): 409–425.

Reed, Howard A. "Perspectives on the Evolution of Turkish Studies in North America since 1946." *Middle East Journal* 51 no. 1 (Winter 1997): 15–31.

Roosevelt, Kermit. *Countercoup: The Struggle for the Control of Iran.* New York: McGraw-Hill, 1979.

Roszak, Theodore, ed. *The Dissenting Academy.* New York: Pantheon Books, 1967.

Russian Research Center. *Ten-Year Report and Current Projects, 1948–1958.* Cambridge: Russian Research Center, Harvard University, 1958.

Ruther, Nancy. *Barely There, Powerfully Present: Thirty Years of U.S. Policy on International Higher Education.* New York: Routledge, 2002.

Safran, Nadav. *Egypt in Search of Political Community: An Analysis of the Intellectual and Political Evolution of Egypt, 1804–1952.* Cambridge: Harvard University Press, 1961.

Said, Edward W. *Orientalism.* New York: Pantheon, 1978.

Samuels, Richard J., and Myron Weiner, eds. *The Political Culture of Foreign Area and International Studies: Essays in Honor of Lucian W. Pye.* McLean VA: Brassey's (US), 1992.

Saunders, Frances Stonor. *The Cultural Cold War: The CIA and the World of Arts and Letters.* New York: New Press, 1999.

Schrecker, Ellen W. *No Ivory Tower: McCarthyism and the Universities.* New York: Oxford University Press, 1986.

Seim, David L. *Rockefeller Philanthropy and Modern Social Science.* London: Pickering & Chatto, 2013.

Sewell, William H., Jr. *Logics of History: Social Theory and Social Transformation.* Chicago: University of Chicago Press, 2005.

Sibley, Elbridge. *Social Science Research Council: The First Fifty Years.* New York: Social Science Research Council, 1974. Accessed February 24, 2015. http://www.ssrc.org/about/history/.

Simpson, Christopher. *Universities and Empire: Money and Politics in the Social Sciences during the Cold War.* New York: The New Press, 1998.

——— "U.S. Mass Communication Research, Counterinsurgency, and Scientific 'Reality.'" In *Communication Researchers and Policy-making*, edited by Sandra Braman. Cambridge: MIT Press, 2003.

Smith, Bradley F. *The Shadow Warriors: O.S.S. and the Origins of the C.I.A.* New York: Basic Books, 1983.

Smith, Neil. *American Empire: Roosevelt's Geographer and the Prelude to Globalization.* Berkeley: University of California Press, 2003.

Smith, Wilfred Cantwell. "The Place of Oriental Studies in a Western University." *Diogenes* 4 no. 16 (December 1956): 104–11.

Social Science Research Council. *World Regions in the Social Sciences.* New York: Social Science Research Council, June 1943.

Solovey, Mark. *Shaky Foundations: The Politics-Patronage-Social Science Nexus in Cold War America.* New Brunswick: Rutgers University Press, 2013.

———— and Hamilton Cravens, eds. *Cold War Social Science: Knowledge Production, Liberal Democracy, and Human Nature.* New York: Palgrave Macmillan, 2012.

Speiser, E. A. "Near Eastern Studies in America, 1939–45." *Archiv Orientální* 16 no. 1 (December 1, 1947): 76–88.

———— "Oriental Studies and Society." *Journal of the American Oriental Society* 66 no. 3 (July–September 1946): 193–197.

———— *The United States and the Near East.* Cambridge: Harvard University Press, 1947.

SRI International. *Defense Intelligence: Foreign Area/Language Needs and Academe.* Washington DC: SRI International, 1983.

Steward, Julian H. *Area Research: Theory and Practice.* New York: Social Science Research Council, 1950.

———— et al. *The People of Puerto Rico: A Study in Social Anthropology.* Urbana: University of Illinois Press, 1956.

Stolper, Matthew W. "George G. Cameron, 1905–1979." *The Biblical Archaeologist* 43 no. 3 (Summer 1980): 183–189.

Sutton, Francis X., and David R. Smock. "The Ford Foundation and Area Studies." *Issue: A Journal of Opinion* 6 nos. 2–3 (Summer-Autumn 1976): 68–72.

Sweet, Louise E., ed. *The Central Middle East: A Handbook of Anthropology and Published Research on the Nile Valley, the Arab Levant, Southern Mesopotamia, the Arabian Peninsula, and Israel.* New Haven: HRAF Press, 1971.

Szanton, David, ed. *The Politics of Knowledge: Area Studies and the Disciplines.* Berkeley: University of California Press, 2004.

Tannous, Afif I. *Village Roots and Beyond: Memoirs of Afif I. Tannous.* Beirut: Dar Nelson, 2004.

Tivnan, Edward. *The Lobby: Jewish Political Power and American Foreign Policy.* New York: Simon and Schuster, 1987.

Turner, Fred. *The Democratic Surround: Multimedia and American Liberalism from World War II to the Psychedelic Sixties.* Chicago: University of Chicago Press, 2013.

United States Department of War. *War Report of the OSS (Office of Strategic Services).* New York: Walker and Company, 1976.

Urban, Wayne J. *More than Science and Sputnik: The National Defense Education Act of 1958*. Tuscaloosa: University of Alabama Press, 2010.

VanDeMark, Brian. *American Sheikhs: Two Families, Four Generations, and the Story of America's Influence in the Middle East*. Amherst NY: Prometheus Books, 2012.

Vitalis, Robert. *America's Kingdom: Mythmaking on the Saudi Oil Frontier*. Stanford: Stanford University Press, 2007.

———— "Aramco World: Business and Culture on the Arabian Oil Frontier." In *Counter-Narratives: History, Contemporary Society, and Politics in Saudi Arabia and Yemen*, edited by Madawi Al-Rasheed and Robert Vitalis. New York: Palgrave MacMillan, 2004.

———— "The End of Third-Worldism in Egyptian Studies." *Arab Studies Journal* 4 no. 1 (Spring 1996): 13–32.

———— "The Noble American Science of Imperial Relations and its Laws of Race Development." *Comparative Studies in Society and History* 52 no. 4 (October 2010): 909–938.

———— *White World Order, Black Power Politics*. Ithaca: Cornell University Press, 2015.

Wagley, Charles. *Area Research and Training: A Conference Report on the Study of World Areas* (Social Science Research Council Pamphlet 6). New York: Social Science Research Council, 1948.

Wallerstein, Immanuel. "The Unintended Consequences of Cold War Area Studies." In Noam Chomsky et al., *The Cold War and the University: Toward an Intellectual History of the Postwar Years*, 195–231. New York: New Press, 1997.

———— et al., *Open the Social Sciences: Report of the Gulbenkian Commission on the Restructuring of the Social Sciences*. Stanford: Stanford University Press, 1996.

Weiner, Tim. *Legacy of Ashes: The History of the CIA*. New York: Doubleday, 2007.

Westad, Odd Arne. *The Global Cold War: Third World Interventions and the Making of Our Times*. Cambridge: Cambridge University Press, 2006.

Wilcox, Clifford. *Robert Redfield and the Development of American Anthropology*. Lanham MD: Lexington Books, 2004.

Wiley, David S., and Robert S. Glew, eds. *International and Language Education for a Global Future: Fifty Years of U.S. Title VI and Fulbright-Hays Programs*. East Lansing MI: Michigan State University Press, 2010.

Wilford, Hugh. *America's Great Game: The CIA's Secret Arabists and the Shaping of the Modern Middle East*. New York: Basic Books, 2013.

———— *The Mighty Wurlitzer: How the CIA Played America*. Cambridge: Harvard University Press, 2008.

Winder, R. Bayly. "Adghath Ahlam." *MESA Bulletin* 4 no. 1 (February 15, 1970): 15–22.

———— "Four Decades of Middle Eastern Study." *Middle East Journal* 41 no. 1 (Winter 1987): 40–63.

Winks, Robin W. *Cloak and Gown: Scholars in the Secret War, 1939–1961.* New York: William Morrow and Company, 1987.

Wise, Gene. "'Paradigm Dramas' in American Studies: A Cultural and Institutional History of the Movement." *American Quarterly* 31 no. 3 (1979): 293–337.

Wolf, Eric R. *Pathways of Power: Building an Anthropology of the Modern World.* Berkeley: University of California Press, 2001.

Worcester, Kenton W. *Social Science Research Council, 1923–1998.* New York: Social Science Research Council, 2001. Accessed February 24, 2015. http://www.ssrc.org/about/history/.

Wosh, Peter J., ed. *Waldo Gifford Leland and the Origins of the American Archival Profession.* Chicago: Society of American Archivists, 2011.

Young, T. Cuyler. "Iran in Continuing Crisis." *Foreign Affairs* 40 no. 2 (January 1962): 275–292.

———— "The Race between Russia and Reform in Iran." *Foreign Affairs* 28 no. 2 (January 1950): 278–289.

———— "The Social Support of Current Iranian Policy." *Middle East Journal* 6 no. 2 (Spring 1952): 125–143.

Zartman, I. William, ed. *Elites in the Middle East.* New York: Praeger Publishers, 1980.

———— et al. *Political Elites in Arab North Africa: Morocco, Algeria, Tunisia, Libya, and Egypt.* New York: Longman, 1982.

Zunz, Oliver. *Philanthropy in America: A History.* Princeton: Princeton University Press, 2012.

Index

Abu-Lughod, Janet, 157, 222

Agency for International Development, 194–195, 235–236, 237

Albright, William F., 82, 162, 164, 168, 309n2

American Association for Middle East Studies (AAMES), 160–170

American Association of Teachers of Arabic, 157

American Council of Learned Societies: 3–4; and area studies, 13–14, 17–18, 33, 37–39, 45, 90–91, 162, 262; Committee on Arabic and Islamic Studies, 15–17, 79–82; Committee on Near Eastern Studies, 82–90, 97, 101; and Far Eastern studies, 6–7; and the foundations, 4–7, 17–19, 22–23, 37–38, 79–83, 85, 88, 91, 270n10; and Latin American studies, 7; and Near Eastern studies, 8–17, 78–91, 105; Near Eastern Translation Project, 88, 90; and the prewar study of the non-Western world, 5–17

American Council on Education, 21, 41

American Middle East Studies Seminar (AMESS), 196, 243, 258, 317n94

American Oriental Society, 3, 8, 10, 15, 136, 171

American Political Science Association, 4, 102, 187, 193

American Research Center in Egypt, 159, 308n84

American Research Institute in Turkey, 159

area studies: and classical studies, 46; and the Cold War, xiii–xiv, 49–53; after the Cold War, 249–251; conflicting visions of, xv, 37–41, 81, 90–91, 97, 117–118; critiques of, xii, 126, 227, 229, 231, 242–243, 251, 257–258; and the disciplines, xi, xvii, xix, 26, 56, 63, 71, 100, 144, 183, 229, 230, 231–232, 252–253, 254; federal government funding for, 92–93, 99–101, 113, 146–150; and interdisciplinarity, xi, 18, 35–36, 47,